F

Program Evaluation

M. E. Gredler
University of South Carolina

Merrill,
an imprint of Prentice Hall
Englewood Cliffs, New Jersey   Columbus, Ohio

To Lee and Gilbert

Library of Congress Cataloging-in-Publication Data
Gredler, Margaret E.
      Program evaluation / M. E. Gredler.
          p.   cm.
      Includes bibliographical references (p.   ) and index.
      ISBN 0-02-346246-9
      1. Educational evaluation—United States. 2. Education planning—United States.   I. Title.
LB2822.75.G74   1996
379.1'54—dc20
                                                    95-7420
                                                      CIP

Cover art: Marjory Dressler
Editor: Kevin M. Davis
Production Editor: Alexandrina Benedicto Wolf
Design Coordinator: Julia Zonneveld Van Hook
Text Designer: Mia Saunders
Cover Designer: Graphica
Production Manager: Patricia A. Tonneman
Electronic Text Management: Marilyn Wilson Phelps, Matthew Williams, Karen L. Bretz, Tracey Ward

This book was set in Garamond by Prentice Hall and was printed and bound by R.R. Donnelley & Sons Company. The cover was printed by Phoenix Color Corp.

ISBN: 0-02-346246-9

Prentice-Hall International (UK) Limited, *London*
Prentice-Hall of Australia Pty. Limited, *Sydney*
Prentice-Hall of Canada, Inc., *Toronto*
Prentice-Hall Hispanoamericana, S. A., *Mexico*
Prentice-Hall of India Private Limited, *New Delhi*
Prentice-Hall of Japan, Inc., *Tokyo*
Simon & Schuster Asia Pte. Ltd., *Singapore*
Editora Prentice-Hall do Brasil, Ltda., *Rio de Janeiro*

Preface

P rogram evaluation as a type of formal inquiry came into existence about 30 years ago with the entry of the federal government into social programming. Lacking a knowledge base for developing timely information about complex social programs, evaluators borrowed methods and procedures from the social science disciplines. Economists developed regression equations to explain program effects and educational researchers compared individuals in social programs with others on selected program indicators.

Dissatisfaction with early evaluation results led to theoretical discussions, analyses of the roles of evaluation in political contexts, adaptations of some methods, and the exploration of others as yet untried. A strong focus on studying outcomes broadened to include study of the implementation of programs and their contexts. From early discussions of methodology, the field moved to addressing also the difficulties of conducting evaluations in political contexts, each with several groups with a stake in the program and the evaluation.

Views of the role of evaluation have expanded from the perspective that the goal is to inform a few key decisionmakers to that of informing both a variety of constituents and the larger evaluation community. Evaluation continues to build a craft from the new methods as well as the experiences of evaluators. Evaluation, above all, is a pragmatic enterprise.

The purpose of this text is to present a framework for evaluation that addresses current methods, important decisions, planning tasks. and ethical issues that face the evaluator. The audiences for this text include practitioners of evaluation, students, and decisionmakers who implement new programs and innovations.

This manuscript has been strengthened by the questions and concerns of my students in evaluation. I am particularly indebted to Joe Ryan, Director of the

Research Consulting Center, Arizona State University West, for his review of the chapter on performance assessment, and Thomas Haladyna, Arizona State University West and Peggy Perkins, University of Nevada–Las Vegas for their invaluable feedback. I would also like to thank the following reviewers for their reviews: James W. Altschuld, the Ohio State University; William M. Bechtol, Southwest Texas State University; Mark A. Constas, University of Colorado; James C. Impara, University of Nebraska–Lincoln; Stephen D. Lapan, Northern Arizona University; Edward Lederman, Eastern Michigan University; and Lani M. Van Dusen, Utah State University.

Contents

PART TWO

Tools of Evaluation   83

PART ONE

Introduction to Evaluation

CHAPTER 1

Overview

A local school board in a midwestern state wishes to know the effects of an additional year of schooling after kindergarten for some children prior to their entry to first grade. The board contracts with two university research faculty to answer the question. Elsewhere, in Washington, D.C., a federal agency is authorizing the installation of alternative high schools for dropouts (and students at risk of dropping out) at different sites to determine their effectiveness.

In the business sector, a major communications conglomerate is dissatisfied with the current first aid training administered to employees. The 10½-hour course requires more than 1 work day per employee. The company contracts with a private firm to develop a course that can be completed in 1 day and that yields scores at the same level as the current first aid training. The staff work several months developing instruction, testing it several times with sample groups of employees, and revising the course based on the tryouts.

These activities and many others are examples of evaluation. Broadly defined, evaluation is the systematic collection of information to assist in decision making. Evaluations may be conducted for any of a variety of decisions about commercial products, works of art, human services, individuals, facilities, and equipment. For example, independent organizations and agencies conduct tests on consumer products to determine effectiveness, efficiency, safety, ease of use, and relative costs. Similarly, building facilities and equipment may be evaluated on such characteristics as adequacy, safety, working environment, and ease of use. Also, employees often are evaluated on their performance by organizations such as businesses, government agencies, and schools. In education, for example, observations typically are used to obtain information about teacher performance and classroom interactions. The purposes may be to identify strengths and weaknesses, to certify the occurrence of particular activities, or to select individuals for particular programs, promotions, or awards.

One broad area of evaluation, referred to as program evaluation, provides systematic information about any of a variety of human services. Among them are workshops, seminars, and other training in industry and business; policies, curricula, programs, and products in education; criminal justice programs and services; and health care services provided by hospitals, nursing homes, and mental health centers. Services provided by local communities, such as libraries and recreational programs for children and adolescents, also are examples.

Program evaluation in education refers to "a careful rigorous examination of any development or system intended to improve or enhance the educational experiences of students. Examples are educational curricula, programs, institutions, organizational variables, or policies" (Walberg & Haertel, 1990, p. xvii). Also included are sets of course materials or teaching resources, computer software, and similar instructional packages. Determining the effects (positive and negative) of an additional year of kindergarten in a school district, documenting the impact of alternative high schools on at-risk students, and revising a first aid course until stated criteria are met are also examples. Still other examples include documenting the strategies undertaken by science students as they work through a computer simulation and the reactions of parents, teachers, and students to a new social studies curriculum.

In other words, educational policies or programs may address a single subject area, a particular learning problem, or a specific age group; or they may address broader problems, such as potential school dropouts. In addition, a program may be implemented in one school or districtwide, or it may be installed in a variety of locations in a state or in different states. Finally, a policy, a course, instructional materials, or a program may be evaluated at any of several phases of development. As indicated in the first aid example, early versions of a course or program were evaluated in order to obtain information to revise the instruction.

THE BIRTH OF PROGRAM EVALUATION

Teachers in several schools that are developing innovative curricula are upset that a standardized test is to be used to evaluate their efforts at the end of the first year. They are concerned that the test measures only recall information, and they are attempting to accomplish more than merely memorization of facts and definitions. Several schools are threatening to leave the study.

The Eight-Year Study

The above event marked the beginning of program evaluation as a systematic area of inquiry. The year was 1932. Thirty schools had elected to develop programs designed to serve the large numbers of teenagers who were remaining in school because they could not find work (50% as opposed to 10% a few years earlier). The schools were allowed 8 years to experiment free of state requirements and college entrance requirements. Effectiveness of the curricula was to be determined by (1) a yearly assessment of student learning and (2) a follow-up appraisal of the students after high school graduation.

As a result of the concern about the use of a standardized test to determine the effectiveness of innovative curricula, Ralph W. Tyler was brought in to direct the project. He was selected because his philosophy was that evaluation should be based on the important learnings that are selected by the school and the teacher.

In the Eight-Year Study, evaluation staff assigned to the schools worked with the teachers to clarify the important abilities, thinking strategies, interests, and attitudes they hoped to foster in students. Tyler recalled that the teachers initially began with trite phrases (Nowalski, 1983). However, the staff probed beneath the surface to uncover goals the teachers were not fully conscious of. The result was sets of goals that went beyond knowledge, skills, and habits to address modes of critical thinking, critical interpretation, and so on. Teachers and the evaluation staff then devised innovative ways of assessing these goals. Performance on the indicators for the goals was used to revise the curriculum and make changes where necessary.

The Eight-Year Study also included a follow-up appraisal of students in the innovative curricula who went to college. A comparison of these students with matched controls indicated that the students in the new curricula performed as well or better academically than their counterparts. Also, they were more likely to be involved in extracurricular college activities than their peers. However, by the time the Eight-Year Study was completed, the United States was on the brink of World War II, and the issues surrounding the high school programs of the prior decade were no longer of major interest.

The Concept of Program Evaluation

The Eight-Year Study is the first comprehensive example of program evaluation. Prior to the study, assessment and evaluation involved the testing of students. Moreover, the focus was on individual differences in defined subject matter areas. The concept of program appraisal—the study of educational programs or curricula as particular entities with associated effects—was a new perspective introduced by Tyler. The Eight-Year Study demonstrated that determining the effectiveness of school programs is an enterprise different from that of appraising an individual student's accomplishments.

Tyler also established three broad principles of curriculum evaluation. First, he differentiated the activities of measurement and evaluation. Measurement is the assessment of some characteristic, trait, or feature that yields a quantitative result. In contrast, evaluation consists of all the activities used to develop substantive information about a curriculum or a program. In other words, evaluation often includes measurement but is not synonymous with it.

Second, human behavior typically is so complex that it cannot be described adequately or measured by a single term or a single dimension (Smith & Tyler, 1942). In other words, paper and pencil tests do not reflect the full dimensions of human behavior. Other useful methods are observations of students by teachers and interviews of students and parents. Further, the collection of themes students have written or the paintings they have made in an art class may serve as evidence of skill and possible student interest in an area. Similarly, the number of books checked out of the library is an appropriate indicator of students' interest in reading (Tyler, 1950).

A third contribution of the Eight-Year Study is the relationship between curriculum development and evaluation. Tyler viewed these processes as integrated activities with each enriching the other. The purpose of evaluation in Tyler's model is "to determine in what respects the curriculum is effective and in what respects it needs improvement" (Tyler, 1950, p. 60). As materials and procedures are developed, they are implemented, their results are appraised, and strengths and weaknesses are identified. These activities are followed by replanning, redevelopment, and reappraisal (Tyler, 1950, p. 89). Thus, he introduced the use of evaluation to provide feedback on the process of curriculum development.

EVALUATION CATAPULTS INTO NATIONAL PROMINENCE

The USSR launched the first space capsule (Sputnik), and the American public, fearful of losing the cold war, questioned the educational system. Were American schools capable of preparing scientists and scholars to close the perceived technology gap?

The Russian feat led to a major shift in the implicit role of public education. The date was October 1957. No longer were school systems to serve only local concerns; instead, they were to be responsive to perceived national priorities as well. The move into national prominence occurred on two separate fronts. One was curriculum redesign, and the other was social reform.

Curriculum Redesign

Ralph Tyler initially conceptualized curriculum development and evaluation as the responsibility of local school personnel. However, the massive federal funding for the development of new curricula ushered in a national role for a variety of school subjects.

Congress enacted the National Defense Education Act in 1958. This legislation provided funding for teacher retraining and the hiring of school counselors, as well as resources to strengthen state departments of education. Also, the National Science Foundation and the U.S. Office of Education began to spend millions of dollars in curriculum redesign.

The extent of the curriculum projects and the method of development reflected the new national priority for education. Projects were concentrated largely in mathematics, science, and foreign languages. Among them are PSSC Physics; Harvard Project Physics; SMSG Mathematics; Project CHEM; BSCS biology; and ALM French, Spanish, and German.

In addition, unlike Tyler's school-based model of curriculum development, this redesign effort involved hundreds of scholars and scientists. The purpose was to update concepts and topics in each subject area and to encourage student inquiry and discovery as a mechanism for intellectual development. The result was comprehensive sets of course materials—textbooks, learning materials, film strips, audio tapes, teacher guides, and tests—as well as teacher training, to be disseminated to local schools. Thus, these new curricula reflected a centralized (rather than a decentralized) model of development.

After the urgency and excitement of the early years had passed, many groups, including Congress, demanded objective evidence of the effectiveness of the new curricula (Walker & Schaffarzick, 1974, p. 83). Several studies were implemented to evaluate the new courses. These studies compared the performance of students in the innovative curricula with that of students in the traditional curricula on paper-and-pencil tests. The results, for the most part, were disappointing. Moreover, the course comparisons suffered from some shortcomings that are discussed in Chapter 2.

The Era of Social Reform

In addition to concerns about the technology race, the 1960s were a period of social unrest in the United States. Civil rights groups focused on the lives of minorities in all areas of American society, and education in particular. The decade also was characterized by optimism about the potential of solving social problems through large-scale programs (Cook & Shadish, 1986). In response to widespread criticism of public education, Congress enacted the Elementary and Secondary Education Act (ESEA) in 1965. This legislation provided billions of dollars to local education agencies for compensatory education and other special programs. The largest single component of the bill, Title I, provided five sixths of the total funding (approximately $1 billion annually) for disadvantaged children in poor schools (McLaughlin, 1975).

ESEA was the first major piece of social legislation to mandate evaluation and project reporting. Specifically, the thousands of local programs funded by Title I and Title III were required to submit project reports in order to receive subsequent funding. The principal architect of the evaluation requirement was Senator Robert F. Kennedy. He viewed the requirement as a way to provide political accountability. He hoped that project reports would provide parents with the information to ensure that poor children were served by Title I dollars (McLaughlin, 1975, p. vii).

In addition to Title I of ESEA, a preschool program for educating disadvantaged children was funded by the Office of Economic Opportunity in 1965. The project was named Head Start. Programs also were enacted in health care, including community health centers, urban renewal, job training, and welfare. Evaluation was mandated for many of these programs.

The Input/Output Concept.   The legislation that provided funding for ESEA, Head Start, and Follow Through initiated a new role for the federal government in education. Accompanying the federal level of funding for new programs was an effort to shift the decision making about the relative effectiveness of programs from the local to the federal level.

A newly created office in 1965, the Assistant Secretary for Program Evaluation (ASPE), established the evaluation philosophy and model for these programs (McLaughlin, 1975). First, the purpose of evaluation was to identify the most effective programs that would then be recommended as universal solutions to particular problems (Rivlin, 1971). Second, the selected model specified that "inputs" (money or resources) yield a set of "outputs," and the programs that maximize outputs for a given level of funding are the most effective (House, 1980; McLaughlin, 1975).

The input/output, or production factor concept, is a managerial perspective drawn from microeconomic theory. Application of this concept to human services programs by ASPE assumed a direct parallel between production in manufacturing and the delivery of human services (House, 1978; McLaughlin, 1975). Use of the input/output model for evaluation was based on the following assumptions:

1. Individuals and organizations act so as to maximize some identifiable outcome or set of outcomes.

2. Consensus can be obtained about the attainable outcomes (outputs).

3. Human services programs can be described in terms of resources and/or amount of funding (inputs).

4. Human services programs are similar to economic decisions in that a stable and quantifiable "production function" exists between inputs and outputs (House, 1980; McLaughlin, 1975).

The output or "payoff" selected for educational programs was test scores. In other words, the most effective programs were the ones that maximized student performance on selected tests, given similar funding or other resources. Excluded from the model is the possibility that different groups legitimately might apply different standards to a program and therefore select quite different indices of effectiveness (House, 1974, pp. 231–232). Reductions in absenteeism, drop-out rate, and school vandalism, for example, are possible choices.

In addition, establishing definitive cause-effect relationships between programs and outcomes required the use of experimental designs and the statistical analysis of data (House, 1980; Rivlin, 1971). Thus, the Westinghouse-Ohio State evaluation of Head Start and the third-year evaluation of the Follow Through projects specified the use of experimental research methods. Hypotheses about each program were tested on selected outcomes using a comparison group. Application of inferential statistics to differences in average effects indicated whether the program "significantly" outperformed the comparison group. These methods were consistent with the production factor priority of identifying the program that maximized test scores.

EVALUATION SEARCHES FOR DIRECTION

Parents, program staff, and others are upset at the trivial outcomes used in the evaluation. Program developers charge that the evaluation does not adequately represent their projects. Researchers question the evaluation conclusions, pointing out serious methodological weaknesses.

The negative reactions occurred in the 1970s in response to the federally mandated evaluations of Head Start and the Follow Through programs. Analyses of these evaluations identified several problems with the application of the production factor concept to social settings. One effect was the development of several evaluation frameworks (referred to as models) that addressed the shortcomings of the production factor concept. These comprehensive frameworks introduced a broad perspective of evaluation that has evolved at present into two major evaluation trends.

Problems With the Production Factor Concept

Implementation of the input/output model for evaluation led to several unanticipated effects. First, the evaluation reports of Title I projects did not yield the managerial information sought by ASPE. Many school systems, lacking research expertise, submitted any available test scores or other data. A subsequent evaluation of Title I reports, TEMPO, identified few programs in which the outcomes were clearly interpretable (McLaughlin, 1975).

Second, as indicated, the evaluations of Head Start and Follow Through were criticized on several fronts. Some noted that the evaluations responded only to bureaucratic concerns, not the needs of clients (Weiss, 1986). Others criticized the categorization of projects under summary labels because many of the sites grouped together were quite diverse, thus distorting the nature of any particular program. Finally, efforts to apply experimental research methods to broad social programs were less than satisfactory.

The underlying problem, however, is that the production factor concept was a poor fit with social reality. First, the paradigm ignores the complex and varied processes of schooling. In other words, the assumption of a direct link between "inputs" and "outputs" was in error.

Second, the model did not acknowledge the different conceptual foundations of many of the programs. Each of the early childhood programs implemented in the Follow Through project developed from a different perspective of the "causes" of poor children's inadequate achievement. The Bank Street approach, for example, assumed that the problem was the child's lack of experience and lack of appropriate stimulation for learning; therefore, the school should provide cultural enrichment. The Bank Street project also emphasized maximum exploration and discovery by the child. In contrast, the Engleman-Becker perspective was based on the assumption that teaching practices were the problem. The project developed small-group highly structured materials in reading and mathematics known as DISTAR.

Third, the production factor concept excludes the pluralistic views that typically are held about innovative programs. That is, programs often are interpreted in different ways by different groups. Federal agencies, for example, viewed the primary aim of Title I, Head Start, and Follow Through as that of enhancing achievement. Congress, however, viewed these programs as efforts to equalize otherwise disparate educational funding for disadvantaged children. Title I, in other words, was analogous to a "rivers and harbors" bill in that the purpose of the funds was to relieve the financial inequities in education for poor districts and the cities (Cohen, 1970). Also, different project sites implement a program in different ways to the extent that considerable variation typically exists between projects with the same general label.

Fourth, the assumption that test scores were legitimate outputs ignores the nature of the programs. They often have broader goals, such as social development, persistence, and self-reliance.

Fifth, the input/output perspective was designed to provide managerial information at the federal level. However, decisions about educational priorities for any particular school district occur at the local level. The evaluations did not provide local decision makers with useful information.

Comprehensive Evaluation Approaches

The federal mandates for evaluation issued in the 1960s allowed no time for researchers and others to develop methods and designs for the informational demands of program evaluation. However, in the early 1970s, psychologists and researchers began to address the need for comprehensive evaluations that would also address issues and concerns raised about the early evaluation studies. Exploration of these problems led to the development of several suggested evaluation approaches or frameworks. These approaches to evaluation were efforts to address the complexities of capturing adequate program descriptions and the need to make credible decisions about programs.

Although referred to as models, Stake (1981, 1991) suggests that the evaluation approaches developed in the 1970s should be referred to instead as persuasions. The term *model* suggests sufficient detail and completeness to plan and implement a satisfactory evaluation. Instead, the authors promote specific concerns and identify a few of the many inquiry opportunities (Stake, 1991, p. 71). Therefore, these evaluation perspectives should not be viewed as methodologies for actually conducting evaluations. They should be viewed as guides for thinking about ways to conduct an evaluation (Borick, 1983).

Two general types of approaches emerged during the 1970s that reflect two different orientations toward evaluation. One group, referred to as utilitarian or management-oriented approaches (Hamilton, 1977; House, 1978) viewed the task of evaluation as that of providing judgmental information about programs to key decision makers. These approaches expanded the rational process of decision making to include program definition, comparisons between intents and observations, available institutional resources for implementation, and the processes of schooling. Four key perspectives in this group are the Provus discrepancy model, the CIPP model, Stake's countenance evaluation approach, and Scriven's goal-free perspective. They are discussed in detail in Chapter 3.

The other perspectives, referred to as intuitionist/pluralist (House, 1978), addressed a different set of evaluation concerns. They viewed the primary role of evaluation as that of enlightening individuals associated with a program and others about the complex dynamics and events that comprise the program. Therefore, these perspectives devoted the maximum evaluation resources to obtaining information about the various interactions stimulated by a program. The purpose of this effort is to understand a program as those affected by it do. Four approaches illustrative of this group are the judicial/adversarial models, Eisner's educational connoisseurship and criticism approach, Stake's responsive evaluation perspective, and illuminative evaluation. They are discussed in detail in Chapter 4.

Current Trends

At present, three trends that impact evaluation may be identified. Two of the trends are outgrowths of the evaluation perspectives of the 1970s. The third trend is the increased interest in and development of alternative assessments that differ substantially from standardized multiple choice tests.

Outgrowths of the 1970s Models.   One trend that emerged from the early evaluation models is the inclusion of qualitative data (such as verbal summaries of open-ended interviews) along with quantitative data to provide a comprehensive picture of programs and processes (see Fetterman, 1982, 1984). An example is the evaluation of kindergarten retention conducted by Shepard and Smith (1985) for a Colorado school district. One purpose of the evaluation was to determine the cognitive and emotional effects of kindergarten retention. The researchers compared the first-grade performance of retained children and retention-eligible children who were promoted after kindergarten. They found no significant differences between the two groups on standardized test scores and teacher ratings of reading achievement, mathematics achievement, social maturity, learning self-concept, and appropriateness of attention to school work.

A literature review prior to the evaluation indicated that some schools and school systems often support kindergarten retention, although the research indicates achievement differences between younger and older children to be small and no emotional or intellectual benefits from retention. Therefore, ascertaining the belief systems that support retention or nonretention in the school district was included in the study. Semi-structured interviews consisting of eight broad categories were conducted with the teachers. The evaluators coded teacher statements according to the different practices and specific beliefs they represented. Synthesis of the qualitative data resulted in the identification of four different belief systems that differed on the two major dimensions of intervention/nonintervention and environmentalism/nativism (see Table 15-4).

The other trend in evaluation is the use of qualitative inquiry. This paradigm seeks to understand the various layers and perspectives of a social milieu as the participants themselves understand it (Guba & Lincoln, 1981; Patton, 1990). Qualitative inquiry begins with open-ended observations; thus, it is exploratory and discovery oriented. Data are rendered in the form of detailed field notes, audio- and video-tapes, photographs, interviews, archival records, and other written human documents and artifacts (LeCompte, Millroy, & Preissle, 1992, p. XV). Analysis dimensions emerge from patterns observed in the data. Data analyses are reported in the form of qualitative narratives that seek to describe a holistic view of a social or cultural milieu. The methods of qualitative inquiry are drawn primarily from anthropology, sociological field studies, and psycholinguistics.

The Alternative Assessment Trend.   The context for the recent emergence of alternative assessments is the high-stakes focus on student achievement that followed the publication of *A Nation at Risk*. This document received national attention with its assertions of the poor quality of American schools. The problems, particularly in inner city and poor rural schools, had existed for some years (Berlak, 1992). However, the report appeared at a time when concerns about a faltering economy were beginning to surface. Rising unemployment, noncompetitive industries, the infusion of foreign wealth, the trade imbalance, and newspaper editorials about the country's second-rate status contributed to the anxiety.

Similar to the earlier Sputnik crisis, the educational system became both the cause and the solution for problems precipitated by political and economic events. However, instead of curricular reform, the 1980s concerns emphasized standards in the form of testing. *A Nation at Risk* recommended standardized tests at major transition points that would certify the student's credentials, and identify both the need for remediation and opportunities for advanced work (p. 28). However, the emphasis quickly became that of accountability, an emphasis sharpened by the publication of "wall charts" by the Secretary of Education in 1983. These wall charts illustrated several types of information for each state and also included state averages on the American College Test and the Scholastic Aptitude Test, even though these tests are inappropriate for such comparisons (Linn, 1989). Within 8 years of *A Nation at Risk,* every state was implementing top-down measures to raise educational standards, the most common of which were statewide testing programs (Berlak, 1992).

The high stakes focus on test results with rankings of classrooms, schools, and districts precipitated some negative effects. In some cases, curriculum was aligned to reflect the focus of the tests (see Smith & Rottenberg, 1991, for an example). Teachers also spent time teaching the types of items on the tests and teaching students to "bubble in" their choices on the answer sheets. Also, some educators selected easier tests instead of those that most accurately measured their educational goals (Linn, 1989).

The high-stakes focus on achievement testing also precipitated criticisms of the multiple choice tests. Among the criticisms were too much emphasis on factual knowledge and on structured decontextualized problems (Linn, Baker, & Dunbar, 1991), the lack of information provided about student progress in developing complex intellectual abilities, and the lack of relationship to classroom activities. The call for more authentic tests of intellectual ability has led to the development of two forms of so-called "alternative" assessment: performance tests and portfolios. Briefly, a performance test requires examinees to demonstrate their capabilities by creating some product or engaging in some activity (Haertel, 1992). Portfolios, in contrast, are collections of samples of student work over a semester or a year that often include reflective comments by the students themselves (Herman, Gearhart, & Baker, 1993).

At present, several states and funded projects are developing alternative assessments. One problem currently facing these developments is the high expectations identified for alternative assessments. Among these expectations are the following:

1. Serving as instruments of school reform (because tests inevitably influence instruction)

2. Providing "lifelike" and, therefore, meaningful tasks for students

3. Representing important teaching activities

4. Functioning as instruments for teacher development

However, little information is available that indicates the assessments can meet these expectations (Frechtling, 1991).

In addition, policymakers are supporting and adapting new assessment systems without solid data about validity and reliability, the unintended effects of these systems, or knowledge about institutional success. Nevertheless, the scope of the developments as well as emergent efforts to address validity and reliability issues are of importance to evaluation.

DEFINITION OF PROGRAM EVALUATION

In education, program evaluation refers to the sets of activities involved in collecting information about the operation and effects of policies, programs, curricula, courses, and educational software and other instructional materials. Of importance is that program evaluation should not be confused with other forms of inquiry or data collection that are conducted for different purposes.

Program Evaluation and Other Forms of Inquiry

Three enterprises with which program evaluation is often confused are educational research, accountability, and accreditation and self-study reviews. Each, however, is conducted for a different purpose than that of evaluation.

Educational Research.   Evaluation and educational research often are confused because they are similar in many ways. Both are forms of disciplined inquiry that seek to develop knowledge. Further, many evaluations also make use of measurement instruments, which are the researcher's primary means of data collection. Educational research, however, differs from evaluation in four major ways. First, the major purpose of educational research is to test principles or theories that may be generalizable across space and time. For example, a particular educational principle to be tested may be, Does reinforcement in an academic setting influence group-responsive behavior? Procedures are then implemented in the study such that the researchers can generalize the findings beyond the sample in the study to the population from which the sample was selected.

A second characteristic of educational research is that the researcher, depending on his/her particular area, determines the nature of the problems to be investigated. These decisions are made consistent with current theory and research in that area. For example, in the area of motivation, attribution theory states that teachers and others send messages in various ways to students about their level of competence. A researcher, therefore, may choose to investigate the effects of classroom priorities on children's competence (see Ames & Archer, 1988; Elliott & Dweck, 1988).

A third characteristic of research is that methods and procedures are implemented so that individual values or preferences do not influence the outcome. The purpose of the research is to determine if a bona fide link exists between the identified independent variable(s), such as reinforcement, and the dependent or outcome variable(s), such as group-responsive behavior.

Fourth, the primary audience for the research is often other researchers and theorists in a particular area of inquiry. Studies of children in performance-oriented and mastery-oriented classrooms, for example, provide information on the different ways that children react to success and failure in different classrooms (Ames & Archer, 1988; Elliott & Dweck, 1988). This knowledge is of particular interest to researchers and theorists in the areas of motivation and attribution theory. In other words, educational research is typically discipline oriented.

In contrast to educational research, evaluation does not test generalizable principles or theories. Instead, evaluations ask particular questions about specific programs. Thus, evaluation is decision oriented (rather than discipline oriented). However, a thoughtful, well-executed evaluation can inform policymakers in other settings about the complexity of issues and alternative courses of action.

Second, evaluation is conducted for a client, such as the school superintendent, a state or federal agency, and so on. Thus, an evaluator is less independent than the typical social scientist (Cronbach & associates, 1980, p. 203). The evaluation is often guided by the major concerns and information needs of the client.

Third, values are an important component of evaluation. Some evaluation perspectives maintain that determining the value or worth of a particular program is a major purpose of evaluation. Other perspectives maintain that the questions of importance depend in large measure on the values and concerns of parties associated with the particular program. Finally, the audience for an evaluation is an identified set of decision makers or the various groups interested in the program.

Accountability.   The major difference between evaluation and accountability is that the purpose of accountability systems typically is to assign responsibility for outcomes among a program's operators (Cronbach & associates, 1980, p. 17). Accountability is thus a measure of control. This perspective is also a restricted view of the reasons for program success or failure.

Managers should be accountable for events that are their responsibility. For example, the manager of a public water system is responsible for water quality to the extent that the technology for keeping the water free from contamination is available (Cronbach & associates, 1980, p. 135).

Findings about social services, however, often are the result of complex influences. A goal of a marriage-counseling service, for example, may be to hold the number of separations of its clients to a minimum (Cronbach & associates, 1980). However, a variety of influences determine whether or not a couple separates. Therefore, the counseling service should not be blamed for a high rate of separations (p. 135). Although evaluations should assist in understanding the reasons for shortfalls, the best use of evaluations is not to bring pressure on public officials for indices that they can only partially influence.

Accreditation and Self-Study Reviews.   A major focus of program evaluation is to determine the effects of an intervention on the recipients. Accreditations, in contrast, typically involve the review of documents to determine if certain prespecified status characteristics are present. (For example, Are course syllabi available in a certain location for student perusal? and What types of physical facilities are available?) Student outcomes (positive or negative) are not analyzed and the program is not examined to determine the ways in which it produces its effects.

Similarly, self-study reports do not assess programmatic effects on students. Although data about number of graduates and other information may be included in the study, the effects of programs on the target group that is served are not considered. Also, self-study reports are typically conducted for internal use. Evaluation, in contrast, is typically conducted to inform a policy-making group or others interested in a particular program.

Key Characteristics of Program Evaluation

Program evaluation in education is a systematic inquiry designed to provide information to decision makers and/or groups interested in a particular program, policy, or other intervention. Examples are, Was the program delivered as planned? (Provus,

1971) Who is the program serving? (Cooley & Bickel, 1986) How does the program work? (Cooley & Bickel, 1986) What are the teacher belief systems that account for decisions about student progress? (Shepard & Smith, 1985) What effect is the program having on students? (Cooley & Bickel, 1986) Does the program produce unintended side effects? (Cronbach & associates, 1980) What revisions of the materials are needed? (Markle, 1967) and so on. Evaluation also is value oriented because judgments about the worth or value of programs are often made.

Evaluations may be conducted at any of several phases of program development and implementation. "An evaluation may be a pilot study of an early version of a program or it may be a review of an established operation with the goal of possible change or termination" (Cronbach, 1982, p. 2).

Michael Scriven (1967) differentiated these two roles of evaluation as *formative* and *summative*. When used as part of the process of curriculum development or teacher self-improvement, for example, the role is formative (p. 41). Examples of questions that may be addressed in formative evaluation are, Is the curriculum clearly communicating basic concepts? and Is the curriculum taking too much time to make an important point? (Scriven, 1967, p. 41). The approach implemented by Ralph Tyler in the Eight-Year Study is an example of formative evaluation.

Another example of formative evaluation is the first aid program at the beginning of this chapter. Staff revised portions of the course and implemented the components with representative samples of workers until the course effectively produced learning in 7½ hours instead of 10½ hours (Markle, 1967).

Summative evaluation is viewed by Scriven (1991) as "done for or by any observers or decision makers who need evaluative conclusions for any reasons other than development" (p. 20). Cronbach and associates (1980) are more explicit in that they view summative evaluation as appropriate only for well-defined explicit interventions. The demonstration projects of alternative high schools for dropouts at the beginning of this chapter is an example. Similarly, the example of the school board commissioning an evaluation to determine the effects of kindergarten retention is a policy study that is a summative evaluation.

SUMMARY

Evaluation was originally conceptualized by Ralph Tyler as a process essential to curriculum development. The purpose was to determine the extent to which the curriculum had achieved its stated goals. Evaluation was the basis for the identification of strengths and weaknesses in the curriculum, followed by replanning, implementation, and evaluation. Tyler also viewed evaluation as school based.

The curriculum design projects and social reform efforts of the 1960s introduced new roles for evaluation. First, evaluation was no longer solely a school-based activity. Federal and state agencies were directed to conduct evaluations of widely disseminated programs. Second, evaluations were conducted to demonstrate program impact as a basis for the identification of the most effective program. In other words, the focus of evaluation shifted to program comparisons rather than program improvement.

Limitations of the input/output concept for meeting the information needs of evaluation led to the development of other approaches to evaluation. Some of these approaches, the utilitarian perspectives, expanded the types of decisions and data sources appropriate for evaluation. Others, the intuitionist/pluralist approaches, addressed the views of various groups interested in a program and/or sought to identify the underlying dynamics of program operation.

Limitations of the input/output concept also led to the identification of key differences between research and evaluation. Research is typically conducted to test principles that are expected to be generalizable over space and time, the researcher selects the problems, and procedures are implemented to reduce sources of bias in reaching conclusions. In contrast, evaluation is conducted to answer particular questions about a specific program, curriculum, set of materials, or policy. Also, the evaluation is conducted for a client whose priorities and concerns in part determine the questions.

In the late 1970s, qualitative inquiry emerged in evaluation. Participant observation and interviews, for example, are used by ethnographers to develop an understanding of social groups and cultures. These methods also are well suited for developing understandings of program implementation in the social setting and are useful in evaluation.

At present, many evaluations combine quantitative and qualitative data where appropriate to provide a comprehensive description and analysis of the program, curriculum, course, or other service undergoing evaluation. Evaluation also is conducted at any of several stages of development and implementation. When conducted for the purpose of providing feedback to developers, evaluation is referred to as formative. When conducted for other purposes, evaluation is referred to as summative.

CHAPTER QUESTIONS

1. According to Tyler, what are the major differences between assessment and evaluation?

2. What are the philosophical differences between Tyler's model of evaluation and the production factor concept of evaluation?

3. In what ways did the production factor concept differ from social reality?

4. What type of inquiry is reflected in detailed notes, videotapes, or archival records?

5. What are some of the events that contributed to interest in alternative assessment?

6. How do educational research and evaluation differ?

REFERENCES

Ames, C., & Archer, J. (1988). Achievement goals in the classroom: Students' learning strategies and motivational processes. *Journal of Educational Psychology*, *80*(3), 260–267.

Berlak, H. (1992). The need for a new science of assessment. In H. Berlak, F. M. Newmann, E. Adams, D. Archbald, T. Burgess, J. Raven, & T. A. Romberg, *Toward a new science of educational testing and achievement* (pp. 1–21). Albany, NY: State University of New York Press.

Borick, D. (1983). Evaluation models: A question of purpose, not terminology. *Educational Evaluation and Policy Analysis*, *5*(1), 61–63.

Cohen, D. (1970). Politics and research: Evaluation of social action programs. *Review of Educational Research*, *40*(2), 213–238.

Cook, T. D., & Shadish, W. R. (1986). Program evaluation. In M. R. Rosenzweig & L. W. Porter (Eds.), *Annual Review of Psychology* (Vol. 37, pp. 193–232). Palo Alto: Annual Reviews Inc.

Cooley, W.; & Bickel, W. (1986). *Decision-oriented educational research*. Boston: Kluwer-Nijhoff.

Cronbach, L. J. (1982). *Designing evaluations of educational and social programs*. San Francisco: Jossey-Bass.

Cronbach, L. J., Ambron, S., Dornbusch, S., Hess, R., Hornik, R., Phillips, D., Walker, D., & Weiner, S. (1980). *Toward reform of program evaluation*. San Francisco: Jossey-Bass.

Elliott, E. S., & Dweck, C. S. (1988). Goals: An approach to motivation and achievement. *Journal of Personality and Social Psychology*, *54*(1), 5–12.

Fetterman, D. (1982). Ethnography in educational research: The dynamics of diffusion. *Educational Researcher*, *11*(3), 17–22, 29.

Fetterman, D. (1984). *Ethnography in educational evaluation*. Beverly Hills, CA: Sage.

Frechtling, J. (1991). Performance assessment: Moonstruck or the real thing? *Educational Measurement: Issues and Practice*, *10*(4), 23–25.

Guba, E., & Lincoln, Y. (1981). *Effective evaluation*. San Francisco: Jossey-Bass.

Haertel, E. (1992). *Performance measurement*. In M. C. Alkin (Ed.), *Encyclopedia of educational research* (pp. 984–989). New York: Macmillan.

Hamilton, D. (1977). Making sense of curriculum evaluation: Continuities and discontinuities in an educational idea. In L. S. Shulman (Ed.), *Review of research in education Vol. 5* (pp. 318–348). Itasca, IL: Peacock.

Herman, J., Gearhart, M., & Baker, E. (1993). Assessing writing portfolios: Issues in the validity and meaning of scores. *Educational Assessment*, *1*(3), 201–224.

House, E. (1980). *Evaluating with validity*. Beverly Hills, CA: Sage.

House, E. R. (1974). *The politics of educational innovation*. Berkeley, CA: McCutchan.

House, E. R. (1978). Assumptions underlying evaluation models. *Educational Researcher*, *7*(3), 4–12.

LeCompte, M. D., Millroy, W. L., & Preissle, J. (Eds.). (1992). *The Handbook of Qualitative Research in Education*. San Diego: Academic Press.

Linn, R. (1989). Current perspectives and future directions. In R. Linn (Ed.), *Educational measurement* (3rd ed., pp. 1–10). New York: American Council on Education/Macmillan.

Linn, R., Baker, E., & Dunbar, S. (1991). Complex performance-based assessment: Expectations and validation criteria. *Educational Researcher*, *20*(5), 15–21.

McLaughlin, M. (1975). *Evaluation and reform: The Elementary and Secondary Education Act of 1965, Title I*. Cambridge, MA: Ballinger.

Markle, D. (1967). The development of the Bell system first aid and personal safety course. Palo Alto: American Institutes for Research (AIR-E81-4/67-FR).

Nowalski, J. R. (1983, May). On educational evaluation: A conversation with Ralph Tyler. *Educational Leadership*, 24–29.

Patton, M. (1990). *Qualitative evaluation and research methods* (2nd ed.). Newbury Park: Sage.

Provus, M. (1971). *Discrepancy evaluation*. Beverly Hills, CA: McCutchan.

Rivlin, A. M. (1971). *Systematic thinking for social action*. Washington, DC: Brookings Institution.

Scriven, M. (1967). The methodology of evaluation. In R. E. Stake (Ed.), *Curriculum evaluation: AERA monograph series on evaluation* (pp. 39–85). Chicago: Rand McNally.

Scriven, M. (1991). Beyond formative and summative evaluation. In M. McLaughlin & D. C. Phillips (Eds.), *Evaluation and education: At quarter century. 90th yearbook of the National Society for the Study of Education, Part II* (pp. 19–64). Chicago: University of Chicago Press.

Shepard, L., & Smith, M. (1985). *Boulder Valley kindergarten study: Retention practices and retention effects*. Boulder, CO: Boulder Valley Public Schools.

Smith, E. R., & Tyler, R. W. (1942). *Appraising and recording student progress*. New York: Harper and Brothers.

Smith, M. C., & Rottenberg, C. (1991). Unintended consequences of external testing in elementary schools. *Educational Measurement: Issues and Practice*, *10*(4), 7–11.

Stake, R. (1981). Persuasions not models. *Educational Evaluation and Policy Analysis*, *3*(1), 83–84.

Stake, R. E. (1967). The countenance of educational evaluation. *Teachers College Record*, *68*, 523–540.

Stake, R. E. (1991). Retrospective on "The Countenance of Educational Evaluation." In M. McLaughlin & D. C. Phillips (Eds.), *Evaluation and education: At quarter century. 90th Yearbook of the National Society for the Study of Education, Part II* (pp. 67–90). Chicago: University Chicago Press.

Tyler, R. W. (1950). *Basic principles of curriculum construction*. Chicago: The University of Chicago.

Walberg, H. J., & Haertel, G. D. (1990). *The international encyclopedia of educational evaluation*. Oxford: Pergamon Press.

Walker, D. F., & Schaffarzick, J. (1974). Comparing curricula. *Review of Educational Research*, *44*(1), 83–112.

Weiss, C. (1986). The stakeholder approach to evaluation. In E. R. House (Ed.), *New directions in educational evaluation* (pp. 145–158). London: Falmer Press.

CHAPTER 2

The Evaluation Reality

The decade of the 1960s marked the beginning of evaluation as a type of inquiry. The period was one of optimism about the government's ability to solve social and educational problems. The optimism, however, was based on several assumptions that later proved to be inaccurate. The result was an initial disillusionment followed by a rethinking of the role and methods of evaluation.

EARLY BELIEFS

The Great Society legislation was based on the belief that educational and social problems could be solved through a process of social engineering. The belief was that problems could be clearly defined, specific solutions would be implemented and evaluated, and the evaluations would develop clear findings about successful programs (Shadish, Cook, & Leviton, 1991, p. 444). Experience indicated, however, that problems are complex and ill defined, programs were implemented in different ways at different sites, and evaluation was not prepared to deal with this complexity.

Evaluators also made assumptions about both the nature of curriculum and program development and the relationship to evaluation. These assumptions were (1) that social science theories could identify both the causes of social and educational problems and indicate likely interventions; (2) that the interventions would be implemented as planned, and evaluations would provide unambiguous answers about their effectiveness; and (3) that policymakers, program managers, and educators would welcome the evaluation results. They would willingly adopt and disseminate the "successes," and radically alter ineffective programs (Cook & Shadish, 1986; Suchman, 1967). In other words, evaluation would provide unequivocal information to decision makers. Acting on this information, decision makers would make go-no-go decisions about the programs.

In addition to basic assumptions about the role of evaluation, the prescribed policy for developing information in federally mandated evaluations was also based on unquestioned assumptions. As indicated in Chapter 1, the production factor concept was believed to apply to social and educational programs as well as manufacturing problems. Inputs, identified as resources or programs, were believed to be directly related to outputs (intended outcomes), which were identified as achievement. Because the evaluation goal was to identify the curriculum or program that maximized achievement, the question guiding the evaluations of the new curricula and the Head Start and Follow Through programs was, "Which [curriculum or which program] works best?"

Identification of the most effective programs, as measured by quantitative outcomes, required experimental (or at least quasi-experimental) designs. Use of the experimental paradigm as an evaluation strategy, however, implies certain conditions. They are:

1. Explicit goals from which causal hypotheses may be derived
2. Stable, homogeneous programs
3. Identification of effects that can be validly measured
4. Feasible designs that rule out spurious interpretations of treatment effects (Cook & Shadish, 1986, p. 217)

Reactions to Evaluation Findings

Multisite quantitative research in the public sector had not been attempted before on such a scale. However, no experience or knowledge base existed on which to question whether these conditions could be met. Therefore, both the funding agencies and the evaluators expected the studies to yield definitive results. Moreover, some advocates who believed strongly in the new programs did not envision situations in which evaluation might indicate little or no effects for an innovation.

For the most part, however, the evaluations indicated "no significant differences" between recipients of the interventions and nonrecipients. Program advocates questioned the relevance of outcome measures, program sponsors of some of the Follow Through models criticized the classifications of their programs in the evaluation, and researchers raised questions about the designs and methodology of the Head Start and Follow Through evaluations.

Subsequent reviews of the curriculum and program evaluations of the late 1960s and early 1970s revealed (1) errors in the basic assumptions about the process of developing solutions to educational problems, (2) problems with the applicability of the input/output model to social reality, and (3) the lack of correspondence between large-scale multisite projects and the essential conditions for experimental studies.

These reviews and discussions led to a rethinking of the role of evaluation in decision making and to an enrichment of the concepts and methods of evaluation.

The problems and issues raised by the early evaluations may be categorized into four major areas. They are implementation issues, measurement of outcomes, evaluation design, and the nature of decision making about new programs.

IMPLEMENTATION ISSUES

An understanding of implementation involves both the nature of the conceptual frameworks from which new curricula and programs are derived and the nature of the implementation process itself.

Nature of the Conceptual Framework

One of the erroneous beliefs about social policy was that social science theory would identify clear causes of social problems and suggest clearly defined solutions to those problems (Cook & Shadish, 1986, p. 195). In reality, the theories on which social interventions are based are not well defined, and information about the workings of society is limited, imprecise, and faulty (Cohen & Garet, 1975).

For example, the social programs of the 1960s were based on the belief that poverty, unemployment, and delinquency were the result of the lack of particular skills and attitudes—reading ability, motivation, and so on. Related assumptions were (1) that schools inculcate these skills and attitudes and (2) that the acquisition of these skills is the key to economic and occupational success. In other words, doing well in school was the key to doing well in life (Cohen & Garet, 1975, p. 21).

However, although education has long been viewed in American society as the key to opportunity, evidence as to the *ways* that education influences future life chances and the extent of that influence was lacking (Cohen & Garet, 1975). Therefore, the direction that compensatory education programs should take was not clear.

Similarly, many of the innovative curricula of the 1960s were not derived from explicit theories of learning. (The DISTAR reading and mathematics curricula and the Ypsilanti cognitive-development preschool curriculum are exceptions.) Many of the curricula were based on a general belief that discovery learning was important in the development of thinking skills. However, components of the curricula were not derived from a specific conceptual framework.

The importance of a conceptual framework for a curriculum or program is that, consistent with existing theory and research, it identifies clear links between the planned program and educational or social change. One problem with the lack of a conceptual framework is the difficulty in explaining ambiguous or negative outcomes of an evaluation. That is, was a curriculum or program less than successful because (1) program elements were not clearly defined, (2) the program was not implemented as intended, or (3) the program has little hope of influencing the selected variables?

In subsequent years, evaluation practice changed in order to be sensitive to these problems. Given that programs often are based on weak theories, one emerging role of evaluation became that of clarifying weaknesses in the conceptual links between beliefs and practice so that they may be tested in the evaluation of a new program.

Nature of the Implementation Process

The new curricula and social programs of the 1970s were disseminated to various schools and communities for implementation. Inexperienced in this process, federal agencies treated the process as simply one of adoption.

The Conception of Adoption.   Classic studies conducted by sociologists addressed the use of relatively simple innovations by different professions. Examples are the use of hybrid corn seed by farmers and the switch from sulphur-based medicines to antibiotics by physicians (Hall, 1992, p. 881). In these examples, the innovation was a particular product, and use required little or no effort. Also, the decision for use involved only a particular individual, that is, a farmer or a physician.

Because use of these new products involved little more than choice, the term *adoption* became associated with their implementation. The term also found its way into education. Early studies of school change, for example, addressed the addition of new offerings to the curriculum. Examples are driver's education and kindergarten, and they were referred to as adoptions. These changes were "add-ons," and they did not seek to change existing decision making or instructional practices. Therefore, the term *adoption* is an accurate description of their introduction into schooling.

Educators also assumed that product adoption would address needed changes in existing curricula. Federal dollars funded the development of complete sets of curriculum materials in a variety of subject areas that were then disseminated to schools. The intent was to update the processes of teaching as well as the content (Hall, 1992). These developments also were intended to be teacher-proof curricula that the individual teacher could not tamper with and, therefore, that would be implemented in hundreds of schools in essentially the same ways.

Similarly, in the area of early childhood education, federal dollars funded the development of several programs intended to address the deficits that disadvantaged children bring to the school setting. In Project Follow Through, the belief was that the models developed in laboratorylike university settings could be easily installed in other sites and that the models would be implemented in the various sites in substantially the same way.

Characteristics of Curricular Change.   Implementation of new curricula or programs differs from the adoption of a new product by a potential user. First, most educational innovations, although they may involve instructional materials, attempt to alter the processes of education. That is, most interventions seek to alter the decisions that are made about students (e.g., retention or promotion) or the ways they are taught. Therefore, implementation involves changes in both responsibilities and activities.

Second, implementation of a curriculum or program involves more than a single decision maker addressing a fairly simple "use/don't use" choice. In the school setting, administrative approval and support in both the local school and the district are essential if the intended changes in activities and responsibilities are to take place. Charters and Jones (1973) identified the levels of decision making and change that are essential for implementation in the classroom. Referred to as the levels of reality of a school program, they are institutional commitment, changes in the structural context, changes in teacher roles, and changes in learning activities. These four levels are summarized in Table 2.1. In other words, institutional commitment and changes in the structural context are not sufficient to indicate that program implementation has occurred.

Therefore, impacting the processes of education depends on factors other than simply the development and introduction of new materials into the classroom. Not surprisingly, the experiences of funding agencies during this period led to the realization that adoption did not ensure successful implementation (Berman & McLaughlin, 1978; Fullan, 1982; Hall & Loucks, 1977; McLaughlin, 1990). The development of exciting new curricula or appealing policies does not lead to successful change processes in schools without addressing the requirements for implementation (Hall, 1992, p. 883).

Table 2.1
Levels of reality of a school program

Level	Description
1. Institutional Commitment	A public announcement that the school intends to introduce a particular program.
2. Structural Context	Changes in formal arrangements and physical conditions. Changes include forming committees, changing job titles, purchasing materials, holding workshops, scheduling classes, and so on.
3. Role Performance	Teacher behaviors must be observed to change as a result of the innovation. The teacher uses instructional packages, for example, rather than simply leaving them in the back of the classroom.
4. Learning Activities	Description or measurement of the educational program enacted by students. Students, for example, conduct independent research projects and report the results.

Summarized from Charters and Jones, 1973.

Systemic Responses to Innovation

Policymakers involved in formulating the federal educational initiatives of the late 1960s and early 1970s assumed a relatively strong relationship between policy "inputs," local responses, and intervention "outputs" (McLaughlin, 1990, p. 11). This policy, however, largely ignored "the 'black box' of local practices, beliefs, and traditions" (p. 11). Since that time, however, policy has matured, and research on planned change has yielded insights on the factors that influence implementation. The Rand change agent study, for example, demonstrated that the extent and direction of change at the local level was the result of local factors that were not under the control of higher level policymakers (McLaughlin, 1990). The study found that local reactions to a new policy or program have a greater significance for outcomes than do characteristics such as technology, program design, funding levels, or government directives (McLaughlin, 1990).

Local beliefs and practices and the extent of institutional support lead to at least five different systemic reactions to innovations that vary from the status quo. Three reactions, identified by McLaughlin (1976, p. 169), are mutual adaptation, co-optation, and non-implementation. A fourth reaction is that of treatment diffusion, or project seepage. A fifth response involves the various types of reactivity by individuals or groups in a situation in which two programs or curricula are perceived to be competing with each other.

Mutual Adaptation.   In mutual adaptation, modification of the project design and changes in the local institutional setting and personnel occur during implementation. Local beliefs and practices influence the ways that the innovation will be interpreted and implemented. For example, the early implementations of Head Start varied in the types of goals, length of the school day, length of the school year, and teacher-pupil ratio. In the Follow Through evaluation, various models of early childhood education were developed and implemented in different sites. The evaluation of Project Follow Through combined the sites implementing a particular model and then compared the aggregation for a model with the other models. However, the analyses indicated that the variation in results among sites using the same model *was ten times the variation across models* (Glass, 1979). Thus, the sites representing a particular model differed from each other more than they differed from sites representing other models.

Co-optation.   In this situation, project strategies are modified to conform in a *pro forma* fashion to the traditional practices the innovation was expected to replace. This situation occurs as a result of either resistance to change by the system or inadequate assistance for the implementers.

One mechanism for preventing co-optation, discovered by Weikart and Banet (1975, p. 65), was to provide an aide or another teacher to assist teachers in the High/Scope Cognitive Development Curriculum. The additional person served as a counterforce to negative reactions of school personnel who were not associated with the Follow Through project. The additional person in the classroom provided intellectual and emotional help to a teacher learning a new method.

Non-Implementation or the "No-Treatment" Project.   The term *no-treatment project* was coined by David Cohen (1970). It refers to projects that are never installed by the system or that break down during the course of implementation. This phenomenon typically occurs in local school sites that are far away from the central policy-making agency (typically, a federal agency) that mandated a new program. According to Cohen, a no-treatment program may occur in any of several ways, for example, when teachers or specialists never see the target children, when books and materials are never unpacked, or when goods or services reach students other than the target group. In other cases, a no-treatment project may occur when program monies are used to pay for goods and services already in use (p. 24).

An example is an evaluation study to assess the effects of differentiated staffing on student achievement that was conducted in the same schools in which others were studying the problems of implementing differentiated staffing (Charters & Jones, 1973). The evaluation study reached the conclusion of no significant difference in achievement gains between differentiated staffing and conventional staffing in two elementary schools. However, the data from the other research project indicated no key differences in the implementation of differentiated staffing and conventional staffing. The study evaluating the effects of the innovation had evaluated a nonevent.

Cronbach (1982) describes a federally supported program of bilingual instruction intended for children of Hispanic origin with a limited command of English. A premise of the program is that children who are more proficient in Spanish would benefit more from education if they were taught to read in Spanish first and then shifted to English (p. 17). The evaluator of the program, American Institutes for Research, discovered that many schools were shunting all Hispanic children with reading problems into the program, even though many of them spoke English better than Spanish. Further, the children were not returned to mainstream instruction after learning to read in Spanish.

Patton (1986, p. 124) describes a program funded by a state legislature to teach welfare recipients the basics of parenting and household management. Because the program became entangled in several political battles, the brochures were never distributed, workshops were not conducted, and caseworkers were not trained to assist recipients.

Treatment Diffusion, or Project Seepage.   An assumption of experimental comparison group designs is that the "treatment" received by one group of subjects differs from that of a no-treatment control (or the alternative treatments received by other groups).

A problem associated with the early curriculum studies is that the innovative curricula were desired products in the school system. One result was that materials from a new program were often borrowed by teachers who were friends of the teachers implementing the innovation. Also, administrators found ways of obtaining the new materials for their teachers. George (1965, p. 298) noted, in reviewing the results of a comparison study of BSCS biology and traditional biology, that "the BSCS program and philosophy have become so widely known that it is nearly impossible to identify a biology teacher that has not been influenced with this philosophy." He concluded that some of the conventional teachers very likely incorporated some of the BSCS materials into their teaching. [Referred to as the seepage effect by Cohen (1970), this phenomenon is also referred to as the "diffusion or imitation of treatment" threat to internal validity.]

In one study, Hall and Loucks (1977) identified the key classroom changes that characterized Individually Guided Education (IGE). They conducted observations in second and fourth grades in 11 IGE schools and 11 non-IGE schools matched by geographic location, socioeconomic factors, ethnic composition, and size (p. 268). Their results indicated that 20% of the IGE schools and 37% of the non-IGE schools were nonusers of the individualized curriculum in reading. Equally important, 80% of the IGE schools and 63% of the non-IGE schools were implementing key features of the innovative curriculum.

These data support Cronbach's concern that the variation among classes using an innovation may be equal to or greater than the variation between the "innovative" and "conventional" classes. Using one-way analysis of variance, Loucks (1975) found no significant differences between IGE and non-IGE schools. In the absence of analysis of use, these data might be erroneously interpreted that IGE did not make a difference.

Reactivity of Study Participants.   Evaluations of the innovative curricula of the late 1960s primarily implemented course comparison studies. As Cronbach (1963) noted, it is impossible for the teachers not to know which curriculum they are implementing. Thus, evaluators were unable to implement the "double-blind" controls used in experimental research. In drug testing, for example, valid results depend, in part, on a situation in which (1) drug and the placebo look alike and (2) both the doctor and the patient are unaware of who is receiving the medication (p. 676).

Three reactive responses associated with the "control" or comparison group in the early curriculum comparisons were identified. One reaction, referred to as the "John Henry" effect, describes the extra effort exerted by teachers in the control group to outperform the innovation (the "steel drivin' machine"). In other words, the teachers who are not teaching with the innovative curricula exert extra effort to demonstrate that their students can learn just as much as those who received the perceived advantage of the new course. [The John Henry effect also is referred to by Cook and Campbell (1979) as the "compensatory rivalry" threat to internal validity.]

Saretsky (1972) maintains that the John Henry effect was operating in the Office of Economic Opportunity study of performance contracting in 1970–71. The Battelle Memorial Institute's interim report cited above-average gains for the control groups in a majority of project sites. The gains were greater than that expected *by up to 1.6 years*. "Interviews with project directors and OEO personnel evoked comments such as 'when you entered the control group school you knew the race was on,' and 'those teachers were out to show that they could do a better job than those outsiders [performance contractors]'" (Saretsky, 1972, p. 580).

The opposite reaction also may occur among control group teachers. Teachers can become demoralized and behave in the classroom in ways that are less effective than their typical teaching. This reaction is referred to as "resentful demoralization" (Cook & Campbell, 1979).

A third reaction arises from the perception that teachers in the experimental group receive goods or services that are desirable. That is, they receive the "new goodies," which may include new materials and/or equipment, an additional planning period, and so on. One reaction to this perception is that administrators tend to compensate for the unequal benefits in the experimental/control groups by providing control group teachers with benefits from other sources. Described as the "compensatory equalization of treatments" (Cook & Campbell, 1979), such actions create an alternate treatment instead of a no-treatment control group.

The ambiguity of results from the early evaluations led to increased emphasis on describing program and project activities, that is, describing the "black box" of implementation (Cook & Shadish, 1986, p. 217). In other words, full explanations of the ways a program achieves particular effects is important because it identifies the factors that must be present if a program is to be effective when it is transferred to other sites (Cook & Shadish, 1986; Cronbach, 1982).

Summary

The curricular and social programs of the late 1960s and early 1970s were based on several assumptions. First, social change can be brought about by social engineering. Second, social science theories can identify the causes of problems, well-defined interventions will be implemented uniformly in different sites, and evaluators can compare the various sites and provide clear-cut information to administrators.

Experience indicated, however, that proposed solutions to social problems were based on weak conceptual frameworks that went untested. For example, education is viewed in America as the key to opportunity. However, the ways that education can contribute to an improved quality of life were not well understood. Further, many of the new curricula were based only on a general belief that discovery, learning, and exploration enhance thinking skills. They were not derived from an explicit conceptual framework.

In addition, the implementation process of innovations that seek to bring about systemic change was not well understood. The concept of adoption applies to simple innovations that involve a single user. In contrast, curricular change involves several stages and is influenced by local beliefs and conditions. Systemic responses to innovations that represent major changes are mutual adaptation, co-optation, non-implementation, treatment diffusion, and reactivity of study participants. These reactions alter the innovation and/or the findings about effectiveness. Subsequent evaluation practice addressed these issues and changed both the focus and breadth.

MEASUREMENT OF OUTCOMES

The production factor policy selected by the Office of the Assistant Secretary for Program Evaluation (ASPE) relied on a single indicator as an index of program effectiveness. Further, the variable selected to represent program effectiveness was achievement. This policy, however, led to problems in the evaluations of early childhood programs and the new subject-area curricula. Three specific problems resulting from this policy were the underrepresentation of program goals, the surrogate variable problem, and the curriculum overlap problem.

Underrepresentation of Program Goals

Legislating broad compensatory education programs, like broad social programs, requires both public pressure and the agreement of several constituencies. To obtain such agreement, all parties must subscribe to some of the program goals. The result is a broad and sometimes conflicting set of aims. Among the diverse aims of Title I, for example, were improving educational services in school districts with many poor children, providing fiscal relief to hard-pressed central cities and parochial schools, reducing minority discontent about the schools, and establishing federal involvement in local school problems (Cohen, 1970).

Given these aims, appropriate evaluation questions for Title I included (1) What was the impact of Title I upon the fiscal situation of the cities and their relationships with adjacent districts? (2) What was the impact of Title I on the fiscal position of parochial schools? and (3) What differences, if any, may be identified in quality education in the target schools as compared with the nontarget schools? (Cohen, 1970) However, the federal policy mandated use of the input/output concept with pupil achievement identified as the outcome indicator of program effectiveness.

Similarly, several different goals also were established for Head Start. They were improving the child's physical health, fostering the emotional and social development of the child, establishing patterns of expectations of success for the child, increasing the child's capacity to relate positively to family members and others, and increasing the dignity and self-worth within the child and the family.

Although idealistic in nature, these goals were logical sources of information for developing indicators of program impact. Logical outcomes to measure for Project Head Start, for example (depending on the emphasis in the particular program's activities), are physical health, social development (as evidenced by types of interactions with others), language development, attention span, and other learning-related skills.

The first evaluation of Head Start was not conducted until 3 years after its inception. However, for the academic year 1969 (the contract was awarded in June 1968), observations of the entering children on the above-named variables could have been made in September. Then observations in May 1969 of these characteristics would have provided the data for an estimate of growth during the year.

However, Cronbach and associates (1980) noted that a particular index was selected for Head Start and "the rest is history. Many of those who heard about the evaluation came to perceive Head Start as a program whose *sole* purpose was to raise children's aptitude. When the results on aptitude variables were unimpressive, the word went out that compensatory education had failed" (p. 173).

Similarly, the choice of achievement as the sole outcome variable for the innovative curricula in mathematics, science, foreign languages, and social studies also only partially represented the curriculum aims. Specifically, these curricula were intended to foster new ways of thinking in students. A one-shot, end-of-year assessment, however, does not adequately assess these process skills. Observations of students in laboratory settings as they attack problems, for example, is one method for addressing process-related curriculum goals.

The new curricula also were updated in new knowledge and the ways that the knowledge structure of the discipline was presented. Thus, another shortcoming of the use of a single summary score is that student failure to master one aspect of the course is masked by success in another direction (Cronbach, 1963).

The Surrogate Variable Problem

One of the long-range aims of compensatory education was to improve the economic and occupational status of poor children (Cohen, 1970). Such outcomes, however, can only be measured in the distant future and evaluations are not long-term studies. Therefore, immediate outcomes were needed that (1) represented program expectations and (2) were logical stepping-stones to later success. In other words, because the long-range outcomes could not be measured, appropriate surrogate or proxy variables were needed.

One assumption of the compensatory education programs was that doing well in school leads to doing well in life. Therefore, achievement or IQ were selected as surrogate variables for the long-range goal of improving the occupational status of poor children. However, other logical variables for disadvantaged children that are related to doing well in school are school attendance, self-confidence in learning, and learning-how-to-learn skills.

Further, achievement was defined as performance on one or more standardized tests. Powell and Sigel (1991) note that IQ scores were the most frequent outcome variables in evaluations of early childhood programs in the 1960s and 1970s. Among the reasons for their use were (1) the well-documented psychometric properties, (2) the relative ease of administration, and (3) the strong relationship to later school success. One limitation of IQ measures, however, is that they may be irrelevant to the program experiences (Powell & Sigel, 1991). For example, the standardized IQ test used in Project Follow Through was Raven's Progressive Matrices. One justification for use of the nonverbal test was that it was "value-free." However, the possibility that an educational program for disadvantaged children in grades 1 through 3 would impact aptitude on abstract reasoning tasks is minimal at best.

A second limitation of standardized IQ and achievement tests for disadvantaged children is that their scores are typically on the low end of the performance range. That is, fewer than 10% of the test items may be at a level of difficulty that most of the children can pass (Clarke-Stewart & Fein, 1983). Such tests, standardized on a diverse population, will be insensitive to individual differences among disadvantaged children (p. 940).

The Curriculum Overlap Problem

The term *curriculum overlap* refers to the match between a curriculum and a particular test (Leinhardt, 1983; Leinhardt & Seewald, 1981). In one study, Leinhardt and Seewald (1981) found that curriculum overlap is second only to prior achievement in explaining current performance on norm-referenced tests. Curriculum overlap becomes a problem when two curricula are compared on outcomes, and the achievement test matches one curriculum more than the other. An analysis of 26 curriculum studies by Walker and Schaffarzick (1974) indicated that "different curricula produce different patterns of achievement, not necessarily greater overall achievement" (p. 97). Groups in the innovative curricula scored higher on tests that favored the new courses. However, groups in the traditional curricula scored higher in comparisons in which test content more nearly resembled their courses.

In a comparison of the CHEM curriculum with traditional chemistry curricula, groups in the innovative curriculum scored significantly higher only on an application subtest of the end-of-course test (Herron, 1966). This performance was consistent with the intent of the CHEM curriculum. Similarly, a study of mathematics curricula indicated that groups in the traditional course scored higher on traditional tests, and groups in the innovative curricula scored higher on a test of skills and applications (Herron, 1966). Thus, the extent to which a particular test matched the curriculum intent influenced the outcomes.

Summary

The production factor concept specified achievement as the appropriate indicator of program effectiveness. This policy led to at least three problems. One is that achievement did not represent the range of program goals of the innovations. The goals for Head Start, for example, addressed the child's physical health, social development, and self-esteem. Similarly, the innovative curriculum developments were intended to foster new ways of thinking. This goal implies process measures as well as outcome measures.

A second problem is that achievement is a poor surrogate variable for the anticipated long-range outcomes of compensatory programs. In contrast, school attendance, self-confidence in learning, and learning-how-to-learn skills are appropriate indicators of the potential for doing well in life. Moreover, achievement in early childhood programs was measured by standardized achievement tests that were not responsive to small changes in the children's cognitive abilities.

A third problem in curriculum comparison studies is the curriculum overlap problem. The problem occurs when the postcourse achievement test matches one curriculum. Because different curricula often produce different patterns of achievement, multiple indicators of curriculum effectiveness should be used.

DESIGN ISSUES

The question asked in the early evaluations was, "Which [curriculum or which program] works best?" School sites were identified as project sites, and the students were compared with a selected nonintervention group. Two problems emerged from this strategy. First, by combining all intervention sites, the effects of strong implementations of a particular innovation were countered by weak or variant implementations. Thus, the observed effect for all sites was less than that of some sites and greater than that of others. In other words, a wash-out effect could occur in which weak implementations outweigh strong implementations of a program.

A different problem faced compensatory programs such as Head Start. Social ethics prevents the denial of treatment to needy subjects. Thus, a typical practice was to first select the treatment group and then to search for a control group from the untreated residual population (Campbell & Boruch, 1975). Control group subjects typically were children from the same neighborhoods or elementary schools who were similar to the program participants in family background, early childhood experiences, and other demographic variables.

However, this procedure did not ensure comparable groups, and the Westinghouse–Ohio State evaluation of Head Start was criticized because the control group was not comparable to the Head Start children. A subsequent suggestion was to choose control group subjects from children on the waiting lists for Head Start. The belief was that, because both groups were chosen from a pool of disadvantaged children, they would be comparable. However, an analysis of Head Start selectees and waiting list children indicated that those chosen for the program were more disadvantaged in both background and initial ability than those who were not chosen (Lee, Brooks-Gunn, & Schnur, 1988). The mothers of the Head Start children had less education and the children lived in more congested quarters and were from larger families than those on the waiting list. In other words, these groups were not equivalent.

One approach to attempting to correct this problem was to adjust posttest scores statistically on the basis of differences in entry characteristics. Analysis of covariance (ANCOVA) was used to adjust the posttest scores on the basis of pretest performance. In essence, ANCOVA subtracts the pretest differences between the groups from the posttest performance.

However, the two groups differed on process characteristics that interacted with instruction, and ANCOVA cannot compensate for such differences. That is, children with a poor knowledge base and inadequate learning strategies are being compared with children who have both an adequate knowledge base and adequate learning strategies. Recent research on Chapter I indicates that low achievers, *even if motivated,* "are likely to learn less and to remember less of what they learn originally, because they rely mostly on rote memorizing and other inefficient learning skills" (Brophy, 1988, p. 262).

Therefore, in comparisons of disadvantaged children with more able children, the more able groups will gain more than the others by virtue of their learning-related skills. This growth pattern may be described as that of the "rich get richer" or

Figure 2.1
Differential growth rates of disadvantaged and able children

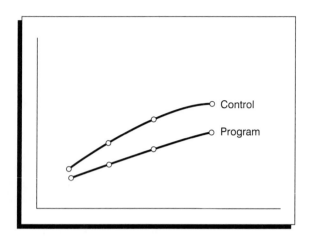

"the able become more able" (Cook & Campbell, 1979, p. 107). The pattern is characterized by an increase in the mean difference between the nonequivalent groups over time, that is, nonparallel growth lines (see Figure 2.1). The result is an estimate of ineffectiveness for the compensatory education program. In other words, when the treatment group and the comparison group are selected from different populations, neither matching on a few selected characteristics nor ANCOVA can compensate for group differences that influence the outcomes of the study.

Discussion

The evaluation question of which program or curriculum worked best predetermined comparison studies in which the innovation was compared with some traditional program or a no-treatment group. However, the new curricula and programs were implemented on a broad scale in different ways and, for some programs, no equivalent comparison group was available.

The underlying problem, however, is that the basic question did not provide the most useful information to decision makers. A more useful question is, Which implementations work best and why? This question implies an in-depth study of program sites in which they are differentiated into strong, moderate, and weak implementations with an evaluation of the effects of each level of implementation. In the case of programs targeted for a disadvantaged group, a pretest-posttest design can provide information on program effects. Outcome data can then be compared with data from more able groups to determine the extent of the deficit that is addressed by the intervention.

Subsequent evaluation practice changed in several ways in response to these and other issues. First, evaluators developed alternatives to the multisite comparison group design. Second, the focus of evaluation broadened to include outcomes that program experiences may be expected to address. Third, multiple indicators of any identified outcome are recommended, rather than relying on one test or type of observation (Cronbach & associates, 1980). Fourth, new programs and policies affect individuals in addition to those directly receiving services. Thus, data are collected on the experiences of program participants, and program effects on teachers and other students are determined as well.

NATURE OF DECISION MAKING

Two early beliefs about the nature of decision making were (1) that solving educational and social problems is an analytical rational process and (2) that policy managers are the sole determinants of action about programs, which typically involve go-no-go decisions. Both beliefs were found to be in error.

The Westinghouse–Ohio State evaluation of Head Start, for example, indicated no significant differences in outcomes between the Head Start and non-Head Start sample. However, the program was not discontinued (as the rational analysis model would predict). Instead, the evaluation results entered a public arena where they were scrutinized and discussed. Social scientists criticized the design and methodology of the evaluation and, therefore, questioned the results. Moreover, the program had a strong constituent clientele. Therefore, the program was continued, although everyone agreed it had not operated "as magically as promised" (Cronbach & associates, 1980, p. 128). Changes were made on the basis of the evaluation, however. The brief summer programs were eliminated, and parents were brought into active participation in the program (p. 128).

The setting for educational decision making differs from the analytical decision making model in at least three ways. First, educational and social problems (unlike problems in geometry) do not have indisputable solutions (Cronbach & associates, 1980). That is, there is no single, easily identifiable right answer to complex problems such as years of poor reading performance.

Second, an evaluation is only one piece of information that enters into discussions and perceptions of programs. Evaluation results become part of a larger context in which many priorities are operating. Examples are the need to be responsible to disadvantaged children or the importance of providing positive reading experiences for first graders. In other words, evaluation information is considered in a context in which needs, priorities, and other types of information also are important.

Third, policy managers are not sole decision makers who act in a vacuum. Instead, their decisions are influenced by program personnel and constituencies. Legislators, school board members, and administrative officers are influenced by teachers, principals, social workers, program staff, program clients, taxpayers, and others. The perceptions and information needs of these groups influence the extent to which evaluation information will impact decision making. For example, critics of the early evaluations contended that much of the data did not address the needs of people involved in programs. Outcome data, in other words, provided little information to staff on ways to improve the program (Weiss, 1986, p. 146).

Two changes observed in evaluation practice between 1965 and 1985 responded to the nature of decision making in a social setting. One change was that of broadening the audience for evaluation findings to a group, referred to by Cronbach and associates (1980) as the policy shaping community. This group consists of the audiences or stakeholders with an interest in the program, that is, teachers, parents, taxpayers, and so on. This change influenced both the issues to be addressed in an evaluation and the ways that evaluation findings are disseminated.

The second change was that of conceptualizing usage more broadly. That is, evaluation may assist in specific decisions, may play a codeterminate role in decisions, may enter both formal and informal debates about policies and programs, and may enhance the enlightenment of all stakeholders in a program (Cook & Shadish, 1986; Cronbach & associates, 1980). Therefore, sources for disseminating evaluation knowledge currently include reports and representations aimed at various audiences and ad hoc media presentations of findings, as well as presentations at meetings and conferences. This view of evaluation provides a role in deepening the understanding of members of the policy shaping community about programs, issues, and problems.

OVERVIEW OF THE TEXT

The chapters in this text are designed to provide information about evaluation practice and methods that have evolved since the 1960s. Among the information needs described in this chapter are the rationale and conceptual framework for a program, the context in which it is implemented, the methods of implementation, and the extent to which program goals are addressed. Chapter 3, Utilitarian Perspectives, describes four approaches for developing this information for decision makers.

Other concerns expressed about the early evaluations were that they failed to address issues important to program constituents and others. Approaches to evaluation sensitive to the pluralistic views of programs are described in Chapter 4, Intuitionist/Pluralist Perspectives.

Part II of the text, Tools of Evaluation, describes the purposes, limitations, and advantages of different types of measurements and methodologies useful in evaluation. Chapter 5 describes various methods for obtaining input from different groups on program needs, goals, interpretations of effects, and other issues.

Chapters 6, 7, 8, and 9 discuss different kinds of assessment. Chapter 6 describes the purpose for which norm-referenced tests were designed and their limitations in evaluation. The two major types of criterion-referenced tests also are described, as well as their advantages and disadvantages for measuring cognitive outcomes. Alternative assessment, a relatively new movement in education, is discussed in Chapters 7 and 8. Chapter 7 describes performance assessment, and Chapter 8 discusses portfolio assessment. Chapter 9 identifies the differences between attitudes and beliefs and the difficulty in obtaining valid assessments. Different methods of assessment are discussed.

One of the neglected aspects of evaluation in the early years was the nature of the program and the culture in which it operates. Chapter 10 provides an overview of qualitative inquiry methods and discusses their utility in developing an insider's view of how a particular program culture is functioning.

Part III of the text, Development of the Evaluation Plan and Implementation of the Evaluation, works through each of the major decision making steps in evaluation. Chapter 11 discusses the important steps in negotiating the evaluation contract and the responsibilities of the evaluator and the client. Developing a program definition is discussed in Chapter 12, along with the importance of this task in identifying potential evaluation questions and avoiding problems in the evaluation. This chapter addresses the need to identify potential weak links in the conceptual framework of a program described in this chapter. Chapter 13 discusses developing the evaluation framework, which includes the differences between formative and summative evaluation, considerations in selecting evaluation questions, selecting an appropriate design, and developing a management plan.

Chapter 14 describes methods for documenting program implementation so that strong sites can be differentiated in the data analysis from weak program implementations. Developing information about program operation and the institutional climate in which the program resides also is discussed. Data analysis and interpretation are discussed in Chapter 15. Both quantitative and qualitative data are included.

An important task in a successful evaluation is the communication of evaluation findings to potential information users. Chapter 16 discusses the importance of communicating findings in nonjargon terminology, ways to visually display data, and various mechanisms for disseminating evaluation information to different audiences. Finally, Chapter 17 addresses ethical issues in evaluation. Ethical issues involve respecting evaluation participants and protecting the confidentiality of information, as well as representing the program fairly in terms of all the groups it is intended to serve. Potential conflicts of interest for the evaluator also are discussed.

CHAPTER QUESTIONS

1. Why should evaluation plans address the links in a program's conceptual framework?

2. Why is the term *adoption* inappropriate for curricular reform efforts?

3. An institution does not go beyond public announcements, distributing materials to teachers, and holding one faculty meeting on a social studies program designed to increase understanding of other cultures. Which type of systemic reaction is this?

4. What are some likely reactions to the introduction in some classrooms of a highly publicized innovation that includes computers and other technology?

5. An early childhood program focuses on involving the parents of disadvantaged children in school advisory councils, in-class activities, and school parent organizations. Why is achievement an inappropriate measure for this program?

6. Describe the design problem faced by compensatory education programs.

REFERENCES

Berman, P., & McLaughlin, M. (1978). *Federal programs supporting change*. Santa Monica, CA: The Rand Corporation.

Brophy, J. (1988). Research linking teacher behavior to student achievement: Potential implications for instruction of Chapter I students. *Educational Psychologist, 23*(3), 235–286.

Campbell, D. T., & Boruch, R. F. (1975). Making the case for randomized assignment to treatments by considering the alternatives. In C. A. Bennett & A. A. Lumsdaine (Eds.), *Evaluation and experiment: Some critical issues in assessing social programs* (pp. 195–298). New York: Academic Press.

Charters, W., & Jones, J. (1973). On the risk of appraising non-events in program evaluation. *Educational Researcher, 2*(11), 5–7.

Clark-Stewart, K., & Fein, G. (1983). Early childhood programs. In M. Haith & J. Compas (Eds.), *Handbook of child psychology: Vol. 2. Infancy and developmental psychobiology* (pp. 917–999). New York: Wiley.

Cohen, D. (1970). Politics and research: Evaluation of social action programs. *Review of Educational Research, 40*(2), 213–238.

Cohen, D., & Garet, M. S. (1975). Reforming educational policy with applied social research. *Harvard Educational Review, 45*(1), 17–43.

Cook, T. D., & Campbell, D. T. (1979). *Quasi-experimentation. Design and analysis issues for field settings*. Chicago: Rand McNally.

Cook, T. D., & Shadish, W. R. (1986). Program evaluation. In M. R. Rosenzweig & L. W. Porter (Eds.), *Annual Review of Psychology* (Vol. 37, pp. 193–232). Palo Alto: Annual Reviews Inc.

Cronbach, L. J. (1963). Course improvement through evaluation. *Teachers College Record, 64*, 672–683.

Cronbach, L. J. (1982). *Designing evaluations of educational and social programs*. San Francisco: Jossey-Bass.

Cronbach, L. J., Ambron, S., Dornbusch, S., Hess, R., Hornik, R., Phillips, D., Walker, D., & Weiner, S. (1980). *Toward reform of program evaluation*. San Francisco: Jossey-Bass.

Fullan, M. (1982). *The meaning of educational change*. New York: Teachers College Press, Columbia.

George, K. D. (1965). The effect of BSCS and conventional biology on critical thinking. *Journal of Research in Science Teaching, 3*, 293–299.

Glass, G. E. (1979). Policy for the unpredictable (uncertainty research and policy). *Educational Researcher, 8*(9), 12–14.

Hall, G. (1992). The local educational change process and policy implementation. *Journal of Research in Science Teaching, 29*(8), 877–904.

Hall, G., & Loucks, S. (1977). A developmental model for determining whether the treatment is actually implemented. *American Educational Research Journal, 14*(3), 263–276.

Herron, T. (1966). Evaluation and the new curricula. *Journal of Research in Science Teaching, 4*, 159–170.

Lee, V. E., Brooks-Gunn, J., & Schnur, E. (1988). Does Head Start work? A one-year follow-up comparison of disadvantaged children attending Head Start, no preschool and other preschool programs. *Developmental Psychology, 24*, 210–222.

Leinhardt, G. (1983). Overlap: Testing whether it is taught. In G. Madaus (Ed.), *The courts, validity, and minimum competency testing* (pp. 153–170). Boston: Kluwer-Nijhoff.

Leinhardt, G., & Seewald, A. (1981). Overlap: What's Tested, What's Taught? *Journal of Educational Measurement, 18*, 85–96.

Loucks, S. F. (1975). *A study of the relationship between teacher level of use of the innovation of individualized instruction and student achievement.* Unpublished doctoral dissertation, University of Texas, Austin.

McLaughlin, M. (1976). Implementation as mutual adaption: Change in classroom organization. In W. Williams & R. Elmore (Eds.), *Social program implementation* (pp. 167–182). New York: Academic Press.

McLaughlin, M. (1990). The Rand change agent study revisited: Macro perspectives and micro realities. *Educational Researcher, 19*(9), 11–16.

Patton, M. (1986). *Utilization-focused evaluation* (2nd ed.). Newbury Park: Sage.

Powell, D., & Sigel, I. (1991). Searches for validity in evaluating young children and early childhood programs. In B. Spodek & O. Saracho (Eds.), *Issues in early childhood curriculum* (pp. 190–212). New York: Teachers College Press, Columbia.

Saretsky, J. O. (1972). The OEO PC experiment and the John Henry effect. *Phi Delta Kappan, 53*, 579–581.

Shadish, W., Cook, T., & Leviton, L. (1991). *Foundations of program evaluation.* Newbury Park: Sage.

Suchman, E. A. (1967). *Evaluative research: Principles and practice in public service and social action programs.* New York: Russell Sage Foundation.

Walker, D. F., & Schaffarzick, J. (1974). Comparing curricula. *Review of Educational Research, 44*(1), 83–111.

Weikart, D., & Banet, B. (1975). Model design problems in Follow Through. In A. M. Rivlin & P. M. Timpane (Eds.), *Planned variation in education: Should we give up or try harder?* (pp. 61–77). Washington, DC: The Brookings Institution.

Weiss, C. (1986). The stakeholder approach to evaluation. In E. R. House (Ed.), *New directions in educational evaluation* (pp. 145–158). London: Falmer Press.

CHAPTER 3

Utilitarian Perspectives

The production factor concept of evaluation imposed by the Department of Health, Education, and Welfare is an example of the social utility perspective. Indicators, such as the gross national product (economics) or mean test scores (education), identify the most useful practices or programs (House, 1978). However, the limited nature of the selected outcomes, the failure to adequately portray the nature of programs, and the lack of attention to the informational needs of decision makers and others led to the development of other evaluation perspectives.

One group of evaluation approaches, referred to as management models (Hamilton, 1977) or utilitarian models (House, 1978), sought to remedy the problems of the production factor concept by improving the process of rational decision making (Hamilton, 1977). The utilitarian perspectives broadened the database used for decision making and expanded the types of decisions beyond that of only student outcomes. These approaches also are referred to as preordinate (Stake, 1975; House, 1978) because they rely on specific designs, identification of objectives, operational definitions of variables, and primarily numerical data.

Although these approaches extended the activities included in evaluation, they share three major characteristics with the production factor concept. First, a key assumption is that the audience for an evaluation is a predetermined decision maker. Second, they rely on predetermined standards as a means of evaluating social utility. Third, the data and performance criteria relate to the total system, rather than to individuals, students, or teachers (Hamilton, 1977).

The utilitarian approaches are the Provus discrepancy model, the CIPP model, Stake's countenance approach, and Scriven's concept of goal-free evaluation. Both the Provus model and the CIPP model are designed for institutions or school districts that have a permanent evaluation staff. Stake's countenance approach and Scriven's perspective address important categories of information in any program evaluation.

THE PROVUS DISCREPANCY MODEL

The model developed by Malcolm Provus (1969, 1971) views the process of evaluation somewhat differently than the other utilitarian models. Specifically, evaluation is viewed as a continuous information-management process that should address program improvement as well as program assessment (Provus, 1969). Thus, the model is similar to the Tyler perspective in that evaluation is treated as a component of program development.

Development of the model began with the identification by Provus (1969) of a problem in program evaluation. He noted that many school programs were quickly formulated and put in place without extensive development or careful planning as to resource needs and utilization (Provus, 1969). Therefore, to compare these "instant installation" programs with existing programs to determine their effectiveness missed the important evaluation question; that is, the first evaluation task is to determine what constitutes a new program. Therefore, the model incorporates program definition and installation as important stages in evaluation.

The model is designed for a school system with a permanent evaluation staff. As a program moves through the various developmental stages, staff may be involved with the program for up to 5 years. Also, like the Tyler model, evaluation and program staff work closely together in generating information about the program.

Provus (1969) described the purpose of evaluation as that of determining whether to improve, maintain, or terminate a program. His model is primarily a problem-solving set of procedures that seeks to identify weaknesses (according to selected standards) and to take corrective actions with termination as the option of last resort.

Components

A key component of the model is the four stages of evaluation that correspond to the four developmental stages of educational programs. They are:

1. Establishment and evaluation of the program definition

2. Evaluation of program installation

3. Verification of the relationships between teacher-student interactions and intermediate program objectives

4. Evaluation of program outcomes (Provus, 1969)

Another major component is the detailed set of questions that are to be applied in each stage.

The model is often referred to as a discrepancy model because, at each of the four stages, program performance is compared with selected standards to determine the discrepancy. This information is then used to identify program weaknesses and to take corrective action (Provus, 1969).

Evaluation Stages.   In Stage I, the basic question is, Is the program adequately defined? That is, the definition should describe a program's purpose, required conditions, and transactions. Also, the evaluation should determine if the program has specified student entry behaviors, staff qualifications and training, media, facilities, and administrative conditions. If not, then this information must be developed.

Next, the evaluators are to analyze the program definition for clarity, internal consistency, and comprehensiveness (Provus, 1969). The importance of subjecting the blueprint of the program to such rigorous analysis is to determine if there is justification for sustaining the program to the next developmental stage (Provus, 1969). A program may be terminated justifiably, for example, if resources do not meet minimal levels to operate the program, program components are inconsistent with each other or other school programs, or the program defies comprehensive definition.

The standard for Stage II evaluation, program installation, is the program definition that is arrived at in Stage I. The key question is, Is the program installed? Observations in the field are compared with the definition, and discrepancy information is used to change installation procedures or redefine the program.

In Stage III, the evaluation staff collect data that indicate the extent to which student behavior is changing in predicted ways. The orienting question for this stage is, Are the enabling objectives being met? Addressing this issue adequately requires flowcharting the relationships between learning activities, enabling objectives, and terminal objectives. Thus, learning activities can be evaluated for their effectiveness, given program assumptions about student readiness and rate of learning. In other words, Stage III evaluation involves building an expanding database of student characteristics, classroom activities, and changing student behavior.

Stage IV evaluation is the assessment of program outcomes. That is, are the program objectives achieved in the implementation? The standard is the terminal objectives of the program, and program performance information is obtained from criterion measures of the objectives (Provus, 1969).

Procedures

The model provides detailed analytical procedures for the four stages of evaluation. This process is illustrated in Figure 3.1. In Stage I, if a discrepancy is discovered between the program definition and the taxonomy, this discrepancy is then analyzed (questions A, B, and C) to identify appropriate corrective action. Follow-up of the corrective action is then conducted (questions 2 through 5). Unless the program is terminated for lack of key components, the evaluation proceeds to Stage II.

Figure 3.1
Summary of the decision process in the Provus discrepancy model

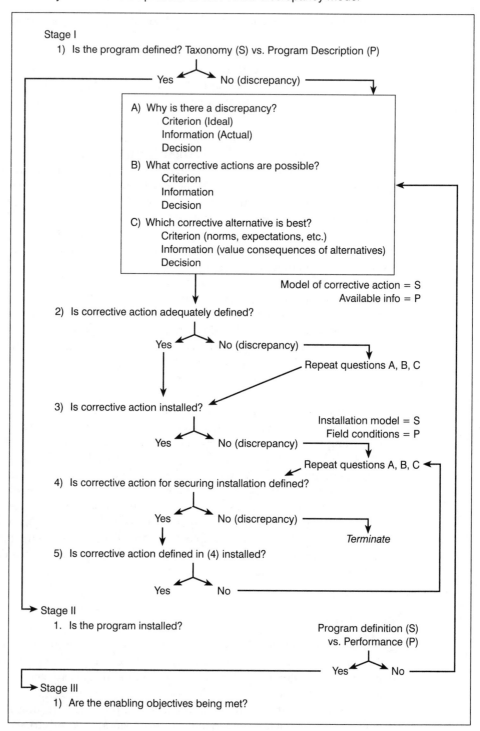

Summarized from Provus, 1969.

A major feature of the model is that the questions asked in Stage I are also a template for the evaluations in Stages II, III, and IV. Question 1 in each stage differs (e.g., the question for Stage II is, Is the program installed?), and the criteria for decision making differ. However, the analytical process is the same.

In addition to the five basic questions asked at each stage of the evaluation, the model also provides an analytical procedure for subquestions A, B, and C. This process is illustrated in Table 3.1. The development of an answer to each question requires establishing a criterion, identifying the actual course of action taken and/or available information, and choosing a course of action to resolve the discrepancy. The fit between this analysis and question 1 in each stage is quite good. However, it is less so for questions 2 through 5. For example, question 2 asks if the corrective action is adequately defined. When the answer is no, then the logical approach is to define the corrective action more adequately instead of undertaking the analysis prescribed in questions A, B, and C.

Strengths and Weaknesses

Major strengths of the Provus model are the emphasis on program definition, analysis of the consistency and comprehensiveness of program definitions, and the focus on evaluating the extent to which the program is installed. These issues, introduced by Provus, continue to be major evaluation issues today. (Chapters 12 and 14 discuss specific steps for addressing these potential problems.)

Another strength of the model is that it introduced the concept of information management and the importance of constructing databases that link student characteristics, classroom processes, and student outcomes. Fifteen years later, Cooley and Bickel (1986), in their description of a long-term evaluation relationship with a large city school system, indicated that they could not begin to provide meaningful information to the administration until they had constructed a similar database.

Table 3.1
Problem-solving analysis of an identified discrepancy

Question	Criterion	Information	Decision
(A) Why is there a discrepancy?	Expected ideal	Actual course of action taken and/or available information	Identify breakdown points
(B) What corrective actions are possible?	Ideal choices	Operational constraints	Choose from the set that satisfies field demands
(C) Which corrective action is best?	Norms, expectations, professional standards	Value consequences of alternative field constraints	Choose alternatives with best value-configuration fit

Summarized from Provus, 1969.

A third strength of the model is that it developed an ongoing partnership between the permanent evaluation staff and program planners and developers. A fourth strength is the use of formative evaluation (revision and correction) to redirect a program in the early stages of development and installation.

One weakness of the model is the extensive time investment required to implement the model. This weakness is related in part to the lengthy sequential questioning that must be undertaken in order to reach a decision. One purpose of the questions was to be able to involve program staff in the process. However, the application of questions A, B, and C to every identified discrepancy is a "force fit" in some cases.

A second weakness is that implementation of Stages III and IV requires the specification of intermediate and terminal objectives for the program. However, many innovative programs are not organized in this way. Finally, the taxonomy identified as a standard for the program definition is simply a listing of categories. The actual standards, such as the amount and timing of teacher training, for example, must be developed elsewhere.

THE CIPP PERSPECTIVE

The CIPP perspective, developed by Daniel Stufflebeam et al. (1971) and updated by Stufflebeam and Shinkfeld (1985), defines the major purpose of evaluation as that of providing useful information for decision making. Secondary purposes are to serve accountability needs and to promote understanding of the program strategy or object being evaluated.

The approach is based on two major assumptions about evaluation. These assumptions are (1) that evaluations have a vital role in stimulating and planning change and (2) that evaluation is an integral component of an institution's regular program. Thus, evaluation is not a specialized activity associated with innovative projects, and the CIPP perspective is not intended to guide the conduct of an individual study (Stufflebeam, 1980). Instead, like the Provus model, the purpose is to provide ongoing evaluation services to administrators and other decision makers in an institution or school district (Stufflebeam & Shinkfeld, 1985, p. 165).

Components

Evaluation in the CIPP perspective is the process of delineating, obtaining, and providing information to judge decision alternatives (Stufflebeam, et al., 1971). These processes are executed for four types of administrative divisions, each of which represents a type of evaluation. These evaluations may be conducted independently or in an integrated sequence. They are as follows:

Planning decisions	–	context evaluation
Structuring decisions	–	input evaluation
Implementing decisions	–	process evaluation
Recycling decisions to judge and react to program attainments (Stufflebeam, et al., 1971)	–	product evaluation

Context Evaluation.   The original focus of context evaluation was to provide a rationale for setting objectives. Desired and actual conditions in the environment were described, unmet needs and unused opportunities were identified, and problems that prevented needs from being met were diagnosed (Stufflebeam et al., 1971). Decisions resulting from context evaluation were identification of the setting to be served, general program goals, and specific objectives.

In contrast, the current expanded focus of context evaluation is to identify the strengths and weaknesses of an institution, a program, a target population, or a person and to indicate direction for improvement (Stufflebeam, 1980; Stufflebeam & Shinkfeld, 1985). The objectives are (1) to assess the object's overall status, (2) to identify its deficiencies and the strengths available to correct the weaknesses, and (3) to diagnose problems that are limiting the object's well being (Stufflebeam & Shinkfeld, 1985, p. 169).

The results of a context evaluation are intended to provide a sound basis for either adjusting or establishing goals and priorities and identifying needed changes (Stufflebeam & Shinkfeld, 1985, p. 172). One suggested use of context evaluation is as a means for a school district to communicate with the public to achieve a shared understanding of the district's strengths, weaknesses, needs, opportunities, and pressing problems. Other uses are to convince a funding agency of the worth of a project, to develop objectives for staff development, to select schools for priority assistance, and to help parents or advisers focus on developmental areas requiring attention (Stufflebeam & Shinkfeld, 1985, p. 172).

Input Evaluation.   The original focus of input evaluation was to provide information for three key decisions. Specifically, Is outside assistance needed to achieve the objectives? Should the project adopt available solutions or develop new ones? and What procedural plan should be used to implement the selected solutions? (Stufflebeam et al., 1971).

The current perspective is that of searching out and critically examining potentially appropriate approaches intended to bring about change (Stufflebeam & Shinkfeld, 1985, p. 173). Thus, an input evaluation identifies and rates relevant approaches and also thoroughly analyzes the one selected for installation. An important component of this analysis is to identify any barriers or constraints in the client's environment that may influence or impede the operation of the program. In other words, the purpose of input evaluation is to help clients consider alternatives in terms of their particular needs and circumstances and to help develop a workable plan for them (Stufflebeam, 1980; Stufflebeam & Shinkfeld, 1985).

Process Evaluation.   The focus of process evaluation is the implementation of a program or a strategy. The main purpose is to provide feedback about needed modification if the implementation is inadequate. That is, Are program activities on schedule? Are they being implemented as planned? Are available resources being used efficiently? and Do program participants accept and carry out their roles? (Stufflebeam & Shinkfeld, 1985, p. 175). In addition, process evaluation should provide a comparison of the actual implementation with the intended program, the costs of the implementation, and participants' judgments of the quality of the effort (Stufflebeam & Shinkfeld, 1985, p. 175).

Although the main purpose is to provide feedback on the extent of implementation, process evaluation can fulfill two other functions. They are (1) to provide information to external audiences who wish to learn about the program and (2) to assist program staff, evaluators, and administrators in interpreting program outcomes.

Important to the success of a process evaluation is an evaluator who is responsible for observing and documenting program activities. Staff and administrators do not have the time required to develop the needed information for a sound process evaluation. Also important, of course, is that the data collection should be as unobtrusive as possible.

Product Evaluation.   The primary function of product evaluation is "to measure, interpret, and judge the attainments of a program" (Stufflebeam & Shinkfeld, 1985, p. 176). Product evaluation, therefore, should determine the extent to which identified needs were met, as well as identify the broad effects of the program. The evaluation should document both intended and unintended effects and negative as well as positive outcomes.

Performance assessments of the program may include test performance compared with preset standards, pretest performance, a profile of assessed needs, or the performance of a comparison group (Stufflebeam & Shinkfeld, 1985, p. 177). Performance should be reported for the total group and subgroups of participants that differ in needs and services received.

In addition, program recipients and observers may complete ratings of the program, and experts may assess work products developed in the program. Hearings or group interviews may be conducted to generate hypotheses about unexpected outcomes, which may then be followed by systematic investigation to support or disconfirm the hypotheses (Stufflebeam & Shinkfeld, 1985, p. 178). Particularly important, however, is that judgments of program success should be obtained from a broad range of people associated with the program.

The primary use of product evaluation is to determine whether a program should be continued, repeated, and/or extended to other settings (Stufflebeam, 1980; Stufflebeam & Shinkfeld, 1985). However, it should also provide direction for modifying the program to better serve the needs of participants and to become more cost effective. Finally, product evaluation is an essential component of an accountability report (Stufflebeam & Shinkfeld, 1985, p. 178).

Strengths and Weaknesses

A strength of the perspective is that it delineates four different types of evaluation. Context evaluation addresses goals, priorities, needs, and problems as a first step toward planning or revising goals and objectives. Input evaluation assesses potential alternatives and analyzes their fit with the client's particular circumstances. Process evaluation documents and assesses implementation, and product evaluation assesses program effects.

Weaknesses are that the specific steps and/or methodology for executing these evaluations are not identified. Further, although aiding decision making is stated as the main purpose, the role of different kinds of records for accountability purposes also is described, and serving accountability needs is a secondary purpose. It is difficult to see how evaluation activities can serve both the program improvement function and accountability because their information needs are quite different.

STAKE'S COUNTENANCE APPROACH

The perspective developed by Robert Stake in 1967 was designed to conceptualize evaluation oriented to the complexities of the evaluation process (Stake, 1967, p. 524). The approach does not identify the measurements to be made in evaluation. Instead, it is background information for an evaluation plan. Stake (1981) also noted that this approach to evaluation should not be referred to as a model. Instead, it is an overview of data available for a study, and his advocacy was for better data selection (p. 84).

Components

The approach describes three major categories of data that correspond to the three phases of an educational program and two important types of information.

Data Categories.   The three data categories are antecedents, transactions, and outcomes. Antecedents are conditions prior to instruction that may be related to outcomes. Student aptitudes, prior experience, and entry skills are examples (Stake, 1967). Transactions consist of the many encounters between students and teachers, parents and teachers, students with students, and others. Transactions, unlike antecedents and outcomes, are dynamic rather than static (Stake, 1967). Presentation of a film, a class discussion, and students working problems are examples of transactions.

Outcomes in this view are conceptualized as more than program effects on students. The impact of the program on teachers, administrators, counselors, and others also should be measured. Also important are such effects as wear and tear on equipment and post-course effects. For example, evaluation of a driver-training program should include post-course accident rates (Stake, 1967).

Types of Information.   Both descriptive and judgmental information are collected about antecedents, transactions, and outcomes. Descriptive data consist of intents and observations. Intents consist of the planned-for environmental conditions and student entry skills (antecedents); the planned-for demonstrations, discussions, and so on (transactions); and the program goals or objectives (outcomes).

Observations involve the documentation of actual events. What were the actual student entry skills and the environment for the program? What program activities were implemented? and What outcomes were achieved? Also important are unwanted side effects and incidental gains (Stake, 1967). In addition to this information, the program rationale also should be documented. The philosophy and purpose of the program (rationale) are important in evaluating intents.

Analysis of the Data.   Stake (1967) identifies two ways of processing the descriptive data. First, the contingencies between antecedents, transactions, and outcomes are determined (see Figure 3.2). For the intents, the contingencies are logical. For example, the innovative curricula of the 1960s assumed that discovery and exploration activities would lead to intellectual development (a logical contingency). Then, observations are made to determine whether or not the expected contingencies occur in practice. For example, did opportunities for exploration and discovery learning enhance intellectual development?

The second stage of processing the descriptive data is to determine the extent of congruence between intents and observations. The cells containing intents and observations should be compared and discrepancies noted to determine the amount of congruence for each row (Stake, 1967). These issues, like the program definition and installation stages of the Provus model, identify the extent to which the implemented program matched the intended program as conceived by program developers.

In addition to descriptive data, the countenance approach also includes judgment of the program according to external standards. Antecedents, transactions, and outcomes are compared with selected standards, and judgment is rendered for each category.

An example of the application of Stake's data matrix is the evaluation of a worksite program in health science and medicine (Shapiro, 1985). Work experiences were a key component in a career awareness program on professions in the health sciences and medicine for talented minority high school students. The primary goal of the project was to increase the students' aspirations for careers in these fields.

Table 3.2 illustrates the intents and observations in Stake's data matrix for the project. The worksite tasks for students were selected exclusively by the worksite supervisors, and data obtained from them indicated that menial tasks were chosen. The data matrix indicates that the intended student characteristics were met, as were the intended tasks. Therefore, the failure to achieve the program goals resulted from

Figure 3.2
Data matrices in the countenance model

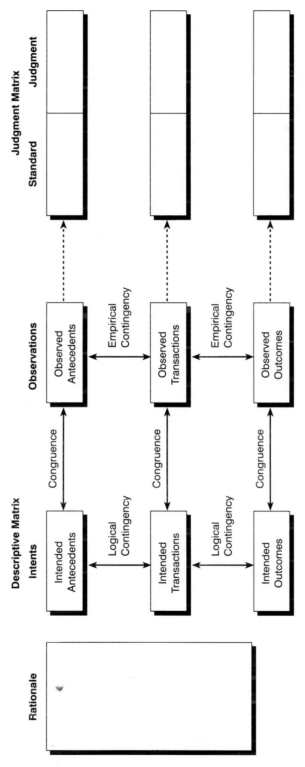

Summarized from Stake, 1967.

51

Table 3.2
Data matrix for the evaluation of worksite experiences in a career awareness program

	Intents	Observations
Antecedents	1. *Student characteristics*: Educationally talented, economically deprived minority students who (a) express interest in careers in health science and medicine and (b) have had no prior work experience in the field.	4. *Student characteristics*: The top 70 of 105 applicants were selected. Group met the stated criteria.
Transactions	2. Questionnaires sent to work site supervisors on intended tasks for students. All site supervisors identified menial tasks.	5. Observations at all work sites using a checklist of intended tasks with space to record observed unintended activities. Data confirmed only intended tasks were implemented.
Outcomes	3. Goals: Increased aspirations for careers in health science and medicine; student contact with, and increased sensitivity to, clients and patients; increased awareness of job opportunities; acquisition of job-related skills; and increased appreciation for the responsibilities of, and satisfaction derived from, working.	6. Administration of Strong Vocational Interest Blank and a survey questionnaire with statements to reflect program outcomes. Students responded using a Likert scale (1 to 4). Data indicated that students (a) acquired new skills from which they derived satisfaction, but (b) the worksite experience was not enjoyable, and (c) attitudes toward health science and medical careers did not change.

Summarized from Shapiro, 1985.

inappropriate work tasks (intended transactions). A subsequent career awareness program based in clinics and community hospitals incorporated more meaningful activities, which resulted in increased career aspirations in health sciences and medicine (Shapiro, 1985).

Strengths and Weaknesses

A major strength of the approach is that it identifies two important categories of information that Cronbach and associates (1980), Patton (1986), and others maintain are essential in program evaluation. They are (1) the conceptual framework for the program (Stake's program rationale and intended goals) and (2) the causal links between program activities and intermediate outcomes (Stake's contingencies that link antecedents, transactions, and outcomes). Another strength is the expansion of the concept of program outcomes to include effects on teachers, administrators, counselors, and others.

A weakness is that examples of observations provided by Stake (1967) were of daily events within the classroom. For a semester or year-long program, observations at this micro-level result in masses of data. In the absence of a framework indicating key types of data, analysis would be difficult at best. Another weakness is that guidelines are not provided for determining logical contingencies between intended antecedents, transactions, and outcomes, nor the congruence between intents and observations.

SCRIVEN'S GOAL-FREE PERSPECTIVE

Goal-free evaluation is not a fully developed model with definitions, structured relationships, and frameworks for data collection (Stecher, 1990). Instead, it is primarily a perspective for reducing a source of bias in the inquiry. Specifically, Scriven (1972) maintains that attention to the stated goals of a program narrows the inquiry into a sort of tunnel vision. When program goals or objectives are used as the basis for an evaluation, the rhetoric of intent is substituted for evidence of success (Scriven, 1972, p. 1). Part of the problem is that goals often are vague or purposefully overstated; but program objectives are often narrow and represent only easily measured outcomes (Stecher, 1990).

Scriven (1973) considers the consumer to be the primary audience for evaluation results, and goal-free evaluation is also referred to as "consumer-based evaluation" (Scriven, 1981). Thus, he views evaluation as similar to consumer product testing. All program effects, including secondary and tertiary effects, are weighted and combined into a summary judgment based on the functional needs of the consumer (House, 1978). Consumer needs are identified through the use of needs assessments.

Determining the merit or worth of a program is similar to a consumer's union report in which a variety of criteria are summarized in an overall rating of poor, fair, good, and excellent. The approach is utilitarian because it generates one judgment of merit leading to the best consumer choice (House, 1978, p. 5).

Components

Scriven identifies two especially important tasks for the evaluator. One is that of ascertaining information about all program effects. The other is that of using methods other than experimental design to identify causal relationships in the program.

Identification of Effects.   As already stated, using program goals or objectives to guide the evaluation can narrow the investigation. Therefore, the evaluator's first task is to discover all the effects of a program, whether they are positive or negative. Scriven (1973, p. 321) indicates that the "so-called side effects can wholly determine the outcome of the evaluation." Further, the terms *side effects* and *main effects* reflect the perspective of the program developers and/or implementers. However, the evaluator's task is not to evaluate intentions, but achievements (p. 321).

Of primary importance in the inquiry is maintaining the independence of the evaluator from that of the program staff. Thus, one of the first steps for the evaluator is to go out in the field before talking to program staff to determine the impact of the program on recipients (Scriven, 1993).

Of course, one may question how the evaluator is briefed about the background, aims, and nature of the project (Scriven, 1976b, p. 146). First, the important information is the effects of the program on the clients. Thus, the evaluator must struggle to find all effects without prejudice. Second, information about the background and goals of the program can be obtained later at a debriefing (Scriven, 1976b, p. 137).

The importance of the goal-free approach, according to Scriven (1976b), is that it moves evaluation toward the double-blind clinical trials used in medicine. In those studies, neither the doctor, the patient, nor the investigator knows which treatment is the placebo and which is the method on trial. In goal-free evaluation, the investigator does not project effects on the group receiving the new program.

Establishment of Cause-Effect Relationships.   Although control-group studies were advocated for social interventions, Scriven (1976a) noted that evaluators must typically make use of nonexperimental data. An appropriate methodology for such situations can be "reconstructed from the methods of the historian, the detective, the anthropologist, and the engineering troubleshooter" (p. 102). Scriven refers to such methods as the *modus operandi* (MO) approach.

Identifying the causes of observed effects in MO analysis depends on a considerable amount of background knowledge. Cause hunting, Scriven (1976a) indicated, is not unlike lion hunting in that respect. Like the automobile mechanic or the detective, the first step in the MO approach is to identify probable causes (*A, A8, A9 . . . A*) for an observed phenomenon *X*.

The second step is to check for the presence of the characteristics and events associated with a particular *A*. The MO of a particular cause is "an associated configuration of events, processes, or properties, usually in time sequence, which can often be described as the *characteristic causal chain* connecting the cause with the effect" (Scriven, 1976a, p. 105). In an autopsy, for example, different characteristics—that is, different MO's—are associated with drowning, poisoning, heart failure, and so on.

An example in educational programs is that of identifying causes for low achievement for students with low pretest scores. One explanation is that the program had no effect. Another is that the posttest items were an "unlucky" set for this student (Scriven, 1976a, p. 115). One MO approach to determining the presence of this cause is to add a question to the test that asks the student if the test tapped his or her knowledge.

If a complete MO is found for only one *A*, then the associated *A* is the cause. If more than one complete MO is found, the associated *A*'s are cofactors. If no complete MO's are present, then none of the *A*'s is a cause.

When the MO approach is used, the evaluator should initiate a "signature" or "tracer" system, such that actions taken by the program or institution are differentiated from those coming from other sources (Scriven, 1976a, p. 109). In evaluating a university bureau designed to improve undergraduate teaching, for example, the evaluator would trace the use of evaluation forms dispensed by the bureau in contrast to those disseminated by department chairs or others.

Another technique useful in evaluating a bureau or service is to identify "information couriers or influence peddlers, people using bureau services and exhibiting some evangelical zeal" (Scriven, 1976a, p. 110). They are interviewed periodically to identify diffusion effects, and hypotheses precipitated by the interviews are also investigated.

An important aspect of MO analysis is the identification of causal links between events and outcomes. These identified links are then used to distinguish between alternative causal hypotheses. For example, a causal link in the studies of the Pygmalion effect in the classroom was that teacher beliefs about student potential influence teacher estimates of the quality of student work. In such a study, MO analysis would ascertain that the essential teacher beliefs existed. (Further discussion of the importance of ascertaining causal links between program events and outcomes is found in Chapter 12.)

Strengths and Weaknesses

The major strength of Scriven's perspective, according to Stecher (1990), is that it sensitizes evaluators to be attentive to a wide range of program effects. A second strength is the identification of likely causes of program effects and checking for the presence of these causes. Included in the identification of alternative causes is the specification of causal links in the program itself (an issue also addressed in the Provus model and Stake's countenance model). A third strength is the introduction of other methodologies as appropriate for evaluation, such as anthropological and historical methods.

Weaknesses of the perspective are the lack of prescribed methods or procedures for implementing MO analysis. The evaluator is left to his or her ingenuity and assistance from other professionals, such as educational psychologists, to identify essential characteristics of potential causes.

SUMMARY

The four utilitarian perspectives each broadened the practice of evaluation by expanding (1) the types of decisions that were made and/or (2) the types of data collected in the evaluation. Key assumptions of all four models are the prior identification of a key decision maker and the identification of accepted standards for the evaluation.

Of the four approaches, the Provus model and the CIPP approach are similar in that (1) they view evaluation as an ongoing process consisting of several stages, and (2) they assume the existence of a permanent evaluation staff to conduct the various stages. The four phases in the Provus model correspond to the four stages of program development. They are:

1. Establishment and evaluation of the program definition

2. Evaluation of program installation

3. Verification of the relationships between classroom activities and intermediate program objectives

4. Evaluation of program outcomes

    At each phase, program performance is compared with selected standards to determine the discrepancy, and corrective action is taken, if necessary. Program termination is the decision of last resort.

    Strengths of the Provus model are:

1. The focus on program definition and installation in particular

2. The development of an ongoing partnership between the permanent evaluation staff and program planners and implementers

3. The use of formative evaluation to redirect programs

4. The focus on constructing databases that link student characteristics, classroom processes, and student outcomes

    Specific weaknesses of the model are the detailed lengthy sets of prescribed procedures and the reliance on intermediate and terminal objectives in Stages III and IV.

The stages in the CIPP approach are organized around the types of decisions that may be made about a program. They are planning decisions (context evaluation), structuring decisions (input evaluation), implementing decisions (process evaluation), and recycling decisions (product evaluation). Currently, context evaluation involves assessing a program's overall status, identifying weaknesses and problems, and identifying strengths available to correct the weaknesses. Input evaluation, in contrast, searches out and rates relevant approaches intended to bring about change. Process and product evaluation are similar to Stages III and IV in the Provus model in that program implementation and outcomes are assessed.

A major strength of the CIPP perspective is the identification of four types of evaluation related to particular decisions that may be implemented together or as separate evaluations. A weakness is the lack of specific procedures for implementing the approach.

The countenance approach, developed by Robert Stake, also recognizes different phases of educational programs. The three phases, referred to as data categories,
are antecedents (e.g., student entry skills and aptitudes); transactions (classroom
interactions); and outcomes, including impact of the program on teachers, administrators, and others.

The countenance perspective also specifies that both intents and observations of
actual events are documented in each of the three data categories. The logical relationships between intended program activities and outcomes are identified, and the
congruence (or lack of it) between intended and observed activities is documented.
Finally, observed antecedents, transactions, and outcomes are compared with
selected standards.

Strengths of the countenance approach are (1) the inclusion of the program
rationale in the conceptual framework, (2) the assessment of the causal links in the
program, and (3) the expansion of program effects beyond student outcome data. A
weakness of the approach is that the transactions are viewed as daily classroom
events without an accompanying mechanism for identifying key events. Another
weakness is that determining the logical contingencies depends, in large measure,
on the evaluator's expertise in and knowledge of program development.

Michael Scriven's goal-free evaluation differs from the other approaches in three
major ways. First, it does not rely on program definitions, intents, or goals as the
framework for evaluation. Second, it identifies the consumer as the audience for
evaluation. Third, a variety of criteria are summarized in one overall assessment of a
program.

The initial task for the evaluator in goal-free evaluation is to assess program
effects on the clients of the program. (Briefings as to the nature and goals of the program may be scheduled later.) Appropriate methodology for determining both positive and negative effects may be found in the methods of the historian, the anthropologist, and others. The evaluator must then undertake an investigation to
determine the causal links that connect particular program events to the identified
effects.

Strengths of goal-free evaluation are (1) the sensitization of evaluators to a wide
range of program effects, (2) the identification of causal links between particular program events and effects, and (3) the use of a variety of methodological sources. A
major weakness is that implementation of this perspective depends, in large measure, on the creativity and ingenuity of the evaluator.

Table 3.3 summarizes the types of decisions and the strengths and weaknesses of
each of the four approaches. Each perspective represents an advancement over the
production factor concept in any of several different ways. A range of real-world decisions at different stages of program development or institutional decision making are
included, the utility of methods other than experimentation are illustrated, the
importance of causal links between program events and outcomes is introduced,
and the assessment of program effects beyond student performance data is
included. Each of these contributions is an important concern in program evaluation
today.

Table 3.3
Summary of utilitarian perspectives

Perspective	Types of Decisions	Strengths	Weaknesses
The Provus discrepancy model	Continue, revise, or terminate a program at each of four stages of development: design, installation, implementation, and outcome.	1. Focus on program definition and installation 2. Development of an ongoing partnership between permanent evaluation staff and program planners and implementers 3. The use of formative evaluation (revise and correct) to redirect a program 4. Introduction of the importance of constructing data bases that link student characteristics, classroom processes, and student outcomes	1. Lengthy set of procedures 2. Dependence on intermediate and terminal objectives
The CIPP perspective	Planning (context evaluation); structuring (input evaluation); implementing (process evaluation); and recycling (outcome evaluation)	1. Identification of four types of evaluation that correspond to particular decisions	1. Lack of specific procedures for implementation

Perspective	Types of Decisions	Strengths	Weaknesses
The countenance perspective	Document intents and observations for program antecedents, transactions, and outcomes. Determine logical congruencies between intents in the three categories and empirical contingencies between observations in the three categories	1. Inclusion of program rationales in the conceptual framework 2. Assessment of causal links in the program 3. Expansion of program effects beyond student outcome data	1. No mechanism is provided for determining key classroom transactions 2. Determining logical contingencies depends on program evaluator's expertise in and knowledge of program development
Goal-free evaluation	Determine the overall merit of the program for the consumer after ascertaining all program effects	1. Sensitization of evaluators to a wide range of program effects 2. Identification of causal links for observed effects 3. Introduction of methodologies, such as historical or anthropological, into evaluation	1. Implementation depends, in large measure, on the ingenuity and creativity of the evaluator

CHAPTER QUESTIONS

1. What characteristics of the utilitarian approaches are shared with the production factor concept?

2. What is the rationale for program definition in the Provus approach?

3. What is the purpose of discrepancy analysis at each stage of the Provus approach?

4. The first task assigned to an evaluation team is to search out the available alternatives designed to address reading deficiencies of first-grade children. The evaluators also are to document the resources essential for each alternative and to recommend one alternative to the client. Which type of evaluation is this in the CIPP approach?

5. What important function is fulfilled by the links between intended antecedents, intended transactions, and intended outcomes in Stake's countenance evaluation?

6. What is one method of observing transactions in Stake's countenance evaluation?

7. According to Scriven, what first step should the evaluator take to avoid bias?

8. What is the chief weakness in Scriven's goal-free evaluation?

REFERENCES

Cooley, W., & Bickel, W. (1986). *Decision-oriented educational research*. Boston: Kluwer-Nijhoff.

Cronbach, L. J., Ambron, S., Dornbusch, S., Hess, R., Hornik, R., Phillips, D., Walker, D., & Weiner, S. (1980). *Toward reform of program evaluation*. San Francisco: Jossey-Bass.

Hamilton, D. (1977). Making sense of curricular evaluation: Continuities and discontinuities in an educational idea. In L. S. Shulman (Ed.), *Review of research in education* (Vol. 5, pp. 318–347). Itasca, IL: Peacock.

House, E. R. (1978). Assumptions underlying evaluation models. *Educational Researcher*, 7(3), 4–12.

Patton, M. (1986). *Utilization-focused evaluation*. Beverly Hills, CA: Sage.

Provus, M. (1969). Evaluating ongoing programs in the public school system. In *NSSE 68th Yearbook, Part II* (pp. 242–283). Chicago: University of Chicago Press.

Provus, M. (1971). *Discrepancy evaluation*. Berkeley, CA: McCutchan.

Scriven, M. (1972). Pros and cons about goal-free evaluation. *Evaluation Comment*, 3(4), 1–4.

Scriven, M. (1973). Goal-free evaluation. In E. R. House (Ed.), *School evaluation* (pp. 319–328). Berkeley, CA: McCutchan.

Scriven, M. (1976a). Maximizing the power of causal investigations: The *modus operandi* method. In G. V. Glass (Ed.), *Evaluation studies review annual* (Vol. I, pp. 101–118). Beverly Hill, CA: Sage.

Scriven, M. (1976b). Evaluation bias and its control. In G. V. Glass (Ed.), *Evaluation studies review annual* (Vol. I, pp. 119–139). Beverly Hills, CA: Sage.

Scriven, M. (1981). *Evaluation thesaurus* (3rd ed.). Point Reyes, CA: Edgepress.

Scriven, M. (1993, April). *The state of the art in evaluation.* Workshop presentation, American Educational Research Association, Atlanta, Georgia.

Shapiro, J. (1985). Evaluation of a worksite program in health science and medicine: An implication of Stake's model of contingency and congruence. *Educational Evaluation and Policy Analysis, 7*(1), 47–56.

Stake, R. (1967). The countenance of educational evaluation. *Teachers College Record, 68,* 523–540.

Stake, R. (1975). To evaluate an arts program. In R. Stake (Ed.), *Evaluating the arts in education: A responsive approach* (pp. 13–31). Columbus, OH: Merrill.

Stake, R. (1981). Persuasions, not models. *Educational Evaluation and Policy Analysis, 3*(1), 83–84.

Stecher, B. (1990). Goal-free evaluation. In H. J. Walberg & G. D. Haertel (Eds.), *The international encyclopedia of educational evaluation* (pp. 41–42). Oxford: Pergamon Press.

Stufflebeam, D. (1980). The CIPP model for program evaluation. In G. Madaus, M. Scriven, & D. Stufflebeam (Eds.), *Evaluation models* (pp. 117–141). Boston: Kluwer-Nijhoff.

Stufflebeam, D. L., Foley, W. J., Gephart, W. J., Guba, E. G., Hammond, R. L., Marriman, H. O., & Provus, M. M. (1971). *Educational evaluation and decision-making in education.* Itasca, IL: Peacock.

Stufflebeam, D., & Shinkfeld, A. J. (1985). *Systematic evaluation.* Boston: Kluwer-Nijhoff.

CHAPTER 4

Intuitionist/Pluralist Perspectives

The utilitarian perspectives responded to some of the criticisms of the production factor concept by expanding the types of decisions to be made and the types of data that may be collected in an evaluation. Nevertheless, these perspectives are management oriented in that they respond to the information needs of identified decision makers. In addition, because only a few decision makers are involved, these approaches to evaluation are based on the assumption that consensus on the standards for judging a program may be easily obtained. Third, the reports consisted of data and performance criteria related to the total system, rather than to individuals, students, or teachers (Hamilton, 1977, p. 334).

In contrast, the intuitionist/pluralist perspectives were based on a different set of assumptions, and they focused on experiences and knowledge bases different from the utilitarian models. First, the intuitionist/pluralist models addressed the information needs and concerns of individuals associated with an innovation or program, rather than simply key decision makers. (One of the criticisms of the early Head Start and the Follow Through evaluations is that they addressed only the questions of interest to the bureaucratic sponsors [Weiss, 1986].)

Second, a uniform standard for determining program worth may not be attainable in many social situations (Hamilton, 1977, p. 238). Specifically, a program does not have a single value. Instead, it is valued differently by different groups and for different purposes (Stake, 1975). Therefore, one role of evaluation is to reflect these diverse perspectives of educational programs.

Third, individuals associated with a program have different experiences, and these experiences are important in any evaluation of a program. Instead of summary information that relates to the overall performance of the innovation or program, individuals' tacit knowledge about the day-to-day workings of a program is important. In other words, developers of the intuitionist/pluralist approaches viewed evaluation as broader than that of applying specific standards to programs and program components.

The four intuitionist/pluralist perspectives discussed in this chapter are the judicial/adversarial models, Eisner's educational connoisseurship and criticism approach, Stake's responsive evaluation perspective, and illuminative evaluation. Each approach, in somewhat different ways, addressed issues of concern to those associated with programs and their experiences.

THE JUDICIAL AND ADVERSARY MODELS

The rationale for the judicial and adversary models is that human judgment and testimony are important types of information about a program or policy. However, the testimony must be understood within a context of facts and situations explored in a systematic way in order to reach a decision about an intervention (Wolf, 1979). Concepts from legal proceedings, for example, fact-finding, adversarial proceedings, cross-examination, evidentiary rules and procedures, and structured deliberations before an audience, were viewed as providing essential dimensions lacking in more conventional evaluations (p. 22). Two similar evaluation approaches, the judicial and adversary models, adapted these concepts from the legal paradigm to the task of evaluation. In the adversary model, the two evaluators representing the pro and con views of the program argue their cases before a jury, which renders a win/lose decision. That is, the jury decision is to either continue or terminate the program (Clyne, 1990).

In contrast, the purpose of the judicial model is to provide a mechanism for the introduction of a broad range of educational evidence in order to clarify the subtle and complex nature of the educational issues in question (Wolf, 1990, p. 79). Further, the task of the jury is to develop a set of recommendations, not to render a win/lose decision.

Components of the Judicial Model

The judicial model was conceptualized (1) to assist educational decision makers in appreciating the complexity of their programs and (2) to provide a complete presentation of available information through the interpretation of a program by two opposing viewpoints (Wolf, 1990, p. 79).

The judicial model consists of four major stages. They are issue generation, issue selection, preparation of arguments, and the clarification forum. Stage one develops a broad range of issues of interest to various groups interested in the program and is viewed as exploratory. In the application of the model to an evaluation of the teacher education program at Indiana University, the key question was, What is the overall impact of the recently formed Department of Teacher Education on the improvement of teacher preparation? (Wolf, 1975, p. 186) Issues related to this focus were generated through 35 interviews of education faculty, students, other university faculty, teacher educators at other agencies, and representatives from the federal funding agency (Wolf, 1975).

In stage two, the range of issues is delimited to a manageable set. The Indiana evaluation administered a survey instrument to faculty, students, and administrators to rank order the issues. A special panel reviewed the final list for relevance and substance and prepared the list in written form (Wolf, 1975).

In stage three, both investigative teams build their cases and prepare their arguments. Specific points of contention are built around each issue so that the teams can present clearly different perspectives (Wolf, 1990). Documents and reports are analyzed, witnesses are selected and interviewed, and formal depositions are taken. Of primary importance in the judicial model, however, is that the purpose of the arguments is not to provoke confrontation (Wolf, 1990, p. 80). Instead, the purpose is to present opposing views in order to clarify complex issues.

Prehearings to share data and evidence between the teams and the clarification forum constitute stage four. Individuals with major responsibility in the implementation develop the rules of evidence and procedures for the clarification forum. The format of the hearing approximates a court of law in that case presenters for each team present opening and closing arguments and examine and cross-examine the witnesses. A hearing officer directs the scheduled flow of evidence and enforces the rules of evidence and procedure (Wolf, 1990, p. 80). Further, the hearing is public.

A panel composed of policymakers and representatives of other groups, such as parents, school personnel, and advocacy groups, hear the evidence. The panel also is permitted to ask questions for the purpose of clarification (Wolf, 1990). At the end of the hearing, the panel deliberates in a closed session and prepares a list of written recommendations.

In addition to the panel, key roles in implementing the judicial model are played by the two investigative teams, the case analyst, the case presenter, the forum moderator, and the panel facilitator. Each investigative team is responsible for building a comprehensive case and preparing challenges to the other team's case. Each team is headed by a case analyst who oversees team activities and also prepares interim reports on the substantive status of interviews and arguments (Wolf, 1979, p. 24). Case presenters, in contrast, present the team's arguments at the clarification hearing and conduct cross-examinations.

At the clarification hearing, the forum moderator directs the flow of events and enforces the rules of evidence. The panel facilitator, in contrast, assists the panel in weighing evidence and clarifies points of confusion during the panel's deliberations (Wolf, 1979, p. 24).

Examples of the Judicial Model

The judicial model was implemented in an evaluation of the teacher education program at Indiana University. This implementation used a diverse 13-member panel and 32 witnesses. A variety of issues about the program were addressed, such as the involvement of Arts and Sciences faculty in planning and implementing programs (Arnstein, 1975; Wolf, 1975). The panel developed a set of recommendations, and the faculty engaged in subsequent study and discussion of the recommendations.

The Mesa Public School System Variation.   The Mesa public school system implemented a variation of the judicial model to evaluate a program for intellectually gifted elementary school students (ELP) and an accelerated program for high-achieving elementary school students (ALP) (Wood, Peterson, DeGracie, & Zaharis, 1986). Instead of the advocacy/adversary presentations, four different advocacy teams, one for each of the district's programs, served as witnesses. The purpose was to avoid the tension and potential negative effects on school climate from the presence of an advocacy and adversarial team visiting each program.

In addition to hearing the evidence presented by the four teams, the 11-person jury panel also developed evidence. Each panel member was required to make a minimum of four school visitations (one to each pilot school and nonpilot school). Attitudinal surveys also were developed and administered to parents, students, teachers, and administrators at the four schools, and a cost analysis was completed for each program (Wood et al., 1986, p. 311).

The evaluation began with a preliminary hearing in which each program presented an overview. The panel visitations to the four programs followed. Next, the advocacy teams made full presentations at a second hearing, which was followed by the administration of surveys and the development of the cost-analysis data. Jury panel members next developed questions for the advocacy teams; these questions were addressed at the third hearing. The panel then developed their recommendations in several working meetings. Their written report was presented at a formal meeting where the advocacy teams and the audience were permitted to ask questions (Wood et al., 1986).

Wood et al. (1986) notes that this version of the judicial model is extremely useful for programs that are highly controversial or political. Although time consuming (the evaluation required 6 months), the superintendent indicated that the time was well spent. All groups that would be implemented or affected by the recommendations were represented, and a broad base of information about the programs was developed. Also, the superintendent accepted all the recommendations of the panel, which combined the strengths of the four programs.

The National Institute of Education (NIE) Variation.   A modified version of the judicial model was supported by NIE to explore the pros and cons of minimum competency testing. However, the hearing did not use a panel; therefore, no concluding recommendations were developed. This modification avoided the unpleasant situation of a federal agency appearing to tell states and districts how to structure competency testing.

Instead of recommendations, videotapes of the 3-day clarification hearing and the transcripts were to be made available to policymakers. However, late in the process the decision was made to develop a 4-hour television program on PBS from excerpts of the hearing. Three major problems with this decision were identified by George Madaus (1982), leader of the team presenting evidence against competency testing.

First, too much clarity and illumination was lost in the editing process. Second, the time limitation for cross-examination meant that questioning ended minutes before a major point was to have been made. A third problem for the team against competency testing was getting witnesses to testify, because their supervisors often were strong supporters of the policy (Madaus, 1982).

However, the major problem with the judicial model in the competency testing issue was one that stemmed from different philosophies (Thurston & House, 1981). The pro position viewed the testing as an external measure to ensure accountability. The con position, in contrast, trusted teachers, parents, and students to monitor the quality of education (p. 88). The judicial model, however, is not equipped to address ideological differences.

The Adversary Model

Unlike the judicial model, which generates a list of recommendations, the adversary model results in a yes/no decision about a program. That is, the key question addressed by the adversary model is, Should the program be continued or discontinued? The win/lose nature of this approach sets a different tone for the proceedings from that of the judicial model. The emphasis becomes that of presenting the best possible case for continuance/discontinuance rather than that of a clarification of issues.

Clyne (1990, p. 78) notes that adversary evaluation represents the "fight theory" concept, whereby opposing views strive to win by producing better (more persuasive) evidence. A major advantage of the approach, according to Clyne (1990), is the cross-examination of witnesses. This process can reveal hidden assumptions or other problems with the opponent's data or logic.

The adversary model was implemented in an evaluation of the Hawaii 3-on-2 program. This program was a team-teaching arrangement for K-3 classes in which three teachers worked with two classrooms. An external evaluator, Northwest Educational Regional Laboratory, directed the evaluation, and the two teams consisted of external evaluators. A coin toss decided the team assignment to the advocacy or adversarial position. As the evaluation progressed, the team assigned to the adversarial approach became uncomfortable with the win/lose nature of the activity. Other positions seemed more sensible, but the evaluators were locked into a "save-it-or-scrap-it choice" (Popham & Carlson, 1977, p. 5).

Strengths and Weaknesses

One strength of both the judicial and adversary models is the opportunities for the participation of nonprofessionals in an educational evaluation. They may serve as witnesses or as members of one of the case teams or the jury panel. Another strength of both models is the breadth of evidence that is presented. That is, the models may reveal information likely to be overlooked in traditional evaluations. A third strength is effective communication with a lay audience.

Particular strengths of the judicial model are (1) the spin-off in enlightened decisions resulting from broad participation (Thurston, 1978), (2) the responsiveness and relevancy of the issues addressed in the evaluation, and (3) the broad hearing given to potentially controversial or political programs (Wolf, 1990).

Three weaknesses of both the judicial and adversary models are (1) the cost, time, and effort involved in the preparation of the cases, (2) the difficulty of obtaining committed and impartial jury panel members, and (3) the potential imbalance in oratorical skills and presentations of the two sides (Wolf, 1990, p. 81).

The adversarial model, as a result of the win/lose nature of the activity, has several limitations. First, differences in oratorical skills, fallible arbiters of the procedures, or the lack of an impartial jury may bias the decision (Popham & Carlson, 1977). Second is the difficulty in framing a proposition in a manner amenable to a win/lose decision (Madaus, 1982; Popham & Carlson, 1977). The model, for example, cannot address philosophical differences.

Third, the jury panel may not attend to crucial variables if it is dominated by the need to reach a verdict of success or failure on issues for which standards of decision making are lacking (Clyne, 1990, p. 79). Fourth, the adversary model can only be used in a summative evaluation, but the judicial model may be used in either a formative or summative evaluation because it generates a list of recommendations. Finally, the adversary model tends to introduce an "indictment mentality" into the process (Worthen & Owens, 1978).

EISNER'S EDUCATIONAL CONNOISSEURSHIP AND CRITICISM PERSPECTIVE

A major purpose of the judicial and adversary models was to open up evaluation to a variety of issues and types of evidence, including the testimony of witnesses. In contrast, the analytic approach developed by Elliott Eisner (1977) focuses on the ongoing interactions within the classroom. The perspective is based on his observation that the range, richness, and complexity of classroom events are far wider than educational measurements can capture.

Therefore, Eisner proposed an approach to educational analysis to serve as a supplement (not as an alternative) to the use of scientific procedures. The model is derived from his belief that improvement in education depends on enabling teachers and others to improve the ways they see and think about classroom life (Eisner, 1977, p. 346). Beneficiaries of educational criticism are teachers, who may wish feedback on their methods; administrators and policymakers, who make decisions about education; and parents and the general public, who can be brought closer to the complexities of education (Barone, 1990, p. 199). Eisner's perspective, like responsive and illuminative evaluation in particular, focuses on the experiences of those individuals directly affected by a program. The original version of the model, however, was confined to classroom interactions.

Components

Eisner's perspective combines two concepts: connoisseurship and criticism. The term *connoisseurship* refers to "that art of perception that makes the appreciation of complexity possible" (Eisner, 1977, p. 346). However, appreciation refers to an awareness and understanding of characteristics and complexities (not a preference). Connoisseurship, in other words, is a judgment that uses knowledge and experience to analyze important attributes of the object or situation under study. In art, for example, attention is given to form, style, and color, and also to the history and social context of the work.

Criticism, the second component, refers to the process of enabling others to understand the qualities possessed by a work of art (Eisner, 1991, p. 6). It is the rich and vivid reporting of one's judgment so as to enlighten practitioners and researchers. The critic renders the essential qualities of the situation, their significance, and the quality of his or her experience when interacting with it (Eisner, 1977, p. 349). Criticism, in other words, is not a negative judgment. Instead, it is reevaluation of essential qualities.

Applied to educational practice, criticism is the art of vividly describing, interpreting, and evaluating ongoing events in the classroom setting (Eisner, 1976). The description may take the form of a narrative that gives the reader the flavor of being present in the classroom. The interpretative aspect of the criticism focuses on understanding the meaning and significance of the various actions in the classroom. An example is, What do the extrinsic rewards for reading mean to the children who keep charts of the numbers of books they read? (Eisner, 1976).

The evaluative aspect of criticism, in contrast, addresses the question of the educational import or value of the observed events. Addressing this question is the primary difference between educational criticism and the work of an ethnographer, psychologist, or sociologist (Eisner, 1976).

The evaluator may focus on any of several aspects of the classroom during his or her observations. Examples are the relationships between the teacher and students in the classroom, the nature of classroom discourse, and the quality of work created by the students (Eisner, 1976). Particular questions that may be addressed are, for example, How is the class paced? How does the teacher respond to students? What level of tension, affect, and spontaneity do teachers display when they teach? Are they approachable and in what ways? and What kinds of values and covert messages do they emphasize? (Eisner, 1977, pp. 350, 352). To answer such questions, the educational critic must astutely observe the classroom. For example, how does discourse in the classroom proceed? Is it an atmosphere of feigned enthusiasm, of dutiful routine? What does the teacher's tone say to students who have difficulty in understanding the material? and so on.

The culminating task for the educational critic is to report his or her findings in such a way as to raise the conscious awareness of others about the complex dynamics in the classroom. The task is to provide a "vivid rendering" that "captures the quality and character of classroom life" (Eisner, 1977, p. 352). Eisner (1977) suggests that the critic must rely on linguistic artistry that makes use of metaphor, contrast, redundancy, and emphasis (p. 352).

Of interest is that classroom events and the underlying bases for their occurrence are among the issues that later were addressed by naturalistic inquiry. The importance of providing rich descriptions of the setting under study is also a purpose of ethnography, a branch of qualitative inquiry that has since been applied to the practice of evaluation.

Similar to the other intuitionist/pluralist approaches, two major concerns of the connoisseurship and criticism perspective are validity and reliability. That is, how representative of classroom life are the descriptions and interpretations, and how consistent are they? Eisner (1985) describes two processes that are essential in developing an educational criticism. These processes are structural corroboration and referential adequacy. Structural corroboration refers to the presence of supportive evidence and the unity and coherence of the picture presented of a program or classroom. Referential adequacy means that the reported insights are based on empirical events that can be observed by others. For example, videotapes of the classroom may be used for comparison.

A problem associated with the observations is that the classroom is a fluid, dynamic setting. However, it does have pervasive qualities that are stable over time. Further, these enduring qualities are likely to be socially significant (Eisner, 1977). Therefore, the educational observer should visit the classroom often enough to be able to identify these pervasive qualities and to be certain he or she is not observing atypical events.

Strengths and Weaknesses

A major strength of Eisner's approach is that it focused attention on an issue neglected in the early evaluations, that of describing and interpreting classroom activities and events in terms of the experiences of the participants. A second strength is that judgments are presented in language and ideas that nonexperts can understand (House, 1980, p. 235).

A weakness of the approach is that the educational criteria to be applied by the evaluator are not specified (House, 1980, p. 236). Further, House (1980) asks if an evaluator has the authority to make judgments based on his or her expertise, and if so, should not the bases for these value judgments be stated (p. 236). The problem is that strongly judgmental criticisms that view the classroom through a particular lens can result in unjust and unfair evaluations.

STAKE'S RESPONSIVE EVALUATION PERSPECTIVE

The countenance approach developed in 1967 by Robert Stake (discussed in Chapter Three) dealt with the question of the types of information that deserve attention in evaluation. Although this perspective addressed the information in the data pool for an evaluation, it did not address the role of clients and audiences in evaluation negotiations and the different kinds of reporting that may be useful in evaluation (Stake in Braskamp & Morrison, 1975).

Consideration of these and other issues by Robert Stake led to the explication of the perspective referred to as responsive evaluation. This perspective is particularly oriented toward the activity, uniqueness, and social plurality of the program being evaluated (Stake, 1990, p. 75). The term *social plurality* refers to the belief that a program has no single true value. Rather, a program has different values for different persons for different purposes (Stake, 1975, p. 27). Therefore, essential features of responsive evaluation are to emphasize "the issues, language, contexts, and standards of stakeholders" (Stake, 1990, p. 77).

Consistent with the concept of social plurality, the orienting question is, What does the program look like to different individuals? (House, 1978, p. 12). Therefore, conceptual organizers for the evaluation are the key issues identified by individuals at the program site (Stake, 1975; 1990). Thus, the questions posed by the program staff, the funding agency, or the research community should be accompanied by issues of importance to stakeholders—those who are personally and educationally affected by the program (Stake, 1990, p. 76).

A primary purpose of responsive evaluation is to increase the usefulness of the evaluation to persons in and around the program (Stake, 1975). Thus, the evaluation responds to audience requirements for information and refers to different value perspectives in reporting the merits and shortcomings of the program (Stake, 1975, p. 14).

Another purpose for addressing stakeholder issues is to prevent the evaluation from being an instrument of any administrative effort to undermine legitimate educational interests (Stake, 1990). Sometimes evaluations are commissioned to protect administrative and program operations from criticism or to promote particular agendas (Stake, 1990, p. 76). However, the inclusion of program concerns from different audiences can serve as a safeguard to such practices.

Components

The three groups of activities in responsive evaluation are (1) the initial planning and focusing of the evaluation, (2) conducting observations, and (3) organizing and reporting. These activities are not divided into phases because observation and feedback (reporting) are important activities from the first week to the last (Stake, 1975, p. 18).

The evaluator's first major task is to become acquainted with the program, in part by talking with students, parents, taxpayers, program sponsors, and program staff (Stake, 1975, p. 19). The evaluator also observes program activities and examines relevant program documents (Stake, 1990, p. 76). The evaluator then selects a few issues around which to organize the study and checks his or her ideas with individuals who are representative of the different audiences. Examples of issues developed for an evaluation of a summer institute for high school students are, "Is the admission policy satisfactory? Are some teachers too permissive? Why do so few students stay for the afternoon? and Is this institute a 'lighthouse' for regular school curriculum innovation?" (Stake, 1975, p. 17).

Once the initial issues are identified, the evaluator selects appropriate approaches for data collection. These decisions are made through discussion of several alternatives and negotiation with program staff and the sponsors of the evaluation (Stake, 1990, p. 76).

A common misunderstanding of responsive evaluation identified by Stake (1990) is the erroneous belief that it is synonymous with qualitative inquiry (p. 76). Instead, the evaluation may be qualitative or quantitative. Of importance is that the selected methods must serve the information needs of the various audiences.

One concern in responsive evaluation is the use of participant testimony as a major data source. Care must be taken to establish the reliability of the data (Stake, 1990). The evaluator obtains the reactions of program personnel to the portrayals and also checks the relevance of evaluation findings with stakeholders. Much of this effort is informal and is ongoing during the evaluation (Stake, 1973).

Organizing and reporting information in a responsive evaluation may occur at various times and in various ways. For example, different reports may be prepared for different groups (Stake, 1990, p. 77). The evaluator often will use portrayals also to provide a vicarious experience of the program. Some portrayals of a program may be short, such as a 5-minute script, a log, or a scrapbook. Longer portrayals, however, may consist of narratives, photographs, maps and graphs, exhibits, and taped conversations (Stake, 1975, p. 23). One issue investigated in an evaluation of an arts program, for example, might be the effect of the program on every student. Case studies of a random sample of students could be developed. They might include taped interviews, art products, and test scores of students' attitudes toward the arts (Stake, 1975, p. 24).

Strengths and Weaknesses

A major strength of responsive evaluation is that it can portray the complexity of educational programs. In this feature, responsive evaluation resembles the illuminative evaluation perspective. (Stake [1990] noted that he drew on the writings of Barry MacDonald, Malcolm Parlett, and David Hamilton in developing responsive evaluation.) Another strength is that the interests, language, and standards of stakeholders are reflected in the evaluation.

A weakness of responsive evaluation, however, is that attention to stakeholder concerns may result in the exclusion of important program information. A second potential problem is that the participation of stakeholders in every aspect of structuring an evaluation, including technical aspects, may lead to a loss of evaluation quality (Scheerens, 1990). In other words, attentiveness to stakeholder concerns in selecting the issues and negotiating the methods may jeopardize evaluation validity.

ILLUMINATIVE EVALUATION

Illuminative evaluation shares a key characteristic with Stake's responsive evaluation view. Specifically, it is the sensitivity to the needs, interests, and questions of different audiences. However, illuminative evaluation differs from Stake's approach in that stakeholders do not have input into the issues for study. Instead, the focus of an illuminative evaluation is holistic. That is, the purpose is to identify and describe the entire network of interrelationships rather than focusing on a few program features (Parlett, 1990, p. 69).

The outcome of the study is some overall model or "map" that strives to make sense of the system as an organized and coherent whole (Parlett, 1990, p. 69). The aim is to increase understanding or "illuminate" the program, instructional innovation, or school setting as a working system as well as the broader context in which it functions. Thus, the evaluator's task is "to unravel the complex scene, isolate its significant features, delineate cycles of cause and effect, and comprehend relationships between beliefs and practices and between organizational patterns and the responses of individuals" (Parlett & Hamilton, 1976, p. 147). In other words, a major purpose of illuminative evaluation is to discover the "invisible realities" of the social organization and the system under study.

Although described as a social anthropology approach, illuminative evaluation is not a standard methodological package. Instead, it is a general strategy in which the problem defines the methods to be used (Parlett & Hamilton, 1976, p. 147). Also, it is an integrated investigative approach and not merely an exemplar of qualitative research or ethnographic field work (Parlett, 1990, p. 69).

The perspective originated in 1967 and 1968 in work at the Massachusetts Institute of Technology and in the early 1970s at the University of Edinburgh. It is the first systematic application of anthropological methods to evaluation (now an accepted paradigm in evaluation practice).

Components

The approach describes three major stages of evaluation and several methods of data collection. The three stages are (1) the exploratory stage of observation, (2) focused questioning and inquiry, and (3) development of explanations and general principles. Data collection methods include nonparticipant observation, open-ended interviewing, unobtrusive measures, questionnaires, focused group discussions, the analysis of program documents, reports of previous studies, and other written information.

Evaluation Stages.   An important preliminary step is that of negotiating the evaluation. Of utmost importance is that the decision makers' reasons for conducting the study must be made explicit. That is, illuminative evaluation places a premium on discovering the hidden agenda. Do the policymakers want to examine management problems, find a scapegoat, reassure committees, satisfy funding agencies, resolve a conflict, or cut down a program to size? (Parlett, 1990, p. 71). Of essential importance is the preliminary discussion and negotiation of the evaluation before delicate policy questions are discovered and opened up for detailed scrutiny (Parlett, 1990).

The first stage of the evaluation is referred to as an "immersion period" (Parlett, 1990). The evaluator becomes thoroughly familiar with the day-to-day reality of the settings(s) under study (Parlett & Hamilton, 1976). It is an exploratory phase in which the evaluator constructs a continuous record of ongoing events, transactions, informal remarks, and discussions between participants (Parlett & Hamilton, 1976, p. 148). The evaluator also uses more systematic observation methods (described in the following section) to gain an understanding of the setting and the ways that participants view the program and function in it and with each other.

For example, in one study of an independent learning project in British secondary schools, Parlett and Hamilton (1976) found that teachers viewed the materials in different ways. Some regarded them as a complete course of study, while others saw them only as supplementary resources to use if necessary.

In the second stage, the study begins to focus on particular themes. For example, in the pilot project on independent learning, Parlett and Hamilton (1976) pursued the different perspectives and uses of the materials by the teachers. Other examples are areas of consensus and disagreement, problems raised by teaching assistants, topics avoided by administrators, and dominant issues in off-duty opinions.

The importance of the emerging themes is that they give direction and shape to the evolving evaluation, and they are analyzed in greater detail as the investigation progresses. Also, they are viewed as "working themes" until the point at which the study must be completed. New themes also are added up to the end of the evaluation (Parlett, 1990, p. 71).

The use of progressive focusing is a key feature of the approach. It provides the criteria for allocating resources in the study and avoids the problem of masses of unanalyzed material, which leads to "not being able to see the forest for the trees" (Parlett, 1990, p. 71). Progressive focusing also allows for attention to unpredictable or unique events (Parlett & Hamilton, 1976).

The third stage is that of a search for general principles underlying the program, identifying patterns of cause and effect, and efforts to place particular findings within a broader explanatory context (Parlett & Hamilton, 1976, p. 148). For example, teachers' views of independent learning materials depended on availability of the materials, prior experience with similar approaches, and whether they viewed the materials as either supporting or supplanting them (p. 148).

The three stages overlap in that a transition occurs when a problem is identified that requires further study. Therefore, the specific evaluation activities cannot be charted in advance. Instead, the evaluator begins with a large database and systematically reduces the focus to allocate attention to emerging questions and issues.

Methods of Data Collection.   Among the primary methods of data collection are observation, unstructured interviews, and document analysis. The evaluator begins in stage one by developing a continuous record of events as described in the previous section. Language conventions, slang, jargon, and other characteristics of conversations are noted because they often indicate important features of the social milieu, such as tacit assumptions and status differences.

Particularly important for identifying problems or issues are unstructured interviews. Individuals may be asked about their work, their views of the use and value of the new program or practice, and so on (Parlett & Hamilton, 1976). Often, interviewing large numbers of individuals is not feasible. However, those with special insight as well as members of various groups should be included (e.g., both successful and marginal students; student counselors; and faculty who are, as well as those who are not, associated with the program) (Parlett & Hamilton, 1976, p. 149).

The exploratory stage also includes codified observation. For example, schedules may be used to record attendance patterns, seating, and utilization of facilities. Classroom observation schedules also may be used to record teacher-student interactions and time utilization (Parlett & Hamilton, 1976).

Analysis of documents also is important because it can provide historical information on individuals' perceptions when the innovation was planned. Committee minutes, proposals for funding, reports, and nonconfidential student records are useful sources of information.

An illuminative evaluation should yield a report that "condenses a maximum amount of valid experience and informative commentary about the system" into a readable form that describes "key topics, unresolved questions, and practical thinking" (Parlett, 1990, p. 72).

The report should circulate freely and facilitate substantive discussion and policy development (Parlett, 1990). Essential conditions for such use are respecting the rights and feelings of participants during the study, observing professional ethics in conducting the study, writing clearly and lucidly for particular audiences, and being attentive to the various contexts in which the report will be circulated (Parlett, 1990, p. 72).

Strengths and Weaknesses

Illuminative evaluation was developed and used primarily in the United Kingdom. Thus, it received scant attention in the United States in the 1970s. This turn of events is unfortunate because the approach demonstrates the application of open-ended observational methods and anthropological fieldwork to evaluation.

A particular strength of the approach is the use of "progressive focusing" to develop themes for further study and to serve as a working framework for further data collection and analysis.

One weakness of the approach involves the skills required of the evaluator. First, he or she must be both knowledgeable and experienced in the use of qualitative research methods. Second, interpersonal skills and communication are at least as important as methodological expertise. A successful evaluation depends on the sensitivity of the evaluator and the participants' trust of him or her.

Another weakness of this view is the concern about the subjectivity of the information that is developed. When open-ended data collection methods are used, the evaluator is, in essence, the data collection instrument. His or her eyes or ears are the conduit for selection, description, and analysis of information. (This issue is discussed in more detail in Chapter 10, which discusses qualitative inquiry.) Although the technique of triangulation (i.e., checking the information through other sources) is used in the investigation, bias can still occur. Omissions and other distortions are not corrected through triangulation.

SUMMARY

A major purpose of the intuitionist/pluralist approaches was to capture and portray the complex dynamics of the programs being evaluated as they affected the individuals most closely associated with them. Thus, the actions and/or testimony of teachers, students, and others, as well as observations of program operation, are key information sources in these models.

The judicial and adversary models are similar in two major ways. First, they adapted some legal concepts and procedures for use in evaluation. Second, they developed a variety of different kinds of information about the particular programs. After the identification of key issues, two opposing teams develop evidence for their position. Witnesses provide testimony and are cross-examined, and documents are introduced at a hearing in which a presenter for each team argues his or her case. In the judicial model, however, the jury panel develops a list of recommendations; but the jury in the adversary model votes to continue or terminate the program.

Strengths of the two models are (1) the opportunities for participation by a diverse group of individuals, (2) communication with a lay audience, and (3) the breadth of evidence that may be presented. Particular strengths of the judicial model are (1) the spin-off in enlightened decisions resulting from broad participation, (2) the relevancy of the issues, and (3) the broad hearing given to potentially controversial or political programs.

A weakness of the two models is the cost, time, and effort involved in the preparation of evidence. Also, two other potential weaknesses threaten the validity of the evaluation. These weaknesses are (1) the difficulty in obtaining an impartial, committed jury panel and (2) the possible imbalance in oratorical skills of the presenters. Weaknesses of the adversarial model are:

1. The indictment mentality introduced by the win/lose decision
2. The difficulty in posing some issues in a win/lose framework
3. The possible failure of the jury panel to attend to crucial variables in their verdict
4. The restriction of use to summative evaluations

The judicial and adversarial models orient activities toward some culminating conclusions or recommendations. In contrast, the focus of Eisner's educational criticism approach is to discover the hidden complexities of classroom life. The purpose is to raise the conscious awareness of teachers and researchers about classroom dynamics. Execution of the approach depends on an astute observer who applies connoisseurship (appreciative perception) and criticism (vivid and rich reporting) to his or her observations of the classroom.

A strength of the perspective is that it addresses a previously neglected issue in evaluation, that of teachers' and students' experiences in a program. Another strength is that it presents judgments in easily understood language. Weaknesses of the approach are (1) that the educational criteria used by the evaluator are not made public and (2) that unfair evaluations can result from strongly judgmental criticisms that apply a particular perspective.

Robert Stake's responsive evaluation perspective is also sensitive to the experiences of individuals associated with a program. His approach, however, addresses the program level rather than the classroom, and it involves different audiences in the evaluation itself. Specifically, those who have an interest in the program are consulted as to their interests, concerns, and information needs. These stakeholders provide feedback to the evaluator on the issues selected for study. Representatives of these groups also may be involved in the discussion of methods to be used. Reporting may take place at several points in the evaluation, and different kinds of reports may be prepared for different audiences. The rationale for such an evaluation strategy is that a program has different value for different persons, and no one perspective is more correct than another.

Strengths of the responsive perspective are (1) the potential to portray program complexity in relation to selected issues and (2) the focus on the interests, language, and standards of the stakeholders. Weaknesses of the model are (1) the possible exclusion of important information, (2) the threat to evaluation validity that may result from stakeholder involvement in the technical aspects of the evaluation, and (3) the need for an evaluator skilled in both qualitative methods and communication.

Illuminative evaluation, although sensitive to the concerns of individuals associated with a program, does not permit stakeholders a voice in the evaluation. Instead, the purpose is to "illuminate the network of cause-effect relationships between beliefs and practices of an innovation or program and the context in which it functions" (Parlett, 1990, p. 69). This purpose is realized through the three stages of evaluation: (1) an exploratory stage, (2) focused questioning and inquiry, and (3) the development of explanations and general principles.

Strengths of the approach are (1) the revelation of the complexities of operation within a system and (2) the use of progressive focusing to serve as a framework for data collection and analysis. Weaknesses of the approach are (1) the need for an evaluator skilled in qualitative methods, interpersonal skills, and communication; and (2) the potential bias in the information that is developed. Potential bias is a problem because the evaluator is both the data collection instrument and the interpreter of the information.

Table 4.1 summarizes the focus and strengths and weaknesses of each of the four perspectives. Despite the weaknesses, a major contribution of all four approaches is that they introduced new perspectives into the purposes and methodology of evaluation. That is, there is no singular reality of program operation awaiting discovery. Instead, programs are characterized by multiple realities that are evidenced in the perspectives of those associated with the program and in the interactions that characterize program operation.

Table 4.1
Summary of intuitionist/pluralist perspectives

Perspective	Types of Knowledge	Strengths	Weaknesses
Judicial and adversary models	Evidence developed and presented by advocacy and adversarial teams to a jury panel	1. Involvement of nonprofessionals in an evaluation 2. Communication with a lay audience 3. Presentation of a breadth of evidence *Judicial model only:* 1. Spin-off in enlightened decisions resulting from broad participation 2. Relevancy of issues 3. The broad hearing given to potentially controversial or political programs	1. Cost, time, and effort of the evaluation 2. Difficulty in obtaining committed and impartial panel members 3. Potential imbalance in oratory skills of the teams *Adversary model only:* 1. The indictment mentality introduced by the win/lose decision 2. Difficulty in framing issues in a win/lose context 3. Possible failure of the jury to attend to crucial variables when dominated by the need to reach a success/failure verdict 4. Restriction of use to a summative evaluation (not formative)

Perspective	Types of Knowledge	Strengths	Weaknesses
Eisner's educational connoisseurship and criticism perspective	Indepth analysis of overt and covert classroom events developed by the evaluator/observer	1. Focus of attention on complex classroom dynamics 2. Presentation of judgments in easily understood language	1. Lack of specific educational criteria 2. Potential bias of the information because the evaluator is both the data collection instrument and interpreter of information
Stake's responsive evaluation perspective	Development of answers to issues, concerns, and information needs of stakeholders in addition to decision makers	1. Portrayal of program complexity in relation to selected issues 2. Reflection of interests, language, and standards of stakeholders in the evaluation	1. Possible exclusion of important information 2. Involvement of stakeholders in technical issues may jeopardize evaluation validity 3. Need for an evaluator skilled in both qualitative methods and communication
Illuminative evaluation	Discovery and illumination of the "invisible realities" of the social organization or program	1. Use of progressive focusing to serve as a framework for data collections and analysis 2. Revelation of the complexities of an innovation or program within an operating context	1. Need for an evaluator skilled in qualitative methods, interpersonal skills, and communication 2. Potential bias of the information because the evaluator is both the data collection instrument and interpreter of information

CHAPTER QUESTIONS

1. What are the assumptions of the intuitionist/pluralist approaches?
2. What is the major weakness of the judicial model? In what types of situations is this model appropriate?
3. Why was the judicial model inappropriate for evaluating minimum competency testing?
4. What types of questions does Eisner's connoisseurship and criticism approach address?
5. What is the focus of Stake's responsive evaluation perspective?
6. What are some ways to portray programs, according to responsive evaluation?
7. What are the three stages of evaluation in illuminative evaluation?
8. What are the primary data collection methods in the illuminative evaluation approach?

REFERENCES

Arnstein, G. (1975, November). Trial by jury: A new evaluation method. II. The outcomes. *Phi Delta Kappan, 57*(3), 188–190.

Barone, T. E. (1990). Curricular implications of educational connoisseurship and criticism. In H. J. Walberg & G. D. Haertel (Eds.), *The international encyclopedia of evaluation* (pp. 197–220). Oxford: Pergamon Press.

Braskamp, L., & Morrison, J. (1975). An interview with Robert Stake on responsive evaluation. In R. Stake (Ed.), *Evaluating the arts in education: A responsive approach* (pp. 33–38). Columbus, OH: Merrill.

Clyne, S. (1990). Adversary evaluation. In H. J. Walberg & G. D. Haertel (Eds.), *The international encyclopedia of educational evaluation* (pp. 77–79). Oxford: Pergamon Press.

Eisner, E. (1976). Educational connoisseurship and criticism: Their form and functions in educational evaluation. *Journal of Aesthetic Education, 3–4*(1), 135–150.

Eisner, E. (1977, February). On the uses of educational connoisseurship and criticism for evaluating classroom life. *Teachers College Record, 78*(3), 345–358.

Eisner, E. (1985). *The educational imagination: On the design and evaluation of school programs* (2nd ed.). New York: Macmillan.

Eisner, E. (1991). *The enlightened eye: Qualitative inquiry and enhancement of educational practice*. New York: Macmillan.

House, E. R. (1978). Assumptions underlying evaluation models. *Educational Researcher, 7*(3), 4–12.

House, E. R. (1980). *Evaluating with validity*. Beverly Hills, CA: Sage.

Madaus, G. (1982). The clarification hearing: A personal view of the process. *Educational Researcher, 11*, 4–11.

Parlett, M. R. (1990). Illuminative evaluation. In H. J. Walberg & G. D. Haertel (Eds.), *The international encyclopedia of educational evaluation* (pp. 68–73). Oxford: Pergamon Press.

Parlett, M. R., & Hamilton, D. (1976). Evaluation as illumination: A new approach to the study of innovatory program. In G. V. Glass (Ed.), *Evaluation studies review annual* (Vol. 1, pp. 140–157). Beverly Hills, CA: Sage.

Popham, W. J., & Carlson, D. (1977, June). Deep dark deficits of the adversary evaluation model. *Educational Researcher*, 6(6), 3–6.

Scheerens, J. (1990). Beyond decision-oriented evaluation. In H. J. Walberg & G. D. Haertel (Eds.), *The international encyclopedia of educational evaluation* (pp. 35–40). Oxford: Pergamon Press.

Stake, R. (1973). Program evaluation, particularly responsive evaluation. Paper presented at the conference, New Trends in Evaluation, Gotesborg, Sweden. Reprinted in G. Madaus, M. Scriven, & D. Stufflebeam (Eds.), *Evaluation models*. Boston: Kluwer-Nijhoff.

Stake, R. (1975). To evaluate an arts program. In R. Stake (Ed.), *Evaluating the arts in education: A responsive approach* (pp. 13–31). Columbus, OH: Merrill.

Stake, R. (1990). Responsive evaluation. In H. J. Walberg & G. D. Haertel (Eds.), *The international encyclopedia of educational evaluation* (pp. 75–77). Oxford: Pergamon Press.

Thurston, P. (1978, July/August). Revitalizing adversary evaluation: Deep dark deficits of muddled mistaken musings. *Educational Researcher*, 3(11), 3–8.

Thurston, P., & House, E. (1981, October). The NIE adversary hearing on minimum competency testing. *Phi Delta Kappan*, 63, 87–89.

Weiss, C. (1986). The stakeholder approach to evaluation: Origins and promises. In E. R. House (Ed.), *New directions in program evaluation* (pp. 186–200). New York: Falmer Press.

Wolf, R. L. (1975, November). Trial by jury: A new evaluation method. I. The process. *Phi Delta Kappan*, 57(3), 185–187.

Wolf, R. L. (1979). The use of judicial evaluation methods in the formation of education policy. *Educational Evaluation and Policy Analysis*, 3(1), 19–28.

Wolf, R. L. (1990). Judicial evaluation. In H. J. Walberg & G. D. Haertel (Eds.), *The international encyclopedia of educational evaluation* (pp. 79–81). Oxford: Pergamon Press.

Wood, K. C., Peterson, S. E., DeGracie, J. S., & Zaharis, J. K. (1986). The jury is in: Use of a modified legal model for school program evaluation. *Educational Evaluation and Policy Analysis*, 8(30), 309–315.

Worthen, B. R., & Owens, T. R. (1978). Adversary evaluation and the school psychologist. *Journal of School Psychology*, 16(4), 334–345.

PART TWO

Tools of Evaluation

CHAPTER 5

Methods of Obtaining Group Input

eedback from groups of individuals associated with an institution or program can be useful at several stages of an evaluation. Among them are the various planning tasks, determining implementation effects and problems, and interpreting results. One planning role for group feedback in the CIPP perspective, for example, is context evaluation. It involves the identification of strengths, weaknesses, needs, opportunities, or pressing problems in an institution, agency, or system. Another role for group input is in the examination and analysis of various program alternatives, referred to, in the CIPP perspective, as input evaluation.

Groups of teachers, students, administrators, and others can provide valuable input to other aspects of evaluation. One aspect is identifying issues to be addressed in an evaluation (Stake's responsive evaluation). Others are providing input to questionnaire designs, reporting perceptions of the conceptual framework of a program, identifying program components that are and are not working, reporting perceptions of program effects, and assisting in the interpretation of results from other data collection methods.

Four methods of obtaining group input are useful in evaluation. They are the focus group interview, the nominal group technique, the Delphi method, and the opinion survey.

THE FOCUS GROUP INTERVIEW

Group depth interviews or focus groups originated in the Office of Radio Research at Columbia University in 1941. Paul Lazerfield and Robert Merton developed the first use in the evaluation of audience reactions to radio programs (Stewart & Shamdasani, 1990). Members of the studio audience listened to recorded radio programs and pressed a red button when they heard anything that evoked a negative response and a green button for a positive response. After the program, members of the audience were asked to focus on the events that evoked a reaction and to discuss their reasons for their reactions (p. 9).

The technique was applied to the analysis of training and morale films during World War II, and the methods for implementation were more fully developed and disseminated. Currently, focus group interviews are used in program evaluation, marketing, public policy, advertising, and communications (Stewart & Shamdasani, 1990, p. 10).

A focus group interview differs from other information-gathering methods in two ways. They are (1) that it seeks to discover in-depth information about a small number of issues and (2) that the group is a device for eliciting information (Goldman, 1962).

Focus groups are not simply general discussions or brainstorming sessions. Also, they are not a mechanism to facilitate group decision making or team building (Krueger, 1993, p. 67). Instead, they are information-gathering processes that seek to discover the perceptions and feelings of participants about a particular topic or experience. Thus, the focus group interview differs from the Delphi method and the nominal group technique. The purpose of those techniques is to provide recommendations or to make decisions among alternatives (Krueger, 1988, p. 29).

A focus group is composed of 7 to 10 or 12 people. The session, from 1½ to 2½ hours, is conducted by a moderator, who asks 6 to 10 open-ended, concrete questions about a particular topic or experience. An important condition for a successful session is an open and permissive atmosphere in which each person feels free to share his or her point of view (Morgan & Krueger, 1993, p. 7). Thus, focus groups produce a rich body of data expressed in the words and context of the respondents (Stewart & Shamdasani, 1990, p. 12).

Uses

Focus group interviews can serve a variety of purposes in evaluation. One purpose is to generate information for use in survey questionnaires (Krueger, 1988; Stewart & Shamdasani, 1990). They are a means to explore the ways that potential respondents talk and think about objects and events. They also may indicate potential problems such as the omission of important questions and response choices (Krueger, 1988; Morgan, 1988). Focus groups also are useful following the analysis of data from a large scale implementation of a quantitative survey (Krueger, 1988; Stewart & Shamdasani, 1990). The focus group can enlighten interpretation of survey responses and provide depth to the responses obtained.

Two other roles of focus group interviews are important in program evaluation. First, focus groups can identify potential problems with a new program, service, or product. Specific implementation problems embedded in a new program or perceptions of the purpose (or potential threat) of a new program that may hinder implementation may be identified through focus groups.

Second, focus groups can provide insights about the effects, advantages, and limitations of a program, curriculum, or set of materials after implementation. Different focus groups, such as a group of teachers and a group of students, can provide information that assists the evaluator in determining why a particular program or set of materials was or was not effective. Useful information for revising or improving the program or materials also can be obtained.

Components

Essential components of a successful focus group are:

1. A carefully selected group of 7 to 10 or 12 participants
2. The interview questions
3. A skilled moderator and an assistant
4. An appropriate environment
5. Verifiable analysis of the data (Krueger, 1993, p. 67)

Participants.   The participants should constitute a homogeneous group with regard to the topic for the interview. The quality of the discussion, and possibly the direction, is determined in large measure by the group composition (Stewart & Shamdasani, 1990, p. 51). Therefore, administrators and teachers should not be participants in the same focus group (or teachers and students or parents and students).

Also, established groups, such as employee work groups, boards of directors, or colleagues, should not be used (Krueger, 1988, p. 97). Similarly, teachers that work closely in the same school should not be selected for the same group. Such groups have formal and informal patterns of relating to one another that may affect their reactions (Krueger, 1988).

Interview Questions.   The questions are the "heart of the focus group interview" (Krueger, 1988, p. 59), and they are critical to the success of the session. Of primary importance is that the purpose of focus groups is to determine the ways that respondents structure their world and not how respondents react to the evaluator's view of the way a phenomenon is structured (Stewart & Shamdasani, p. 65).

Therefore, the interview questions are *not* a verbal version of a questionnaire. Instead, they are concrete, open-ended questions to which the respondent structures the direction and content of the answers. Examples are, How do you feel about *XYZ* program? and What thoughts went through your head when you first read through the materials? The dimensions or issues raised first by respondents are those that are likely to be the most memorable and important to them (Stewart & Shamdasani, 1990, p. 63).

Questions to avoid are "yes/no" questions, abstract or philosophical questions, and "why" questions. The problem with "why" questions is that participants will provide answers that appear rational. However, decisions are often not the result of a rational process (Krueger, 1988, p. 63). Instead, when people describe their feelings, they are providing information about "why."

The maximum number of questions that can be addressed in a 2-hour session is 10. However, typically, a focus interview will consist of a total of 5 or 6 questions. The questions are listed on an interview guide with the most general questions first. For example, a question such as, How do you feel about the in-service training (for program *XYZ*)? would not be the first question. The interview guide ensures the inclusion of all the important topics and a consistent ordering of questions across groups (Morgan, 1988).

The Moderator and Assistant.   In addition to the interview questions, the moderator is critical to the success of a focus group. He or she must be skilled in group processes, be a good listener, have a warmth and liking of people, and be able to communicate clearly and precisely both orally and in writing. In addition, the moderator must have an adequate background knowledge of the topic to be able to follow up on critical points of concern (Krueger, 1988; 1993). In a school setting, the moderator should not be an administrator, a representative from the central office, or the chief evaluator. These individuals will precipitate socially desirable answers from the respondents.

The moderator's initial task is to create a nonthreatening environment. Introductions are followed by a brief statement of the purpose of the group and the importance of each person's thoughts.

An important task for the moderator is to manage potential "problem participants," such as the self-appointed expert, dominant talkers, shy respondents, and ramblers (Krueger, 1988). Another key task is to be sensitive to participants' nonverbal cues (such as puzzlement or stopping in midsentence) and their vague answers. These reactions to a question are signals to probe further for information. The skilled moderator reacts with questions such as, Would you explain further? Can you describe what you mean? and Is there anything else? (Krueger, 1988, p. 83). The moderator also avoids comments such as "correct" or "that's good" and also limits head-nodding tendencies to avoid influencing the participants (p. 83).

The role of the assistant to the moderator is to take comprehensive notes, respond to any interruptions, and operate the tape recorder (Krueger, 1988, p. 75). (Although the session may be videotaped, this practice is not recommended because the equipment is intrusive and may inhibit responding.) The assistant also may be called on at the end of the session to summarize briefly the main points that were expressed. The moderator asks if this summary is correct and watches participants' body language for indicators of agreement, hesitation, or confusion. The moderator then asks for any additional thoughts or if anything has been omitted (Krueger, 1988, p. 80).

Environment.   The setting should be a neutral location (not the teachers' lounge) that is accessible to the participants. The room should be comfortable, and the furniture should be arranged so that participants can establish eye contact with each other and the moderator. Typically, a U-shaped table arrangement or a large conference table is used. Also important is that the confidentiality of responses must be assured (Krueger, 1993).

Data Analysis.   The first step in the data analysis is the transcription of the interview. The moderator and the assistant then may supplement the transcript with additional observational data, if needed (Stewart & Shamdasani, 1990, p. 104). When focus groups are used in marketing research or social science research on sensitive topics, content analysis or coding of the transcript is required (Knodell, 1993). Coding is the process of identifying the concepts and ideas stated by the participants, developing a code for each, and keying each use of the concept by the particular code. Data analysis is then organized around the terms identified in the content analysis or the codes.

In evaluation, however, the topics pursued in a focus group typically generate issues, problems, strengths, and weaknesses relative to an institution, program, curriculum, or set of materials. Data analysis can be organized typically around the issues generated or questions pursued in the interview.

Regardless of method, the data analysis should be systematic and verifiable. The goal is data reduction, not data confusion (Krueger, 1993). Also, another evaluator should be able to arrive at the same summary, given the interview transcript.

Advantages and Limitations

Several advantages have been identified for focus groups. They are as follows:

1. Focus groups place people in more natural situations than one-on-one interviews.

2. Focus groups provide data from a group of individuals more quickly and with less cost than individual interviews.

3. The format allows the moderator to interact directly with respondents and to explore unanticipated issues.

4. The open response format yields a rich set of data in the respondents' everyday language.

5. Focus groups allow participants to react to and build on the responses of other participants (Krueger, 1988; Stewart & Shamdasani, 1990).

Limitations of focus groups are:

1. Trained moderators are required.

2. The moderator has less control than the interviewer in a one-on-one interview.

3. The open-ended nature of the responses make summarization and interpretation difficult.

4. The moderator may bias the responses by knowingly or unknowingly providing cues about the nature of desirable responses (Krueger, 1988; Stewart & Shamdasani, 1990).

THE NOMINAL GROUP TECHNIQUE

Both the Nominal Group Technique (NGT) and the Delphi technique are special purpose methods for situations in which individual recommendations must be tapped and pooled (Delbecq, Van de Ven, & Gustafson, 1975, p. 4). In evaluation, examples are identifying issues, needs, problems, and strengths and weaknesses.

The NGT was developed by Andre Delbecq and Andrew Van de Ven as a technique to facilitate the involvement of disadvantaged citizens in community action agencies funded by the Office of Economic Opportunity (Delbecq et al., 1975, p. 77). The technique then spread to business, government agencies, and other settings because it overcame some limitations of typical group planning meetings. Two such limitations are the tendency to offer solutions before all the problems are identified and the dominance of the discussion by highly vocal participants.

The NGT is a structured group of seven to nine individuals that is designed to provide equal opportunity for the participation of all the members and equal consideration of all ideas. The term *nominal* in the title refers to the nature of the group, that is, a group in name only (Delbecq et al., 1975, p. 7). The usual verbal exchange that characterizes typical groups does not occur.

The first activity is the silent development of a set of ideas by each group member in response to the stimulus question. Then, in round-robin fashion, each person contributes an idea, which is recorded on a flip chart or laptop computer with a large screen. Serial discussion of the recorded ideas follows, and the session concludes with each member rank ordering the ideas on the list.

Uses in Evaluation

The NGT is a structured group technique that generates a range of ideas for consideration. It is often used as an introductory planning mechanism. For example, the Missouri Department of Mental Health used the NGT to develop lists of needs by the regional advisory councils for their regions (Pokorny, Lyle, Tyler, & Topolski, 1988).

In evaluation, the NGT is useful in identifying institutional or system needs, goals, or priorities (context evaluation in the CIPP approach). Also, recall from Chapter 4 that the judicial model and Stake's responsive evaluation focus on issues identified by individuals associated with the program to be evaluated. The nominal group technique is a useful mechanism for this task. The technique is also useful in identifying issues or concerns to be addressed in a questionnaire or survey, and it is sometimes used to generate the items to be addressed in the Delphi technique.

The NGT technique also is useful in identifying weaknesses or problems in courses and programs. In an evaluation of an educational studies course, the NGT process revealed 10 prioritized weaknesses that were not revealed by a standard questionnaire (O'Neil, 1981, p. 52).

Components

Prior to the group meeting, the evaluator or staff develops the question to be addressed by the group. The question should be phrased as simply as possible

(Moore, 1987). For example, a good question is, What obstacles do you see to the installation of Program *X*? or What are the issues the evaluation of Program *Y* should address? A complex question such as, What are the goals to be achieved and projects to be undertaken by the county health department? should not be used.

Although the NGT can accommodate only seven to nine individuals, several groups can be conducted simultaneously in separate rooms or, if necessary, in one large meeting room. If possible, each group should be seated around a U-shaped table with the flip chart or computer screen at one end. Other required supplies are paper and pencil for each participant and a pack of 3 × 5 cards for each table.

Table 5.1 illustrates the sequence of activities in the NGT session. After welcoming the group and emphasizing the importance of their input, the moderator distributes the written question and reads it aloud. Participants are instructed to write phrases or brief sentences and to work independently. As indicated in Table 5.1, at the end of 5 minutes, each participant in turn contributes an idea to the group list. When completed, the list may consist of from 12 to 25 items.

In the round-robin reporting of ideas, the group leader emphasizes that the purpose is to map the group's thinking (Delbecq et al., 1975, p. 49). If duplicate items are suggested, however, they should be omitted by the group (not the group leader).

Table 5.1
Sequence of activities in the NGT

Component	Description
Silent generation of ideas	Question is presented to each participant in writing, and the group works independently for 5 minutes
Round robin recording of ideas	In turn, each participant contributes an idea, which is recorded on the flip chart or laptop computer, until all ideas are recorded and numbered (usually 12 to 25 items)
Serial discussion for clarification	Each idea is briefly explained by the writer (ideas are not debated)
Preliminary vote on item importance	Each participant selects, from the list, the top five priority items and writes the number and phrase of each on a 3 x 5 card. Each participant then rates the selected items from 5 (top priority) to 1 (least important)
Discussion of preliminary vote	Votes are recorded and group members briefly may comment on inconsistencies or surprises
Final vote	Each participant lists the five most important items in rank order on a rating form and rates each on a 0 to 10 scale of relative importance

Summarized from Delbecq, Van de Ven, and Gustafson, 1975.

The rule of thumb for allocating time to the serial discussion is 2 minutes times the number of items (Moore, 1987). The total time for the discussion is announced to the group. Each item is addressed in turn, and any participant can comment or provide clarification. The moderator, however, should resist efforts to combine several items into broader categories because some of the meaning may be lost (Moore, 1987).

Some descriptions of the NGT conclude with a single vote in which participants choose the seven most important ideas and rate each as to relative importance on a 7-point scale. Other single-vote procedures use a rank ordering of the top five items from 5 to 1. This method is recommended by Moore (1987) because the results can be quickly tallied. Delbecq et al. (1975), however, recommend both a preliminary and a final vote. The purpose of the preliminary vote is to discuss briefly any surprises that may result from other information held by participants. However, the additional time involved and the possibility of social pressure by some group members may outweigh this advantage.

When a large group has been subdivided into several NGT sessions, the small group votes may be consolidated into a master list after the serial discussion. This process may require up to 2 hours because the wording will be different on the different lists (Moore, 1987). The groups should then convene in a plenary session (scheduled after a long lunch break, perhaps) to vote on the items.

A variation of the NGT is suggested by Lapine (1987) for use in formative evaluation. Each group addresses three questions in turn. The first two questions are addressed in the same session with a short break. These questions are, What are the problems and challenges facing this program? and What are the strengths of the program in your opinion? (Lapine, 1987, p. 16). Addressing the second question after a brief break facilitates a positive feeling about the program and also puts the problems in perspective (p. 16). After compilation of the information from these questions, a second session may be scheduled to address the third question, which is to identify actions that can be taken to improve the program.

Advantages and Limitations

Several benefits have been identified for the NGT. Among them are:

1. Avoidance of choosing between ideas prematurely
2. Avoidance of competition, status pressures, and conformity pressures
3. Maximum opportunity for identification of a range of ideas
4. Ease in learning and using the technique (Delbecq et al., 1975; Moore, 1987)

In evaluation, NGT sessions often identify obvious problems that are difficult to document in other ways. An example is the lack of communication between staff members, which may be obvious to an observer but difficult to document (Lapine, 1987, p. 17).

One limitation of the technique, resulting from its ease of implementation, is that it may be overused in situations where it is not appropriate. A second limitation is that the quality of ideas is likely to vary greatly; that is, some will be shallow or impractical. Therefore, the NGT should be regarded as a starting point for idea development (Moore, 1987). Also, of absolute importance is that the items identified by the group be addressed in some way.

THE DELPHI TECHNIQUE

The Delphi method was developed in the early 1950s at the Rand Corporation as a process for technological forecasting (Helmer, 1967). The technique is named for Delphi, the site of the oracle of Apollo in ancient Greece, whose priests were believed to be able to divine future events.

The principal use of the Delphi technique for several years was to make future predictions and forecasts. However, it is useful whenever a pooled judgment is desirable.

Like the nominal group technique, the Delphi is a means of aggregating the judgments of a number of individuals (Delbecq et al., 1975). An advantage of the Delphi, however, is that individuals who cannot be brought together for a meeting can participate.

The Delphi is a series of questionnaires to which individuals respond anonymously. Each questionnaire also includes summary information on the group's prior responses as well as individual comments about particular statements. Thus, respondent decisions on subsequent questionnaires are made in light of others' decisions. The typical number of questionnaires is three, but a maximum of five rounds may be used. The process ends when consensus is approached, if consensus is the goal, or when sufficient information exchange has occurred (Delbecq et al., 1975, p. 83).

Moore (1987) differentiates between a conventional Delphi and a real-time Delphi. In a conventional Delphi, questionnaires are mailed to respondents with intermittent time allowed for data analysis. At least 45 days must be allowed to complete a conventional Delphi. In contrast, a real-time Delphi occurs during the course of a meeting or computer conference. Respondents attend the meeting or are connected by means of computer terminals so that time spent in distribution and collection of questionnaires is minimal (p. 51). The widespread use of microcomputers and the use of electronic mail can also minimize the time required to implement a conventional Delphi.

Uses

Use of the Delphi may be warranted for reasons such as the following:

1. A problem resolution can be facilitated by the collective judgments of one or more groups.
2. The groups are unlikely to communicate adequately without an intervening process.

3. Frequent group meetings are not practical.

4. One or more groups of participants are more dominant than others (Uhl, 1990, p. 82).

The Delphi also has been used as a preconference planning tool to clarify positions and delineate views of different reference groups (Delbecq et al., 1975, p. 11).

Like the nominal group technique, the Delphi has been used to help identify problems and to set goals and priorities. In the university setting, for example, the Delphi has served as a means of involving faculty in planning and decision making for the future of the institution.

The Policy Issues Committee of the Evaluation Network (a professional organization of evaluators that later merged into the American Evaluation Association) used a two-round Delphi survey with its 18 members to identify priority areas for study. On the first round, members listed priority areas for committee attention. These identified priorities were listed on the second questionnaire and were ranked by the members. The top-ranked activities were used to form the eight working subcommittees. The Delphi also is useful in identifying issues of concern to stakeholders in an evaluation, particularly when a group meeting is difficult or impractical to schedule.

Components

Table 5.2 summarizes the stages in the Delphi technique. As indicated, the decision makers, policymakers, or others develop the broad question to be addressed. This step is very important because, if the question is vague, unfocused, or confusing, the respondents may answer inappropriately or become frustrated and lose interest (Delbecq et al., 1975, p. 86). Thus, decision makers should clarify exactly the information that is needed and how it will be used (p. 86).

The nature of the question, of course, will vary, depending on the purpose of the Delphi. For example, planners for a conference on the role alignment of nurses used a Delphi to identify participants' views of nursing responsibilities in 10 years. In program planning, the question may be, What are the goals or priorities that program X should address? In planning an evaluation, various stakeholders might be asked to complete the sentence, The questions that the evaluation of Program X should address are ___.

The second step, selection of respondents, is also important. In order to obtain useful information, planners and evaluators must ensure, as much as possible, that the respondents feel personally involved in the issue or problem, have relevant information on the issue or problem, and are motivated to take the time to participate. Also, they must feel that the pooled information resulting from the Delphi will include information that they value and to which they would not otherwise have access (Delbecq et al., 1975, p. 83).

After the respondents are selected and contacted, the first questionnaire is prepared and mailed with a cover letter and a stamped, self-addressed envelope for returning the questionnaire. The cover letter is very important because it is the only contact between the staff and the respondent. The letter should thank the respon-

Table 5.2
Summary of major components in the Delphi technique

Component	Description
Development of broad question	Decision makers, policymakers, and others identify the issue, concern, and problem to be addressed.
Questionnaire #1	Questionnaire #1 is typically an open-ended instrument in which respondents generate responses to a broad question, issue, or problem.
Analysis of respondents' answers by evaluation staff and development of questionnaire #2	The list of items identified by participants is reduced to a set of generic statements and randomly listed for questionnaire #2.
Administration of questionnaire #2	Respondents either rank order the items or rate each item on a Likert scale and comment on any item they wish.
Analysis of respondents' answers and development of questionnaire #3	Total vote scores (or medians and modes of Likert rankings) are tabulated. These summary data and comments for any items are included in questionnaire #3.
Administration of questionnaire #3	Participants review items and accompanying data and rerank or rerate the items.
Data analysis and reporting to respondents and decision makers unless other rounds are required	Provide a summary of the data to respondents and decision makers.

dent for participation, ensure anonymity, explain the importance of the respondent, explain the purpose of the Delphi, provide instructions, and name the return date for the questionnaire (usually 2 weeks).

When the questionnaires are returned, the suggestions of the respondents are grouped in sets that essentially convey the same ideas. An easily understood complete sentence is then written for each group (for inclusion on the second questionnaire). Delbecq et al. (1975) suggest placing each item identified by respondents on a 3 × 5 card. The cards may then be placed in stacks and each set identified by a label that guides the development of the generic statement. Of importance is that the statements should be as concrete as possible. General statements are subject to misinterpretation and do not capture the interest of the respondents (Moore, 1987).

In responding to the second questionnaire, participants react to a compilation of the problems, issues, goals, or program alternatives initially identified by the group. The rank orderings or median ratings of participants, as well as comments, obtained in the second round, are provided on the third questionnaire. Participants are asked to consider this information as they review their rankings or ratings in round three. If necessary, the process may include up to five rounds.

Three conditions are critical for successful implementation of the method. One is adequate time. For questionnaires that are not sent by electronic mail to participants' computers, a minimum of 45 days is needed for a three-round Delphi. Second, the participants must be skilled in written communication. Third, high partici-pant motivation is essential (Delbecq et al., 1975). Effective participation depends on respondent interest in the issue or problem and belief in the value of the process.

Questionnaire Format.   Either of two somewhat different formats and rating methods may be used. In one approach, participants select the 10 items they believe most important and assign a value of 10 to the most important item, 9 to the next most important item, and so on (Delbecq et al., 1975, p. 98). A "comments" column is also provided on the instrument where participants may express disagreement, agreement, or clarification of any item. The data analysis consists of summing the individual item scores for a total item score and counting the numbers of individuals that voted for each item. One item, for example, with votes of three 10s, three 9s, and a 6 has an item vote of 63. The total votes and comments are included in the third questionnaire.

The other format is to construct a 5-point Likert scale on a priority continuum (most to least important) for each item. (Some implementations have used a 7-point scale, although the advantage of this variation is not clear.) When a scale is used, the information added to the third questionnaire consists of either (1) the mode for each item plus the respondent's prior rating or (2) the group median and interquar-tile range for each item. Also, when completing the third questionnaire, respondents are asked to state the major reason for any item they believe should be excluded from consideration.

Both of these methods are a mechanism for summarizing group priorities. A dis-advantage of the priority vote is that tabulating item totals for a large group of respondents is cumbersome. A disadvantage of the Likert format is the calculation of the median or the mode for a large number of items.

One often-used variation of the Delphi sequence is to begin with the second questionnaire. That is, the first query to the respondents consists of the basic ques-tion and a listing of items to be rated or ranked by the participants. When this proce-dure is followed, the nominal group technique is often used to identify the question-naire items.

Another variation, if the first and second questionnaires involve an identification of major problems or needs, is to use the third questionnaire for an identification of possible solutions. This variation is similar to the NGT modification suggested by Lapine (1987).

Advantages and Limitations

Among the advantages of the Delphi are that it allows adequate time for thinking and reflection; it avoids the undue influence of psychological factors, such as spe-cious persuasion of the loudest voice or the greatest supposed authority; and it pro-vides anonymity. It also overcomes the limitations of the "one-shot" rating of priori-ties, which does not allow for rethinking of the issues by participants. In addition, it allows for the participation of more people than would be effective in an interacting group (Linstone & Turoff, 1975).

One disadvantage is that the technique is logistically cumbersome to implement, particularly with large samples. The required time frame, data analysis, mailing, and follow-up of questionnaires are a costly investment for evaluation staff.

One criticism of the Delphi is that some respondents may allow their true opinions to be influenced by their perception of "expert" opinions reported in the rounds. Other criticisms focus on the data analysis, which encourages conforming answers. Nevertheless, the Delphi is a useful technique for involving similar or dissimilar groups in a complex exercise—that of identifying major issues, establishing policy alternatives, or exploring assumptions underlying a key issue.

THE OPINION SURVEY

The focus group interview and the nominal group technique are designed to obtain feedback from small groups of respondents. Although the Delphi technique can be implemented with somewhat larger samples, the data analysis and administration become more cumbersome as the group size increases. When group input is sought from a large sample, an opinion survey is appropriate.

An opinion survey is similar in many ways to attitude measurement (Hills, 1981). A major difference, however, is that the intent of an opinion survey is to obtain information on a group's position on particular issues, policies, program characteristics, and so on. Also, the items differ subtly in the phrasing. For example, an attitude measurement may ask the question, When you should be studying arithmetic and you're not, how do you feel about it? (Hills, 1981, p. 373). In contrast, an opinion survey may include an item such as, How long before first period should the school's outside doors be opened to students? (Hills, 1981, p. 374).

In evaluation, an opinion survey is appropriate when input is sought from a large sample on (1) institutional or system needs, goals, or priorities or (2) advantages and disadvantages of a program or perceived program effects. An example is the 1981 needs assessment of 10 Pittsburgh middle schools by the Learning Resources Development Center (LRDC) at the University of Pittsburgh. Perceptions from a wide variety of middle school constituencies about the conditions of the schools and ways to improve them were obtained. Twelve hundred adults were surveyed, and the respondents included board members, bus drivers, cafeteria workers, counselors, custodians, paraprofessionals, parents, principals, psychologists, school clerks, secretaries, security guards, social workers, and teachers (Cooley & Bickel, 1986, p. 224). The results were disseminated during meetings to several groups, and they became a part of the action plans of area managers in the school system.

Development and Use

The six stages in the development and use of an opinion survey are:

1. Generation of issues or topics

2. Item or question construction and pilot testing (instrument development)

3. Selection of the sample(s)

4. Administration

5. Data analysis

6. Dissemination of results

Instrument Development.   Like the other group methods discussed in this chapter, a clear purpose for use of the results is an essential prerequisite. For example, the 1981 districtwide and middle-school assessments of needs in Pittsburgh city schools were initiated by a new superintendent, hired from outside the district. Surveys of various groups were used as a means of assisting him to establish an agenda and a plan of action. The focus of the needs assessment was to identify problems and solutions that were within the district's capabilities to influence and implement (Cooley & Bickel, 1986, p. 183).

Critical to obtaining useful information is the development of issues or topics that are nontrivial and phrased in terminology the respondents understand. Equally important is that the items must be derived from an understanding of the policy, program, or institution that is the object of the survey and the context in which it operates. Topics for the districtwide needs assessment in the Pittsburgh schools were developed by a 30-member task force (half were community leaders and half were representatives of district employee groups). A smaller task force participated in the middle school needs assessment a few months later. Ideas and topics were then refined into survey items by the LRDC evaluation staff and reviewed by each task force.

Three essential characteristics of the items are that they must be understandable, answerable, and interpretable (Hills, 1981, p. 365). Each question must address a single element, and use of the word *not* should be avoided. Conditional clauses, which complicate and confuse the question, and catch words also should be avoided (Hills, 1981).

Items may be constructed in a declarative or interrogative form. The item may be followed by either four choices or a continuum that ranges from most to least important or from strongly agree to strongly disagree (a Likert scale).

One issue in developing the rating scale is whether or not to provide a middle ground or neutral position for respondents, for example, "don't know" or "no opinion." Hills (1981) notes that forcing respondents to one side or the other (by excluding a neutral position) when a neutral position is feasible distorts the results. However, when a middle ground is available on an issue in which respondents do not hold strong opinions, it will be selected by large numbers of them (p. 375). The decision as to response options must be made by the developers for their particular situation.

When completed, the items should be grouped into some logical organization. The completed instrument should then be pilot tested with representatives of selected respondent groups. The Pittsburgh districtwide needs assessment survey organized statements of educational conditions by major educational topics, for example, school climate, instructional leadership, facilities, and parent-school relations (Cooley & Bickel, 1986, p. 46). Also, at the end of each section, respondents were asked to select and rank order the two most important problems within that topic.

Size of the sample and group representation in the sample depend on the purpose of the survey. Information about perceived strengths and weaknesses of an innovative program, for example, may be obtained from program staff, administrators, teachers, parents, and students. Surveys of institutional or system weaknesses or problems typically involve a range of constituent groups and large samples. One purpose, in addition to obtaining information, is to communicate the complexities of the system to constituents. In the districtwide needs assessment in Pittsburgh schools, all the board members and community leaders were interviewed, and 5% of 10 other groups were sampled, for a total of approximately 1,400 potential respondents.

Administration, Data Analysis, and Dissemination.   When small groups, such as school boards, are sampled, the opinions may be obtained in a telephone interview and recorded by the interviewer. Otherwise, the survey should be mailed to respondents with a brief letter that stresses the importance of their input and the anonymity of their participation. The letter should also state that the results will be shared with them. Self-addressed, stamped envelopes must be included for the return of the questionnaires.

Although the questionnaires are completed anonymously, the return envelopes can be coded so that they may be matched to the name of the particular respondent. When the opinion surveys are returned, they are separated from the envelopes, and the data are coded for analysis. In the event that the response rate is low, or if a high participation rate is essential, the returned envelopes are matched to the respondent list. A follow-up request can then be sent to those who did not respond.

Data analysis for the items typically consists of means and standard deviations for topical areas (e.g., school climate) and medians for each issue (item) within a subscale. Data should be reported for different stakeholder groups, as well as for the total sample. If respondents are asked to choose the two most important issues within a topical area, as in the Pittsburgh needs assessment, then the issues within each area should be rank ordered according to the number of participants selecting each issue.

Dissemination of needs assessment results should inform the various stakeholders and also be presented in ways to precipitate action. The dissemination implemented by LRDC in the Pittsburgh school district is an example. First, as preliminary analyses were completed, results were informally communicated to the superintendent. The final results were communicated by interactive slide presentations in addition to written reports. Eight interactive slide presentations were conducted over a 6-week period and presented first to the superintendent and then to the superintendent and the president of the school board. Other presentations followed with the school board, the central administration, the building administrators and supervisors, the teachers, the task force, and lastly, the media at a scheduled press conference (Cooley & Bickel, 1986, p. 192). The presentation to the school board involved a 1-day retreat with the members. The district's 3,000 teachers, in contrast, viewed a 1-hour television presentation in their buildings at a special faculty meeting that was followed by a discussion.

A major advantage of an opinion survey is that input can be obtained in an efficient manner from large samples of respondents. However, unless a mechanism is also incorporated by which respondents indicate top priority issues, the data may be difficult to interpret. Another limitation is that the data will not be meaningful unless the items are concrete, simply stated, and phrased in ways the respondents can understand.

SUMMARY

Four well-known methods of obtaining group input are useful in various phases of planning and conducting evaluations. The four methods are the focus group interview, the nominal group technique, the Delphi technique, and the opinion survey. The focus group interview and the nominal group technique obtain information from small groups of individuals who convene together. In contrast, participants in the Delphi method and respondents to opinion surveys do not meet face to face.

The purpose of the focus group interview is to discover the perceptions and feelings of a small group of individuals about a particular topic or experience. Essential components are a skilled moderator, a limited set of open-ended concrete questions, a homogenous group of participants, a neutral setting, and an open atmosphere. Implementation of the focus group interview results in a rich body of data expressed in the words and context of the respondents.

Advantages of focus groups are:

1. Focus groups place people in more natural situations than one-on-one interviews.

2. Focus groups provide data from a group of individuals more quickly and with less cost than individual interviews.

3. The format allows the moderator to interact directly with respondents and to explore unanticipated issues.

4. The open response format yields a rich set of data in the respondents' everyday language.

5. Focus groups allow participants to react to and build on the responses of other participants (Krueger, 1988; Stewart & Shamdasani, 1990).

Limitations of the technique are:

1. Trained moderators are required.

2. The moderator has less control than the interviewer in a one-on-one interview.

3. The open-ended nature of the responses make summarization and interpretation difficult.

4. The moderator may bias the responses by knowingly or unknowingly providing cues about the nature of desirable responses (Krueger, 1988; Stewart & Shamdasani, 1990).

In contrast to the focus group interview, the purpose of both the nominal group technique and the Delphi method is to identify and establish priorities for issues, goals, needs, problems, or strengths and weaknesses. The NGT is referred to as "nominal" because the typical verbal exchange characteristic of groups does not occur. Instead, a small group (or simultaneous small groups) first silently develops written responses to an open-ended question asking them to name issues, problems, or goals, and so on. In round-robin fashion, group members then list the ideas on a flip chart. Serial discussion of the ideas follows, and the session concludes with a rank ordering of the listed items.

Advantages of the NGT are:

1. The avoidance of choosing between ideas prematurely

2. The avoidance of competition and status and conformity pressures

3. Ease in learning and using the technique

4. The maximum opportunity for identification of ideas

Limitations of the technique are (1) the range in the quality of ideas that are developed, (2) the potential for misuse in situations where it is not appropriate, and (3) the difficulty in compiling data from several simultaneous groups.

Like the NGT, the Delphi method is a mechanism for aggregating the judgments of a number of individuals. It is used when participants cannot meet face to face and consists of a series of questionnaires with summary information on prior responses and individual comments about particular statements. Participants first generate ideas in response to an open-ended request to identify issues, problems, goals, strengths, or weaknesses. Each of the subsequent questionnaires lists the ideas in sentence format with a rating or ranking mechanism. After the second round, each questionnaire reports either the rank orderings or median rankings of each item. The process ends when consensus is reached or sufficient information is obtained.

Advantages of the Delphi are:

1. The avoidance of status pressure and specious persuasion

2. The adequate time allowed for reflection

3. The rethinking of issues provided by the subsequent questionnaires

4. The allowances for large numbers of people

A limitation of the technique is that it is cumbersome to implement, and this problem increases as samples become larger.

The opinion survey is appropriate when input is sought from large samples on (1) institutional or system needs, goals, or priorities and (2) advantages and disadvantages of a program or perceived program effects. The six stages in the development and use of an opinion survey are:

1. Generation of issues and topics
2. Item or question construction and pilot testing (instrument development)
3. Selection of the sample(s)
4. Administration
5. Data analysis
6. Dissemination of results

A major advantage of the opinion survey is that input can be obtained in an efficient manner from large samples of respondents. A limitation is that items must be carefully constructed with a mechanism for respondents to indicate top priority issues for the data to be meaningful.

All four methods are appropriate for various tasks in the planning, conduct, and results interpretation phases of evaluation. Of the four methods, the focus group interview is the most versatile in evaluation. The NGT, the Delphi, and the opinion survey, however, are appropriate whenever issues, problems, goals, needs, or strengths and weaknesses must be identified and rank ordered by groups of individuals (see Table 5.3).

Table 5.3
Summary of group input methods and uses in evaluation

Uses	Methods
Planning	
Identifying instructional or system needs, goals, or priorities	NGT, Delphi, opinion survey
Identifying issues an evaluation should address	NGT, Focus group interviews, Delphi
Providing input to design a quantitative survey	Focus group interviews, NGT
Documenting Implementation and Effects	
Perception of conceptual framework and rationale of a program by teachers, administrators, and others	Focus group interviews
Program strengths and weaknesses	Focus group interviews or NGT + opinion survey
Information on program effects	Focus group interviews, NGT
Interpretation of Results	
Interpreting questionnaire results	Focus group interviews
Interpreting program outcomes	Focus group interviews

CHAPTER QUESTIONS

1. How does the purpose of the focus group interview differ from that of the Delphi method and the nominal group technique?

2. What actions should the moderator of a focus group take care to avoid?

3. Which group technique is best suited to discovering the perceptions of a program's conceptual framework by teachers? Why?

4. What do the nominal group technique and the Delphi method have in common?

5. What are the three conditions essential for successful implementation of the Delphi technique?

6. How does an opinion survey differ from the measurement of attitudes?

7. What are the essential characteristics of items on an opinion survey?

REFERENCES

Cooley, W., & Bickel, W. (1986). *Decision-oriented educational research*. Boston: Kluwer-Nijhoff.

Delbecq, A., Van de Ven, A., & Gustafson, D. (1975). *Group techniques for program planning*. Glenview, IL: Scott, Foresman.

Goldman, E. (1962). The group depth interview. *Journal of Marketing, 26,* 61–68.

Helmer, O. (1967). *Analysis of the future: The Delphi method*. The Rand Corporation.

Hills, J. R. (1981). *Measurement and evaluation in the classroom* (2nd ed.). Columbus, OH: Merrill.

Knodell, J. (1993). The design and analysis of focus group studies. In D. L. Morgan (Ed.), *Successful focus groups* (pp. 35–50). Newbury Park: Sage.

Krueger, R. A. (1988). *Focus group: A practical guide for applied research*. Newbury Park: Sage.

Krueger, R. A. (1993). Quality control in focus group research. In D. L. Morgan (Ed.), *Successful focus groups* (pp. 65–88). Newbury Park: Sage.

Lapine, L. (1987). Using the nominal group technique in formative evaluation. *Evaluation Practice 8*(3), 15–18.

Linstone, H. A., & Turoff, M. (Eds.). (1975). *The Delphi method: Techniques and applications*. Reading, MA: Addison-Wesley.

Moore, C. (1987). *Group techniques for idea building*. Newbury Park: Sage.

Morgan, D. L. (1988). *Focus groups as qualitative research*. Newbury Park: Sage.

Morgan, D. L., & Krueger, R. A. (1993). When to use focus groups and why. In D. L. Morgan (Ed.), *Successful focus groups* (pp. 3–19). Newbury Park: Sage.

O'Neil, M. (1981). Nominal group technique: An evaluation data collection process. *Evaluation Newsletter*, 45–61.

Pokorny, L., Lyle, K., Tyler, M., & Topolski, J. (1988). Introducing a modified nominal group technique for issue identification. *Evaluation Practice 9*(2), 40–44.

Stewart, D. W., & Shamdasani, P. N. (1990). *Focus groups: Theory and practice*. Newbury Park: Sage.

Uhl, N. (1990). Delphi Technique. In H. J. Walberg & G. D. Haertel (Eds.), *The international encyclopedia of educational evaluation* (pp. 81–82). Oxford: Pergamon.

CHAPTER 6

Indicators of Academic Achievement

ormal schooling, as a social institution, is a centuries-old tradition. However, educational and psychological measurement of the effects of schooling is a relatively new concept. Prior to the twentieth century, information about academic achievement was in the form of highly subjective judgments about student responses on oral and essay examinations (Thorndike & Hagan, 1969).

The application of measurement to the educational setting introduced new methods to making decisions about students. Specifically, measurement consists of (1) defining the quality or attribute of interest, (2) determining the set of operations that serve as indicators of the attribute or quality, and (3) establishing a set of procedures for translating observations of the indicators into quantitative estimates of degree or amount (Thorndike & Hagan, 1969, p. 9). Currently, two major approaches to the measurement of educational and psychological attributes are in use: norm-referenced and criterion-referenced measurement. Each emerged in response to a different need, and each can be useful in program evaluation.

THE BIRTH OF NORM-REFERENCED MEASUREMENT

Experimental psychologists and the research of Sir Francis Galton introduced the measurement of human characteristics in the late nineteenth century. Experimental psychologists measured sensory and mental functions such as seeing, hearing, and response time to mental tasks.

Galton, in contrast, researched individual differences and collected data on 10,000 people on attributes such as height. He demonstrated that the normal curve represented the distribution of certain physiological and psychological characteristics of the population. In other words, few individuals are at the extreme values of the particular characteristic, and a large number cluster around the average or midpoint of the range of scores or values.

The concept of norm-referenced measurement was introduced to the educational setting by way of the Binet intelligence test. Developed in France to identify children with mental retardation, the Binet test was further refined and tested at Stanford and became the first comprehensive measure of intelligence. Known as the Stanford-Binet, the test yields an intelligence quotient for each examinee. The individual's score, in comparison to the population, may be interpreted as below average, average, or above average intelligence.

The Stanford-Binet served as the model for numerous norm-referenced aptitude and achievement tests at all levels of education. These tests were used extensively in the first half of the twentieth century because they were compatible with the general purpose of education. Specifically, that purpose was selection. Of the students entering the educational system, only approximately 5% were considered by nature or by nurture to benefit from higher education (Bloom, Hastings, & Madaus, 1971, p. 21). Students, therefore, formed a pyramid, with many at the lower levels and a few at the apex. A major task of the school was to determine, at each level, who should continue to more advanced education. Norm-referenced tests, which indicate fine differences in student performance and rank students on a continuum, were particularly appropriate for this purpose.

THE EMERGENCE OF CRITERION-REFERENCED MEASUREMENT

In the early 1960s, criticisms about the overuse of norm-referenced tests began to surface. Among them were the overuse of tests for grouping and the potential for eliminating good job applicants who had limited cultural backgrounds (Thorndike & Hagan, 1969). In addition, several of the new curricula developed in the post-Sputnik reform emphasized the mastery of identified skills. The norm-referenced standardized tests selected to evaluate the new curricula often did not reflect program goals. Moreover, the tests were found to be relatively insensitive to differences between schools and/or programs, primarily because of their psychometric properties and their less than complete content coverage (Madaus, Stufflebeam, & Scriven, 1983, p. 13).

These concerns led to the development of tests variously labeled criterion referenced, mastery, competency, proficiency, or objectives-referenced tests. These tests were designed to answer the question, What skills has the student mastered?

Efforts to develop mastery tests for important skills were aided by the taxonomy of educational objectives conceptualized by Benjamin Bloom (Bloom, Engelhart, First, Hill, & Krathwohl, 1956). The taxonomy consists of six levels of cognitive skills sequenced from simple to complex. The definitions for each of the levels serve as the basis for developing mastery test items.

In addition to measuring program outcomes, another role for criterion-referenced testing emerged in the 1970s. Fueled largely by a perceived decline in student performance on college admission tests (underscored by media reports of student deficits [Gray, 1980]), the belief developed that high school graduates lacked the essential skills to function in society. During the 1970s, many states enacted legislation that required students to pass competency tests either (1) to pass from one grade to another or (2) to receive a high school diploma. According to Baker and Choppin (1990), the minimum competency tests are almost always based on objectives that describe the general type of skill to be tested and consist of items assembled to measure that skill (p. 500). A cut-off score or band is established to differentiate pass and no-pass on the test.

Both norm-referenced and criterion-referenced measurement can fulfill useful roles in program evaluation. This chapter discusses their characteristics and uses, as well as other data sources that can provide information about achievement.

NORM-REFERENCED ASSESSMENT

Norm-referenced tests, like the Stanford-Binet, provide information about an examinee's performance relative to an identified comparison group. Important issues in norm-referenced assessment are the basic characteristics, scoring and interpretation, types of achievement tests, and the decisions for which they are appropriate.

Basic Characteristics

Both the theoretical foundations of norm-referenced measurement and the defining features of the tests are important in understanding their function in relation to schooling.

Theoretical Foundations.   The basis for norm-referenced measurement is trait theory or the theory of individual differences. This concept began with the research of Sir Francis Galton (Cronbach, 1970; Taylor, 1994). He concluded from his research that major physical attributes (referred to as traits) are distributed in the population in the form of normal curves (Taylor, 1994).

Psychological measurement applied Galton's concept to the development of assessments of traits such as intelligence. The methods developed for measuring intelligence (viewed as a stable trait) were then extended to the development of achievement tests, even though learning is a goal-directed activity (Taylor, 1994). The rationale for this transition was the fairly strong correlation between ability tests and subsequent school achievement (.60 to .70) and between broad-range achievement tests and subsequent school performance (.70 to .80).

Definition.   The key features of norm-referenced tests are (1) the capability to spread out the examinees so that performance differences can be clearly identified and (2) the availability of performance norms (usually population means) (Vincent, 1990, p. 111). The norm, however, is only typical performance; it does not imply a desirable standard. Norm-referenced tests estimate individual performance relative to this typical or average performance.

Scoring and Interpretation

The quantitative score reported for each examinee is a comparison score such as percentiles, grade equivalents, or standard scores. A score at the 60th percentile, for example, indicates that the student scored higher than 60% of the students in the norming group. For grade norms, the score 3.0, for example, is assigned to average performance at the beginning of third grade, 3.5 to average performance in the middle of the grade, and so on (Thorndike & Hagan, 1969). One problem with grade equivalent scores, however, is that they are sometimes misinterpreted. A grade equivalent score of 5.8 in mathematics earned by a fourth grader does not indicate that the student has mastered fifth-grade mathematics. He or she only earned a score as high as the average pupil at the end of fifth grade (Thorndike & Hagan, 1969, p. 219).

Standard scores, in contrast to percentiles and grade equivalents, are expressed in standard deviation units above or below the mean. For example, a score of 0.52 is half a standard deviation above the mean. Standard scores may be developed in any of several scales. The College Entrance Examination Board, for example, uses a mean of 500 and a standard deviation of 100.

Applied at a class or group level, norm-referenced measurement can be informative about the range as well as differences in achievement (Vincent, 1990, p. 113). However, efforts to bring "all pupils up to the grade norm," are doomed to defeat. The very nature of relative scores results in as many examinees below average as above. That is, when the norm is defined as the average of the reference group, it is a statistical necessity that approximately half the group will be below average (Thorndike & Hagan, 1969, p. 246). Suppose that a sudden and major improvement in educational effectiveness occurred and students scored considerably higher on a selected norm-referenced test. The next time that new norms are established, a higher absolute level of performance would be required to "read at the sixth-grade level," for example. The norm or average would be higher, and again half the students would be at or below average (p. 247).

Technical Specifications

Development of a standardized norm-referenced test begins with the identification of common concepts in the major textbooks in the subject area. The test blueprint, referred to as a table of specifications, lists the concepts as column headings. Broad cognitive abilities, such as recall and problem solving, identify rows in the table. Items are written for cells in the table that represent major emphases across textbooks. A term mentioned briefly, for example, may be tested only at the recall level.

Approximately three times the needed number of items are developed initially. The items selected for the test are those that maximize examinee differences on the test (Taylor, 1994; Vincent, 1990). In other words, items are selected for their power to discriminate between examinees with higher and lower total scores on the test (Taylor, 1994, p. 240). If items do not function as discriminators, they are eliminated. For example, an item that may be considered important in the curriculum will be eliminated from the test if it is answered correctly by all fourth graders. Such an item does not differentiate between the test takers. In addition, an item might be chosen because it differentiates between the 95th and 99th percentiles rather than for its representation of a critical concept in the curriculum (Taylor, 1994, p. 240).

Traditional methods of establishing the validity of the test are content reviews of the items and correlational methods. Performance on the test is correlated with performance on a test that measures the same thing and/or an identified real-world behavior the test is to predict. Recent discussions of test validity emphasize that validity does not reside in a test but must be established for each use of a test (Messick, 1989; Shepard, 1993). Thus, an essential question in test validity is, "Does the test do what it claims to do?" (Shepard, 1993, p. 444). For example, justifying the use of IQ tests to place low-scoring children in separate classrooms requires evidence that (1) the treatment is more beneficial than regular classroom instruction and (2) the benefits outweigh the social stigma (Messick, 1984; Shepard, 1993). In other words, like the Federal Drug Administration, the test developer is responsible for documenting both anticipated effects and side effects of the product before it is released for widespread use (Shepard, 1993, p. 426).

Once test validity is established, reliability of the test must be documented. Methods include calculating correlations between forms of the test or by formulas applied to one test administration.

Decisions

Norm-referenced tests were developed to provide information about an individual relative to a population to which he or she belongs. Appropriate uses are (1) to compare a student's performance in different subject areas and (2) to inform a teacher of a new student's relative performance in an academic area. Norm-referenced tests, when used in conjunction with other information, also can assist in certain academic decisions, such as diagnosing individual learning disabilities. In addition, when administered to a group, norm-referenced tests can provide information about the range of performance within the group and differences in achievement (Vincent, 1990).

For programs that target broad areas of performance, such as reading, norm-referenced tests can provide information about growth. However, the tests should not be used to make decisions about the termination of particular programs because the tests are insensitive to specific program objectives. Tyler (1990, p. 734) noted that the topics that are not common to programs or curricula are more numerous than the common topics for which items are written. Thus, the fit between a test and any particular curriculum is questionable (Haertel, 1990).

Some problems also have been identified with the use of norm-referenced tests for accountability purposes. Accountability refers to the comparison of classrooms, schools, and school districts on student scores. First, as already stated, the tests are not designed to assess the range and variety of the goals and priorities of a particular curriculum (Haertel, 1990). Second, they are limited to forms of learning that can be tested with multiple-choice items (p. 486).

Third, groups should only be compared on output when input is taken into consideration (Thorndike & Hagan, 1969). Input consists of the earlier status of the student, the relative emphasis on different goals, and the resources committed to the classroom or school. However, this information is rarely provided.

Fourth, some educators indicate that the increased use of standardized tests for high-stakes decisions (the assignment of positive and negative consequences based on test scores) has led to negative effects on schools and students (Darling-Hammond & Wise, 1985; Haertel, 1990; Haladyna, Nolen, & Haas, 1991; Shepard, 1991a; Smith & Rottenberg, 1991). Among these negative effects are a focus on drill-and-practice exercises to the neglect of other activities (Smith & Rottenberg, 1991), pressures to increase test scores, and the use of some activities that are unethical. Among the activities documented by researchers are using commercial test preparation materials that teach or review the skills to be tested, teaching items from the current year's test, dismissing low-achieving students on test days, allowing additional time and giving hints during the test, and aligning the curriculum to test items (Haladyna et al., 1991; Mehrens & Kaminski, 1989). Haladyna et al. (1991) refer to the effects of these practices on test results as test score pollution. Scores are increased or decreased with no connection to the constructs represented by the test (p. 2).

Interpretation of Group Performance

In program evaluation, norm-referenced achievement tests can be used to subdivide a sample of students on prior achievement into high, average, or low. They can also provide estimates of general ability levels of students who are being compared in a study. For example, the Boulder Valley retention study compared the achievement in first grade of previously retained and matched nonretained children. Two indices of first-grade achievement were obtained for each group. One was a teacher rating of their pupils' achievement and adjustment. The other was the scores on a standardized test of reading and mathematics. The use of norm-referenced scores as a posttest measure of achievement was appropriate in this particular situation. The rationale for retention is that simply providing additional time will enable children to perform better in subsequent years. Therefore, a comparison of retained children with a group that met the requirements for retention but were not retained on a norm-referenced test was appropriate. The results indicated only an average 1-month gain in reading for the retained children and no difference in mathematics.

Scores on norm-referenced tests can provide school districts with information about potential problems when high-stakes consequences are not associated with test performance. For example, New Orleans Public Schools (1993) analyzed student performance on the California Achievement Test by high-risk and low-risk categories and also related performance to other factors. High-risk students are those in each age cohort who have been retained at least once *or* received Chapter I services for at least one full school year. The median percentile of low-risk students in reading for grades 1 through 6 ranged from 51 to 60, while the median percentile for high-risk students in those grades ranged from 22 to 27. The report suggests that systematic differences may exist at the classroom level and recommends an analysis of instructional variables.

A contributing factor appears to be absenteeism—29% of the low-risk group was absent an average of 12 to 18 days per school year, while 41% of the high-risk students were absent an average of 12 to 18 days. Further, analysis of the data from students receiving free lunch questions the assumption that low socio-economic status (SES) is associated with poor achievement (New Orleans Public Schools, 1993, p. 39). Many of the students who receive free lunch are low-risk students, and their median percentile rank in reading for grades 1 through 6 ranged from 51 to 59. The report recommends an analysis of instructional variables to gain a better understanding of these findings (p. 39).

Summary

The research of Sir Francis Galton established the theoretical foundation for norm-referenced measurement. Specifically, individuals can be measured on traits such as intelligence and ordered on a continuum according to the amount of the trait they possess. The concept of trait measurement was soon applied to both ability and achievement testing, and the tests assisted in the selection of individuals who should go on to higher levels of education.

A norm-referenced test is constructed to yield a ranking of students on a continuum. The performance of representative samples of students, referred to as the norming group, is used as the basis for ranking the performance of other examinees.

The scores reported for students are percentiles, grade equivalents, or standard scores. A particular problem with grade equivalents, however, is that they may be misinterpreted as years of school work completed. Standard scores, in contrast, represent student performance in standard deviation units above or below the mean.

Important in interpreting student scores is the basis for their construction. The tests are designed to yield 50% of the scores above and below the mean. In other words, although major concepts and terms to be tested are identified in advance, items are selected to discriminate among examinees.

Appropriate uses of norm-referenced tests are (1) to compare a student's performance in different subject areas, (2) to inform a teacher of a new student's relative performance in an academic area, and (3) when used with other information, to provide information for different educational decisions. Norm-referenced tests may be used in program evaluation to subdivide a sample of students on prior achievement into high, average, or low. For programs that target broad areas of performance, the tests can provide information about growth.

Comparisons of programs, schools, or districts on norm-referenced tests may be misleading because the tests do not assess program goals, are restricted to limited forms of learning, and typically are not reported in relation to differential inputs. Finally, high-stakes testing leads to increased pressure to increase performance and to some questionable practices. In contrast, one appropriate use of norm-referenced data at the district level is to identify potential problems for further study.

CRITERION-REFERENCED ASSESSMENT

Criterion-referenced assessments were developed initially in response to the needs of instructional development. Curriculum designers required tests that would provide information about the skills and competencies learned by the students and which would discriminate between masters and nonmasters (Glaser, 1963).

Some writings on criterion-referenced assessment have interpreted the term *criterion* to mean "standard of performance." However, the term does not refer to the performance standard or cut-off score set for the test. Instead, the criterion refers to the behaviors or tasks that are the basis for the test (Hambleton, 1990; Nitko, 1984). Some researchers suggest that criterion-referenced score interpretations are possible from clusters of related items on a norm-referenced test. However, their value is limited because of the typically small numbers of items measuring any skill (Hambleton, 1990, p. 115).

Basic Characteristics

The theoretical foundation and definition of criterion-referenced tests differ from those of norm-referenced tests.

Theoretical Foundation.   The theoretical basis for criterion referencing is a continuum of knowledge in a well-defined domain. The goal is to be able to place an individual's attainment on the continuum on the basis of proficiency measures (referred to as criterion-referenced tests) (Glaser, 1963). In other words, the basis for evaluating the student's performance is not how well other students performed on the test. Instead, it is a particular set of behaviors or tasks on which the student demonstrates proficiency.

The continuum of knowledge in a domain may be ordered in any of several ways (Nitko, 1984). Some domains, such as spelling, may be ordered on the basis of the difficulty of the subject matter. Other domains, such as writing narratives, debugging computer programs, and interpreting X rays, can be organized on quality of performance from novice to expert (see Chi, Glaser, & Farr, 1988). That is, an expert's performance is both qualitatively and quantitatively different from that of a novice.

One mechanism for identifying a continuum of cognitive abilities is the levels of cognitive learning identified by Bloom et al. (1956) referred to as Bloom's taxonomy. These levels can serve as a mechanism for writing or organizing course objectives and developing test items (see Table 6.1).

Table 6.1
Levels of Learning in Bloom's Taxonomy

Types of Learning	Definition
Knowledge	Recall of (1) specifics and universals such as structures and generalizations that dominate a subject field and (2) methods and processes
Comprehension	
translation	Restatement by paraphrasing of a communication
interpretation	Explanation or summarization of a communication
extrapolation	Extension of trends or tendencies beyond the given data that are in accordance with the original communication
Application	The use of abstractions (ideas, procedures, generalized methods, or technical principles) in particular concrete situations
Analysis	The deconstruction of a communication into its elements or parts so that the relations among ideas are made explicit
Synthesis	Arrangement and combination of elements and parts to form a pattern or structure not clearly evident before
Evaluation	Use of a standard of appraisal to develop judgments about the value of material and methods for stated purposes

Summarized from Bloom, Hastings, and Madaus, 1971.

Definition.   Criterion-referenced tests are designed to measure representative samples of tasks drawn from the particular domain (Nitko, 1984). For example, an important domain for radiologists is interpreting chest X rays. This domain can be analyzed on a novice-expert continuum with identified, wide variations in proficiency from novice performance to expert diagnoses. Novices make decisions based on perceptual data, intermediate students begin to use cognitive reasoning with many errors, and so on (Lesgold et al., 1988).

In developing a test for the classroom or evaluation of a program, the knowledge continuum may or may not be fully developed in advance. However, the type of domain and a general sense of placement of the particular skills to be assessed is important. The two mechanisms for designing a particular test are objectives referencing and domain referencing. They are appropriate for different types of domains. A third type of criterion-referenced assessment is that of minimum competency testing.

Objectives-Referenced Assessment

In the model developed by Ralph Tyler (1950), broadly stated end-of-course objectives served as the basis for assessments. Tyler (1950) cautioned that objectives were not references to isolated bits of behavior. Instead, they should be "more than knowledges, skills and habits; they should involve modes of thinking or critical interpretation, emotional reactions, and interest" (Tyler, 1950, p. 19). Examples are "application of principles in science" and "sensitivity to art values" (Smith & Tyler, 1942). These complex skills are the end points of instruction in a particular curriculum and depend on the learning of prior skills in the course.

One end-of-course objective identified by the teachers for both junior and senior high school students was that of interpreting data. Table 6.2 illustrates the assessment tasks for the junior high school level. Note that because objectives are general statements, the first task is to describe the aspects of that skill to be tested. Then, test situations are developed to assess those aspects.

Recently, Michael Scriven (1994) has advocated the use of items similar in format to measure higher level cognitive skills. He refers to the two-stage process he is recommending as multiple-rating items. An example is to provide a student with a prose passage and five summaries. The student grades the summaries, which is a higher order cognitive task, and also selects a rationale for the grades from a set of reasons. Another example is to provide the student with a set of data and a set of explanations about the data, which the student grades. Such items assess higher order cognitive skills; are resistant to multiple guessing (efforts to eliminate wrong answers);

Table 6.2
Description of test situations for making inferences from data

Objective:	The ability to make inferences from data
Skills involved:	The ability to make comparisons, to see elements common to several items of data, to recognize prevailing tendencies or trends in the data, and to recognize the limitations of given data.
Content:	Data pertinent to such topics as heredity, crop rotation, immigration, government expenditures, and health.
Test items:	Data presented in various forms, including tables, charts, and different kinds of graphs.
	Each set of data is followed by 15 statements that purport to be interpretations. The student is asked to place the statement in one of three categories as follows:
	(a) true (b) insufficient data (c) false
	(At the senior high level, students selected their answers from five options. In addition to the above were (d) sufficient to indicate the statement is probably true and (e) sufficient to indicate the statement is probably false.)

Summarized from Smith and Tyler, 1942.

and avoid the problem of verbal fluency, which may mask deficiencies in subject area knowledge (Scriven, 1994).

Course objectives are not limited to skills that only may be tested by paper-and-pencil tests. Logical objectives in science, for example, are using equipment and measuring instruments, and designing and conducting experiments. Performances of these capabilities is assessed through observation and the analysis of student reports.

Domain-Referenced Testing

Domain-referenced testing is a special case of criterion-referenced measurement (Baker, 1990). Of importance is that the term *domain* in domain-referenced testing does not correspond to the domains described by Bloom et al. (1956). In Bloom's well-known taxonomy of objectives, the domains refer to broad areas of competency (Baker, 1990, p. 365). Instead, domain refers to the specifically circumscribed universe or subarea of content to which performance is expected to generalize (p. 365). Thus, the basis for the test is the content the learner will address and the form of the student's response.

Domain-referenced testing is appropriate when the basis of ordering the domain is difficulty of the subject matter. An example is spelling. A key aspect, however, is the specification of the content rules or limits. Such rules specify the common characteristics of eligible examples for the test (Baker, 1974). For spelling, the types of words and difficulty level would be specified.

Another form of domain-referenced testing is the certification examinations developed in various professional fields. An example is a 4-hour credentialing examination for respiratory care practitioners. The examination consists of a set of 10 patient-management problems in which the examinee identifies and analyzes the problem and takes appropriate steps toward solution. Each problem is a sequential decision-making task in which the examinee may access any of several information sources in the identification and analysis. The nature of the problems and the expertise required are drawn from a content matrix that lists essential types of data, equipment, and therapeutic procedures required of respiratory care therapists. The range of possible choices presented at each decision point in the problem are weighted from plus 4 to minus 4 (optimal to harmful), and a score equal to or greater than the mastery score set for the test is required for credentialing (Cavanaugh & McGuire, 1988).

Scoring and Interpretation

Norm-referenced tests yield scores that indicate an examinee's standing relative to an identified reference group. The score earned by any particular student is dependent on the performance of the selected comparison group. In contrast, the reference for the interpretation of a student's performance on a criterion-referenced test is the behavior domain from which the test was drawn. In other words, the meaningfulness of examinee performance is not dependent on the performance of others.

The scoring of criterion-referenced tests may be either (1) mastery or nonmastery or (2) the level of proficiency attained in reference to a continuum of performance. Scoring for mastery requires the prior identification of a standard of proficiency representing competent performance. Documentation of mastery requires performance that is equal to or exceeds the standard established for the skill (Hambleton, 1990). For example, in situations in which the student is making predictions from sets of data, mastery involves the proportion of the student's logical predictions in relation to the established proficiency standard. For a procedure, such as using the microscope, mastery consists of the completion of the essential steps and the avoidance of any actions that damage the slide or the microscope.

For domains ordered from novice to expert performance, examinees may be evaluated on a continuum such as naive, novice, intermediate, and expert. Situations in which computer programming students are asked to debug flawed programs are examples; the computer routines range from simple to complex.

Sometimes a standard for a course or program may be expressed in a statement such as, 80% of the students will master 80% of the curriculum concepts. The problem with this approach is that it obscures the different levels and patterns of performance in the classroom (Tyler, 1990). Instead, for a class in writing composition, for example, the report should indicate that 15% are in the top level in clarity, 50% at the middle level, and 25% at the low level. The same information can be reported for other writing criteria.

Technical Specifications

Of primary importance is the clear specification of the behaviors (objectives-referenced tests) or content (domain-referenced tests) that define each competency to be measured (Hambleton, 1990, p. 116). The mechanisms by which competencies are defined, however, may vary. District leaders, for example, may identify a small set of broad competencies (e.g., reading comprehension) for high school graduation tests. An objectives-based program, in contrast, may rely on a two-dimensional matrix that matches content topics with types of skills. Objectives are written for the cells and then reviewed and revised (p. 116).

In addition to a concise statement of the content or behaviors, test specifications also should include (1) a statement of test purpose, (2) an example of test directions and a model test item, and (3) a detailed description of the structure and content of the item pool. This information guides item writers in test preparation and reviewers who initially evaluate test items for congruence with the objectives or domain (Hambleton, 1990).

After preliminary review of the draft test items by curriculum and measurement specialists, the items should be pilot tested with appropriate groups of examinees. Items that may need revision are (1) those that are easier or harder than other items measuring the same skill and (2) items with negative discriminating power (students passing the draft test miss the particular item).

For mastery tests, a standard typically is established for the test after the initial pilot testing and item revision. Berk (1990) notes that more than 20 different standard-setting procedures are suggested in the literature. All of the methods, however, involve human judgment. Some of the approaches, referred to as state models, assume that mastery is an all-or-nothing state or 100% performance. Deviations from this performance are assumed to be the result of classification errors.

Many of the state models use judgmental-empirical methods to adjust the cut-off score downward to minimize classification errors (Berk, 1990, p. 493). That is, the items are administered to groups of examinees identified as masters and non-masters. Few, if any, of the items should be completed correctly by the non-masters, and a high number of the masters should answer each item correctly (Hills, 1981). Such evidence is essential in justifying the cut-off score and also is used as evidence of the construct validity of the test. Also important in establishing construct validity is that results should be comparable to the results from other tests developed from the objective (Moy, 1990).

Other approaches to the concept of mastery are referred to as continuum models (Berk, 1990). Skills that are ordered on a continuum require definitions of the different proficiency levels and the development of tasks or scoring rubrics that represent the increasing levels of expertness. First, panels of experts develop the tasks and scoring mechanisms. Then, the tasks are administered to samples of students already identified by other means as representing the different levels of expertise. Their performance on the tasks is documented, and test revisions are made based on their performance. The revised test is then administered to a subsequent sample representing a range of expertise. If problems persist in the items or tasks, the process is repeated.

Several methods of addressing the reliability of criterion-referenced test items have been proposed (Berk, 1990). However, most of these methods are derivations of methods used with norm-referenced tests and are dependent on deviations of student scores. Criterion-referenced tests, however, are developed to provide information about well-defined domains or competencies and are not designed to produce variability in student performance. Reliability of criterion-referenced items, therefore, may be determined by the consistency of classification of examinees across parallel forms of the test.

Decisions

A basic use of criterion referencing is to generalize an examinee's status from the items on the test to the larger behavior domain from which the items were sampled (Nitko, 1984). That is, a properly developed criterion-referenced test can indicate the level of proficiency of the student with respect to identified objectives or tasks.

In addition to describing examinee performance, two other uses are (1) to assign individuals to mastery or nonmastery states and (2) to describe the performance of particular groups in program evaluation studies (Hambleton, 1990, p. 113). Assignment to mastery or nonmastery states may be a component of specific courses, or it may be the decision that is made in credentialing examinations or minimum competency examinations.

In program evaluation, the performance of the students is typically described in two ways. The first is in reference to the achievement goals set for the program. Also of importance in measuring course or program achievement is that outcomes are multidimensional (Cronbach, 1963). Therefore, summarizing student performance as a single score is misleading. As stated earlier, the percentage of students that attained a particular level of performance or met a particular standard is appropriate.

Second, the evaluation also may report student achievement in related areas. That is, the evaluation should include measures of other types of proficiency that may be reasonably expected in the program (Cronbach, 1963). For example, a new mathematics course in trigonometry may not emphasize computational skills. However, determining student proficiency in computing in their efforts to solve problems about right triangles is reasonable. If the results indicate that students completing the new course are fairly proficient in computation despite the lack of direct teaching, this finding is important. Otherwise, the evidence indicates that something is being sacrificed in the new course (Cronbach, 1963, p. 480).

Summary

Criterion-referenced assessment developed in response to curriculum needs. Efforts to develop instruction to facilitate mastery of cognitive skills required assessments that would indicate the skills and competencies learned by the students. The foundation for criterion-referencing is a continuum of knowledge in a well-defined domain. Four typical mechanisms for ordering a knowledge domain are:

1. Extent of aesthetic quality
2. Difficulty of the subject matter
3. Novice to expert skills
4. Defined prerequisite capabilities

A criterion-referenced test is constructed to be interpretable in terms of the continuum established for that domain. Of importance is that the criterion is the competencies or skills to be demonstrated, not the cut-off score or standard of performance.

The three broad types of criterion-referenced tests are objectives-referenced, domain-referenced, and minimum competency tests. Objectives-referenced tests consist of the perspective of the Tyler model (broadly stated learnings) and the cognitive levels of learning perspective. Domains of learning, in contrast, are identified subareas of content; and minimum competency tests address basic skills. In addition to a clear specification of the competencies to be tested, test purpose, test directions, item pool, and both expert review and pilot testing are essential in establishing construct validity. Reliability may be determined by the consistency of examinee performance on parallel forms of the test. Criterion-referenced tests may be used to assign students to mastery or nonmastery states and to describe student proficiency in program evaluation.

OTHER DATA SOURCES

Tests, whether norm referenced or criterion referenced, establish standardized questions or tasks for students. The examinees respond directly to the presented items, and their responses are recorded and scored according to the psychometric requirements of the test. Other data sources that do not require the presentation of specific stimulus situations also provide information about academic achievement. They are (1) systematic observations and judgments by others and (2) secondary indicators of student performance.

Systematic Observations and Judgments

Whenever possible, program evaluation should make use of multiple indicators of program outcomes (Cronbach and associates, 1980). In addition to test scores, sources of information about achievement consist of (1) evaluations of student products, (2) observations of students engaged in cognitive activities, and (3) teacher judgments about student competence. Evidence of problem-solving abilities in science, for example, may be obtained from laboratory notebooks of experiments, observations of students conducting experiments, and student projects, if available. Also, in composition or literature courses, student essays or written research reports are important sources of information.

Two methods of recording information about student accomplishments are (1) checklists and (2) rating scales. When used to evaluate cognitive activity, the checklist is designed to record the occurrence or nonoccurrence of important behaviors. For example, procedural tasks, such as using the microscope, are analyzed into the set of essential behaviors, and each statement is followed by "yes" and "no." The observer records the actions of the student as he or she completes the procedure by checking or circling "yes" or "no." A checklist to evaluate the use of a microscope, for example, consists of statements such as, "wipe cover glass properly," "adjust light and concave mirror," "use coarse adjustment properly," and so on.

Rating scales, in contrast, list statements or categories, each of which is evaluated on a continuum, such as from 1 to 5. Rating scales often are used to evaluate attitudes and social characteristics of individuals (discussed in Chapter 9). Scoring rubrics are also used with performance assessments of students that reflect stages of proficiency and complexity in student products (discussed in Chapter 7).

Teacher judgment about students' levels of achievement may also be useful. An example is the Boulder Valley retention study in which first-grade teachers rated the children in their classes on reading and mathematics achievement (in addition to pupil adjustment characteristics). For reading and for mathematics, the teacher made two judgments about each child. One was an *absolute* rating in comparison to grade level standards. The teacher rated each child on a 4-point scale from "recommend to repeat first grade because of performance" to "above grade level." The other was a *normative* comparison in relation to the other children in the class. The 4-point scale ranged from "bottom group (lowest five children in this class)" to "top group (top children in this class)" (Shepard & Smith, 1985).

The teacher ratings contribute key information in the study, given the published research on retention. Specifically, when negative empirical evidence for retention has been reported, advocates of the practice typically have stated that the research did not address achievement and adjustment differences between retained and nonretained children that the teachers observe (Gredler, 1992). Thus, the ratings by first-grade teachers of the retained and nonretained children in their classrooms were important in this study.

Secondary Indicators

Supporting information for program effects on achievement also can be obtained from sources referred to as secondary indicators. Examples are number of retentions and number of students assigned to special programs. They are referred to as secondary indicators because they are logical by-products of achievement. They are logical indirect effects. If a program for disadvantaged children is effective, the number of students that are retained should decrease.

Secondary indicators should be interpreted with caution, however. One reason is that they are corruptible indicators (Cooley & Bickel, 1986, p. 6). That is, the indicator can be affected without accompanying changes in the underlying phenomenon that the indicator represents. Retention, for example, may be influenced by factors other than a new program. These factors are changes in school policy, perceived pressures to change typical practices, and so on. Therefore, school climate, staff perceptions, and other factors that may influence secondary indicators, should be documented in a program evaluation. Secondary indicators also can be contaminated; that is, they are the result of causes other than the new program or policy. This phenomenon is discussed in Chapter 9.

SUMMARY

Three events contributed to the emergence of educational and psychological measurement. They are Galton's research on individual differences and the normal curve, the beginning of experimental psychology, and the development of the Binet test of intelligence. By the 1960s, norm-referenced achievement and aptitude batteries had become a staple in educational and personnel decisions. A major role of testing was to provide information for the selection of the few students who would advance to the next level of education.

Criticisms of norm-referenced tests in the 1960s and the development of new curricula that emphasized mastery of identified skills led to the development of different kinds of tests. Referred to as criterion-referenced or mastery tests, these assessments answered the question, What can the student now do?

Concerns about the skills of high school graduates in the 1960s and 1970s led to legislative requirements for competency testing. This development was followed by pressure for accountability in education. The result was increased testing with state reports providing information on districts and, in some cases, schools.

In program evaluation assessment has moved from a reliance on norm-referenced tests in the 1960s to other indices of cognitive achievement. In addition, evaluation assesses the goals, inputs, implementation, and delivery of services.

The development of norm-referenced tests is based on trait theory, which states that individuals differ on identified characteristics or traits; and these traits are normally distributed in the population. Psychological measurement of intelligence was soon followed by the development of broad-range achievement and aptitude tests.

The two defining characteristics of norm-referenced tests are (1) the capability to spread out the examinees and (2) the availability of performance norms for the comparison of individual performance. The quantitative score reported for examinees may be a percentile, grade equivalent, or standard score. One shortcoming of grade equivalents, however, is that they may be misinterpreted. Unlike the other scores, standard scores are reported in standard deviation units about the mean.

Development of a broad-range achievement test begins with a blueprint that identifies concepts drawn from the major textbooks in the area. Items are selected for the test for their power to discriminate between examinees with higher and lower total scores on the test. Validity is often documented by correlational methods and also should include information about the consequences of test use for suggested decisions. Reliability of the test is documented by correlational methods.

Norm-referenced tests are appropriate for comparing a student's performance in different subject areas, informing a teacher of a new student's relative performance in an area, and providing information related to other decisions.

Problems associated with the use of norm-referenced tests for accountability purposes are the lack of fit with a particular curriculum, the limited forms of learning that are assessed, and the failure to relate output (scores) to resources and other inputs. Some educators indicate that the use of norm-referenced tests for high-stakes decisions has led to negative effects on schools and students. They focus on drill-and-practice exercises in the classroom and the use of questionable practices to raise scores.

In program evaluation, scores can be used to subdivide a sample on prior achievement and to provide information about growth. They also can provide information to school districts about potential problems. However, efforts to bring all students up to the norm are self-defeating. First, the tests are designed so that 50% of the examinees will be above and 50% will be below the mean. Second, after substantial improvement, when the tests are renormed, the average performance on the test will be higher. Then, groups will be striving to reach a higher benchmark.

Criterion-referenced tests, in contrast, were developed to provide information about the mastery or nonmastery of identified skills. Some writers interpret the word *criterion* to mean "standard of performance." However, criterion refers to the behavior or tasks that are the basis for the test. The basis for criterion-referencing is a continuum of knowledge in a well-defined domain. The domain may be ordered on the basis of the difficulty of the subject or on quality of performance from novice to expert.

In developing a test for the classroom or evaluation of a program, the knowledge continuum may or may not be fully developed in advance. However, the type of domain and a general sense of the placement of the skills to be measured is important. The two mechanisms for designing a test are objectives referencing and domain referencing. End-of-course objectives serve as the test basis in objectives referencing. Identifying a subarea of content is the basis for domain-referenced tests. The scoring of criterion-referenced tests may be either mastery or nonmastery or the level of proficiency attained in reference to a continuum of performance.

Development of mastery tests begins with clear specifications of competencies, test purpose, and the item pool. Expert review of draft items and pilot testing are essential in establishing construct validity of the test. Skills ordered on a continuum require definitions of the proficiency levels, reviews by panels of experts, and administration to students already identified as representing the different levels of expertise. Consistency of the classification of examinees across parallel forms of the test may be taken as evidence of reliability.

Uses of criterion-referenced tests are (1) to describe examinee skills, (2) to assign individuals to mastery or nonmastery states, and (3) to describe the performance of particular groups in program evaluation studies. In program evaluation, student performance may be described in reference to program goals and student achievement in related areas of competency. Typically, student performance is reported in terms of the percentages of students that achieved certain objectives or attained identified levels of performance.

Other data sources that can provide evidence of cognitive achievement are (1) systematic observations and judgments by others and (2) secondary indicators. Evidence of problem solving in science, for example, may be obtained from laboratory notebooks of experiments, observations of students, and student projects. Checklists and rating scales may be used for observations, and rating scales may be used for teacher judgments about performance. Examples of secondary indicators are number of retentions, number of promotions, and number of students assigned to special programs. A disadvantage of these indicators is that they are corruptible. The indicator can be affected without accompanying changes in the underlying phenomenon. When used with other sources of information, they can corroborate program effects.

CHAPTER QUESTIONS

1. What is the contribution of Galton's research to the development of norm-referenced tests?

2. What are the two defining features of norm-referenced assessments?

3. On what basis are items retained on a norm-referenced test?

4. For what types of decisions are norm-referenced tests appropriate?

5. What is the foundation for developing criterion-referenced tests? How do they differ from norm-referenced tests?

6. How are criterion-referenced tests scored and interpreted? How are they used in program evaluation?

7. Name some other indicators of academic performance that may be useful in program evaluation.

REFERENCES

Baker, E. (1974). Beyond objectives: Domain-referenced tests for evaluation and instructional improvement. In W. Hively (Ed.), *Domain-referenced testing* (pp. 16–30). Englewood Cliffs, NJ: Educational Technology Publications.

Baker, E. (1990). Domain-referenced testing. In H. J. Walberg & G. D. Haertel (Eds.), *International encyclopedia of educational evaluation* (pp. 365–367). Oxford: Pergamon Press.

Baker, E., & Choppin, B. H. (1990). Minimum competency tests. In H. J. Walberg & G. D. Haertel (Eds.), *The international encyclopedia of educational evaluation* (pp. 499—502). Oxford: Pergamon Press.

Berk, R. (Ed.). (1980). *Criterion-referenced measurement: The state of the art.* Baltimore: The Johns Hopkins University Press.

Berk, E. (Ed.). (1984). *A guide to criterion-referenced test construction.* Baltimore: The Johns Hopkins University Press.

Berk, R. (1990). Criterion-referenced testing. In H. J. Walberg & G. D. Haertel (Eds.), *The international encyclopedia of educational evaluation* (pp. 490–495). Oxford: Pergamon Press.

Bloom, B., Engelhart, M., First, E., Hill, W., & Krathwohl, D. (1956). *Taxonomy of educational objectives: Handbook I: Cognitive domain.* New York: David McKay.

Bloom, B., Hastings, J., & Madaus, G. (1971). *Handbook on formative and summative evaluation of student learning.* New York: McGraw-Hill.

Cavanaugh, S., & McGuire, C. (1988, April). *Written simulations, professional education, and evaluation: Current practices, problems and future directions.* Minicourse session presented at the American Educational Research Association, New Orleans.

Chi, M., Glaser, R., & Farr, M. (Eds.). (1988). *The nature of expertise.* Hillsdale, NJ: Erlbaum.

Cooley, W., & Bickel, W. (1986). *Decision-oriented educational research.* Boston: Kluwer-Nijhoff.

Cronbach, L. J. (1963). Course improvement through evaluation. *Teachers College Record, 64,* 672–683.

Cronbach, L. J. (1970). *Essentials of psychological testing* (3rd ed.). New York: Harper & Row.

Cronbach, L. J., Ambron, S., Dornbusch, S., Hess, R., Hornik, R., Phillips, D., Walker, D., & Weiner, S. (1980). *Toward reform of program evaluation.* San Francisco: Jossey-Bass.

Darling-Hammond, L., & Wise, A. E. (1985). Beyond standardization: State standards and school improvement. *The Elementary School Journal, 85*(3), 315–336.

Glaser, R. (1963). Instructional technology and the measurement of learning outcomes. *American Psychologist, 18*, 519–521.

Gray, D. (1980). *Minimum competency testing: Guidelines for policy makers and citizens.* Washington, DC: Council for Basic Education.

Gredler, G. R. (1992). *School readiness: Assessment and educational issues.* Brandon, VT: Clinical Psychology Publishing Company.

Haertel, E. H. (1990). Achievement tests. In H. J. Walberg & G. D. Haertel (Eds.), *The international encyclopedia of educational evaluation* (pp. 485–489). Oxford: Pergamon Press.

Haladyna, T. M., Nolan, S. B., & Haas, N. S. (1991). Raising standardized achievement test scores and the origins of test score pollution. *Educational Researcher, 20*(5), 2–7.

Hambleton, R. K. (1990). Criterion-referenced assessment in evaluation. In H. J. Walberg & G. D. Haertel (Eds.), *The international encyclopedia of educational evaluation* (pp. 113–118). Oxford: Pergamon Press.

Hills, J. (1981). *Measurement and evaluation in the classroom* (2nd ed.). Columbus, OH: Merrill.

Lesgold, A., Robinson, H., Feltovich, P., Glaser, R., Klopfer, D., & Wang, Y. (1988). Expertise in a complex skill: Diagnosing X-ray pictures. In M. Chi, R. Glaser, & M. Farr (Eds.), *The nature of expertise* (pp. 311–342). Hillsdale, NJ: Erlbaum.

Madaus, G., Stufflebeam, D., & Scriven, M. (1983). *Evaluation models.* Boston: Kluwer-Nijhoff.

Mehrens, W. A., & Kaminski, J. (1989). Methods for improving standardized test scores: Fruitful, fruitless, or fraudulent? *Educational Measurement: Issues and Practices, 8*, 14–22.

Messick, S. (1984). Assessment in context: Appraising student performance in relation to instructional quality. *Educational Researcher, 13*(3), 3–8.

Messick, S. (1989). Validity. In R. L. Linn (Ed.), *Educational measurement* (3rd ed., pp. 13–103). New York: American Council on Education and Macmillan.

Moy, R. (1990). Standardized tests. In H. J. Walberg & G. D. Haertel (Eds.), *The international encyclopedia of educational evaluation* (pp. 495–498). Oxford: Pergamon Press.

New Orleans Public Schools (1993). *Norm-referenced test results of the New Orleans Public Schools: A report on their relationship to major student characteristics.* New Orleans Public Schools.

Nitko, A. (1984). Defining "criterion-referenced test." In R. Berk (Ed.), *A guide to criterion-referenced test construction.* Baltimore, MD: The Johns Hopkins University Press.

Scriven, M. (1994, April). Death of a paradigm: Replacing multiple choice with multiple ratings. Invited address, American Educational Research Association, New Orleans.

Shepard, L. (1991a). Will national tests improve student learning? *Phi Delta Kappan, 73*(2), 232–238.

Shepard, L. (1993). Evaluating test validity. In L. Darling-Hammond (Ed.), *Review of research in education* (Vol. 19, pp. 405–450). Washington, DC: American Educational Research Association.

Shepard, L., & Smith, M. (1985). *Boulder Valley kindergarten study: Retention practices and retention effects.* Boulder, CO: Boulder Valley Public Schools.

Smith, E. R., & Tyler, R. W. (1942). *Appraising and recording student progress.* New York: Harper Brothers.

Smith, M., & Rottenberg, C. (1991). Unintended consequences of external testing in elementary schools. *Educational Measurement: Issues and Practice, 10*(4), 7–11.

Taylor, C. (1994). Assessment for measurement or standards: The peril and promise of large-scale assessment reform. *Review of Educational Research, 31*(2), 231–262.

Thorndike, R., & Hagan, E. (1969). *Measurement and evaluation in psychology and education* (3rd ed.). New York: Wiley.

Tyler, R. (1950). *Principles of curriculum construction.* Chicago: University of Chicago Press.

Tyler, R. (1990). Reporting evaluations of learning outcomes. In H. J. Walberg & G. D. Haertel (Eds.), *The international encyclopedia of educational evaluation* (pp. 733–738). Oxford: Pergamon Press.

Vincent, D. (1990). Norm-referenced assessment. In. H. J. Walberg & G. D. Haertel (Eds.), *The international encyclopedia of educational evaluation* (pp. 111–113). Oxford: Pergamon Press.

CHAPTER 7

Alternative Methods of Assessment: Performance Assessment

A lternative assessment began as a mechanism for developing curricula that emphasize meaningful learning. It has recently captured the attention of policymakers concerned about the achievement of American students. Three components that are contributing to the interest in and development of alternative assessments are provisions in the Goals 2000: Educate America Act. One is the creation of a National Education Standards and Improvement Council (NESIC) "to develop model standards and certify state standards and assessments" (Linn, 1994, p. 2). The second component consists of three types of standards identified by the legislation: context, student performance, and opportunity-to-learn standards. Third, performance standards are described as concrete examples and descriptions of student knowledge and student proficiency outlined in the content standards (Congressional Record, March 21, 1994, H1626, in Linn, 1994). This legislation lends support to efforts already under way that involve a greater use of alternative assessments such as performance assessments and portfolios.

GENERAL CHARACTERISTICS OF ALTERNATIVE ASSESSMENT

Three critical attributes establish major goals for alternative assessments. First, they should measure complex intellectual capabilities. That is, they should not be surrogates or proxies for important capabilities.

Second, they should focus on important and teachable learning processes (Baker, Freeman, & Clayton, 1991, p. 135). Examples are (1) developing a persuasive argument and (2) conducting experiments in which two variables interact to influence an outcome. Third, alternative assessments should inform teaching practice about students' strengths and weaknesses in relation to complex cognitive skills. The cues provided by an assessment should indicate weaknesses (such as an inadequate knowledge base, misconceptions, or poor learning strategies) that can be addressed through instruction.

Some proponents indicate that, in such a system, "teaching to the test" becomes a positive (not a negative) effect of assessment because the skills being taught are those that are assessed. However, one cannot assume that more "authentic" assessment automatically will lead to classroom activities supportive of learning (Linn, Baker, & Dunbar, 1991). For example, an assessment that requires students to write an essay might lead to classroom time devoted to producing highly rated essays in a 20-minute time limit (p. 17).

The search for alternative assessments has led to the use of open-ended problems, essays, hands-on science tasks, computer simulations of unstructured real-world problems, and portfolios of student work (Linn et al., 1991, p. 15). Although already in use in several settings, many of these assessments have yet to be evaluated on the critical attributes.

EXPECTATIONS FOR ALTERNATIVE ASSESSMENT

Proponents of performance testing hold high expectations for education through the use of these assessments (Linn, 1994). One is that testing will become productive, rather than reductive or punitive assessment (Wolf, LeMahieu, & Eresh, 1992, p. 9). The hope is that by focusing classroom effort toward "genuine" intellectual challenges (instead of the rote learning of information) alternative assessments can guide reform (Wiggins, 1989; Wolf et al., 1992).

Another expectation is that the tasks will be meaningful to students because they indicate the actual challenges typically faced by writers, business people, scientists, community leaders, or designers (Wiggins, 1989). Among such tasks are writing essays and reports, designing proposals, and conducting individual and group research (p. 704).

However, Messick (1994) cautions that a richly contextualized assessment task is not necessarily uniformly good for all students. Contextual features that motivate some students (thereby facilitating task performance) may alienate and confuse others, thus distorting their performance (p. 19). For example, certain types of content or subject matter in reading passages lead to different performance consequences as a function of gender and ethnicity. Also, some data from the National Assessment of Educational Progress (NAEP) analyses indicate that students differ by ethnicity in their rates of attempting more open-ended items (Baker, O'Neill, & Linn, 1993, p. 1214). Therefore, development of alternative assessments must be accompanied by research data on the motivational aspects of these assessments and the effects of different contexts and content references.

Finally, alternative assessments are expected to influence the professional development of teachers. In some schools, districts, and states, groups of teachers meet together to score the assessments. This activity can increase teacher understanding of the capabilities involved in complex performance as well as ways to modify classroom instruction (Mitchell, 1992).

Current approaches to alternative assessment are typically grouped into two major categories: performance assessment and portfolios. A performance assessment measures cognitive abilities at a specified administration. Portfolios, in contrast, are collections of a student's work (often accompanied by student reflections and teacher comments) over an extended period of time, such as a semester or a year.

OVERVIEW

Historically, the term *performance test* referred to nonverbal psychological tests, such as the Block Design subtest of the WISC-R. In the 1960s, performance assessment also referred to "the process of gathering data by systematic observation for making decisions about an individual" (Berk, 1986, p. ix). Typical examples are work sample tests in which an employee's performance is observed and scored while he or she demonstrates tasks essential to the job (Siegal, 1986). Currently, performance assessment is defined as "a type of testing that calls for demonstration of understanding and skill in applied, procedural, or open-ended settings" (Baker et al., 1993, p. 1211).

Basic Characteristics of Performance Assessment

A performance assessment is, first, one that requires examinees to demonstrate their capabilities by creating some product or engaging in some activity (Haertel, 1992). An example is conducting an experiment on the absorbency of different paper towels. Second, and equally important, the behavior or product is valued in its own right outside of the test setting (Haertel, 1992). Examples are measuring and comparing the weight of different substances and writing a letter in a foreign language to a pen pal in that country.

The choice of whether to evaluate a performance or a product depends in large measure on the nature of the domain (Messick, 1994). In the performing arts, such as acting and dancing, the performance and the product are essentially the same. Thus, the task is basically that of evaluating the performance. In other domains, such as creative writing, in which several modes of accomplishing a task are acceptable, evaluating the product is the focus. Some domains, however, in which both the outcomes and procedures are important, require evaluation of both product and performance. Examples are auto mechanics and chemical experimentation (Messick, 1994, p. 14).

A term sometimes applied to performance assessments is that they are direct measures of cognitive capabilities. However, all measurements of skill and knowledge are indirect because they are mediated by judgment (Messick, 1994). Thus, the term *direct assessment* should not be used because it promises too much (p. 21).

Relationship Between Authentic and Performance Assessment

Some performance tasks are important because they are key intellectual performances in the particular subject area or are essential prerequisites to discipline-related capabilities. Examples are asking students to measure and weigh materials or to design and conduct an experiment to determine the absorbency of paper towels. Such tasks are referred to as "academic" by Champagne and Newell (1992).

In contrast, authentic assessments consist of real-world tasks or problems. Observing and rating a teacher's conduct of lessons in the classroom is both a performance and an authentic assessment of the teacher's subject matter knowledge. In contrast, asking the teacher to critique the knowledge base of a particular textbook is a performance assessment. It is not authentic for the typical classroom teacher because critiquing texts is not part of his or her customary duties.

Also important, according to Meyer (1992), is that both the task *and* the conditions of assessment must represent real-world situations. For example, a 4-day writing exercise (guided by teachers with a carefully scripted manual) that proceeds from topic introduction to editing and final copying is a performance assessment. The task is not authentic because of the prescribed testing conditions. In contrast, papers developed during the semester with as much or as little time allocated to each stage by the student is an authentic assessment. The key dimensions, context and student behavior, also are known as stimulus fidelity and response fidelity (Fitzpatrick & Morrison, 1971). An authentic assessment is one that is high in both characteristics.

EXAMPLES

Performance assessments in school subjects have been implemented in a variety of settings. Among them are NAEP; specific projects in particular subject areas; and school, district, and statewide assessments in history, mathematics, science, and writing. At present, however, wide differences exist in both the design and purpose of performance assessments (Linn, 1994).

History

One project in eleventh-grade history was undertaken to develop an essay assessment that measured students' deep understanding and to develop and validate content-quality scoring criteria (Baker et al., 1991, p. 137). Primary source material served as the reading material for the task because available texts treated possible topics superficially. The selected material, the Lincoln Douglas debates on popular sovereignty and slavery, met four important criteria:

1. Significance in the history curriculum
2. Amenability to multiple interpretations
3. Potential relationships to other events
4. Brevity (Baker et al., 1991, p. 39)

The first day of the assessment consisted of a brief knowledge test on relevant concepts, followed by reading the debates, and a brief multiple-choice test on the material. The purpose of the test was (1) to assist students in accessing relevant knowledge and (2) to indicate students' knowledge deficiencies related to essay development. On the second day, the students wrote an essay to an English cousin explaining two problems facing the United States at that time.

Initial efforts to establish a scoring rubric by relying on experts' statements about grading priorities were unsuccessful. Interrater agreement on scores was quite low. The researchers then constructed a scoring rubric derived from recordings of experts' "think-aloud" strategies as they developed answers to essay questions. (This method is recommended by Cronbach [1990].) The revised rubric consisted of overall content quality, prior knowledge, principles/themes, text detail, and misconceptions. Argumentation was added at the request of raters to acknowledge presentation quality (Baker, 1994).

Interrater reliabilities for project staff in a tryout with 250 eleventh graders were .85 to .98. (Scores ranged from 3 [fully elaborated] to 1 [incorrect or incoherent response].) Intercorrelations among the subscales (-.20 to .60) supported the premise that the rubric addressed different aspects of students' content quality (Baker et al., 1991). Factor analysis across the samples of students and raters indicated that prior knowledge, principles, and overall content quality formed one factor; and text detail and misconceptions formed the other (Baker, 1994, p. 103). Also, Advanced Program students scored twice as high as the slower students on overall essay scores and more than three times higher on the use of principles. In addition, the successful training of four history teachers to use the rubric (interrater reliabilities of .80 to .90 except for misconceptions [0.68]) indicates the potential for classroom use.

Writing

Contrary to popular belief, no consensus exists for the characteristics of student essays that represent increasing levels of skill development (Quellmalz, 1984a). Moreover, a determination of competent writing first requires a differentiation of realistic standards for minimum competence from the more rigorous high school standards and from criteria applied in critiques of professional writing and literature (p. 64).

Large-scale assessments currently track writing development at two levels (Quellmalz, 1984a). One is a minimum level measured by competency tests that examine a few skills within a restricted range (Quellmalz, 1984b). A more advanced level is used in status testing that reflects the broad range of writing skill emphasized in secondary education. An example is the Illinois writing assessment, which tests students' abilities to develop convincing points of view or ideas. Students respond to a single prompt with a time limit of 25 minutes. An analytic scoring guide is used (the Rating Guide for Functional Writing), which measures focus, support, organization, mechanics, and overall effectiveness (Chapman, Fyans, & Kerins, 1984).

The California Learning Assessment Scale (CLAS) (used in 1994) and writing assessment programs in Milwaukee, Wisconsin, and Arizona also require students to develop some form of essay. Milwaukee ninth graders are given 90 minutes to write a business letter (such as a job application or consumer complaint) and an essay on a topic such as problems with their friends, neighborhood, or school (Archbald & Newmann, 1992).

The CLAS and the Arizona Student Assessment Program (ASAP) link writing assessment to a particular reading. In the ASAP, students first read and respond to a particular piece of literature or narrative writing (such as a personal narrative about Helen Keller) and then write an essay on an issue or topic related to the reading (Mitchell, 1992). The CLAS provided a class period in which students in small collaborative groups discussed a work using a series of questions. The next day they received either the same document or a series of related tasks and wrote a critical essay or expressive response (DeVise, 1994).

Various scoring rubrics and methods are used in these assessments. California used a modified primary trait system in which points are assigned according to the presence of essential traits for the particular writing type. For example, one scoring rubric has a set of paragraphs; each paragraph describes a level of achievement (from 1 to 6). Minimal achievement (1 on the scale) for an evaluation essay consists of a description of the subject, but no judgment, or a general personal evaluation that lacks supporting evidence. In contrast, adequate achievement (level 4) consists of an adequately argued evaluation in which the student identifies, describes, and judges the subject. The writer also provides at least one moderately developed reason in support of the argument; but the piece lacks the authority and polish of commendable (level 5) or exceptional (level 6) achievement (Mitchell, 1992, p. 35).

In contrast, the Milwaukee public schools use an analytic scoring guide. The analytic approach uses sets of characteristics that can be applied across writing types. The performance levels for scoring ninth-grade English essays range from 0 (no response, illegible, or an off-the-point paper) to competent or clear mastery (level 4). A highly flawed paper (level 1) lacks a clear main idea, rambles, lacks content, uses inappropriate language for the task, and does not demonstrate sentence or paragraph development. Capitalization, punctuation, and spelling errors also are prevalent.

The two approaches to scoring rely on the publisher who developed the test and on using classroom teachers in a configuration described as group grading (Mitchell, 1992). The teachers assemble in teams and agree on standards. A group of sample papers representing a range of performance and graded by experienced raters serve as "benchmark papers" for grading practice sessions (Archbald & Newmann, 1992). In the actual scoring, all papers are scored by two readers; and, in cases of disagreement, a third reader is used.

Mathematics and Science

A major impetus for alternative assessments is the emphasis on multiple assessment methods, advocated by the National Council of Teachers of Mathematics (NCTM) (1989). In addition to written, oral, and demonstration formats, assessment should be an integral part of teaching and should focus on a broad range of tasks. For example, one exercise used in a statewide assessment involves both group and individual activity in a 2-week research project. In addition to the group activity, each student reports his or her contributions orally to the class, submits a log of activities and ideas to the teacher, and then solves "a near-transfer task which applied the same skills and procedures in a different context" (p. 156).

Individual performance assessments often require the student to demonstrate an understanding of some algorithm *and* explain his or her understanding of the situation. Sample questions from the 1994 CLAS test are examples (see Figure 7.1). A similar approach from the 1991 International Assessment of Educational Progress (IAEP) asks students to make a 15 gram lump of clay from a larger mass, using a two-pan balance and two weights (20 grams and 50 grams). Students also must explain the procedure they used (Stemple, 1992). Other tasks in the IAEP, in contrast, are fairly straightforward measurement situations, such as measuring the perimeter of a rectangle to the nearest millimeter and measuring three angles using a 180 degree protractor.

At present, there is no consensus on the goals of school science (Champagne & Newell, 1992); and performance tasks vary considerably in their focus, complexity, and breadth. In one example, the student assumes he or she is stranded on a mountainside in cold, dry, windy weather. The task is to determine which of two fabrics would keep him or her warmer (Archbald & Newmann, 1992, p. 157). The assessor also is permitted to give the student suggestions, for example, to use a container filled with warm water so as to test the warmth protection of each jacket fabric. Students are scored from 1 to 3 in each of seven areas, including approach, control, temperature measurements, and data recording.

Many of the science tasks require the student to manipulate materials and to conduct either simple or complex experiments. Examples are (1) to set up a filtering apparatus shown in a drawing and to filter muddy water and (2) to use a magnet to identify magnetic and nonmagnetic items (and to explain their differences) (Stemple, 1992).

Summary

Interest in alternative assessments has emerged from efforts to restructure curricula for student construction of meaning. Three critical attributes of alternative assessments are (1) that they should measure complex intellectual abilities, (2) that they should focus on important and teachable learning processes, and (3) that the cues provided by the assessments should indicate weaknesses that can be remedied through instruction. Three expectations voiced for authentic assessments are (1) that they should guide reform by focusing classroom effort toward more intellectual tasks, (2) that they should be more meaningful to students because they indicate real-world challenges, and (3) that they should influence the professional development of teachers.

Figure 7.1
Examples from the 1994 CLAS test

"Predicting the difference"
A game involves two cubes with sides numbered 1 through 6. After throwing the two cubes, the smaller number is subtracted from the larger number to find the difference. If a player throws the cubes many times, what difference will occur most often? Provide a diagram and written explanation that you could use to explain to a friend.

Mathematics grade 8

"Double the dotted line segment"
Part 1
For each of the figures shown, draw a new enlarged figure that has the same shape. The dotted line segment in each new figure should be double the length of the dotted line segment in the original figure.

Part 2
Describe mathematically how the pairs of old and new figures are the same and how they are different.

Mathematics grade 4

"The vending machine"
Maria wants to buy a 75-cent snack from a vending machine. The machine takes only nickels, dimes and quarters. Maria has 7 nickels, 5 dimes and 2 quarters.
Part 1
Show all of the different ways she could pay for the snack. You may use words, diagrams or charts.
Part 2
Which of your ways uses the fewest number of coins? Explain why this is true.

From "How Three Different Grade Groups Took the 4-Section CLAS Exam" by D. DeVise, March 10, 1994, *Press-Telegram,* Los Angeles, CA.

One major type of alternative assessment is performance assessment. Earlier, performance assessment has referred to nonverbal tasks and tests such as work samples. Currently, it refers to any assessment in which examinees demonstrate their capabilities by creating a product or engaging in some activity. In addition, the behavior or product has value outside of the test setting. The choice of whether to evaluate a performance or product depends, in large measure, on the nature of the domain. In the performing arts, product and performance are the same. In writing, however, the focus is typically the product.

Of importance in understanding performance assessments is that they should not be referred to as direct assessments. All assessments of cognitive abilities are indirect because they involve judgment. Also, performance assessments may or may not be described as authentic. Performance assessments are authentic if they are real-world problems or tasks and are assessed under real-world conditions.

Among the areas in which performance assessments have been developed are history, writing, science, and mathematics. An eleventh-grade history project developed a 2-day assessment in which students read primary source historical material and wrote an essay that required interpretation. Student knowledge of concepts relevant to development of the essay also was tested.

Large-scale assessments in writing vary in focus. Some are minimum competency examinations and others test students' abilities to express ideas. Scoring methods and rubrics also vary. A primary trait system is one in which points are assigned for the presence of characteristics of the particular task. In contrast, analytic scoring guides consist of generic qualities applicable to a variety of tasks.

Both mathematics and science implement a variety of performance assessments. The tasks range from specific measurement situations to tasks that require the student to demonstrate an understanding of an algorithm and to explain it. Many of the science tasks require the student to manipulate materials and to conduct either simple or complex experiments. In summary, across the various subject areas, tasks vary in terms of scope, complexity, and type of required response.

ISSUES IN DESIGNING AND USING PERFORMANCE ASSESSMENTS

Evaluators may be called upon to assist schools, districts, and states as they explore the development of alternative assessments. Key issues in development are validity, reliability, and fairness. An important issue for implementation is resource needs.

Validity

The open-ended nature and the complexity of many performance assessments leads to particular problems in obtaining validity evidence that are not found in the development of multiple-choice tests. They are the task complexity/ability inference problem, the confounding of abilities problem, the focus of the scoring rubric, and the domain representation issue.

The Task Complexity/Ability Inference Problem.   A key validity question is, What psychological or social processes is the assessment intended to reflect? (Wiley, 1991). When measures are derived from actual performance, the erroneous assumption often made is that they are more valid than multiple-choice tests (Linn et al., 1991). However, responses to the surface features of performance assessments do not guarantee that complex thinking processes are involved (Baker et al., 1993; Linn et al., 1991). A complex-appearing task may hinge on the recall of a particular content item, or it may depend on a flash of insight unrelated to a teachable process.

Further, hands-on tasks may not necessarily encourage the use of sophisticated mental models (Kulm, 1990, p. 19). For example, the goal of one science task was for children (1) to observe the characteristics (size, color, and shape) of several lima beans, kidney beans, pinto beans, peas, and corn and (2) to classify them into two logical groups based on their observations. However, one child, using a different framework, responded "good for chili" and "good for soup" (Mitchell, 1992).

Proponents of performance assessment have yet to offer explicit frameworks for generating measures or to document the cognitive processes used by students (Baker et al., 1993). At present, development often is task driven rather than construct or process driven. However, proposed tasks should undergo both expert review and tryout to identify the actual processes applied by students in working through the situations.

The Confounding of Abilities Problem.   One problem in developing performance assessments is the difficulty of disentangling component skills from complex functioning by judgment alone (Messick, 1994, p. 20). Examples are tasks that require linguistic competence or communication in addition to the basic processes required to solve the problem. The linguistic requirements of many performance-based assessments, even in areas such as mathematics, frequently are substantial (Linn, 1994, p. 22) (see Figure 7.1).

The breadth and scope of subject matter knowledge also is a component in tasks that focus on interpretation and writing and tasks that require complex problem solving. Research indicates, for example, that knowledge of a topic contributes to variable writing performance (Breland, Camp, Jones, Morris, & Rock, 1987; Quellmalz, 1984b). Cognitive research indicates that successful problem-solving performance depends on (1) the availability of relevant domain knowledge and (2) the student's capability of accessing that knowledge. These factors are critical differences between expert and novice problem solvers (see, for example, Chi, Glaser, & Farr, 1988; Tuma & Reif, 1980). Therefore, problem-solving performance tasks should provide a mechanism for identifying each of the component(s) that may be responsible for poor performance.

Also important in the development of problem-solving tasks is to document the strategies of both successful and unsuccessful students (Baker et al., 1993). An example is a computer simulation in which students were asked to predict which combination of five variables affected the oxygen and waste concentration of water in a water treatment system (Lavoie & Good, 1988). Poor problem-solving performance was related to any of three factors: the level of initial knowledge, the level of academic achievement, and the level of Piagetian reasoning. In addition, the researchers identified 21 problem approach activities that differed between successful and unsuccessful problem solvers. In the absence of pilot testing problem-solving tasks, the number and variety of student strategies and responses may go undetected.

Focus of the Scoring Rubric.   Another potential problem in designing performance assessments is that the scoring rubric may not capture the fully functioning complex skill (Messick, 1984). The different criteria in scoring rubrics typically reflect aspects of performance quality (such as clarity of expression) rather than different components of a complex skill (p. 20). Thus, a key question is, "By what evidence can we be assured that the scoring criteria and the rubrics used in holistic, primary trait, or analytic scoring of products or performances capture the fully functioning complex skill?" (Messick, 1994, p. 20).

Domain Representation.   In the development of standardized multiple-choice tests, the domain is often synonymous with a subject area or content discipline, such as history, social studies, mathematics, and science, and so on. A two-way matrix that matches major topics with levels of skill (e.g., recall, applications, and inference) is used to document domain coverage.

Some states exploring performance assessment and the committees involved in NAEP have developed frameworks for different subject areas. Scientific literacy for the 1990 NAEP assessment, for example, is conceptualized as a two-way matrix in which three fields of science (earth, physical, and life science) are crossed with the three general skill areas of conceptual understanding, scientific investigation, and practical reasoning. However, these curriculum frameworks are broad in scope and require further interpretation by teachers and test developers.

In the absence of domain specifications for areas of study, Baker et al. (1993) suggest a strategy that permits the review of task comparability. Assessment development should be guided by a specification of task format, content quality, cognitive demands, and scoring criteria. In this way, the comparability of different performance assessments can be determined.

This approach also can be useful in the domain of writing, which is defined in different ways, depending on the purpose of the assessment. One perspective is based on literary theories of discourse. Tests developed from this perspective require lengthy compositions that reflect quality of ideas, originality, organization, and style (Quellmalz, 1986, p. 49). The pragmatic view, in contrast, focuses on functional writing tasks, such as writing a letter of application. Tests tend to emphasize paragraph length responses that meet functional criteria, such as clarity, cohesiveness, and correctness (p. 494). A third approach considers writing as a process of creating meaning. The focus for this perspective is the student's prewriting activities, drafting, and revising. Criteria emphasize effectiveness, sensitivity to audience, and authenticity of voice.

Summary.   Performance assessments are open-ended tasks that require constructed and often lengthy responses that address several parameters. Among the issues to be addressed in obtaining evidence of validity are the task complexity/ability inference problem, the confounding of abilities problem, the focus of the scoring rubric, and the issue of domain representation. First, tasks that appear complex on the surface do not necessarily require complex thinking processes or the use of mental models. Assessment should undergo both expert review and tryout to identify the actual processes used by students.

Some tasks, in contrast, may require more than one ability, such as linguistic competence and mathematical ability. Problem-solving tasks require relevant domain knowledge and skill in accessing that knowledge in addition to problem-solving strategies. Assessment should be designed to provide information about component abilities as well. In addition, the scoring rubric should be reviewed and tested to determine the extent to which it captures the complex skill.

Because the development of performance assessments often is task driven, questions of relationship to a larger domain of expertise are yet to be answered. Some development efforts have designed broad curriculum frameworks for different subject areas, but they are not detailed specifications. In the absence of domain specifications, assessment development should be guided by a specification of task format, content quality, cognitive demands, and scoring criteria.

Reliability

The key question with respect to reliability is, To what extent is the student's score a reflection of his or her true ability (and not the result of measurement error)? The test developer's goal is to design the assessment, the conditions for administration, and the scoring so that student performance is neither assisted nor hampered by situational artifacts unrelated to the capability being measured. Well-known sources of measurement error are inadvertent cues that give away the answer, confusing or poorly written directions, use of unfamiliar terminology not covered during instruction, and inaccurate scoring.

Particularly problematic for performance assessment are:

1. Variations in the accuracy of observers rating group performance or individuals completing manipulative tasks

2. Student unfamiliarity with the mechanical apparatus in a manipulative task

3. Student unfamiliarity with the topic addressed in the assessment

4. Variability in the scoring of performances or products by different individuals

However, Linn (1994, p. 25) notes that several studies have demonstrated that the error resulting from different raters can be minimized when well-defined scoring rubrics are used and care is exercised in training the raters.

A serious problem for performance assessments, however, is the error of measurement resulting from task variability (Linn, 1994). In writing tasks, for example, sources of variability are:

1. Features of the essay prompt

2. Types and extent of prewriting activities

3. Nature of the topic

4. Writing purpose and range

5. Time allowances

6. Conditions of administration (Moran, Myles, & Shank, 1991)

Different topics and different purposes, for example, make different demands on the writer (Quellmalz, 1984b). Further, Conlan and Chambers (1987) report that the pretesting of writing prompts has led to many being discarded because they resulted in unintended interpretations by the students. For example, some elementary school children, when asked in an essay examination to describe their favorite person, responded with, "He is six feet tall, has brown hair and blue eyes" (Mitchell, 1992).

The variability across tasks in other domains also is considerable (Linn, 1994; Shavelson, Baxter, & Pine, 1992). This variability can lead to the misclassification of student performance and limits the inferences that may be made to broad domains or general constructs (Linn, 1994).

Fairness

Among the potential roles proposed for performance assessment are certification and grading and selecting students (Baker et al., 1993). For these situations, in which high-stakes decisions are made about individuals, fairness of the assessment is an important consideration.

Three issues to be addressed in determining fairness are (1) comparability of assessments, (2) availability of needed equipment, and (3) opportunity to learn. If assessments provide a range of topic options or assignments, validity evidence should document the comparability of the assessments (Baker et al., 1993, p. 1215).

Availability of equipment required in an assessment impacts the fairness concern in two ways. One is the lack of essential equipment at the time of testing, such as substituting rulers for missing yardsticks to calculate the area of the classroom (Phillips, 1994). The other is student access to equipment during learning. A non-threatening assessment such as NAEP may include calculator-active problems, although student access to calculators may be inequitable (Linn et al., 1991, p. 17). For tests intended to profile a particular student's capabilities, however, equitable access is an important consideration.

Some evidence indicates relatively low levels of student performance in almost every precollegiate subject area on performance assessments (Baker et al., 1993). Also, some data indicate lower rates of attempting open-ended tasks for some ethnic groups. The implications for fairness are twofold. First, resources must be allocated to instruction to ensure that important learning priorities are addressed. Second, cultural diversity and experiences can lead to different group performances on some tasks. Therefore, changes in the allocation of resources and instructional strategies may be necessary to prepare students for complex open-ended assessments (Linn et al., 1991, p. 18).

POTENTIAL ROLES IN PROGRAM EVALUATION

A rapidly changing policy context has generated interest in the concept of alternative assessment. It is a core feature of the proposed national examination system, is promoted as a major effort in some state reforms, and has attracted commitments from organizations of subject matter specialists (Baker et al., 1993, p. 1210). Further, several different roles currently are proposed for alternative assessment. Among them are (1) serving as a model for curriculum reform and a vehicle for staff development and (2) functioning as a means of formative evaluation for instructional improvement.

Implementing performance assessment in the classroom requires time for teacher training and support and other resources (Flexer, Cambo, Borko, Mayfield, & Marion, 1994; Lamme & Hysmith, 1991). An important task for program evaluation is to conduct formative evaluation of performance assessment to determine the extent to which it is being utilized in the classroom and the classroom effects. Then, when performance assessment is integrated into the school's practices, it can serve as a mechanism for evaluating curriculum and instruction.

Evaluation of the Implementation of Performance Assessment

An evaluation of the implementation of performance assessment in classrooms should address the nature of teacher training activities, the adequacy of performance assessment examples provided to teachers, the nature of teacher support, the nature of the assessments developed by the teachers, and the effects of this policy in the classroom and on the teachers. Similarly, if a school or district is relying on district-level testing to serve as a mechanism for staff development and classroom change, these same questions are also relevant. In these contexts, performance assessment is the object of the evaluation.

Adequacy of Assessment Examples.   Criteria described earlier should be used to evaluate the examples and related information provided to the teachers. Rationale for the assessment tasks, the psychological or social processes the assessments are intended to reflect, and the development of the scoring rubrics should be explained and illustrated. The rationale for assessing related component abilities should be explained as well as ways to test component abilities, such as a prior knowledge test.

Nature of the Assessments Developed by Teachers.   The extent of implementation of performance assessment in the classroom may vary according to the particular discipline and the availability of assessments from other sources. In some domains, such as art, musical performance, and creative writing, performance is an integral component of both learning and assessment. During instruction, students produce creative works or interpretations and receive feedback as they successively refine their work. Developing assessments to determine student achievement on curriculum outcomes for such domains is consistent with the already established course focus and should present minimal implementation and validity problems.

In other subjects in which analysis and synthesis are emphasized, the development of performance assessments will require both the identification of meaningful tasks and the development of scoring rubrics. Provision also must be made for assessing component abilities in problem-solving tasks.

Other subject domains, particularly mathematics and science, are currently undergoing major shifts in conceptualization, focus, and the roles of both the student and the teacher. Some curriculum frameworks in mathematics, for example, view the discipline as a method of inquiry rather than a set of truths to be learned. Students are asked to formulate problems and evaluate alternative mathematical claims, and the teacher's role is to serve as a facilitator of these activities. Time will be required to adequately conceptualize performance assessment in this context. Given the extent of curriculum refocus, time will be required to develop meaningful performance assessments.

Classroom Effects.   One year-long project in which an 11-member team worked with 14 teachers to help them develop performance assessments in mathematics and reading documented teacher difficulties with performance assessment. Among the problems were initial lack of knowledge about implementation and being "overwhelmed" in attempting to change both assessment and instruction in mathematics and reading. Moreover, the new assessments and instruction were initially viewed as "add-ons" (instead of a shift in focus). Another pressure was the perceived expectation of upper-grade teachers for the children's performance on computational timed tests (Flexer et al., 1994). For curricular and assessment efforts to change, Flexer et al. (1994, p. 27) note that teachers need support, permission to go slowly, and time for the changes to be measured in years, not months.

Formative Evaluation of Instruction

A role for performance assessment suggested by Baker et al. (1991) is that of instructional improvement. That is, performance assessments will be administered to students, and on the basis of performance data, instructional plans and processes will be designed for subsequent cohorts of students (p. 1213). Such evaluations, in which achievement data (and often other information) is used to revise a curriculum or a program, is referred to as formative. In this context, performance assessment is a means of evaluation. This role for performance assessment depends on the integration of the assessments into school and classroom practice and requires matching assessments to curriculum goals.

When performance assessments are used to estimate the performance of groups for the purposes of program evaluation, the issue of comparability of tasks becomes less important. However, the standards used to classify successful and unsuccessful students must be validated (Baker et al., 1993, p. 1215).

SUMMARY

Alternative assessment began as a mechanism for restructuring curricula and recently has attracted support as a means of assessment. These assessments often are open-ended or hands-on tasks that are intended to measure complex cognitive abilities. The tasks should be designed to provide information about students' strengths and weaknesses in relation to complex cognitive abilities. One expectation for alternative assessments is that they can guide curriculum reform because they direct classroom effort toward "genuine" intellectual challenges. Another is that they will be meaningful to students and, therefore, serve as motivators. However, preliminary data indicate that such tasks are not motivating for all students. A third expectation is that they can influence the professional development of teachers.

Performance assessments require students to demonstrate their capabilities by creating a product or engaging in some activity. Some performance tasks are academic in that they are key intellectual processes in the subject area. Others are referred to as authentic because the tasks represent real-world situations.

Teachers and evaluators are developing performance assessments for a variety of settings. Among them are history, writing, mathematics, and science. However, in most disciplines, consensus has yet to be reached on the complex capabilities that represent pivotal authentic accomplishments in the field. At present, performance tasks in mathematics and science vary widely in scope, complexity, and breadth. Some are group research tasks, others require that the student demonstrate an algorithm and explain the answer, others involve basic measurement or manipulation of materials, and others depend on logic and reasoning. Also, writing performance may be conceptualized as basic competencies or the abilities associated with more advanced writing.

Important criteria to be considered in the design of performance assessments are validity, reliability, and fairness. The open-ended nature and the complexity of many performance assessments lead to particular problems in establishing validity not found in the development of multiple-choice standardized tests. One is the task complexity/ability inference problem. That is, a task that appears to be complex on the surface may not require the use of complex cognitive processes. The second issue is the confounding of abilities problem. For example, performance on a complex task in mathematics or science may be inextricably entwined with linguistic competence. Similarly, many problem-solving tasks depend on the student's domain knowledge and the ability to recall that knowledge when needed. Thus, performance assessments should be designed to assess component capabilities as well. Other key validity issues are the focus of the scoring rubric and the extent of domain representation. Specifically, the scoring rubric may not capture the fully functioning complex skill, and relying on broad curriculum frameworks or tasks developed from general ideas may omit key intellectual processes in the domain.

Issues in the reliability of scores on performance assessments are:

1. Variability in the scoring of performances or products by different individuals
2. Student unfamiliarity with task requirements (e.g., unfamiliarity with the mechanical apparatus in a manipulative task)

3. Unfamiliarity with the topic addressed in the assessment

4. Variability of the different tasks

Error resulting from rater variability can be minimized through well-defined rubrics and targeted training of raters. However, measurement error resulting from task variability is a major issue and can lead to misclassifications of student performance.

Also important in performance assessment are the issues of fairness and costs. At present, data are needed on the relationships between cultural diversity, prior experiences, and performance on alternative assessments. Data also are needed on the curricular effects of performance assessment, although a preliminary study indicates the changes will take time and effort.

Two roles for performance assessment of most interest in program evaluation are serving as a model for curriculum reform and serving as a means of formative evaluation in instructional improvement. Evaluating performance assessment as a curriculum reform mechanism involves addressing teacher training activities, the adequacy of assessment examples, implementation activities, the nature of teacher-developed measures, and classroom effects. Using performance assessment to revise instruction involves matching assessments to classroom goals and recommending changes in classroom activities based on performance data.

CHAPTER QUESTIONS

1. What are the major goals expressed for alternative assessment?

2. What are the basic characteristics of performance assessment?

3. What is one difference between analytic scoring guides and primary trait rubrics?

4. What are some of the validity interpretations associated with open-ended complex tasks?

5. What are some of the sources of unreliability of performance tasks?

6. What are the requirements for relying on performance assessment as a formative evaluation of curriculum?

REFERENCES

Archbald, D., & Newmann, F. (1992). Approaches to Assessing Academic Achievement. In H. Berlak, F. M. Newmann, E. Adams, D. Archbald, T. Burgess, J. Raven, & T. A. Romberg, *Toward a new science of educational testing and achievement* (pp. 139–180). Albany, NY: State University of New York Press.

Baker, E. (1994). Learning-based assessment of history understanding. *Educational Psychologist, 29*(2), 97–106.

Baker, E., Freeman, M., & Clayton, S. (1991). Cognitive assessment of history for large-scale testing. In M. Wittrock & E. Baker (Eds.), *Testing and cognition* (pp. 131–153). Englewood Cliffs, NJ: Prentice Hall.

Baker, E., O'Neill, H., & Linn, R. (1993). Policy and validity prospects for performance-based assessment. *American Psychologist, 48*(12), 1210–1218.

Berk, R. A. (1986). *Performance assessment: Methods and applications.* Baltimore, MD: Johns Hopkins University Press.

Breland, H., Camp, R., Jones, R., Morris, M., & Rock, D. (1987). *Assessing writing skill. Research monograph no. 11.* New York: College Entrance Examination Board.

Champagne, A., & Newell, S. (1992). Directions for research and development: Alternative methods of assessing scientific literacy. *Journal of Research in Science Teaching, 29*(8), 841–860.

Chapman, C., Fyans, L., & Kerins, C. (1984). Writing assessment in Illinois. *Educational Measurement: Issues and Practice, 3*(1), 24–26.

Chi, M., Glaser, R., & Farr, M. (Eds.). (1988). *The nature of expertise.* Hillsdale, NJ: Erlbaum.

Congressional Record. (1994, March 21). Conference report on H.R. 1804. *Goals 2000: Educate America Act.* Washington, DC: U.S. Congress.

Conlan, G., & Chambers, P. (1987). Selecting the best essay topic. In K. Greenburg & V. Slaughter (Eds.), *Notes from the national testing network in writing* (pp. 5–6). NY: City University of New York.

Cronbach, L. J. (1990). *Essentials of psychological testing* (5th ed.). New York: Harper and Row.

DeVise, D. (1994, March 10). How three different grade groups took the 4-section CLAS exam. *Press-Telegram*, Los Angeles, CA.

Fitzpatrick, R., & Morrison, E. (1971). Performance and product evaluation. In R. L. Thorndike (Ed.), *Educational measurement* (2nd ed., pp. 237–270). Washington, DC: American Council on Education.

Flexer, R., Cambo, C., Borko, H., Mayfield, V., & Marion, F. (1994). How "messing about" with performance assessment in mathematics affects what happens in classrooms. Paper presented at the annual meeting of the American Educational Research Association, New Orleans.

Haertel, E. (1992). *Performance measurement.* In M. C. Alkin (Ed.), *Encyclopedia of educational research* (pp. 984–989). New York: Macmillan.

Kulm, G. (1990). Assessing higher order mathematical thinking. In G. Kulm (Ed.), *Assessing higher order thinking in mathematics* (pp. 1–4). Washington, DC: American Association for the Advancement of Science.

Lamme, L., & Hysmith, C. (1991). One school's adventure into portfolio assessment. *Language Arts, 68*, 629–640.

Lavoie, D., & Good, R. (1988). The nature and use of prediction skills in a biological computer simulation. *Journal of Research in Science Teaching, 25*(5), 335–360.

Linn, R. (1994, April). Performance assessment: Policy promises and technical measurement standards. Invited address, Division D, annual meeting of the American Educational Research Association, New Orleans.

Linn, R., Baker, E., & Dunbar, S. (1991). Complex performance-based assessment. Expectations and validation criteria. *Educational Researcher, 20*(5), 15–21.

Messick, S. (1984). The psychology of educational measurement. *Journal of Educational Measurement, 21*, 215–237.

Messick, S. (1994). The interplay of evidence and consequences in the validation of performance assessments. *Educational Researcher, 23*(2), 13–22.

Meyer, C. (1992). What's the difference between authentic and performance assessment? *Educational Leadership, 49*(8), 39–40.

Mitchell, R. (1992). *Testing for learning*. New York: The Free Press.

Moran, M., Myles, B., & Shank, M. (1991). Variables in eliciting writing samples. *Educational Measurement: Issues and Practice, 10*(3), 23–26.

National Council of Teachers of Mathematics (NCTM) (1989). *Curriculum and evaluation standards for school mathematics*. Reston, VA: NCTM.

Phillips, S. E. (1994). Opportunity for success. *NCME Quarterly Newsletter*. Washington, DC: National Council on Measurement in Education.

Quellmalz, E. (1984a). Designing writing assessments: Balancing fairness, utility, and cost. *Educational Evaluation and Policy Analysis, (6)11*, 63–72.

Quellmalz, E. (1984b). Toward successful large-scale writing assessment: Where are we now? Where do we go from here? *Educational Measurement: Issues and Practice, 3*, 29–33.

Quellmalz, E. (1986). Writing skills assessment. In R. Berk (Ed), *Performance assessment* (pp. 492–501). Baltimore: Johns Hopkins University Press.

Shavelson, R., Baxter, G., & Pine, J. (1992). Performance assessments: Political rhetoric and measurement reality. *Educational Researcher, 21*(4), 22–27.

Siegal, A. (1986). Performance tests. In R. Berk (Ed.), *Performance assessment: Methods and applications* (pp. 121–142). Baltimore, MD: The Johns Hopkins University Press.

Stemple, B. (1992). *Performance assessment: An international experiment*. Princeton, NJ: Educational Testing Service.

Tuma, D., & Reif, F. (Eds.). (1980). *Problem-solving and education: Issues in teaching and research*. Hillsdale, NJ: Erlbaum.

Wiggins, G. (1989). A true test: Toward more authentic and equitable assessment. *Phi Delta Kappan, 70*(9), 703–713.

Wiley, D. (1991). Test validity and invalidity reconsidered. In R. Snow & D. Wiley (Eds.), *Improving inquiry in social sciences: A volume in honor of Lee J. Cronbach* (pp. 75–107). Hillsdale, NJ: Lawrence Erlbaum.

Wolf, D., LeMahieu, P., & Eresh, J. (1992). Good measure: Assessment as a tool of reform. *Educational Leadership*, 8–13.

CHAPTER 8

Alternative Methods of Assessment: Portfolio Assessment

Performance assessment is one component of the assessment trend referred to as "alternative." Performance assessments are administered at established times, and the tasks typically are standardized in that all the students complete the same tasks with the same apparatus or equipment.

Portfolio assessment is the other major component of the current alternative trend. When used within the classroom, a portfolio is a collection of student work that reflects growth and also indicates some of the diversity of student accomplishments. Like performance assessment, portfolios should measure intellectual capabilities, they should focus on important and teachable learning processes, and they should inform teaching practice about students' strengths and weaknesses (Baker, Freeman, & Clayton, 1991, p. 135). However, portfolios are intended to address some intellectual processes that differ from those targeted by performance assessments.

Portfolio assessment has attracted widespread interest for some of the same reasons as performance assessment; that is, the authenticity of the tasks, the alignment with the curriculum, and the potential for teacher development (Valencia & Calfee, 1991). Because portfolios are collections of student work, their appeal also may stem, in part, from their apparent ease of use (Mitchell, 1992).

In addition to the expectations identified for alternative assessments, particular expectations have been voiced for portfolios. Among them are the opportunities to provide student involvement and some ownership of the assessment process; opportunities to accommodate schoolwide projects, such as artwork and writing; opportunities for teachers to observe and document student growth over a period of time (Mitchell, 1992); and opportunities for less traditionally skilled students to develop their abilities (Wolf, Bixby, Glenn, & Gardner, 1991).

At present, portfolios are implemented as within-classroom research projects and assessment tools and as district and statewide assessments. However, little is known about the needed technical specifications for large-scale assessment purposes or the effects of different uses and formats on teachers and students. Key topics in portfolio assessment are the basic characteristics; the various formats in current use; and the issues of purpose, implementation, and interpretation.

TYPES OF PORTFOLIOS

Portfolios have been advocated for a variety of purposes, from that of altering the quality of the student's learning experience in the classroom to that of large-scale assessment. The formats and types of entries in the portfolio vary somewhat, according to the particular purpose.

Basic Characteristics

The concept of portfolios began with their use by artists and, later, photographers. For these professions, portfolios serve as portable collections of work samples to show prospective clients. They are transportable showcases of one's talents. In the educational setting, a portfolio in its simplest form is a purposeful collection of student work. *When used within the classroom,* a portfolio differs from a folder or collection of work in three major ways. First, a student's portfolio (1) illustrates longitudinal growth as evidenced in the changes from the student's earlier to later work and (2) indicates breadth through the samples of different kinds of work that are included. In language arts, for example, a portfolio may contain journal entries, essays, poems, narratives, and tape recordings of class presentations.

Second, the portfolio provides an opportunity for the student and teacher to review ongoing work and to select new goals for the student (Gearhart, Herman, Baker, & Whittaker, 1992). In the classroom, portfolios can be designed to function simultaneously as a teaching tool and as an assessment (Mitchell, 1992).

The third important characteristic of within-class use is that changes in portfolio entries over time should reflect important changes in the student's intellectual processes. Among them are students' abilities "to formulate new questions, pursue work over time, and arrive at standards of excellence" (Wolf, 1987/1988, p. 29).

Since the inception of student portfolios in the 1980s, they have been implemented in different contexts. As a result, portfolios are viewed as fulfilling different purposes, depending on their use. Some educators maintain that the purpose is to assist in developing autonomous learners who can assess their strengths and weaknesses and, as a result, develop in different directions. Others view portfolios as rich examples of student effort and progress in the classroom. Others consider portfolios as a mechanism of documenting student progress toward curriculum goals or of demonstrating student accomplishments or achievement in (an) identified area(s).

Although portfolios contain examples of student performance, they differ from performance assessments in at least four key respects (Herman, Gearhart, & Baker, 1993, p. 203). First, portfolios contain samples of class work, rather than student responses to a stimulus presented under standardized conditions. Second, portfolios represent multiple opportunities to demonstrate competence across a range of contexts. Third, student work in the portfolio often represents different types of tasks. In writing, for example, the selections typically represent different genres and topics. Fourth, portfolio samples are often the result of continued effort to refine the product, such as revising early drafts of a narrative or a summary.

The "Ideal" Format

One goal expressed for alternative assessments is that they should assess thinking, rather than the possession of information. They should serve as the basis for sophisticated judgments about students' understanding of significant ideas and processes (Wolf et al., 1991, p. 33). Questions that assessment should assist the teacher in answering are, Does the student have a hold on the kinds of thinking processes it takes to sustain long-term serious work? Can the student pose interesting questions or solve problems outside the comforting, familiar structure of school assignments? and Can the student step back and reflect on his or her own work? (Wolf, 1987/1988, p. 24).

The "ideal" portfolio is so named because it is designed to address these and similar questions. Developed in the arts and humanities, the portfolio targets two major aims. One aim is to model individual and personal responsibility in questioning and reflecting on one's own work. The second aim is to capture growth in order to assist learners to become thoughtful and informed evaluators of their own histories as learners (Wolf, 1989, p. 36). Implemented in the Pittsburgh public schools as a part of Project PROPEL, the portfolio is primarily an instrument for enhancing the quality of learning (Archbald & Newmann, 1992).

The "ideal" portfolio consists of three major components. They are biographies of works, a range of works, and reflections (Wolf, 1989). A biography of a work is the documentation of the development or production of a major project (Wolf, 1989). Because students save the various phases of their work, the portfolio illustrates the microgenesis, or unfolding, of their ideas within a selected project (Wolf, 1987/1988, p. 27). Portfolio items in art may be a series of sketches from the student's sketchbook, with accompanying notes. The portfolio of a music student may contain several tape recordings of a particularly difficult selection; whereas a writing portfolio may contain notes, diagrams, drafts, reflections, and the final version of a narrative.

In addition to documenting progress in a major project, the portfolio also reflects a variety or range of student work. In language arts, for example, a portfolio may contain journal entries, essays, poems, narratives, and tape recordings of class presentations.

The third portfolio component consists of student reflections. At different times during a semester, the teacher asks the students to review their collections from the perspective of an informed critic or biographer. Students describe characteristic features of their work, the changes that have occurred, and progress or work yet to be achieved (Wolf, 1989, p. 37).

In the classroom, the portfolio functions in two ways. First, it contributes to the development of student self-reflection and self-assessment. This goal is addressed through the compilation of selections that reflect (1) growth in student knowledge and capabilities in the subject area *and* (2) growth in students' abilities to analyze and assess their work. Moreover, a particular advantage of this form of portfolio-based assessment is that it can provide a context in which students can learn to view assessment as an occasion for learning (Wolf et al., 1991).

Second, the portfolio is not simply a repository of completed works or thoughts. Instead, it is an ongoing source of information for both the teacher and the student. In the larger classroom context, teachers and students often discuss the processes involved in creating worthwhile work, elements of a helpful critique, and ways to utilize comments into ongoing work (Wolf et al., 1991, p. 58). Thus, the port-folio provides a continuous body of work that teachers and students may access as the students are developing their writing or musical skills, for example. Students may return to earlier works for later revision or to make comparison with later works. At the end of the year, a final selection of biographies, reflections, and final pieces is made that become a part of a permanent record of their development (Wolf et al., 1991, p. 58).

Portfolios also are messy, and they require work. However, they can offer partic-ular strengths over other classroom mechanisms. Briefly summarized, these strengths are:

1. Development of student responsibility for learning

2. Expansion of the dimensions of learning

3. Renewed emphasis on process

4. Focus on a developmental view of learning (Wolf, 1989)

Other Portfolio Formats

The purpose of the initial portfolio use in the arts and humanities is to serve as a learning tool for students and as a planning mechanism for classroom teachers. Since that inception, others have begun to view portfolios as mechanisms for demonstrating or exhibiting the student's efforts, progress, or achievements in a par-ticular area. Given this expanded function, various alterations in the original format have been made. For example, the essential elements of a portfolio, according to Meyer, Schumann, and Angello (1990) are:

1. Student participation in the selection of content

2. Criteria for selection

3. Criteria for judging merit

4. Evidence of student self-reflection

In this view, although self-reflection is mentioned, merit, rather than growth, becomes a major focus for the portfolio.

General Types.   Valencia and Calfee (1991) identify four different portfolio formats, each of which reflects a different purpose. In their analysis, the broad classifications are:

1. The showcase portfolio

2. The documentation portfolio

3. The evaluation portfolio

4. The class portfolio

The four classifications as well as the "ideal" portfolio are summarized in Table 8.1. As indicated, the showcase portfolio consists of the student's best or favorite work selected by the student. Sometimes the showcase portfolio is developed from the student's ongoing working portfolio that is maintained throughout the year. Some teachers in one elementary school, for example, used expandable folders for the showcase portfolios, which the students decorated; and others used classroom collection books (Lamme & Hysmith, 1991). Of primary importance, however, is that the showcase portfolio should represent the student's view of what is good about his or her learning (p. 634). When the student provides reasons for a decision of a particular piece of work as a good effort, he or she can begin to develop some ownership of the assessment process. However, teachers should be sensitive to the fact that students often do not select the stronger pieces for the portfolios (Moss et al., 1992; Simmons, 1990).

The documentation portfolio, in contrast, is an ongoing record of student progress, and it may contain teacher checklists and observations in addition to student work, self-reflections, and other information. For example, students may maintain a list of the books they read during the year, evaluating each on a 5-star scale (Lamme & Hysmith, 1991). The documentation portfolio also may be viewed as a working portfolio when students use it to collect and store their ongoing work.

Both the evaluation and the class portfolio are mechanisms to report to parents, administrators, and others about student work. In the evaluation portfolio, both the contents and criteria for each entry are predetermined. In contrast, the class portfolio is a summary of each student's work in the class with reference to individual portfolios. Also, the class portfolio described by Valencia and Calfee (1991) differs from the other external reporting types in that it also documents the complexity and nature of the curriculum.

The classifications in Table 8.1 are general categories that highlight key differences among different implementations of portfolios. However, examples of these categories rarely exist in pure form (Valencia & Calfee, 1991). For example, the Vermont portfolio assessment in mathematics consists of five to seven of the student's best pieces selected by the students and teachers (a characteristic that resembles the showcase portfolio). However, the set of best pieces also must include three types of

Table 8.1
Categories of portfolios

Type	Description	Focus
"Ideal" portfolio[1]	A collection of student work and self-reflections that represent (1) growth in student knowledge and capabilities and (2) growth in students' abilities to analyze and assess their work.	To enhance the quality of learning and to assist learners to become thoughtful and informed evaluators of their own histories of learning by capturing growth over time.
Showcase portfolio[2]	A collection of the student's best or favorite work selected primarily by the student. Self-reflection and self-selection are more important than standardization.	To provide a sampling of student work for exhibition to parents and others.
Documentation portfolio[2]	A systematic ongoing record of student progress. Some entries are accompanied by student self-reflections, and others are evaluated by external raters. Observations, checklists, anecdotal records, and performance tests also are included.	To provide a systematic record in terms of student products and quantitative and qualitative evaluations.
Evaluation portfolio[2]	A generally standardized collection of student work with direction from the teacher, administrator, or district. Although some self-selection may be permitted, the portfolio largely consists of pre-scribed entries. Criteria for evaluation also are predetermined.	To provide a largely standardized reporting of student achievement in terms of student products to parents and administrators.
Class portfolio[2]	A three-section binder that consists of (1) summary sheets for all students, describing performance in terms of curriculum goals; (2) the teacher's detailed notes and observations for each student referring to student works, test data, conference notes, and notes on the instructional activities for each student; and (3) the teacher's curriculum and instructional plans for the year, with comments on extension and revision.	To communicate to parents, administrators, and others the teacher's judgments about student accomplishments in an interactive and situational context.

[1]Summarized from Wolf, 1989; [2]Summarized from Valencia and Calfee, 1991.

problems: puzzles, investigations, and applications. The specification of types of entries is a characteristic of the evaluation portfolio.

Basic Differences.   The four general models illustrate some of the diverse aims and features of the portfolio concept. As indicated, purposes vary from enhancing the quality of learning to that of standardized reporting by districts or states or communicating the complex nature of student accomplishments to parents, school board members, and others.

The portfolio types also illustrate three other major differences in the ways the concept is implemented. One is the different emphases on individual student growth and standardization. Specifically, the documentation, evaluation, and class portfolios do not emphasize student self-reflection and the development of self-analysis skills. For the documentation and evaluation portfolios, the focus is that of reporting student accomplishments or achievement. This purpose differs from that of developing autonomous learners and fostering individual growth as a primary goal. A focus on documenting accomplishments directs selection of the student's best pieces with some support information as to the process of development. A focus on individual growth, however, directs selection to works that demonstrate a breakthrough in the student's thinking, and the pieces may not be overall examples of excellence. Moss et al. (1992) note that growth in writing, for example, is often manifest in "changes in the complexity of the problems that students undertake, which may involve losing control over other features of the writing like organization or mechanics" (p. 13). One student, for example, included two pieces of expository responses to literature in her portfolio. While the second is less well organized, it is an example of her growth because it is a richer interpretation (Moss et al., 1992).

The second major difference across the four portfolio categories is the amount of student work that is included. The "ideal" portfolio consists of student products and their analyses of those products, but the class portfolio only includes references to student work. A third difference is the extent of student input into the selection of their work for inclusion in the portfolio. Students are responsible for the decisions in the ideal and showcase portfolios, and they share the decision making with the teacher in the documentation portfolio; but they have little or no input in the evaluation portfolio. Moss et al. (1992) note that students can be required to include certain types of writing in their portfolio, for example, at least two pieces of writing from at least two genres. However, this practice reduces the student's sense of ownership and risks undermining the pedagogical and motivational plus of the portfolio creation process (p. 19).

One potential problem with the evaluation portfolio is that it may be simply a collection of different assessments. Purves (1993, p. 177) notes that the portfolios used by many districts and states more closely resemble multiple measures in a domain than portfolios. That is, a state or school district may specify the types of entries with specified criteria for each. Thus, a portfolio that contains only a brief narrative, a business letter, and a persuasive essay, for example, is a collection of multiple assessments. This approach is consistent with Darling-Hammond's (1989) bureaucratic model of accountability, which seeks evidence of teacher adherence to stated policies (Moss et al., 1992, p. 13). In these assessments, the student's goal is likely to be that of demonstrating competence, rather than developing his or her own purposes for learning (Moss et al., 1992).

The Vermont Portfolio Assessment.   The purpose of the Vermont statewide assessment system is (1) to provide high-quality data about student achievement that can permit the comparison of schools or districts and (2) to induce improvement in instruction (Koretz, Stecher, Klein, & McCaffrey, 1994, p. 5). At present, the assessments are confined to writing and mathematics in grades 4 and 8. The system is referred to as "bottom up" because teacher committees developed the operational plans, established the guidelines limiting teacher and student portfolio choices, and designed the scoring rubrics.

The centerpiece of the assessment system consists of student portfolios. In mathematics, students and teachers select five to seven best pieces from the student's year-long portfolio for scoring. The pieces are scored on seven 4-point scales (three relating to communication and four addressing problem solving). Teachers other than the student's own teacher score the selections in regional or state meetings (Koretz et al., 1994).

Writing portfolios consist of a single best piece and three pieces selected by the student; a letter explaining the composition and selection of the best piece; a poem, short story, or personal narrative; a personal response to a book, event, current issue, mathematical problem, or scientific phenomenon; and a prose piece from a subject area other than English or language arts (Koretz, Stecher, & Deibert, 1992, p. 6). The best piece and the rest of the portfolio are scored on the same five dimensions. They are purpose, organization, details, voice/tone, and usage/mechanics/grammar. Scorers use a 4-point scale to evaluate each of the five dimensions. In 1993, teachers scored portfolios of students other than their own in a statewide meeting (Koretz et al., 1994). A random sample of both mathematics and writing were selected for rescoring by second raters. The portfolios are complemented by standardized assessments that are not entirely multiple choice.

SUMMARY

Portfolio assessment is a major component of the trend referred to as alternative assessment. Among the distinct advantages advocated for portfolio assessment are that it can promote some student ownership of the assessment process, that it provides opportunities to observe student growth, and that it provides opportunities for students at all skill levels to develop their abilities. When implemented within the classroom, changes in portfolio entries should reflect important changes in students' intellectual processes.

The "ideal" format for the portfolio is designed (1) to model individual responsibility in questioning and reflecting on one's own work and (2) to assist learners to become thoughtful evaluators of their own learning. To this end, the portfolio consists of biographies of works, a range of works, and student reflections. The portfolio also serves as an ongoing source of information during the year for the teacher and the student.

Other portfolio formats are the showcase, documentation, evaluation, and class portfolios. The showcase format provides a sampling of student work for exhibition, but the documentation portfolio provides a systematic record of both qualitative and quantitative assessments. The evaluation format is a standardized reporting to administrators and parents, and the class portfolio is a summary record of a teacher's class with detailed notes on each student.

The Vermont statewide portfolio assessment was developed to address instructional needs as well as standardized reporting to administrators. At present, the concept is implemented in reading and mathematics in grades 4 and 8.

ISSUES IN PORTFOLIO ASSESSMENT

At present, portfolios are implemented for either of two different purposes: to foster student growth and development or to assess student accomplishments or achievement. Unresolved issues about portfolio assessment include the need for data on technical specifications for each of these two purposes, implementation issues, the relationship to equity, and the possible role in systemwide assessment.

Nurturance of Student Growth and Development

The early use of portfolios in the classroom in the 1980s was for the purpose of serving as a working document. Typically, entries change throughout the year as the student develops maturity and insight into the subject. Also, early entries serve as focal points for teacher-student conferences about possible directions for the student to pursue (Wolf, 1987/1988). Student growth is determined by a qualitative analysis of early versus later works.

Currently, researchers are exploring methods of providing quantitative summaries of the teacher's interpretative judgments. In the area of writing, Moss et al. (1992) suggest an interpretative approach to the analysis of student portfolios. The analysis culminates in a narrative summary of a sequence of the student's writing. A sequence consists of a final draft or product and all related drafts or plans. The teacher's narrative is based on a coding scheme that incorporates important writing features categorized into five clusters (see Figure 8.1).

The coding scheme documents the extent to which particular revisions increased or decreased evidence of a particular feature and the extent to which a particular feature is present in the final product. The symbols (+, -, and /) indicate the relationship between drafts and particular features, and the 4-point scale indicates the presence of that feature in the final product.

The purpose of the framework is not to score the student's writing. Instead, it is to serve as a guide for the teacher in developing a narrative description of the stu-

Figure 8.1
Suggested coding scheme for interpretative analysis of portfolios

STUDENT: *Barry* TOPIC: *On Lord of the Flies* GENRE: *Response to Literature* WHY SELECTED? *Unsatisfying*						
	FINAL	**REVISE**	**SELF**	**TEACHER**	**OTHER**	**COMMENTS**
date	1/18/90					
length/number	1 page	4 drafts	1	1	0	
VISION						
something to say	3			1		*T: explain, why would you rather*
voice	2					*be with Ralph, not Jack?*
seeing beyond ordinary	2					
conceptual framework	2					
autobiography	1					
intertextuality						
DEVELOPMENT						
elaboration	3					
specificity	3					
explanations	3			−		
focus	2					
structuring	3	+		+		*T: you confuse Ralph & Jack in*
comprehensiveness	2			−		*2nd paragraph*
movement	3	+		+		
multiple perspectives	1					
CRAFT: LANGUAGE/FORM						
word choice	3	+	−			*S: I'd like to bring in more*
sentence structure	3	+				*fancy words*
clarity/cohesiveness	3	+				
form approp. to genre	3	+				
standard conventions	3	+				
CRAFT: LITERARY STYLE						
sound						
figurative language						
concrete imagery	1					
shape						
show-not-tell	1					
tone						
READER'S RESPONSE						
compelling/interesting	2					
believable	3					
accessible	3					
shared context	3					
SENSE OF WRITER						
engagement/interest			1			
comfort						
gen'l self-evaluation						
purpose awareness						
genre awareness			+			*S: It's not like creative writing*
audience awareness						*It's more concrete*
use of comments						
revising						
development						

FINAL	REVISE	SELF, TEACHER, OTHER
1 some evidence of feature	+ revision increases evidence of feature	+ positive mention
2 extended evidence of feature	/ revision doesn't change evidence of feature	/ neutral mention
3 appropriately sustained evidence	− revision reduces evidence of feature	− change suggested
of feature		
4 integrated/sophisticated	single sign = some revision	single sign = some mention
evidence of feature	double sign = extended revision	double sign = extended mention

"Portfolios, Accountability and an Interpretative Approach to Validity" by P. Moss, J. Beck, C. Ebbs, B. Matson, J. Muchmore, D. Steele, C. Taylor, R. Herter, 1992, *Educational Measurement: Issues and Practice, 11*(3), 16. Copyright 1992 by the National Council on Measurement in Education. Reprinted by permission of the publisher.

dent's work. This type of coding scheme provides more information about student growth than either holistic or analytic scores. Holistic scores are not sensitive to subtle changes in student work, and analytic scores cannot adequately represent growth.

Another example of a mechanism to record growth in writing was developed by K-2 elementary school teachers in a Florida school. The scale consists of 11 levels and begins with simple activities, such as "attempts to write in scribbles or draw patterns" (level 1) and "child copies words he/she sees around the room" (level 3), and moves to more complex items, such as "child writes the start of a story" (level 7) and "child writes original poetry." One difficulty in interpreting this scale, however, is that it combines both processes the child is expected to engage in, such as "child uses both phonics and sight strategies to spell words" (level 7) and features of the writing product itself. An example is "writing includes details or dialogue, a sense of humor, or other emotions" (level 9) (p. 631).

Validity and Reliability.   Coding schemes for portfolios to document student growth should meet several criteria. First, the categories should be clear and unambiguous. They should not be subject to a variety of interpretations. Second, the benchmarks that are selected should reflect major growth changes, and they should occur in the stated sequence. Third, empirical data should be provided to support both the selection of categories and the hypothesized sequence. For example, the placement of "child uses commas, quotations, and apostrophes" at a higher level than "child willingly revises" in the K-2 writing growth scale should be verified.

To date, little information is available on the reliability of analytic schemes for assessing student growth. In the study conducted by Moss et al. (1992), two readers each analyzed work for 10 student writing portfolios. Content analysis of the summaries, however, indicated substantial differences across readers in their emphasis on the drafts or revisions.

Assessment of Student Accomplishments or Achievement

Portfolios to assess student accomplishments tend to emphasize different examples of student capabilities rather than selections that demonstrate improvement. A writing portfolio, for example, may consist of narratives, summaries, business letters, poetry, or essays. The Vermont statewide portfolio assessment in mathematics consists of entries in three categories. They are puzzles, applications, and investigations. Also, unlike portfolios established to determine growth, portfolios to assess accomplishments consist of examples of the student's best work.

Scoring Rubrics.   The scoring rubrics currently proposed for portfolio assessment may be any of three general types. One type identifies key features of the particular product or plan that may occur to a greater or lesser degree. For example, a scoring rubric for an essay may address purpose, organization, details, voice/tone, and mechanics/grammar. The writing is scored on a scale, such as 1 to 4, for each of the features.

A second type is an analytic scale, with sets of characteristics associated with different scores in the range. An example is the scale described by Herman et al. (1993). Level 1 writing (minimal achievement) is characterized by no overall organizational plan, minimal development with few or no transitions, incomplete sentences, and mechanical errors. Level 4 writing (adequate achievement/competent writer) is characterized by the presence of an overall plan or controlling ideas; logical transitions; some realistic, clear detail; and vivid details that may lack depth (p. 212).

A third type identifies broad dimensions, such as "uses appropriate structures" or "presents information/ideas clearly," for which levels of accomplishment also are identified. Purves (1993) describes such a rubric, in which the particular skill levels for each dimension are identified as basic, proficient, or advanced. Basic performance for "uses appropriate structures" is the capability to manage a simple sequence. Proficient performance requires that the student manage complex sequences, such as cause/effect and comparison. Supporting hypotheses, using complex arguments, and mixing modes of organization to gain effect constitute advanced performance for that dimension (p. 189). This rubric can, in a general way, indicate a pattern of performance in that the student may be at a basic level for one or more dimensions and at another level for other dimensions.

Validity.   The primary validity question for portfolios that document student accomplishments is the capabilities or constructs that are represented by the works in the collection. Also, the capabilities reflected in a narrative or summary in which the rubric emphasizes purpose, organization, voice, or mechanics should be identified. Koretz et al. (1994) note that clear definitions of the domains the assessments are intended to tap and adequate measures of related constructs are needed to establish validity.

In the absence of domain specifications, one approach to obtaining some validity information is to correlate the scores from portfolios with those of similar assessments in the domain. Three studies have correlated writing portfolio scores with scores on standard writing assessments.

Gentile (1992) found that the relationship between students' school-based portfolio scores and NAEP writing assessment scores was essentially chance. Correlations between mathematics portfolio scores and a standard math assessment and writing portfolio scores and a standard writing assessment ranged from .31 to .38 in the 1992 Vermont portfolio assessment.

Herman et al. (1993) found no correlation between scores on total portfolio collections and a standard writing assessment and correlations from .13 to .31 between scores on elements of the portfolio collection and the standard assessment. In addition, the portfolio scores were higher than the scores on the standard performance assessment. (The performance assessment was included in each portfolio collection but was not labeled as such.) The consistently higher ratings assigned to classroom assignments instead of the responses to a standard timed prompt may reflect any of several possibilities. First, classroom work may overestimate some students' knowledge and skills. Second, standardized tasks may fail to capture students' capacities that become evident when sufficient time and encouragement are present (Herman et al., 1993). Third, the higher ratings for classroom work may reflect the extent of instructional support from teachers or peers and the resources available in the classroom. In other words, one concern associated with portfolios used as a measure of student accomplishments is, Whose work is it? (Herman et al., 1993, p. 220).

They also found that the scores for the portfolio collections were higher than the average of the ratings of single pieces. That is, students' average scores for their more competent writing pieces were often lower than the single scores assigned to the entire portfolio (p. 219). This finding raises the question that raters may be looking for some evidence of capability rather than for typical performance. In other words, the portfolio score reflected the more competent pieces in the collection.

Reliability.   Koretz et al. (1994) note that *reliability* has many meanings. The Vermont portfolio assessment used rater agreement—the consistency with which raters assign scores to particular pieces of work—as information about reliability (p. 7). In 1992, classroom teachers initially rated the writing and mathematics portfolios, and volunteer teachers provided second ratings for samples of portfolios. Spearman rank order correlations for the writing portfolios ranged from .28 for voice to .57 for usage. In mathematics, correlations ranged from .23 for language of mathematics to .44 for procedures. Potential contributing factors to the low reliability are:

1. Unclear or inconsistent terminology in the scoring rubrics
2. Complexity of the rubrics
3. Insufficient training of raters
4. Lack of standardization of tasks and administrative conditions (Koretz, McCaffrey, Klein, Bell, & Stecher, 1992, pp. 22, 23)

During benchmarking sessions for the writing portfolios, considerable confusion was observed among the teachers about the interpretation of the rubrics. Raters also sometimes disagreed about the applicability of some scoring dimensions to specific attributes of a particular piece (Koretz et al., 1994, p. 12). The lack of standardization of tasks also required raters to stretch general purpose rubrics to the scoring of a wide variety of tasks (p. 120). In contrast, the NAEP writing portfolio trial used unstandardized tasks, but applied genre-specific scoring rubrics. High levels of rater reliability were obtained (Gentile, 1992).

Implementation Issues

Several issues about implementation have been identified in the early applications of portfolio assessment. One is the tension between the different purposes of portfolios in assessment. Koretz et al. (1994) note that the two goals of the Vermont program, quality measurement and instructional improvement, are somewhat in conflict. To improve a program's performance toward one goal may degrade performance in terms of the other (p. 13). Further, raters in one scoring situation, for example, felt constrained by the exclusion of prewriting and early drafts and the lack of student self-assessments. Thus, one concern is that a "top-down" portfolio structure that imposes comparability of contents as a standard could negate some of the "bottom-up" appeal of portfolios for teacher use (Gearhart et al., 1992, p. 25). One proposed solution to this problem is to provide system-level information in another way. First, teachers would maintain portfolios with all their students, and they would be accompanied by the teacher's goals and interpretations of student work. Random samples of classroom portfolios would be collected, and committees of teachers and researchers would develop categories to describe both content and quality of work. Information provided in such an analysis would be the types of projects students are completing, the criteria and standards teachers are using, and the extent of critical or creative thinking encouraged by the projects (Moss et al., 1992, p. 20).

Another issue, as yet not fully addressed, is that of the facets of student accomplishment that can best be portrayed in portfolios. One observation is that the portfolio structure has yet to achieve its potential. Among the important dimensions of portfolios are creativity, perseverance or investment, excitement or interest, and risk taking or willingness to try difficult assignments (Gearhart et al., 1992, p. 22).

A third issue is the time investment associated with implementing portfolio assessment. Studies of classroom use report extensive out-of-class time required to implement portfolios as well as effort to plan individual time with students about their work (Gomez, Grave, & Block, 1991; Lamme & Hysmith, 1991). Also, monitoring the system, keeping up to date, and establishing a routine are difficult (Lamme & Hysmith, 1991, p. 638). In addition, the use of an interpretative approach to the analysis of student portfolios adds about 30 minutes per portfolio in which six to seven writing sequences are addressed (Moss et al., 1991). If portfolio assessments become class and school requirements, adjustments in teacher schedules and/or the assistance of aides for other duties will be required in order to implement portfolios appropriately for all students.

Equity

One of the expectations of portfolios is that they will provide opportunities for less traditionally skilled students to develop their abilities (Wolf et al., 1991). In one study, an analysis of three papers selected by a random sample of fifth graders from their writing portfolios revealed that the lowest writers on a timed writing test showed the biggest gain on the portfolio. Their gain of 2 points on a 6-point scale placed their portfolio scores on the level of the average writers. Also, the lowest group worked the longest (16 days) on papers nearly as lengthy as the highest groups, 410 and 440 words respectively (Simmons, 1990).

However, implementing portfolio assessment in the classroom will not necessarily introduce equity in learning opportunities or evaluation in culturally diverse classrooms. Ball (1993) found, in an analysis of teacher ratings of formative essays, that students who used orally based organizational patterns received lower ratings than those who used linear, explicit, and impersonal writing (p. 264). She described the need for research to investigate the relationship between students' informal usage patterns and the requirements of academic discourse so that bridges may be built in the classroom from one to the other. In the absence of such analyses, differences in communication can lead to inaccurate assessments of students' intentions, capabilities, and motivation (Ball, 1993, p. 274).

Potential Role in Evaluation

At present, four uses of portfolios have been suggested:

1. To showcase students' best work
2. To develop autonomous self-reflective learners
3. To document student growth in relation to major classroom goals
4. To provide a largely standardized reporting of student accomplishments and achievement

Documenting student growth and providing a standardized reporting of student achievement are viewed also as potential mechanisms for systemwide assessment.

Portfolios that showcase students' best work and those used to develop self-reflective autonomous learners are appropriate in developing case studies of programs suggested in Stake's (1973; 1980) responsive evaluation. Stake (1980, p. 294) notes that sometimes the purpose of a program is to provide artistic experiences for *intrinsic* value alone. Thus, the evaluators should not presume that only measurable outcomes provide evidence about a program's worth. Examples of such programs are art, writing, musical performance, and literature. Evaluations of such programs may develop case studies of a random sample of students that consist of portfolios of their work, including the self-reflections and teacher commentaries. Other information included in the case study consists of taped interviews with the students, their parents, and teachers; prose descriptions of student involvement and interest in class activities; and results of attitude questionnaires about the class.

Portfolios used to develop self-reflective learners and those used to document student growth toward curriculum goals can also illustrate intrinsic program value in another way. Moss et al. (1992, p. 20) suggest the collection of random samples of student portfolios accompanied by statements of teacher goals that are then analyzed qualitatively. Categories developed to analyze the portfolios might answer such questions as, What kinds of projects are students working on? Do they encourage self-reflection and revision? Are the teachers' goals reflected in the student work? What criteria and standards are teachers using to evaluate student work? and How are they documenting the validity of these evaluations? (p. 20). Prose summaries of the responses to these questions developed from a coding scheme analysis of the portfolios and reflections can serve as one source of information about the nature of a program.

The difficulty, at present, in using portfolios in program evaluation is the proposed role of providing a standardized reporting of student accomplishments across classrooms, schools, and, perhaps, districts. This role is one of providing evidence of student outcomes of a curriculum or a program; it is problematic, at present, in two ways. First, portfolios imply a different emphasis in the curriculum and a different teaching emphasis. Students are expected to be proficient at tasks that reflect a different philosophy and require a redirection of teacher effort in the classroom. As Chapters 2 and 14 indicate, implementing new ways of thinking and teaching is a difficult and lengthy process. Adequate time and assistance are needed to provide the kinds of teaching essential to fostering the types of outcomes emphasized in portfolio assessment. Until this redirection is implemented, judging a curriculum or a program on the outcomes reflected in the portfolio is problematic at best.

Second, standardized reporting of student accomplishments must meet criteria of validity, reliability, and uniform conditions of administration. For example, one would not want School A to appear to be doing a superb job simply because it uses easy assignments or because students get extensive help at home with their portfolios (Herman et al., 1993, p. 22). Therefore, portfolios with prescribed types of entries should, at present, only be viewed as multiple within-classroom assessments that can provide some indications as to the types of activities implemented in the classroom. Observations of in-class activities may be developed from the portfolio entries to determine the congruence between classroom emphasis and type of student work in the portfolio. Also, portfolio entries can provide information as to the kinds of student performance to seek out in other indicators. For example, a mathematics portfolio may include puzzles to test reasoning and applications to demonstrate student capabilities in solving new problems that incorporate previously taught principles. Therefore, a legitimate evaluation question is, To what extent is class time devoted to developing logical reasoning skills and providing experiences in student transfer of important concepts to new situations?

SUMMARY

Issues identified in portfolio assessment are (1) needed technical specifications for portfolios intended to foster student growth and those intended to document accomplishment, (2) implementation, and (3) potential role in evaluation. At present, two methods have been suggested for evaluating portfolios for fostering student growth. One is a coding scheme that lists important features of a type of work and the extent to which successive student efforts reflect that feature. The other involves the development of scales that reflect progressive stages of the student's development.

An important validity question for both methods is the meaning of terms that are used. The selection of categories and subcategories as representing important characteristics also should be verified through the collection of empirical data. A validity question specific to growth scales is the extent to which the identified stages are major benchmarks of growth and whether they occur in the hypothesized sequence.

Portfolios to assess student accomplishment typically consist of examples of different kinds of student work that are scored to indicate level of achievement. Scoring rubrics may address specific features of the particular work, or they may be clusters of characteristics that represent different levels of competence. Thus, student work may be scored on a single 4-, 5-, or 6-point scale, or different dimensions of the capability may be rated from 1 to 4 or greater on each dimension. The primary validity question for the scoring mechanisms is the constructs or processes that the student example represents.

At present, however, validity has been examined from the perspective of validating portfolio scores with scores assigned to student responses to standardized prompts. Portfolio scores tend to be higher; and the portfolio score also is greater than the average of the scores assigned to individual pieces in the portfolio. Other validity concerns include the extent of external support received by the student, the time involved in working on particular pieces, and so on. Reliability data reported for portfolio assessments in writing is adequate in some situations and less than adequate in others. Other concerns to be addressed are providing for the teacher's time and effort involved in implementing portfolios and the necessity for ensuring equitable assessment of all students.

The lack of technical specifications verified by empirical data limits the use of portfolios in program evaluation. Portfolios that showcase students' best work and those used to develop self-reflective learners can be used in evaluations in which the purpose is to document the intrinsic value of the program. That is, in art, writing, musical performance, and literature, case studies may be developed in which portfolios, taped interviews, and prose descriptions of student involvement document the nature of the program.

Portfolios used to develop self-reflective learners and those used to document student growth also may be analyzed qualitatively. The analysis may address questions about the kinds of projects students engage in, the extent to which self-reflection influences revision, the nature of teacher goals, and so on.

Portfolios intended to provide a standardized reporting of student accomplishments across classrooms, schools, and districts have yet to meet the standardization, validity, and reliability criteria for use in verifying student outcomes. Therefore, at present, they should be viewed as multiple within-class assessments that can indicate the types of classroom observations to conduct. As research and development continues on portfolio assessment, these roles for evaluation may be expanded in the future.

CHAPTER QUESTIONS

1. What are the major differences between performance assessment and within-classroom uses of portfolio assessment?
2. How does the "ideal" format differ from the other types?
3. How do the different uses of portfolio assessment create tension when the same entries are used?

4. What are some of the implementation issues with regard to portfolio assessment?

REFERENCES

Archbald, D., & Newmann, F. (1992). Beyond standardized testing: Assessing authentic academic achievement in the secondary school. In H. Berlak, F. M. Newmann, E. Adams, D. Archbald, T. Burgess, J. Raven, & T. A. Romberg, *Toward a new science of educational testing and assessment* (pp. 139–180). Albany, NY: State University of New York Press.

Baker, E., Freeman, M., & Clayton, S. (1991). Cognitive assessment of history for large-scale testing. In M. Wittrock & E. Baker (Eds.), *Testing and cognition* (pp. 131–153). Englewood Cliffs, NJ: Prentice Hall.

Ball, A. (1993). Incorporating ethnographic-based techniques to enhance assessments of culturally diverse students' written exposition. *Educational Assessment, 1*(3), 255–281.

Darling-Hammond, L. (1989). Accountability for professional practice. *Teachers College Record, 91*(10), 59–80.

Gearhart, M., Herman, J., Baker, E., & Whittaker, A. (1992). *Writing portfolios: Potential for large-scale assessment.* Los Angeles: Center for the Study of Evaluation, University of California.

Gentile, C. (1992). *Exploring new methods for collecting students' school-based writing: NAEP's 1990 portfolio study.* Washington, DC: National Center for Educational Statistics.

Gomez, M., Grave, M., & Block, M. (1991). Reassessing portfolio assessment: Rhetoric and reality. *Language Arts, 68,* 620–628.

Herman, J., Gearhart, M., & Baker, E. (1993). Assessing writing portfolios: Issues in the validity and meaning of scores. *Educational Assessment, 1*(3), 201–224.

Koretz, D., McCaffrey, D., Klein, S., Bell, R., & Stecher, B. (1992, December). *The reliability of scores from the 1992 Vermont portfolio assessment program, interim report.* Santa Monica, CA: The Rand Institute on Education and Training.

Koretz, D., Stecher, S., & Deibert, E. (1992, July). *The Vermont Portfolio Assessment Program: Interim report on implementation and impact, 1991–92 school year.* Santa Monica, CA: Rand Corporation.

Koretz, D., Stecher, B., Klein, S., & McCaffrey, D. (1994). The Vermont portfolio assessment program: Findings and implications. *Educational Measurement: Issues and Practice, 13*(3), 5–16.

Lamme, L., & Hysmith, C. (1991). One school's adventure into portfolio assessment. *Language Arts, 68,* 629–640.

Meyer, C., Schumann, S., & Angello, N. (1990). *NWEA white paper on aggregating portfolio data.* Lake Oswego, OR: Northwest Evaluation Association.

Mitchell, R. (1992). *Testing for learning.* New York: The Free Press.

Moss, P., Beck, J., Ebbs, C., Matson, B., Muchmore, J., Steele, D., Taylor, C., & Herter, R. (1992). Portfolios, accountability and an interpretative approach to validity. *Educational Measurement: Issues and Practice, 11*(3), 12–21.

Purves, A. (1993). Setting standards in the language arts and literature classroom and the implications for portfolio assessment. *Educational Assessment, 1*(3), 175–200.

Simmons, J. (1990). Portfolios as large-scale assessment. *Language Arts, 67*(3), 262–268.

Stake, R. (1973, October). Program evaluation, particularly responsive evaluation. Paper presented at the conference *New Trends in Evaluation*, Goteborg, Sweden. Reprinted (1980) in G. Madaus, M. Scriven, & D. Stufflebeam (Eds.), *Evaluation models*. Boston, MA: Kluwer-Nijhoff.

Valencia, S., & Calfee, R. (1991). The development and use of literacy portfolios for students. *Applied Measurement in Education, 4*(3), 333–346.

Wolf, D. (1987, December/1988, January). Opening up assessment. *Educational Leadership, 45*(4), 24–29.

Wolf, D. (1989). Portfolio assessment: Sampling student work. *Educational Leadership, 46*(7), 35–39.

Wolf, D., Bixby, J., Glenn, J., & Gardner, H. (1991). To use their minds well: Investigating new forms of student assessment. In G. Grant (Ed.), *Review of Research in Education, Vol. 17* (pp. 32–73). Washington, DC, AERA.

CHAPTER 9

Assessment of Affective Characteristics

Affective characteristics are nonobservable internal characteristics of persons that arise from or include an emotional component. Affective characteristics consist of appreciations, attitudes, adjustments, interests, and values, as well as feelings about oneself, such as self-concept, self-esteem, and self-efficacy.

Affective characteristics are constructs that are indirectly related to behavior. Self-efficacy, for example, is the belief that one can be successful in or master particular situations (Bandura, 1986). Students with high self-efficacy strengthen their effort in the face of difficulties, focus attention on the demands of the situation, and exhibit persistence. Students with low self-efficacy, in contrast, slacken their efforts, may give up entirely when faced with difficulties, and focus their attention on their perceived personal deficiencies (Bandura, 1986).

During the period of rapid development of norm-referenced achievement tests in the early twentieth century, efforts also were directed toward developing instruments to measure affective characteristics. One expectation was that information about attitudes might be used to predict subsequent behavior. However, this expectation was not realized for several reasons. First, defining the nature of affective constructs is a difficult task. Social attitudes, for example, may be taken to mean any or all of the following: concern for the welfare of others, respect for laws, respect for the property of others, sensitivity to social issues, concern for social institutions, and the desire to work toward social improvement (Linn & Gronlund, 1995).

Second, establishing links between affective characteristics and particular actions is difficult. Third, responses to paper-and-pencil measures of affective characteristics can be influenced by a range and variety of unrelated factors. Thus, behavioral changes in personal-social development are particularly difficult to assess with paper-and-pencil tests (Linn & Gronlund, 1995, p. 265).

167

Some interventions establish affective objectives in addition to cognitive objectives. Frequently, however, these objectives are not measurable because they can only be realized sometime in the future or are stated in vague terms. The Head Start goal of fostering social development is an example. Such goals should be translated into observable behaviors that are realistic for the project to achieve, such as the children learning to take turns and helping one another.

Some programs, such as the Minnesota Outward Bound Program, may be designed primarily to impact the thoughts and feelings of participants. Others, particularly new curricula, consider that contributing to the development of positive attitudes toward a subject area or discipline is an important objective.

Evaluation staff should carefully consider the nature of affective objectives and their importance when planning a study of an intervention. Some states have laws prohibiting the use of personality tests in the schools. A homemade questionnaire that attempts to assess growth in self-esteem could easily be viewed by some as in the category of a personality test (Henerson, Morris, & Fitz-Gibbon, 1987, p. 17).

CATEGORIES OF AFFECTIVE CHARACTERISTICS

Affective characteristics are constructs. Like cognitive constructs, such as ability and aptitude, they are hypothesized characteristics that are indirectly related to observable events. Affective characteristics, in other words, are inferred from the statements or actions of individuals.

Major Types

The domain of affective characteristics may be conceptualized in different ways. Table 9.1 illustrates one useful analysis. A component of appreciations, for example, is feelings of satisfaction or enjoyment toward broad areas of accomplishment, such as music. Interests, in contrast, are preferences for engaging in particular activities, such as working with computers, camping, and so on. Adjustments refer to interactions with peers and authority figures and one's reactions to social situations. Attitudes are tendencies to respond favorably or unfavorably to particular targets, such as school and school subjects or different ethnic groups. Values are beliefs that are abstract standards for behavior. In contrast, self-attitudes are positive or negative self-worth beliefs constructed by the individual.

Affective characteristics differ from each other in intensity, stability, and presumed influence on behavior. Self-esteem and self-concept, for example, begin to develop in early childhood, are formed over several years, are highly stable, and influence students' achievement-related actions (Bandura, 1986). Interests, in contrast, may change at different ages and in different contexts. For some individuals, interests involve the casual choice of leisure-time activities while, for others, they develop into intensive avocations.

Table 9.1
An analysis of the affective domain

Affective Category	Definition
Appreciations	"Feelings of satisfaction and enjoyment expressed toward music, art, literature, outstanding social contributions" (Linn & Gronlund, 1995, p. 266)
Attitudes	Learned predispositions to respond favorably or unfavorably to an object (Fishbein & Ajzen, 1975; Gagne, 1977)
Adjustments	"Relationships to peers; reactions to praise, criticism, and authority; emotional stability; social adaptability" (Linn & Gronlund, 1995, p. 266)
Interests	Preferences for engaging in particular activities
Values	Abstract standards that may be aesthetic, economic, political, social, or theoretical (Rokeach, 1973)
Self-attitudes	Positive or negative self-worth beliefs constructed by the individual (includes self-esteem, self-concept, and self-efficacy)

Attitudes Toward Subject Areas

A concern of program developers is the attitudes toward a subject area or discipline that may be generated by new materials or interventions. Of importance, for example, is that an intervention not produce competency at the expense of negative attitudes toward the subject.

Also important is that attitudes toward a subject area should not be confused with course satisfaction. Attitudes are "meanings or beliefs, not mere expressions of approval or disapproval" (Cronbach, 1963, p. 678). One's attitude toward science, for example, consists of (1) ideas about the matters on which science can provide definitive information and (2) the benefits that can be derived from various scientific endeavors, such as interplanetary exploration, genetic studies, and so on.

Another important component of attitudes toward a subject is the match between the student's self-concept and his/her concept of the field. For example, What roles does science offer someone like me? Would I want to marry a scientist? In other words, learning activities can contribute to perceptions that reach beyond any one subject, such as the student's sense of his/her own competence and desire to learn (Cronbach, 1963, p. 679). Instruments developed to assess attitudes toward a subject should also address these issues.

Course Satisfaction

As already stated, course satisfaction differs from attitudes toward a content area or discipline. Important dimensions of a comprehensive course satisfaction instrument are relevance of the topics, likes and dislikes, strengths and weaknesses, and recommendations.

Instruments that assess course, program, or workshop satisfaction typically ask participants to rate key aspects of the experience. However, they often address information that is interesting or nice to know, but such information is not useful in program evaluation. Instead, items should address information related to decisions to be made about the course, workshop, or program. The three general categories of program-related decisions are (1) content, (2) instructional activities, and (3) logistics. For example, program participants can indicate which topics were most relevant for them and which activities contributed most to their learning. Participants also should be asked to evaluate the strengths and weaknesses of the program, workshop, or course.

Information for a formal questionnaire should first be obtained from a focus group of participants or interviews with selected representatives of the target group. In this way, the items included in the instrument will be meaningful to the participants. Then the procedures described in Chapter 5 for the development of opinion surveys should be followed. In addition, any instrument assessing participant opinions about a course should include a separate sheet asking for respondents' comments and recommendations.

Opinions Versus Feelings

In obtaining information from individuals about courses, programs, or other interventions, opinions and feelings are sometimes confused (Patton, 1990). For example, in an interview, the question, "How do you feel about that?" may be followed by the answer, "I think it's the best we can do under the circumstances" (p. 291). Although the question addressed feelings, the response was an opinion. Interviewers should understand the difference so that they will know when the question they are asking has been answered. Understanding the difference is also important for instrument construction. Measuring attitudes involves obtaining information about predispositions that involve feelings. Typically, the purpose also is to determine the strength and direction of the attitude. An example of an item on an attitude questionnaire is, "I would like to take a course that teaches me to write poetry" (Hills, 1981, p. 373).

In contrast, an opinion survey seeks to obtain information on a group's position on particular issues, policies, program characteristics, activities, and so on. An example for students is, "I think students should be chosen to clean erasers on the basis of their good behavior" (Hills, 1981, p. 373). The choices may be simply "agree/disagree" or "strongly agree," "agree," "disagree," "strongly disagree." Results of an opinion survey are reported as the percentages of the total group that chose each option, because the purpose of the survey is to identify group perspectives, not individual scores.

Summary

Affective characteristics are nonobservable, internal characteristics of persons that arise from or include an emotional component. Affective characteristics are constructs that are indirectly related to behavior. One expectation of the early test development of attitude measures was to be able to predict behavior. However, this expectation was not realized.

Some interventions establish affective objectives that are distant goals or broad statements. These objectives should be translated into observable behaviors that are realistic for the intervention to accomplish. Evaluation staff also should carefully consider the nature of affective objectives for an intervention and their importance when planning a study. Some states prohibit the use of personality tests, and project-developed instruments to test constructs such as self-esteem may be suspect.

The domain of affective characteristics can be conceptualized in different ways. One analysis is appreciations, interests, adjustments, attitudes, and values. Of importance in program evaluation is that attitudes toward a subject area should not be confused with course satisfaction. Attitudes are meanings or beliefs about a subject area or discipline that also include the match between the student's self-concept and his/her concept of the field. Course satisfaction instruments, in contrast, should ask participants to rate key aspects of the course, program, or workshop. Key dimensions of a comprehensive course satisfaction instrument are relevance of the topics, likes and dislikes, strengths and weaknesses, and recommendations.

Important in obtaining information from participants about interventions is that opinions differ from feelings. Attitudes involve feelings, but opinions reflect an individual's perspective on particular issues, policies, and so on.

MEASUREMENT OF INTERESTS AND ATTITUDES

In addition to course satisfaction, assessing interests and attitudes may be a component in program evaluation. Types of instruments that can be useful in measuring these characteristics are rating scales and observation systems.

The development and validation of affective instruments is a lengthy and time-consuming process. Therefore, the evaluator is advised to review commercially available instruments rather than to undertake development, unless the project is a multiyear effort. A useful source of test reviews is *Test Critiques,* which is published by Test Corporation of America every 2 to 3 years. The exception to the rule of avoiding the instrument development process is the design of classroom observation scales or checklists that are tailored to the particular intervention (see the following section).

Rating Scales

A scale is a set of related statements, questions, or adjectives that is constructed to yield information about a single affective characteristic. The most frequently used type of scale is the Likert scale. Instruments that use the Likert scale format typically list an equal number of positive and negative items. Each item is followed by a set of response options that usually consist of "strongly agree," "agree," "undecided," "disagree," and "strongly disagree." For some statements, the responses "often," "frequently," "seldom," and "never" are appropriate. A variation on the original Likert format is to use incomplete statements for which adjectives or other terms are the choices for completion of the statement (Anderson, 1990). An example is, When art class is canceled, I feel (a) very sad, (b) sad, (c) happy, (d) very happy.

Numerical values are assigned to the responses for each item; for example, 5 = strongly agree, 4 = agree, and so on. After the instrument is administered, and prior to scoring, the weights assigned to the responses for the negative items are reversed. In other words, "strongly agree" for the negative statements becomes 1, "agree" becomes 2, and so on. The purpose of reversing the values attached to the negative statements is that *agreement* with a negative statement represents *disagreement* with the basic construct, and should be recorded as such. The numerical values for the respondents' answers to positive items and the reversed values for negative items are then summed for a total score.

Chapter 6 discussed the use of rating scales in relation to student achievement. Rating scales also are used to determine attitudes, interests, teacher and student behaviors, and constructs such as classroom climate. The two general types are self-report measures and judgements by others.

Self-Report Scales.   A self-report is any measurement technique in which an individual serves as both the observer and the object of the observation (Newfield, 1990, p. 146). Typically, self-report scales consist of a set of statements, questions, or adjectives. Respondents are asked to indicate the extent of agreement or disagreement with each statement, an answer to each question, or whether they would use the adjective to describe some object, activity, or idea.

The major problem with self-report scales is that respondents may provide misinformation. Two major factors that contribute to misinformation are social desirability and acquiescence. Social desirability refers to situations in which individuals may provide answers that they believe the researcher is seeking. Or they may respond in ways that appear to them to be socially desirable or important. Social desirability tends to increase when the instrument includes very personal questions and when the information is to be used for selection of individuals for a job, a promotion, or entry into a school program (Anderson, 1981). The social desirability factor can be reduced by (1) excluding or reworking items from the scale that are likely to elicit socially desirable responses, (2) ensuring the anonymity of respondents, and (3) instructing the participants that there are no right or wrong answers (p. 70).

The problem of acquiescence refers to the tendency to respond positively to statements or questions when the respondent is uncertain or ambivalent (Cronbach, 1970). Acquiescence is likely to occur when the respondent has no strong feelings about the program, topic, or issue or lacks understanding of it (Anderson, 1981). This tendency can be controlled to a degree by using an instrument with an equal number of favorable and unfavorable items that are arranged in random order (Anderson, 1981).

Judgments by Others.   Rating scales also may be developed for individuals to make decisions about the characteristics of objects, events, or other individuals. However, in program evaluation, instruments in which students choose in rank order the others they most want to work with should not be used. (These instruments are referred to as sociometric devices.) The use of such instruments can lead to adverse effects on those identified as unpopular when participants discuss their choices among themselves (Henerson et al., 1987, p. 17).

Other types of judgement scales are useful, however. Recall in Chapter 6 that judgement scales were developed for first-grade teachers to evaluate the achievement of the children in their classes.

A typical use of rating scales in program evaluation is for trained observers to spend time in the classroom using instruments to rate the presence or frequency of certain behaviors. Rating scales typically require the observer to watch the object of the observation for a set period of time (Stallings & Mohlman, 1990, p. 640). The time may be 5 to 60 minutes. Then, the observer rates the prevalence of specific behaviors observed during that period (p. 640).

Ratings may be used to assess high-inference behaviors that can be observed over continuous time. Examples are teacher enthusiasm or student cooperativeness. Subjectivity is one disadvantage of the rating scale, however. Therefore, specific definitions of the different scale points are needed. In addition, observers must undergo training until acceptable interrater agreement is obtained (Stallings & Mohlman, 1990).

Quality of Rating Scales

An affective scale should meet five important criteria prior to use. They are communication value, objectivity, validity, reliability, and interpretability (Anderson, 1981). Communication value refers to the extent that the directions are clear and the target group can read and understand the items. The directions should clearly state the nature of the task and specify the general purpose of the scale. They also should indicate that there are no right or wrong answers. Although readability formulas should be applied to the scale, formative evaluation with members of the target group also is essential to assess communicability.

Objectivity refers to the extent to which a person's score on an instrument is free of scorer error or bias. With Likert scales, the typical format for rating scales, the scoring rules are explicit, and objectivity is typically not a problem. Points are assigned to the ratings indicated by each respondent (negative items are scored inversely), the scores for the items are summed. (Some scales specify that the total is divided by the number of items.)

Validity.   Validity refers to the appropriateness of the inferences that may be made from scores obtained on an instrument. Validity is jeopardized by vague descriptors that require interpretation by the respondents, complex sentences that are difficult to understand, and a lack of relationship between the statements on the instrument and the affective characteristic being measured. Therefore, statements that are ambiguous or use the word *not* should be avoided. Each statement also should consist of only one idea and be in the form of a simple sentence. The developer of the instrument also should describe the process by which items were selected to reflect the affective characteristic.

Rating scales that are used to assess important pupil characteristics, such as self-esteem, self-concept, and anxiety, also should be subjected to empirical validity analyses. Two important approaches are factor analysis and the method referred to as known-group comparisons. Factor analysis is a correlational technique that identifies the items on a test that cluster together, and each cluster reflects a separate factor. (The test developer must examine the items in each cluster to determine the nature of the construct that is measured.) Of importance is that only items with at least a correlation of .40 with the factor should be retained on the final form of the instrument.

The method of known-group comparisons first requires the identification of groups that are believed to differ on the affective characteristic under consideration (Anderson, 1981, p. 133). For example, high and low achievers would be expected to differ in motivation and academic goal orientation. The affective instrument is then administered to members of the two groups. Performance of the two groups on the affective instrument should differ. Students with a high or low interest in reading, for example, should differ in their responses to an instrument measuring attitude toward reading.

Instruments to assess affective characteristics that are commercially available or disseminated to interested individuals should be accompanied by manuals that document the method of development. Validity information provided in the manual should describe the characteristics of the groups that participated in the validation studies and the methods used to determine the validity of the instrument.

Reliability.   The two types of reliability that are often determined for affective instruments are internal consistency and stability. One internal consistency approach is to divide the scale into two parts (odd and even items) and compute the correlation between the scores on the two sections. This method, however, reduces the length of the original scale, which reduces the reliability estimate.

Internal consistency also can be determined using Cronbach's alpha coefficient. This coefficient is appropriate for items in which more than two answers are possible. Formulas used with achievement tests, in which the answers are either right or wrong, are not appropriate for affective scales.

Determining the stability of an affective instrument requires administering the instrument at two different points in time to the same group and calculating the correlation between the two sets of scores. The stability coefficient is likely to be higher, however, if the time period between testing is a few weeks rather than several months or longer.

Reliability coefficients for affective instruments, unlike reliability estimates for standardized achievement tests, rarely exceed the mid .80s. Also, reliabilities often are sample specific and may range from .48 to .79 (Anderson, 1981). Therefore, a careful comparison of the sample used for the reliability estimate for a standardized instrument with the group in the proposed study or evaluation is important prior to selection of a particular scale.

Observation Systems

Observations of behavior may serve as the basis for documenting the types of activities individuals engage in, their actions, and the kinds of interactions they have with others. Observations also may serve as the basis for inferences about individuals' affective characteristics. In the classroom, the focus of an observation may be, for example:

1. The teacher

2. Teacher's interactions with individual students, a small group, or the class

3. Individual students

4. Student interactions with one or more other students (Henerson et al., 1987, p. 120)

Examples of behaviors that may be the focus of the observation are nonverbal aspects of interactions, such as smiling, number and type of interactions, types of statements or questions, attentive-inattentive behaviors, and types of vocal expression (such as praising) (p. 121).

Several elements are common to all observational techniques. These elements are illustrated in Table 9.2. The importance of operational definitions is to guide observers to assign the same value or category to the observed event (Stallings & Mohlman, 1990, p. 639). Comparison of observer identifications to a stated criterion is a mechanism for determining the validity of observer inferences. Typically, interrater agreement is accepted as evidence of reliability. Of importance is that training procedures for observers are essential to ensure consistency of decisions.

Types of observation systems are rating scales (discussed in the prior section), narrative descriptions (Chapter 10), interactive coding systems, and checklists. An interactive coding system permits the observer to record all the actions and oral statements of the teacher or student during a specified time segment (Stallings & Mohlman, 1990, p. 642). The typical time segment is 5 minutes spaced evenly throughout the class period. Categories of teacher and student talk and a coding system that identifies sequences as well as the speaker are essential for this method of observation. Disadvantages of interactive coding systems are (1) that some of the quality of the interaction is not captured in the observation, (2) that the content of the lesson is lost, and (3) that 5- to 7-day training sessions are essential for reliable data collection (p. 643).

A checklist is a set of key behaviors that represent the construct of interest. The number should be fewer than 10, and the behaviors should be arranged in a logical sequence (Henerson et al., 1987, p. 121). The observer may be required to simply check the occurrence of the behavior or record a tally each time the behavior is observed. A more sophisticated form of a checklist is a two-dimensional chart that can combine activities and materials, for example. An advantage of checklists is that observers can be easily trained to use them. A disadvantage is that only a limited set of events can be recorded (Stallings & Mohlman, 1990, p. 640).

Table 9.2
Common elements of observation systems

Element	Description
Purpose	May be research; evaluation of teacher performance; evaluation of a child's social, physical or cognitive development; or program implementation.
Operational Definitions	State explicitly the behaviors that represent each attribute.
Training Procedure	Paired observers record the same events in the natural settings; calculate inter-rater agreement and compare observer identifications to a correct criterion.
Observation Focus	Teacher, aide, child, class, or activities.
Setting	Classroom, school grounds, hallways, cafeterias, staff room, and so on.
Unit of Time	Seconds, minutes, hours, or days.
Observation Schedule	Pretest/posttest or more frequently, and a set time of day for several days.
Methods of Recording Data	Audiotape, videotape, optical scan forms, or paper-and-pencil forms.
Methods of Processing Data	Frequency counts, percent of occurrences, scores on rating scales, presence or absence of events, or quality statements.

Summarized from Stallings and Mohlman, 1990.

Summary

Two types of instruments for assessing attitudes and interests are rating scales and observation systems. A rating scale is a set of related statements, questions, or adjectives that is constructed to yield information about a single affective characteristic. The most frequently used type is the Likert scale. The instrument lists an approximately equal number of positive and negative items with a set of response options for each. The options represent a range of reactions, typically from "strongly agree" to "strongly disagree." A variation is the incomplete statement format in which adjectives are the set of possible responses.

The two major types of rating scales are self-report and judgement by others. The major problem with self-report scales is that respondents may provide misinformation. Two contributing factors to this problem are social desirability and acquiescence. Methods for reducing these problems are (1) ensuring anonymity of respondents, (2) instructing participants that there are no right or wrong answers, and (3) using an instrument with an equal number of favorable and unfavorable items arranged in random order.

Rating scales also are developed for individuals to rate objects, events, or other individuals. However, in program evaluation, instruments in which students rank order others they most want to work with should not be used. Referred to as sociometric devices, these instruments tend to precipitate negative effects when students informally discuss their choices among themselves.

A typical use of rating scales in program evaluation is by trained observers. The individual watches the object of the observation for a set period of time and then rates the specific behaviors observed during that time period. Rating scales also may be used to asses high-inference behaviors, such as student cooperativeness. Because subjectivity is a disadvantage of these instruments, observers should undergo training until acceptable agreement is obtained.

The five important qualities for an affective scale are communication value, objectivity, validity, reliability, and interpretability. Communication value refers to the clarity of the directions, and objectivity refers to the extent the individual's score is free of bias.

Validity refers to the appropriateness of the inferences that may be made from the scores. It is jeopardized by vague descriptors, complex sentences, and a lack of relationship between statements on the instrument and the characteristic being measured. Rating scales used to assess important pupil characteristics, such as self-esteem and anxiety, should be subjected to empirical validity analyses. Two important empirical approaches are factor analysis and known-group comparisons. The methods used to determine validity also should be reported in the test manual for the instrument.

Reliability refers to the consistency or stability of the instrument in measuring the particular characteristic. A frequently used method for classroom observations is interrater agreement. Methods used for self-report instruments are internal consistency (Cronbach's alpha coefficient) and test-retest reliability. Reliability coefficients for affective measures, unlike standardized achievement tests, rarely exceed the mid .80s.

Rating scales may be self-report instruments or judgments by others. Rating scales used by individuals to record events in a particular setting are one type of observation system. Others are narrative descriptions, interactive coding systems, and checklists. Interactive coding systems may be constructed to record teacher-student exchanges for specific time segments, but both lesson content and some interaction quality are lost. They also require several days for training. A checklist is a set of key behaviors that represent the construct of interest. The observer may be required to simply check the occurrence of the behavior or record a tally each time the behavior is observed. Although observers can be easily trained to use checklists, they address only a limited set of events.

OTHER METHODS OF DETERMINING ATTITUDES AND INTERESTS

Methods of obtaining information about interests and attitudes other than formal instruments are semi-structured and standardized open-ended interviews, nonreactive measures, and secondary indicators. Semi-structured interviews, which also may be used in relation to belief systems, are discussed later in this chapter.

Standardized Open-Ended Interviews

The standardized open-ended interview consists of (1) a set order of carefully worded questions and (2) clarifications, elaborations, and probing follow-up questions (Patton, 1990, p. 285).

Standardized open-ended interviews are useful in program evaluation in several ways. First, in formative evaluation, they can assist in determining which program components elicited negative reactions and which components were perceived as effective. Second, through the inclusion of follow-up questions, the interviews can probe unexpected reactions or feelings that may go undetected with a questionnaire. Third, they are important when (1) the major purpose of a program or project is to impact the thoughts and feelings of program recipients and (2) the participants can only be interviewed before and after program implementation (Patton, 1990). In such a situation, the preselected questions readily provide for an analysis of prepost differences.

A disadvantage of interviews is that they are time consuming to administer; the data analysis is time consuming as well. Another is that training and practice are essential for effective interviewing.

Example.   The Minnesota Outward Bound Course for the Disabled was developed to impact the thoughts and feelings of participants. The evaluators implemented pre-post standardized open-ended interviews to assess the effects. The precourse interview consisted of nine questions, with some subquestions. Topics included:

1. How the student became involved in the course
2. The process in deciding to participate
3. Feelings about the decision
4. Course expectations
5. Thoughts about different relationships with nondisabled and disabled participants
6. Ways the interviewee typically faces new situations

The general questions also were accompanied by probing subquestions. For example, question 3 asked, "Now that you've made the decision to go on the course, how do you feel about it?" The subsequent probes were "(a) How would you describe your feelings right now?" and "(b) What lingering doubts or concerns do you have?" (Patton, 1990, p. 364).

The precourse interview addressed expectations and feelings about the decision to participate. The immediate postcourse interview addressed the extent to which students' expectations were realized and their feelings about the program. They also were asked, "What is it about the course that makes it have the effects it has?" and "What happens on the course that makes a difference?" (Patton, 1990, p. 365). Finally, the students were asked what they would say to a government agency that expressed interest in sponsoring a similar course. A follow-up interview 6 months later focused on their feelings at that point in time and their view of the main components of the course.

Interview Construction.   Of importance is that questions should not be "yes/no" questions. Instead, they should be open ended to elicit the interviewee's perspective. Also, "why" questions should be avoided unless a specific reason for the question is identified. In other words, the question, "Why did you join this program?" should be replaced with the more focused question, "What is it about the program that attracted you to it?" (Patton, 1990, p. 315).

Questions also should be value neutral and not contribute to a response set by the interviewees. In the Career Intern Program, students were asked, "What do you think of CIP?" "What do you like about the program?" and "What do you dislike about the program?" (Fetterman, 1980, p. 36).

Table 9.3 illustrates the content areas that can be addressed in a standardized interview. As indicated, the questions can provide information about the nature of program activities as well as student feelings about the program.

Essential Requirements for Conducting Interviews.   Preparation for the interview is as important as conducting the interview itself. First, the interviewer should contact the prospective respondents personally; this task should not be left to a secretary (Guba & Lincoln, 1981, p. 172). A follow-up letter that confirms the purpose, date, place, time, and approximate length of the session should be sent to each respondent. Second, the draft interview script is implemented with trial respondents prior to actual use. This step is very important because the placement and wording or probes must be adjusted to the variations that respondents offer in their answers

Table 9.3
Content areas for interview questions

Areas[1]	Examples
Examples	"If I had been in the program with you, what would I have seen you doing?" (Patton, 1990, p. 290)
Opinion	What do you think about the inservice program? "Would you recommend that other schools adopt this program? What do you see as the most important components of the program?"
Feelings	How did you feel about working on class projects with a group?
Sensory	"When you walk through the doors of the program, what do you see?" (Patton, 1990, p. 292)
Knowledge	What activities are in the program?
Background/Demographic	Age, education, occupation, years of experience, etc.

[1]Summarized from Patton, 1990.

(Goetz & LeCompte, 1984, p. 128). After tryouts and revisions are completed, the interview guide is ready for use in the study itself.

The key to quality information in interviews is a genuine interest in the perspectives of others, the skill of careful listening, and skill in constructing and implementing interviews (Guba & Lincoln, 1981; Patton, 1990). Perhaps the most important skill is the ability of the listener to become immersed in the respondent's frame of reference and to "hear" on most of the levels on which the respondent is speaking (Guba & Lincoln, 1981, p. 176).

The surroundings for the interview should be comfortable, and if possible, a private office should be used. The interviewer should preface the session by (1) stating again the purpose of the study, (2) assuring the respondent of anonymity, and (3) explaining the importance of the respondent's thoughts and observations (Bernard, 1988, p. 226). At this point, permission should be obtained from the interviewee to record the session. The use of a tape recorder increases the accuracy of the data and allows the interviewer to be more attentive to the respondent (Patton, 1990, p. 348). The interviewer should take notes about the interview itself, where hesitation occurred, relevant body language of the respondent, and so on.

Most interviewers begin with demographic questions because they are addressed easily by the respondent. Also, they serve to relax the interviewee prior to the introduction of more complex questions (Goetz & LeCompte, 1984). The more difficult or controversial questions are usually placed either in the middle or toward the end of the interview, after rapport has established with the respondent (p. 129). At the conclusion of the session, the interviewer should thank the respondent for his or her time and information. A thank-you letter also should be sent to the respondent immediately (Guba & Lincoln, 1981, p. 183).

Unobtrusive or Nonreactive Measures

Self-report instruments and interviews present questions, events, and other information to which individuals respond. They are, therefore, referred to as reactive measures. A problem with such measures is that individuals may be influenced by the process of measurement itself. They then respond in ways that do not reflect their true attitudes.

Another approach to obtaining information about attitudes is that of unobtrusive or nonreactive measures. These measures consist of (1) physical traces of behavior and (2) archival records and other documents. An example of physical traces is the wear and tear on vinyl tiles around an exhibit of live, hatching chicks in the Chicago Museum of Science and History (Webb, Campbell, Schwartz, & Sechrest, 1966). The exhibit was so popular that the tiles had to be replaced every six weeks.

The documentation of physical traces and the analysis of written documents are referred to as qualitative methods because they yield data in the form of words (see Chapter 10). In the Career Intern Program (CIP) for minority youth dropouts, documentation of the presence or absence of graffiti in the rest rooms served as an indicator of student respect for "their" building. Student reactions when graffiti was found also indicated attitudes toward and involvement with the program (Fetterman,

1980, p. 40). Students at two sites stated "this was not right . . . this is not no dump and we won't let it be either" (p. 40).

Documentation of student poetry published in the school newspaper in the CIP program also provided evidence of student attitudes. An example is the selection entitled "CIP Means" (Fetterman, 1988).

> CIP means people who care. CIP means people who share. CIP means a step along the way. CIP means looking forward to a better day. CIP means a great deal. CIP means being for real. . . . But most of all, CIP means success (p. 56).

Secondary Indicators

Secondary indicators are behaviors that are not direct outcomes of the interventions but are logical hypothesized indirect outcomes. Examples are tardiness, absenteeism, and number of students participating in clubs related to a subject area.

Some researchers refer to secondary indicators as unobtrusive measures because the participant is not confronted with a form of assessment. However, unobtrusive measures are traces of prior behavior that are presumed to be spontaneous; that is, they are not reactions to institutional pressures or the evaluation itself.

In contrast, secondary indicators, because they are human behaviors, may be either "contaminated" or "corrupted." A contaminated indicator is one that can be the result of other causes. For example, a student may enroll in a club because her friends also have enrolled, and not because of interest in the topic or subject. Similarly, the number of times books on art or painting are checked out of the library often is cited as an example of possible secondary effects of a new art appreciation course. However, the students may be enrolled in other humanities courses that require projects on aesthetic contributions of other cultures. Several students may choose art as their topic because of familiarity from the prior course, not increased interest.

Corruptible measures, in contrast, are those behaviors that may be affected without affecting the underlying phenomenon (Cooley & Bickel, 1986, p. 61). For example, school suspensions may be monitored as an index of school climate. If a high number of suspensions is likely to lead to questions about the principal's leadership, some principals may modify their behavior in issuing or reporting suspensions (p. 61). The school climate, however, is unchanged.

Indicators are more likely to be corrupted if rewards or punishments are associated with extreme values on the measures. Therefore, choosing indicators of program or school characteristics that are part of an administrator's or supervisor's professional responsibility should be avoided. In addition, secondary indicators should be used only in conjunction with other measurements. Also, potential alternative causes should be identified.

Summary

Methods other than formal instruments for assessing attitudes and interests are interviews, unobtrusive or nonreactive measures, and secondary indicators. The standardized open-ended interview consists of a set order of carefully worded questions that have been developed in advance. Interviews are useful in program evaluation in several ways. They can provide information about students' perceptions of program components, and they can probe students' unexpected reactions or feelings. They are important when (1) the major purpose of a program is to impact the thoughts and feelings of program recipients and (2) the participants can only be interviewed before and after program implementation. Disadvantages of interviews are that both the administration and data analysis are time consuming.

Interview questions should be open ended to elicit the interviewee's perspective. They also should be value neutral and not contribute to a response set by the participants. The key to quality information in interviews is a genuine interest in the perspectives of others, the skill of careful listening, and skill in framing and using the questions.

Unobtrusive or nonreactive measures can also provide information about attitudes. Unobtrusive measures consist of physical traces of behavior and archival records and other documents. Examples are defacement of school property and articles or poetry published by students in the school newspaper. Secondary indicators are behaviors that are not direct outcomes of the intervention but which may be influenced by the intervention. Some researchers refer to secondary indicators as unobtrusive measures because the participant is not confronted with a form of assessment. However, unobtrusive measures are traces of prior behavior that are presumed to be spontaneous; that is, they are not reactions to institutional pressures or the evaluation itself. Secondary indicators, in contrast, may be either contaminated or corrupted. A contaminated indicator is one that can be the result of other causes. Corruptible measures are those behaviors that may be altered without affecting the underlying phenomenon. For example, the reporting of school suspensions may change even though the school climate has not changed.

ASSESSING VALUES AND BELIEF SYSTEMS

Values are generally considered to be more complex than predispositions toward or away from a particular class of objects, events, or activities. The term *middle-class values,* for example, refers to a strong work ethic, responsibility for one's behavior, and, typically, a belief that success depends on one's own efforts.

A belief is a person's disposition with respect to the truth of a proposition. Smith and Shepard (1988, p. 308) note that beliefs are similar to emotional attitudes, because one may believe a proposition without realizing it, and beliefs can be unconscious or repressed. Beliefs differ from knowledge in that knowledge is based on fact. In the elementary school classroom, teacher beliefs refer to the propositions about development and early learning that the teacher holds to be true (p. 309).

Some instruments to assess values for research purposes have been developed. An example is the *Survey of Work Values,* which assesses the meaning that a person attaches to work in a general sense in contrast to attitudes toward a particular job.

Two methods of determining values or beliefs appropriate for program evaluation are semi-structured interviews and judgment-capturing experiments.

Semi-Structured Interviews

The semi-structured interview is based on an interview guide in which the issues to be explored are outlined in advance. The purpose of the guide is to ensure that basically the same information is obtained from all of the respondents. The interviewer, however, is free to use a conversational format.

Semi-structured interviews are appropriate in program evaluations in which the same types of information are needed from interviewees. Among the examples are student perceptions of and reactions to materials and activities in a formative evaluation and parent perceptions of a new curriculum or program.

Semi-structured interviews also are useful in determining the belief systems of individuals. Belief systems are often tacit knowledge. For example, teachers may not be able to articulate the specific propositions to which they ascribe. However, teachers are able to describe the characteristics of successful children, the ways that school can be helpful in children's development, and so on. When used to determine tacit knowledge, the respondents' statements are coded according to categories that arise from the data (see Chapter 10). The data are then recontextualized according to the explanatory constructs.

An example is the use of confidential clinical semi-structured interviews in the Boulder Valley retention study. The interviews were conducted with the 42 kindergarten teachers in the district to assess the ways that they address particular cases. Teacher beliefs were inferred from their case knowledge. The rationale for the interviews was that the most valid and least reactive data are those expressed in the teachers' own words that are prompted by neutral fact-oriented questions (Smith & Shepard, 1988, p. 311).

A series of indirect questions that tapped the teachers' case knowledge was developed. Teachers were asked to recall specific children in their classes who were not ready for school and to describe those children in concrete terms. The teachers also were asked to think of particular children who had not been ready for school and to describe reasons for their lack of preparation. The fact-oriented questions related types of information to eight categories that were specified in advance. The categories were:

1. Characteristics of children who are unprepared for first grade
2. Timing at which these characteristics appear
3. Best evidence of lack of preparation
4. Whether any remedies can assist unprepared children
5. Perceived causes of good or poor preparation
6. Teachers' views of first grade and their school
7. Teachers' theories of child development

8. Teachers' views of the benefits and weaknesses of school retention (Shepard & Smith, 1985, p. 126)

Data from the 1-hour interviews were coded according to 47 categories developed from the initial research questions and categories that emerged from earlier parent interviews and from reading one third of the interview transcripts (see Chapter 10). The coded data were then organized around the eight types of information listed in the prior paragraph. From this compilation, four distinct teacher belief systems were identified that varied on two broad dimensions. The dimensions were (1) perceptions about the fundamental processes of child development and (2) the extent to which teachers can alter the level of preparation of individual children who come to kindergarten (Shepard & Smith, 1985).

The four belief systems form a continuum from nativists (development is a physiological process that cannot be altered) to remediationists (within broad limits, readiness is a function of experience). The two intermediate belief systems, diagnostic prescriptives and interactionists, vary on the extent to which specific entry abilities can be assessed and corrected (Smith & Shepard, 1988). These four belief systems are presented in Table 15.4.

The importance of discovering teacher belief systems about child development and the role of the school is that these beliefs were instrumental in accounting for differences in pupil retention across the district. (Some schools retained 16% to 25% of kindergarten children and others retained 0% to 4%.)

Judgment-Capturing Assessments

Judgment- or policy-capturing studies are designed to identify the ways in which a rater combines and implicitly assigns weights to dimensional information in arriving at an overall rating or a decision about employees, students, or others (Hobson & Gibson, 1983). In an educational setting, information can be obtained, for example, about the characteristics or events that are important in making decisions about students. Such an approach can indicate the rater's basic values about which characteristics or features are most important in the decision.

The method consists of three basic steps. First, simulated cases, profiles, or vignettes are developed (Shavelson, Webb, & Burstein, 1986). Second, the supervisor or teacher is instructed to review each case, profile, or vignette and make a decision that best represents the available information. Third, the researcher uses multiple regression analysis (1) to calculate the extent to which the supervisor's or teacher's overall decision is predictable given the information provided on the separate dimensions and (2) to compute the relative importance of each single dimension in the overall decision (Hobson & Gibson, 1983, p. 640). The technique is useful (1) for determining the unique information processing behavior of decision makers, (2) for determining the basic value system of the decision maker, and (3) for comparing stated decision making policies with those actually used (p. 640).

One use of this approach documented the relative importance of six student characteristics in fourth-grade teachers' judgments about pupils who would be successful in fifth grade (Borko & Cadwell, 1982). Another study determined the extent to which six external pressures influenced teachers' decisions about curriculum content (Floden, Porter, Schmidt, Freeman, & Schwille, 1981).

The kindergarten teachers in the Boulder Valley retention study were presented with 45 pupil cases in the form of profiles of pupil characteristics. All were simulated cases of children completing 1 year of kindergarten. The profiles presented gender, kindergarten entry age, physical size (reported in percentiles), a rating of academic skills, and a rating of social maturity. The teachers were asked to recommend (1) placement for the following year and, if no other programs were available, (2) the likelihood of the child's success in first grade. Although no particular pupil was represented, all of the cases were realistic and could be matched to actual pupil records (Shepard & Smith, 1985).

Each teacher's decision data were analyzed using multiple regression. The implicit weight assigned to each pupil dimension in making recommendations about retention was estimated by determining the extent to which variance on the dimension predicts the particular judgment score. Recommended placement decisions were scored on a scale of 1 to 4 (from repeat kindergarten to pass to first grade), and the likelihood of success in first grade was scored on a scale of 1 to 10. The consistency of teacher judgments was indicated by the multiple Rs, which were .76 and above.

The policy weights (Beta weights) for each variable in the 88 equations (44 teachers and two decisions per teacher) indicated the relative importance of the five characteristics in retention decisions and estimates of success. The data indicate considerable variability across teachers in their decisions. The results are illustrated in Figure 16.3.

Summary

Values are generally considered to be more complex than predispositions toward or away from a particular class of objects, events, or activities. A belief, in contrast, is a person's disposition with respect to the truth of a proposition. Beliefs differ from knowledge in that knowledge is based on fact. Beliefs also can be unconscious or repressed.

Two methods for assessing values and beliefs are semi-structured interviews and judgement-capturing studies. The semi-structured interview is based on an interview guide in which the issues to be explored are outlined in advance. The interviewer, however, is free to use a conversational format. Semi-structured interviews are appropriate in program evaluations in which the same types of information are needed from interviewees. Semi-structured interviews may be used for any of several purposes. Among them are to determine student perceptions of a new program or curriculum and individuals' tacit belief systems about policies and issues. When used to determine tacit knowledge, the respondents' statements are coded according to relevant categories that arise from the data (see Chapter 10). The data are then recontextualized according to the explanatory constructs.

Judgement-capturing assessments are designed to identify the ways in which a rater combines and implicitly assigns weights to dimensional information in arriving at an overall rating or a decision about employees, students, or others. The method consists of three basic steps. First, simulated cases, profiles, or vignettes are developed. Second, the rater reviews each profile and makes a decision. Third, the researcher uses regression analysis to compute the relative importance of each dimension in the overall decision.

CHAPTER QUESTIONS

1. What are the major differences between attitudes toward the subject matter and course satisfaction?

2. What is the method referred to as known-group comparisons?

3. What are the important considerations in training observers to use a rating scale or checklist?

4. What are some of the content areas that interviews can address?

5. What is the major disadvantage in using secondary indicators to assess affective change?

6. What are the steps in developing a judgment-capturing assessment?

REFERENCES

Anderson, L. W. (1981). *Assessing affective characteristics in the schools.* Boston: Allyn & Bacon.

Anderson, L. W. (1990). Likert scales. In H. J. Walberg & G. D. Haertel (Eds.), *The encyclopedia of educational evaluation* (pp. 334–335). Oxford: Pergamon Press.

Bandura, A. (1986). *Social foundations of thought and action: A social-cognitive theory.* Englewood Cliffs, NJ: Prentice Hall.

Bernard, H. R. (1988). Research methods in cultural anthropology. Newbury Park: Sage.

Borko, H., & Cadwell, J. (1982). Individual differences in teachers' decision strategies: An investigation of classroom organization and management decisions. *Journal of Educational Psychology, 74*, 598–610.

Cooley, W., & Bickel, W. (1986). *Decision-oriented educational research.* Boston: Kluwer-Nijhoff.

Cronbach, L. J. (1963). Course improvement through evaluation. *Teachers College Record, 64*, 672–683.

Cronbach, L. J. (1970). *Essentials of psychological testing* (3rd ed.). New York: Harper and Row.

Fetterman, D. (1988). Ethnographic educational evaluation. In. D. Fetterman (Ed.), *Qualitative approaches to evaluation in education* (pp. 45–67). New York: Praeger Publishers.

Fetterman, D. (1980). Ethnographic techniques in educational evaluation: An illustration. *Journal of Thought, 15*(3), 31–48.

Fishbein, M., & Ajzen, I. (1975). *Belief, attitude, and behavior: An introduction to theory and research.* Reading, MA: Addison-Wesley.

Floden, R. E., Porter, A. C., Schmidt, W. H., Freeman, D. J., & Schwille, J. R. (1981). Responses to curriculum pressures. *Journal of Educational Psychology, 73*, 129–141.

Gagne, R. (1977). *The conditions of learning* (3rd ed.). New York: Holt, Rinehart.

Goetz, J., & LeCompte, M. (1984). *Ethnography and qualitative design in educational research.* New York: Academic Press.

Guba, E., & Lincoln, Y. (1981). *Effective evaluation.* San Francisco: Jossey-Bass.

Henerson, M., Morris, L., & Fitz-Gibbon, C. (1987). *How to measure attitudes.* Newbury Park, CA: Sage.

Hills, J. R. (1981). *Measurement and evaluation in the classroom* (2nd ed.). Columbus, OH: Merrill.

Hobson, C. J., & Gibson, F. W. (1983). Policy capturing as an approach to understanding and improving performance appraisal. *Academy of Management Review, 8*(4), 640–649.

Linn, R., & Gronlund, N. (1995). *Measurement and assessment in teaching* (7th ed.). Englewood Cliffs, NJ: Prentice Hall.

Newfield, J. W. (1990). Self-report. In H. J. Walberg & G. D. Haertel (Eds.), *The international encyclopedia of educational evaluation* (pp. 146–147). Oxford: Pergamon Press.

Patton, M. (1990). *Qualitative evaluation and research methods.* Newbury Park: Sage.

Rokeach, M. (1973). *The nature of human values.* New York: Free Press.

Shavelson, R. J., Webb, N. M., & Burstein, L. (1986). Measurement of teaching. In. M. Wittrock (Ed.), *The handbook of research on teaching* (3rd ed., pp. 50–91). New York: Macmillan.

Shepard, L., & Smith, M. (1985). *Boulder Valley kindergarten study: Retention practices and retention effects.* Boulder, CO: Boulder Valley Public Schools.

Smith, M., & Shepard, L. (1988). Kindergarten readiness and retention: A qualitative study of teachers' beliefs and practices. *American Educational Research Journal, 25*(3), 307–333.

Stallings, J., & Mohlman, G. G. (1990). Observation systems. In H. J. Walberg & G. D. Haertel (Eds.), *The international encyclopedia of educational evaluation* (pp. 639–644). Oxford: Pergamon Press.

Webb, E. J., Campbell, D. T., Schwartz, R., & Sechrest, L. (1966). *Unobtrusive measures: Nonreactive research in the social sciences.* Chicago: Rand McNally.

CHAPTER 10

Qualitative Methods of Inquiry

T wo early evaluation approaches raised evaluators' awareness of the complexity of the settings in which innovations are introduced. They are Eisner's criticism/connoisseurship approach and the illuminative evaluation perspective. In the last 30 years, the emergence of qualitative inquiry from a marginal position in the social sciences to a more central role introduced methods that address these concerns (Hammersley, 1992).

THE NATURE OF QUALITATIVE INQUIRY

The term *qualitative inquiry*, or *qualitative research*, refers to research traditions or paradigms (1) that are nonmanipulative and (2) that collect data in the form of words. Some qualitative studies analyze documents only and do not involve observations of human subjects. Examples are archival research and literary criticism. Other perspectives that study groups and settings through direct contact with individuals are referred to as field based. Field-based perspectives cross the disciplines of anthropology and sociology and, more recently, educational research and evaluation.

Major assumptions of field-based qualitative research are (1) that setting has an important influence on human behavior and (2) that human behavior has a subjective dimension (Jacob, 1988). Researchers obtain richly detailed chronicles of human interactions and the settings in which the behaviors occurred. Some qualitative traditions, for example, cultural anthropology, also obtain detailed information on individuals' beliefs, assumptions, and values.

Firsthand field research emerged in 1886 with Franz Boas, a cultural anthropologist. He collected extensive data while living with the Kwakiutl Indians of Vancouver Island, Canada. Prior to that time, armchair anthropologists interpreted the information provided by explorers, missionaries, colonial administrators, and travelers.

The relevance of qualitative methods for contemporary issues began with sociologists at the University of Chicago in the 1920s. A landmark work, *The Polish Peasant in Europe and America* by W. I. Thomas and Florian Znaniecki, is the first use of document analysis to portray sociological differences. The 2,232-page study used newspaper accounts, records from social agencies and Polish-American organizations, and hundreds of letters to and from immigrants in America.

In contrast to *The Polish Peasant,* Nels Anderson's (1923) study of homeless men, *The Hobo,* was based on informal interviews and observations (Bulmer, 1984). Anderson played the role of a hobo in the heart of Chicago's "Hobohemia," but he did not reveal his research purpose to the homeless men. (This practice is not sanctioned under current ethics principles [see Chapter 17].) The purpose of Anderson's research was to portray the hobo in a self-created milieu within a society that viewed him largely as an outcast (Bulmer, 1984, p. 99).

Since these early studies, sociologists have studied particular topics or issues within an organization or setting. An example is the study of the efforts of a small midwestern town to adapt to a declining regional economy (Janes, 1961). Cultural anthropologists, in contrast, have focused on understanding a community or group from the perspective of the group members. Gradually, education has emerged as a major focus within the cultural perspective. The work of Solon Kimball and George Spindler formalized educational anthropology as an area of study in the 1960s. Subsequent studies explored explicit social structures, implicit conceptual systems, patterns of interpersonal interactions and participation in educational settings, and the effects of government policies on cultural patterns and education (Goetz & LeCompte, 1984, p. 22).

In the 1970s, the anthropological perspective and other qualitative methods were introduced into educational evaluation. Early examples are the Career Intern Program (CIP) for minority youth dropouts (Fetterman, 1988a, 1988b) and the experimental schools program (Messerschmidt, 1984). Currently, qualitative methods are an accepted approach to evaluation issues.

Clarification of Terminology

Terms that have been used interchangeably in some discussions of qualitative inquiry are *naturalistic research, fieldwork,* and *ethnography.* However, their meanings are somewhat different. The term *naturalistic research* refers to the "investigation of phenomena within and in relation to their naturally occurring contexts" (Willems & Rausch, 1969, p. 3). *Naturalistic inquiry,* therefore, is another term for *field-based qualitative inquiry.* Fieldwork involves entering a particular setting and establishing direct contact with the participants for an extended period of time. Observing subjects carry out their daily job responsibilities, interviewing subjects, tape recording verbal interactions, and participating in a group's activities while conducting observations are examples.

Some sociologists use the term *ethnography* to refer to the richly detailed reports that result from fieldwork. However, ethnography refers to a particular research framework (Wolcott, 1992). An ethnography is an analytic description or reconstruction of an intact cultural scene or group that "delineates the shared beliefs, practices, artifacts, folk knowledge, and behavior of some group of people" (LeCompte & Goetz, 1982, p. 382). The hallmark of ethnographic research is the commitment to cultural interpretation (Wolcott, 1992, p. 271). The test of an ethnography is whether it enables one to anticipate and interpret the events occurring in a society or social group as accurately as one of the members (Wolcott, 1982, p. 82).

Although ethnography and field study may use the same research techniques, "ethnography is field study plus something special in the nature of interpretative emphasis" (Wolcott, 1992, p. 21). Thus, a researcher may use the basic methods used by ethnographers but does not necessarily conduct an ethnographic study. One is "doing ethnography" (cultural interpretation) and the other is "borrowing ethnographic techniques" (Wolcott, 1992, p. 28).

Four Field-Based Perspectives

Several qualitative perspectives have contributed methods and insights to an understanding of human behavior. Four that have implications for education are cultural or holistic anthropology, sociological fieldwork, the ethnography of communication, and ecological psychology. These perspectives differ in basic assumptions, scope of inquiry, and the use made of different qualitative methods (see Table 10.1).

Cultural or holistic ethnography seeks to analyze and interpret the various layers of implicit meanings in cultural practices, rituals, economic and political structures, and so on. Microethnographers analyze verbal and nonverbal communications in particular settings in order to interpret cultural rules. For example, Phillips (1972) and Erickson and Mohatt (1982) found that the communication structure of the classroom imposed requirements on Indian children that differed from their culture. The children reacted with silence, nervous giggling, and failure to answer questions in the controlling environment of the classroom (Erickson & Mohatt, 1982, p. 140).

In contrast, ecological psychologists record behavioral sequences to determine the influence of different settings on behavior. LeCompte & Goetz (1984) note that the methodology can generate important information about the actual manipulation of materials in the classroom and the implementation of teaching strategies (p. 50).

Summary

In the last 30 years, qualitative inquiry has acquired a more central role in the social science disciplines. Field-based qualitative methods that began in cultural anthropology were introduced into sociology and then education. Of importance in under-

Table 10.1
Four qualitative field-based research perspectives

	Assumptions	Methodology	Scope	Examples
Cultural or holistic ethnography	Immersion and participation for an extended period is essential to understanding a culture from an insider's perspective.	Participant observation for months or years; detailed records of observations and interviews of key informants	Cultural interpretation: language, kinship, patterns, rituals and beliefs, economic and political structure, childrearing, life stages, arts, crafts, and technology	Malinowski (1922) *Argonauts of the Western Pacific*
Sociological fieldwork	Fieldwork is essential to understanding important issues in collective life.	Participant observation, interviewing	Social topics of interest within an organization or setting	Janes (1961) Analysis of a small mid-western community undergoing economic change; data obtained as a new resident in the community
Ethnography of communication (microethnography; constitutive ethnography)	1. Culture is a set of standards for perceiving, believing, and behaving. 2. Values and cultural patterns are revealed in face-to-face interactions.	Audiovisual records of both verbal and nonverbal communication; participant observation and conversational analysis	Verbal and nonverbal communication as observed in particular cultural scenes	Erickson and Mohatt (1982) Cultural organization of participant structures in two classrooms of Indian students
Ecological psychology	Psychological events and environmental actions and components are interrelated in the same way that a generator is part of an engine and a bat of a ball game (Barker, 1965, p. 34).	Videotapes and observations to construct stream-of-behavior chronicles; chronicles analyzed into units reflecting goal-directed behavior	Analysis of behavioral sequences to identify the influence of different settings	Barker and Gump (1964) *Big school, small school*

standing the various perspectives is that fieldwork refers to methods of direct contact with subjects. Ethnography refers to fieldwork that results in cultural analysis and interpretation. Naturalistic research indicates any field-based nonmanipulative study that primarily uses qualitative methods.

Four qualitative perspectives with implications for evaluation are holistic or cultural ethnography, sociological fieldwork, microethnography, and ecological psychology. Although they overlap in methods, they differ in focus and scope.

PARTICIPANT OBSERVATION

Participant observation is the primary research method used by anthropologists and the early sociologists. Formally defined, participant observation is a process in which the researcher (1) is in a face-to-face relationship with the observed and (2) gathers data by participating with them in their natural setting (Schwartz & Schwartz, 1969, p. 91). Participant observation is useful for any of several specific purposes. They are (1) reconstructing events or a series of events; (2) developing case histories of an individual, classroom, school, organization, or community; and (3) conducting pilot inquiries into a new problem (Schwartz & Schwartz, 1969).

The purpose of participant observation in sociological studies is, typically, to address a particular problem, such as the ways a small midwestern town is coping with economic change. In ethnographic studies, the purpose is to discover and interpret the cultural setting from the insider's perspective. This task involves determining people's "definitions of reality and the organizing constructs of their world" (Goetz & LeCompte, 1984, p. 110). This focus requires going beyond the surface appearance of activities and interactions (manifest events) to the unspoken rules, expectations, and values that guide participants' actions (latent events).

A crucial element in this process is a familiarity with the language variations or argots used by participants. Members of bridge clubs speak differently from devotees of pool halls, and a particular group of bridge or pool players will differ from others of the same general type.

Role of the Participant Observer

The researcher may take a role in the setting that is either formal or informal and integral or peripheral to the social structure (Schwartz & Schwartz, 1969). A sociologist studying a hospital ward, for example, may observe interactions on the floor, only occasionally asking informal questions, and participate directly with patients only in games in the recreation area. In contrast, a participant observer in a preschool volunteered to help with tasks such as putting on the children's coats and distributing materials and was soon regarded as a member of the "staff family" (Cosaro, 1981). In the CIP program for minority dropouts, participant observers informally interacted with staff and students in their homes, "hung out" in the streets, attended Pentecostal church services and wrestling matches with students, and danced at a CIP disco (Fetterman, 1980, p. 34).

Participant observation in anthropological studies typically involves long-term residence in the setting. In evaluation, however, residence may not be continuous. Nevertheless, each period of contact with participants should be long enough to prevent loss of good relations, and the observations should extend over a sufficient period of time to permit cultural patterns and interpretations to emerge. In the CIP program, contact was maintained with project sites between visits with frequent and lengthy telephone conversations with staff and students. Regardless of the type of role or duration of contact, the researcher attempts to share the life of the observed on a human level as well as on the designated role level.

Entry Into the Field

The researcher first obtains formal entry through the sanction of responsible administrators and then begins the informal process of entry into the field. This informal process can be facilitated by an informant or guide who introduces the researcher to individuals in the setting (Schatzman & Strauss, 1973, p. 35).

The initial phase of field entry is referred to as "mapping" (Schatzman & Strauss, 1973) or "shagging around," that is, "casing the joint" (LeCompte, 1969). The researcher begins to develop a "social map" of individuals and their roles; a "spatial map" of centers of work and activity; and a "temporal map" of the ebb and flow of events, including special assemblies, rituals, and routines (p. 36). A daily ritual for teachers in a school, for example, may be coffee in the cafeteria prior to homeroom.

Mapping or shagging around also allows the researcher to begin to sort and categorize the individuals who can serve as primary data sources (Goetz & LeCompte, 1984, p. 90). Particularly important for an ethnographic study is to begin collecting the anecdotes, stories, and myths that make the rounds in the teacher's lounge or student groups (Goetz & LeCompte, 1984). This information assists the researcher in developing preliminary conceptual categories that may be used later in analyzing the data.

Entry into the field is a continuous process that involves developing and establishing relationships over a period of time, particularly in relatively complex sites (Schatzman & Strauss, 1973). Initially, different individuals are likely to exhibit different degrees of receptivity, and the researcher does not press for their participation. Messerschmidt (1984), Fetterman (1984), Thorne (1980), and others who conduct ethnographic evaluations report being viewed by some project personnel as spies. A sincere desire to learn about the program from the participants' perspectives and extended time on-site can contribute to overcoming these perceptions.

Data Collection

Entry into the setting may be accompanied by the feeling that it is impossible to "get it all down" (Goetz & LeCompte, 1984, p. 111). The participant observer does not yet know how the data will be coded; thus, more information typically is collected initially than is used later. However, of importance in the data collection is that the researcher does not enter the setting with the goal of recording every minute detail. Instead, data collection is guided by a general conceptual framework such as to discover the latent rules of group conduct or ways that communication patterns reflect the culture. Or the study may address a major topic, such as child-rearing practices, that provides an orientation for data recording.

The raw data of participant observation are the events and interactions that occur in the setting under study. Relevant data may consist of the form and content of verbal interactions between participants and with the researcher, as well as nonverbal behavior and patterns of action and nonaction (Wilson, 1977).

Basic Rules.   Bernard (1988, pp. 181–182) identifies five basic rules for data collection in an ethnographic study. They are as follows:

1. Do not put notes into one long commentary. Instead, use plenty of paper and make many shorter notes.

2. Maintain four physically separate sets of notes. They are field jottings, field notes, a field (personal) diary, and a field log. Field jottings are the immediate shorthand-type notes of ongoing interactions and activities. Field notes are the fleshed-out jotted notes with contextual and other information added. The diary is a personal record of thoughts and feelings. The log is a running daily account of how the researcher plans to spend time and how time actually was spent.

3. Record field jottings all the time, not simply at appointed times. In other words, take notes on the spot, and do not rely on memory.

4. Do not be afraid of offending people by taking notes. Simply ask for permission to take notes while talking with people.

5. Write up field notes from jottings at a set time of day, and allow 1 to 2 hours to write up field notes and complete the diary. Do not write up the day's notes the next day because too much will be lost.

Particularly important is to record events in concrete terms and not overgeneralize. For example, the researcher should not record that the student was angry at the instructor's critique. Instead, the student's verbal and nonverbal reactions should be recorded.

The breadth and depth of information that is recorded in field notes will vary somewhat depending on the underlying purpose of the study, for example, cultural interpretation or the analysis of particular problem-solving processes in an institution. However, the purpose should not be that of documenting events or a series of events. The resulting data will be only at the level of superficial description, lacking contextual and interpretative analysis.

Ethnographic Studies.   In addition to verbal and nonverbal interactions, holistic ethnographers collect information about rituals, myths, rites of passage (if appropriate to the setting), and other data that can indicate participants' belief systems. Photographs also may be a part of the data record. In the CIP intern project, Fetterman

(1988b) photographed students intermittently over a 3-year period, thus documenting visually the changes in their posture and apparel.

Ethnographers also often construct one or more context maps of the location, whether classrooms, playgrounds, or offices. Erickson and Mohatt (1982) used context maps of two classes to illustrate the teachers' movement patterns in assisting children during individual seat work. These maps illustrated key differences between the teachers in length of time spent with each child and the smoothness of movement patterns within the classroom.

Potential Problems

Several potential problems may arise in participant observation. One is the reactive effects of members of the group to the evaluator's presence. If the evaluator is perceived as a critical outsider, a management spy, or a close friend, individuals may modify their conduct accordingly. Also, individuals may react to personal characteristics of the observer, such as gender, race, or level of education (McCall, 1969).

Another potential problem is applying one's own categories to situations. This is particularly a concern in settings in which a common basic language is shared and both the researcher and the subjects are in the same discipline, such as education or health care. Because different individuals attach different meanings to the same words, such as *cooperative learning, individualized instruction,* and so on, the researcher must be sensitive to the meanings and intents of the subjects.

A third potential problem is the researcher's overidentification with a particular faction in the setting. The extreme example is referred to as "going native," which is the complete identification with the group under study and a complete loss of distance and objectivity. Safeguards against overidentification with a particular faction involve (1) checking later field notes to determine changes in perception from earlier notes that indicate increasing bias and (2) checking the observer's interpretations with top informants in relevant subgroups. If possible, perceptions should be checked with knowledgeable outsiders (McCall, 1969, p. 132). Some researchers suggest that observers should report the extent to which they were changed by a study, thus making public altered values and beliefs (Guba & Lincoln, 1981, p. 208).

Summary

Participant observation is a primary data collection strategy in fieldwork. The role of the participant observer may vary from formal to informal and may be either integral or peripheral to the social structure of the setting. Ideally, residence in the setting should be continuous but may be discontinuous if the visits are of sufficient length.

Important initial tasks for the participant observer are gaining entry into the field and focusing the data collection. Field entry involves establishing good relations with the participants and becoming oriented to the setting. Focusing the data collection involves developing a frame of reference for the study, such as microethnography and/or identifying a major topic to pursue.

The participant observer collects data by recording the details of events in a record referred to as field notes. These notes should be concrete and avoid overgeneralizations. In addition to field notes, ethnographers typically maintain a daily log and a personal diary.

Potential problems in participant observation are (1) the reactive effects of group members to the researcher, (2) the application of the researcher's own system of meaning to events, and (3) the researcher's overidentification with subgroups in the setting. Checking observations with top informants and knowledgeable outsiders can guard against interpretative errors and overidentification.

NONPARTICIPANT OBSERVATION

Nonparticipant observation does not involve interactions with the subjects of the study; the observer attempts to be as unobtrusive as possible. However, unless conducted from behind one-way glass, the presence of the observer (or video camera if the setting is being taped) is likely to influence the participants initially. Time should be allowed for the observer and/or equipment to become accepted as part of the setting. An example of nonparticipant observation is a psychologist on a school playground looking for instances of frustration in children (Guba & Lincoln, 1981, p. 190).

Nonparticipant observation may also address broader issues. LeCompte (1978) documented teachers' verbal behaviors and actions in four classrooms to determine the norms and standards emphasized by individual teachers.

Types of Nonparticipant Observation

Three general types of nonparticipant observation are (1) proxemics and kinesics, (2) interaction analysis protocols, and (3) stream-of-behavior chronicles. Briefly, proxemics and kinesics address the social uses of space and the use of bodily movements (Goetz & LeCompte, 1984). Context maps that document movement and the uses of space are an example. In the Erickson and Mohatt (1982) study, context maps documented particular dimensions of teacher-student interactions. One teacher moved quickly and somewhat erratically from child to child in the classroom while also disciplining others at a distance. A second teacher moved more slowly from child to child and did not discipline children across the classroom.

Interaction analysis protocols are behavior rating systems that record certain aspects of classroom exchanges. These instruments address particular predefined categories of behavior and are limited to a few behaviors. Some projects develop their own protocols that reflect important behaviors the project is to address. For example, observers in an evaluation of early childhood bilingual models recorded children's utterances that reflected program objectives (Chesterfield, 1986). The key behaviors were linguistic use (e.g., plural nouns), functional use, and concept development (p. 180).

Stream-of-behavior chronicles were developed by Barker (1963) and other ecological psychologists. They are minute-by-minute accounts of a participant's actions and statements. LeCompte (1975) used stream-of-behavior chronicles to record teacher behavior in a study of teacher norms.

Audio or video recording equipment should be used in conjunction with an observer to develop stream-of-behavior chronicles. This procedure guards against missed dialogue and allows the observer to note the times of switches from one activity to another, as well as nonverbal communications, such as gestures, facial expressions, and body movements.

Advantages and Disadvantages of Observation

Advantages of observational methods are:

1. They make possible the recording of events as they occur.
2. They can maximize discovery and description.
3. They enhance the observer's ability to understand complex situations.
4. They permit data collections in situations where communication is not possible.

   Examples are infant studies and situations in which the subject is unable or unwilling to speak (Guba & Lincoln, 1981, p. 193).

Several disadvantages of observational methods have been identified. One, already mentioned, is that observation can lead to reactivity in the setting or on the part of group members (House, 1978). Another is that the methods, particularly participant observation, are not readily adapted to large, complex settings (Guba & Lincoln, 1981). Four other disadvantages of observation arise from the use of the researcher as the instrument of observation:

1. The researcher can experience the setting in a biased way.
2. Involvement in the setting can lead the researcher to take meanings for granted and, therefore, fail to record them (Guba & Lincoln, 1981).
3. The field notes from participant observation constitute masses of undigested data that are time consuming to analyze and interpret.
4. Adequate implementation requires discipline and training (Patton, 1990).

Summary

Like participant observation, nonparticipant observation is a primary data collection method. However, nonparticipant observation does not involve interactions with participants. The three types of nonparticipant observation are proxemics and kinesics, interaction analysis protocols, and stream-of-behavior chronicles.

Among the advantages of observational techniques are the recording of events as they occur, the enhancement of the observer's ability to understand complex situations, and the opportunities for discovery and data collection in situations where communication is not possible. Disadvantages, in addition to reactivity of the subjects, are the lack of fit to large, complex settings; the time and effort required to analyze the data; and difficulties arising from the researcher serving as the instrument of data collection.

INTERVIEWS AND OTHER METHODS

Observation can indicate actions, customs, social interactions, and patterns of behavior within organizations, groups, and cultures. Other methods, however, are important to corroborate data collected in observations or to discover information that is not accessible through observation. These methods are interviews, unobtrusive measures, document analysis, and enumerative listing.

Interviews

A major purpose of interviews is to gain information about individuals' thoughts, feelings, concerns, intents, or interests (Guba & Lincoln, 1981; Patton, 1990). Interviews can take more than one form, from conversational to a highly structured fixed-response format. However, the fixed-response interview is nothing more than an orally administered questionnaire. The four major types of open-ended interview structures are informal conversational, unstructured, semi-structured, and standardized open ended (Patton, 1990).

Informal Conversational Interviews.   The exchange in an informal conversational interview is spontaneous, and it is not a question-and-answer interchange (Guba & Lincoln, 1981). In many cases, the individual may not realize that an interview is being conducted. The key characteristic is that only the general focus is determined in advance, not the specific questions. The purpose of the informal conversational interview is to provide information about respondents' perceptions of observed events.

Unstructured Interviews.   The unstructured interview is based on a clear plan, but the interviewer exercises minimal control over the informant's responses. The purpose is to let people express themselves in their own terms (Bernard, 1988, p. 204). The interviewer keeps the conversation focused on a topic, but the informant defines the content of the discussion (p. 207).

Unstructured interviews are typically used to develop oral histories and to obtain information from special or "key" informants (Goetz & LeCompte, 1984; Guba & Lincoln, 1981; Patton, 1990; Zelditch, 1962). A key informant is a member of the group who can provide accurate information about rules and practices of the group and events that the researcher does not have access to (Zelditch, 1962). For instance, the researcher cannot be everywhere at the same time; and he or she cannot be "everywhere in time." Events occur prior to the researcher's arrival or during his or her absence from the site that are not observed. Also, parts of the social structure will not be penetrated by the researcher. Thus, the informant serves as "the observer's observer" for these gaps in the researcher's knowledge (p. 569).

Although a necessary source of information, respondents and key informants can present problems. They are lack of knowledge, reportorial skills, and potential bias of the respondent or informant. Biases may arise from ulterior motives of the individual or other factors, such as mood or subgroup identity.

Fetterman (1980) suggests four ways to ensure the quality of information. First, develop good rapport to decrease fabrication. Second, ask for the beliefs of the informant and the informant's views of others' beliefs. This step provides information for cross-checking. Third, ask the same questions in subsequent interviews. Fourth, confirm the information by checking with other sources and using other methods of data collection (p. 35). In the CIP project, staff perceptions were checked with intern (student) perceptions, which were checked by program monitor observations (Fetterman, 1980, p. 39).

Semi-Structured and Standardized Open-Ended Interviews.   These two types of interviews were discussed in Chapter 9 as methods for obtaining information about respondent attitudes and belief systems. The semi-structured interview is based on an interview guide with the issues identified in advance. The interview proceeds in a conversational format, however. The semi-structured interview is useful in developing knowledge of participants' perspectives of their cultural setting and organization. Spradley (1979) suggests the use of three types of questions in such interviews. Descriptive questions address a respondent's representation of some aspect of culture. Structural questions are designed to discover or substantiate the constructs respondents use to portray their world. Finally, contrast questions focus on eliciting respondents' meanings of and relationships among constructs (Goetz & LeCompte, 1984, p. 125).

The standardized format consists of a set order of carefully worded questions along with clarifications and follow-up probes. Advantages of this format are that interviewer variation is minimized, responses to particular issues are easily summarized, and available time is carefully used (Patton, 1990).

Other Data Sources

Two other important sources of information are unobtrusive measures and enumerative listing. Included in unobtrusive measures are physical traces, archival records, and other documents. As indicated in Chapter 9, the CIP program documented the amount of rest room graffiti as an indicator of student attitudes toward and involvement in the program. Staff and intern apparel also indicated possible affiliations and were cues to probe further. Specifically, a Borsolini hat indicated possible gang affiliation, and rabbit fur coats and layers of jewelry suggested possible identification with pimps or prostitution. Changes in student wardrobes over the length of the project indicated changes in self-presentation skills (Fetterman, 1980, p. 40).

Documents can be rich sources of information about a group or cultural setting, as indicated by *The Polish Peasant,* a sociological analysis of immigrant life.

Important documents in instructional programs are curriculum guides, classroom materials and assignments, student projects, programs of student-planned activities, and similar materials. Among the documents that can provide information on events the evaluator is unable to observe are journalistic accounts, archives, and official statistics and reports. Also, minutes of faculty or staff meetings can indicate decisions and directions previously taken that influence present events. However, the researcher should remember that official documents convey partisan or official views.

Ethnographers associated with the CIP program collected samples of learning packets, examples of student poetry from the school newspaper (see Chapter 9), and records of CIP-is-HIP awards (Fetterman, 1980). Records of the monthly CIP-is-HIP day corroborated observations of this event as a rite of solidarity for the interns (students). Prizes were awarded in a variety of categories, including most talkative, best attendance, teacher's pet, likely to succeed, class participation, sleeping in class, leadership ability, and so on (p. 50).

In contrast to unobtrusive measures and document analysis, enumerative listing is a method for eliciting information from participants. The researcher asks the participant to tell him or her all the members of a particular category of things (Goetz & LeCompte, 1984, p. 123). In a community study, for example, the researcher may ask for all the kinds of food eaten by the people or all the gift exchange occasions in the calendar (p. 123). In one study, LeCompte (1980) used photographs of activities and asked young children to tell her all the things they thought they and their teacher would do in kindergarten. The data led to the development of a typology of children's perceptions of teacher and pupil roles (p. 123). Enumerative listing is particularly useful in determining the inclusiveness of certain categories of information and also for determining the ways that participants structure their views of certain activities and events.

Summary

In addition to observational techniques, other important data sources are interviews, unobtrusive methods, document analysis, and enumerative listing. Interviews are important supplements to observations because they can provide information about individuals' internal thoughts, feelings, concerns, intents, or interests. The four types of open-ended interviews are the informal conversational, unstructured, semi-structured, and standardized open ended. Informal interviews are used to check information with participants, whereas unstructured interviews obtain information from key informants. The semi-structured interview also may be conversational, but the researcher prepares an interview guide in advance. A standardized open-ended interview consists of a set of carefully worded questions and follow-up probes. This format provides for an analysis of pre-post differences.

Unobtrusive measures consist of evidence available in the setting that does not require intrusion by the researcher. Examples are the condition of school buildings and rest rooms and modes of dress. Unobtrusive measures can provide information about participant attitudes and values.

Analysis of documents such as journalistic accounts, curriculum materials, project records and statistics, and minutes of meetings can provide information about events the researcher is unable to observe. They also may indicate goals and directions, and some may provide information about attitudes, such as examples of student poetry. Of importance in the use of official documents is that they may present a partisan or official view of events.

Enumerative listing, in contrast, is a method for eliciting responses from participants. Specifically, the researcher asks the respondent to tell about all the things in a particular category, such as the kinds of food in the community. The technique is useful for establishing (1) the boundaries of a particular category and (2) the ways that participants structure their views of events and activities.

DATA QUALITY CONTROL

A hallmark of field-based qualitative methods is (1) that the researcher is the data collection instrument and (2) that the research involves unstructured observation of and interactions with others. The process is dependent, to a great extent, on the insights and conceptual capabilities of the researcher (Patton, 1990). Thus, the potential exists for data that are distorted and/or incomplete.

Several mechanisms to enhance the credibility of the data should be implemented in conducting the research. One general strategy suggested by Webb et al. (1966) and explicated by Denzin (1978) is that of *triangulation*. The process consists of four techniques used in data collection and analysis:

1. Implementing multiple methods for obtaining data
2. Consulting multiple data sources
3. Using more than one researcher to collect data
4. Relying on additional researchers for the analyses

An example of multiple data sources is the checking of staff perceptions in the CIP project with intern (student) perceptions and with the observations of program monitors.

Other strategies that contribute to the credibility of the data are listed in Table 10.2. As indicated, each serves an important function in the research process. These strategies (1) serve as checks against narrow or distorted data collection and analysis and (2) enhance opportunities to obtain richly contextualized information.

Particularly important in checking the data are the testing of rival hypotheses and the search for negative cases. Sadler (1981), in a discussion of the information processing limitations of humans, cites research that indicates people tend to not process information that conflicts with an already held hypothesis. The issue is not that people deliberately ignore disconfirming instances. Instead, these instances are simply not perceived (p. 28). Thus, the conscious search for rival hypotheses and negative instances is important.

Table 10.2
Mechanisms for enhancing data quality

Strategies	Purpose
Data collection:	
Prolonged engagement in the field	To identify possible sources of distortion and salient events for participants
Persistent observation	Permits in-depth pursuit of possible salient events
Multiple data collection methods	To compensate for omissions or distortions that may arise from the use of one method
Multiple observers	To provide a check on the intrusion of researcher perceptions and/or emerging beliefs
Data verification:	
Test rival hypotheses	To identify alternative explanations of the emerging constructs
Search for negative cases	To identify individuals or situations that differ from the emerging constructs
Check information with other sources	To check the accuracy and completeness of data obtained from one individual
Share deductions with key informants and stakeholders	To check the accuracy of the portrayal of a group or situation and the accuracy of researcher's deductions
Data analysis:	
Multiple analysts	To ensure the use of categories appropriate for the data

Summarized from Goetz and LeCompte, 1984; Lincoln and Guba, 1987; Patton, 1990.

The use of multiple analysts may be undertaken in either of two ways. One approach is for researchers to analyze the data independently and then compare their findings. The other is for researchers from the different sites to meet as a committee to determine the coding categories and typologies appropriate for the data. (See Chapter 15 on data analysis.)

Some discussions of triangulation give the impression that the use of multiple methods, observers, and sources serve to corroborate the data. Instead, they may tap into different aspects of a social phenomenon. For example, primary teachers in one project received cards containing brief math activities that were appropriate for transitional and noninstructional class time. Although teachers reported extensive use of the activities, observations of 200 classrooms indicated that only 14 activities of the total set were used (Mathison, 1988, p. 16). The explanation is that the teachers were positive about use of the activities but would find they had no unplanned time and did not want to reduce the time spent on other goals. Thus, implementation was difficult for them (p. 16).

The importance of triangulation is that all of the outcomes, whether convergent, inconsistent, and contradictory, should be filtered through other knowledge about the context, the program, and the larger social world to arrive at an explanation (Mathison, 1988). In other words, triangulation rarely provides a singular view of a situation, but it can provide a rich and complex picture of the phenomenon under study (Mathison, 1988, p. 15).

In summary, several mechanisms to enhance the credibility of the data should be implemented. Among them are the testing of rival hypotheses, the search for negative cases during data collection, and triangulation. The process of triangulation consists of implementing multiple methods, data sources, researchers, and analyses of the data. Of importance, however, is that triangulation rarely provides a unitary view of a situation. However, it can provide information about the complexity of the setting.

QUALITATIVE METHODS IN EVALUATION

Two general approaches to incorporating qualitative research methods in evaluation may be identified. They are ethnographic evaluation and "formalized" qualitative research.

Ethnographic Evaluation

The ethnographic evaluator, like the conventional ethnographer, must be immersed in the field in order to develop an interpretation of a culture or subgroup from the perspective of the group members (Fetterman, 1988, p. 42). Britain (1978) refers to ethnographic evaluation as contextual evaluation because it provides a wealth of information about the following:

1. The context in which the program is attempting to function
2. The actual activities of the program
3. The perceptions of participants
4. The factors influencing the direction of the innovation

The ethnographic evaluator is a hybrid, with one foot in each camp (Fetterman, 1986). As an ethnographer, he or she must remain nonjudgmental and maintain confidentiality. As an evaluator, the individual is assessing the functional or dysfunctional qualities of the program or situation (p. 37). Unlike the ethnographer, the evaluator has a responsibility to the taxpayer. The acceptance of government funds introduces an ethical and contractual obligation to fulfill the responsibilities in the contract.

Several characteristics distinguish ethnographic evaluation from other evaluations of program processes:

1. Extended on-site evidence
2. The use of participant observation, interviews, and other ethnographic methods to construct field notes of the culture

3. The development of explanatory constructs from the data itself
4. The development of a cultural interpretation of the program context

An example of an ethnographic evaluation of program context is the CIP study, an evaluation of an alternative high school for minority dropouts. Ethnographic data collection methods were used in 2-week visits to each site every 3 months for 3 years. Most visits were made by teams of two persons. They conducted structured and unstructured interviews with interns (students), CIP staff, federal agency staff, and relevant community leaders; observed CIP classroom and nonclassroom activities; and reviewed documentation and observations pertaining to the earlier prototype development and implementation. The ethnographers collected extensive notes, tape recordings, and photographic records. Observations were discussed at length at the conclusion of each visit. Contact was maintained between visits through lengthy telephone calls with students and staff (Fetterman, 1988a, pp. 264–265). Literature in both sociology and anthropology also was reviewed to identify relevant concepts.

One contribution of the ethnographic component of the evaluation is the analysis of the mechanisms of cultural transmission in the CIP program. The latent functions of the program were for the students to climb the social ladder of success and to acquire black middle-class values (Fetterman, 1988b, p. 49). Key program components were a supportive environment, high expectations, and the preservation of ethnic identity. Also important were the rites of solidarity in the program, such as the student council elections, sports events involving staff and students, and the monthly CIP-is-Hip day when students received awards in a variety of categories. Among these categories were likely to succeed, class participation, and sleeping in class.

Another contribution of the ethnographic perspective was the insights provided into the crime ridden neighborhoods of the students and the rivalry between sponsoring and managing federal agencies that complicated program implementation. The evaluation also developed an analysis of adaptive and maladaptive characteristics of program operation, external management, and the community (Fetterman, 1988a).

"Formalized" Qualitative Evaluation

The term *formalized qualitative research* was coined by Firestone and Herriott (1984) to signify the standardizing of qualitative data collection and data reduction procedures. Three major characteristics distinguish formalized qualitative research from ethnography. First, like sociological fieldwork, the major question is identified in advance. A sociological study may ask, for example, How is a small midwestern town coping with changes in the regional economy? In evaluation, the key questions typically are, How is the program being implemented? and Why is it being implemented in this way?

Second, formalized qualitative evaluation often identifies specific questions of interest. For example, the study of parental involvement in federal programs asked,

What is the nature of parental participation in project decision making? What factors contribute to or inhibit the decision making? and What impact does that involvement have on parents, students, and the schools? (Smith & Robbins, 1984, p. 121).

Third, the research tends to emphasize standardization of data collection procedures through the use of semi-structured interviews and observation protocols. An example is the 1979–80 evaluation of bilingual Head Start programs. Observers recorded the verbal interactions of randomly selected children in each classroom in different contexts (mealtime, independent play, and in large and small group activities) (Chesterfield, 1986). The field notes were coded for the language used and for behaviors identified as curriculum objectives. Examples of key behaviors were linguistic use, such as using plural nouns; functional competence, such as giving verbal instructions or describing feelings; language comprehension, such as telling events from a story; and concept development (p. 150). In addition to frequency counts across classrooms and sites of the key behaviors, the data provided a progress record in English for the children who preferred Spanish at the beginning of the year.

Formalized qualitative data collection in multisite projects can contribute to knowledge about program operation. However, it is accompanied by some problems. First, although comparable data across sites is obtained, too much structure defeats the purpose of collecting qualitative data (Smith & Robbins, 1984, p. 123). Second, the danger exists that important data will be lost in the effort to reduce the amount of information to be analyzed.

SUMMARY

Field-based qualitative inquiry began in anthropology with the interpretative studies of other cultures. Anthropological methods of participant observation, document analysis, and interviews spread to sociology in the early 1920s. At present, qualitative inquiry perspectives also consist of educational anthropology, microethnography, ecological psychology, and ethnographic evaluation.

Primary qualitative methods are participant observation, nonparticipant observation, interviews, and unobtrusive measures. Issues in participant observation are the observer's role, entry into the field, and data collection. The participant observer's role may be formal or informal and integral or peripheral to the social structure. Also, the observation may be continuous or intermittent. Of importance, however, is to develop an understanding of the setting from the participants' perspectives.

Entry into the field is a process in which the participant observer becomes familiar with the physical and social structure of the setting and begins to establish rapport with participants. Data collection consists of recording interactions and activities in jotted note form, which are later fleshed out in field notes. Ethnographers also maintain a daily log and a personal diary. Potential problems in participant observation are participant reactivity and possible bias of the researcher.

Nonparticipant observation does not involve interaction with participants. The three types of nonparticipant observation are proxemics and kinesics, interaction analysis protocols, and stream-of-behavior chronicles. Advantages of observational methods are the recording of events as they occur, the potential to maximize discovery and understanding, and the opportunity to collect data in situations where communication is not possible. In addition to reactivity and the potential for researcher bias, another disadvantage of observational methods is that the data are time consuming to analyze.

The advantages of interviews is that they can reveal an individual's internal thoughts, feelings, concerns, intents, or interests. The four types of interviews are informal conversational, unstructured, semi-structured, and standardized open ended. Informal conversational interviews are spontaneous and typically provide clarification of some event. The function of unstructured interviews is to construct oral histories and to obtain detailed information from knowledgeable key informants. Semi-structured and standardized open-ended interviews are used when the same information is sought from all members of a group. The semi-structured interview is informal, whereas the standardized format follows a set order of questions.

Unobtrusive measures consist of physical traces and available documents. In contrast, enumerative listing is a method that asks the participant to name all the members of a particular category of things.

Qualitative methods yield data in the form of words, and the researcher is the primary data collection instrument. Thus, quality control of the data is an important issue. Methods for enhancing the credibility of the data consist of methods of triangulation, the testing of rival hypotheses, and the search for negative cases.

Qualitative methods are appropriate for developing information about the nature of an implementation, social structures in the program setting, and interactions among program staff and recipients. Two approaches to the application of qualitative methods to evaluation are ethnographic evaluation and formalized qualitative evaluation. Ethnographic evaluation develops a cultural interpretation of the dynamics of the innovation and the settings in which it is implemented. Formalized qualitative evaluation, in contrast, specifies the types of data to be collected and standardizes the collection and analysis across project settings.

CHAPTER QUESTIONS

1. What are the major assumptions of field-based qualitative inquiry?
2. What is the major difference between ethnography and other fieldwork-based studies?
3. The data collected by an inexperienced evaluator lists the various activities that occur in a classroom during several math classes. What major error, in terms of understanding classroom processes, has he or she made?
4. What are the defining characteristics of participant observation? What are the potential problems?
5. How do interaction analysis protocols differ from stream-of-behavior chronicles?

6. What potential problems does unstructured interviewing present? What are the solutions?

7. Name some strategies to ensure the credibility of data obtained in fieldwork.

8. How does ethnographic evaluation differ from formalized qualitative evaluation?

REFERENCES

Barker, R. G. (Ed.). (1963). *The stream of behavior.* New York: Appleton.

Barker, R. G. (1965). Exploration in ecological psychology. *American Psychologist, 10,* 1–14.

Barker, R., & Gump, P. (Eds.). (1964). *Big school, small school.* Stanford: Stanford University Press.

Bernard, H. (1988). *Research methods in cultural anthropology.* Newbury Park, CA: Sage.

Britain, G. (1978). The place of anthropology in program evaluation. *Anthropology and Education Quarterly, 6*(4), 28–34.

Bulmer, M. (1984). *The Chicago school of sociology.* Chicago: University of Chicago Press.

Chesterfield, R. (1986). Qualitative methodology in the evaluation of early childhood bilingual curriculum models. In D. Fetterman & A. Pitman (Eds.), *Educational evaluation* (pp. 145–168). Beverly Hills, CA: Sage.

Cosaro, W. (1981). Entering the child's world—research strategies for field entry and data collection in a preschool setting. In J. Green & C. Wallat (Eds.), *Ethnography and language in school settings* (pp. 117–146). Norwood, NJ: Ablex.

Denzin, N. (1978). *Sociological methods.* New York: McGraw Hill.

Erickson, F., & Mohatt, G. (1982). Cultural organization of participant structures in two classrooms of Indian students. In G. Spindler (Ed.), *Doing the ethnography of schooling* (pp. 132–174). New York: Holt, Rinehart, & Winston.

Fetterman, D. (1980). Ethnographic techniques in educational evaluation: An illustration. *Journal of Thought, 15*(3), 31–48.

Firestone, W., & Herriott, R. (1984). Multisite qualitative policy research: Some design and implementation issues. In D. Fetterman (Ed.), *Ethnography in educational evaluation* (pp. 63–88). Beverly Hills, CA: Sage.

Fetterman, D. (1984). Guilty knowledge, dirty hands, and other ethical dilemmas: The hazards of contract research. In D. Fetterman (Ed.), *Ethnography in educational evaluation* (pp. 211–238). Beverly Hills: Sage.

Fetterman, D. (1986). The ethnographic evaluator. In D. Fetterman & A. Pitman (Eds.), *Educational evaluation* (pp. 21–47). Beverly Hills, CA: Sage.

Fetterman, D. (1988a). A national ethnographic evaluation: An executive summary of the ethnographic component of the Career Intern Program study. In D. Fetterman (Ed.), *Qualitative approaches to evaluation in education* (pp. 262–276). New York: Praeger.

Fetterman, D. (1988b). Ethnographic educational evaluation. In D. Fetterman (Ed.), *Qualitative approaches to evaluation in education* (pp. 45–67). New York: Praeger.

Goetz, J., & LeCompte, M. (1984). *Ethnography and qualitative design in educational research.* New York: Academic Press.

Guba, E., & Lincoln, Y. (1981). *Effective evaluation.* San Francisco: Jossey-Bass.

Hammersley, M. (1992). *What's wrong with ethnography?* London: Routledge.

House, E. R. (1978). Assumptions underlying evaluation models. *Educational Researcher*, 7(3), 4–12.

Jacob, E. (1988). Clarifying qualitative research: A focus on traditions. *Educational Researcher*, 17(1), 16–24.

Janes, R. (1961). A note on the phases of the role of the participant observer. *American Sociological Review, 26,* 446–450.

LeCompte, M. (1969). The dilemmas of inner city school reform: The Woodlawn Experimental School Project. M.A. Thesis. University of Chicago.

LeCompte, M. (1978). Learning to work: The hidden curriculum of the classroom. *Anthropology and Education Quarterly, 9*, 22–37.

LeCompte, M., & Goetz, J. (1984). Ethnographic data collection in evaluation research. In D. Fetterman (Ed.), *Ethnography in educational evaluation* (pp. 37–59). Beverly Hills, CA: Sage.

Lincoln, Y., & Guba, E. (1987). But is it rigorous? Trustworthiness and authenticity in naturalistic evaluation. In W. Shadish & C. Reichardt (Eds.), *Evaluation studies review annual* (Vol. 12, pp. 425–436). Newbury Park, CA: Sage.

McCall, G. (1969). Data quality control in participant observation. In G. McCall & J. Simmons (Eds.), *Issues in participant observation* (pp. 128–141). Reading, MA: Addison-Wesley.

Malinowski, B. (1922). Argonauts of the Western Pacific: An account of native enterprise and adventure in the archipelagos of Melanesian New Guinea. London: Routledge and Kegan Paul.

Mathison, S. (1988). Why triangulate? *Educational Researcher, 17*(2), 13–19.

Messerschmidt, D. (1984). Federal bucks for local change: On the ethnography of experimental schools. In D. Fetterman (Ed.), *Ethnography in educational evaluation* (pp. 89–113). Beverly Hills, CA: Sage.

Patton, M. (1990). *Qualitative evaluation and research methods.* Newbury Park, CA: Sage.

Phillips, S. (1972). Participant structures and communicative competence: Warm Springs children in community and classroom. In C. Cazden, D. Hymes, & V. John (Eds.), *Functions of language in the classroom* (pp. 370–394). New York: Teachers College Press.

Sadler, R. (1981). Intuitive data processing as a potential source of bias in naturalistic evaluations. *Educational Evaluation and Policy Analysis, 3*(4), 25–31.

Schatzman, L., & Strauss, A. (1973). *Field research.* Englewood Cliffs, NJ: Prentice Hall.

Schwartz, M. S., & Schwartz, C. G. (1969). Problems in participant observation. In G. C. McCall & J. L. Simmons (Eds.), *Issues in participant observation* (pp. 89–105). Reading, MA: Addison-Wesley.

Smith, A., & Robbins, A. (1984). Multimethod policy research: A case study of structure and flexibility. In D. Fetterman (Ed.), *Ethnography in educational evaluation* (pp. 115–132). Beverly Hills, CA: Sage.

Spradley, J. P. (1979). *The ethnographic interview.* New York: Holt, Rinehart, & Winston.

Thorne, B. (1980). "You still takin' notes" fieldwork and problems of informal consent. *Social Problems*, *27*(3), 284–297.

Webb, E. J., Campbell, D. T., Schwartz, R., & Sechrest, L. (1966). *Unobtrusive measures: Nonreactive research in the social sciences*. Chicago: Rand McNally.

Willems, E., & Rausch, E. (Eds.). (1969). *Naturalistic viewpoints in psychological research*. New York: Holt, Rinehart, & Winston.

Wilson, S. (1977). The use of ethnographic techniques in educational research. *Review of Educational Research*, *47*(1), 245–265.

Wolcott, H. (1982). Mirrors, models, and monitors: Educator adaptations of the ethnographic innovation. In G. D. Spindler (Ed.), *Doing the ethnography of schooling* (pp. 68–95). New York: Holt, Rinehart, & Winston.

Wolcott, H. (1992). Posturing in qualitative research. In M. LeCompte, W. Millroy, & J. Preissle (Eds.), *The handbook of qualitative research in education*. San Diego: Academic Press.

Zelditch, M. (1962). Some methodological problems of field notes. *American Journal of Sociology, 67,* 566–576.

PART THREE

Development of the Evaluation Plan and Implementation of the Evaluation

CHAPTER 11

Negotiation of the Evaluation Contract

The first major step in planning an evaluation is to negotiate the evaluation contract with the client or sponsor who commissioned the study. This task is important for both parties for two reasons: (1) to prevent misunderstandings and (2) to establish the obligations and responsibilities of both parties. For the evaluator, the contract is one important safeguard against ethical dilemmas. The other safeguard is to be personally and financially able to decline to conduct evaluations in settings in which such agreements cannot be made (Sieber, 1980). "The hallmark of being ethical in program evaluation is planning so that the context does not produce dilemmas" (p. 58).

PRELIMINARY TASKS

Prior to negotiating the contract, the evaluator should develop a preliminary knowledge base about the intervention. The evaluator should review the program description that is provided by the funding agency or sponsor and conduct at least a brief literature review on the program or on similar programs.

Also important is to note the budget amount allocated to the evaluation and the allotted time frame for completion of the study. Either the financial allocation or the time frame may be insufficient to conduct a meaningful evaluation.

The evaluation may be part of a developmental project in which funds were allocated to design and implement an innovation, or it may be fixed-price evaluation. Ideally, in a project budget, the amount allowed for the evaluation should range from 7% to 10% of the total project budget. If the allowable amount is less than 3% of the project budget, the evaluator may be forced to rely on existing testing programs for outcome data and may be unable to conduct an evaluation of program implementation. If the evaluator is considering a response to a Request for Proposal (RFP), he or she must decide if meaningful information can be developed for the client within the specified framework.

TYPES OF CONTRACTS

Evaluations and evaluation contracts may vary from one setting to another. A contract for an evaluation may be awarded after responses to an RFP issued by the sponsor or funding agency. Interested parties submit evaluation proposals to the agency or institution to evaluate an existing program, and one is chosen by the client.

In other situations, a school, a school district, or another group may be engaged in program development, and an evaluation component is a requirement in the proposal. The evaluator may work with the school in defining the evaluation activities. On other occasions, an individual may be contacted about conducting an evaluation of a project and informational materials are forwarded for his or her review. If the individual is agreeable to conducting the evaluation, formal meetings are arranged for negotiating the contract.

The evaluation contract may be as simple as a letter of understanding signed by all parties, or it may be an elaborate document. Regardless of format, the purpose is to specify clearly the obligations and responsibilities of both the client and the evaluator. Gunn (1987) notes that the challenge is to write a contract in which the contractor can conduct an evaluation of the program "with enough contractor independence to ensure the credibility of the study and enough client control to ensure that the contractor does not go off on a wild tangent" (p. 12).

Three major types of information should be addressed in the contractual document. They are (1) the context of the evaluation, (2) the conduct of the evaluation, and (3) the technical specifications. Although discussed separately, these components are interdependent.

CONTEXT OF THE EVALUATION

Information that defines the context consists of the identification of the sponsor or client, the identification of the evaluation contractor, the description of the entity to be evaluated, and the purpose of the evaluation.

Identification of the Client

The client may be a federal, state, or private agency; a school district; an institution of higher learning; or a business or industry in the private sector. The client commissioning the evaluation as well as his or her authority to initiate and contract for an evaluation should be clearly established. For example, a community organization does not have the authority to conduct an evaluation of a school system without the school board's consent (Guba & Lincoln, 1981, p. 271). In situations where an agency receives funding from another agency, approval for the evaluation should be obtained from all responsible parties (p. 271).

Identifying a specific client for the evaluation is important in other contractual situations as well. An example of the failure to identify a primary client occurred in the evaluation of Project Pass in the Pittsburgh public schools (Cooley & Bickel, 1986). Project Pass was established for students scheduled for retention or for those who had failed a grade (grades 1 to 9). The intent was to provide intensive individualized instruction so that students could either rejoin their cohorts or at least be promoted at the end of a year. Because the classes were not necessarily in the student's home school, the hope was that the project would improve racial balance in the schools (p. 171).

The evaluation team, already under contract to the school board, developed several important findings about the program. Among these findings were the following:

1. Only 8% of the elementary school participants were advanced a grade so they could rejoin their peers.

2. Of the previous participants, 14% remained in Pass, although it was to be a 1-year program.

3. Many of the students assigned to Pass had serious emotional and behavioral problems.

4. In grades 6 to 9, one fourth of the Pass students were absent one third of the time (Cooley & Bickel, 1986, p. 180).

However, the evaluation reports did not have a major impact. Cooley and Bickel (1986) concluded that the evaluation suffered from the lack of a primary client. The board sought a summative evaluation so as to make decisions about the program, whereas the central administrative staff wanted continuance of the program as a desegregation tool. The supervisors, from another point of view, wanted assistance in implementing a program to substantially help needy students. Thus, the reports were of little interest to any group because none had identified with the inquiry.

Identification of the Contractor

The contractor who seeks to conduct the evaluation may be a corporation (such as Educational Testing Service), an institute associated with a university (such as the Center for Instructional Research and Curriculum Evaluation [CIRCE] at Illinois), a university faculty member, or an independent evaluator.

Both the evaluator and the level of expertise of the agency or individual should be supported by documentation such as vitae of the evaluation team or a public record of prior evaluations conducted by the agency. Fetterman (1986) describes a case in which he was asked to review a "qualitative" study. The report, however, was a "meaningless hodge-podge of pieces of information" (p. 24). The evaluators took a contract for which they had no expertise. Their unethical actions cost the program a just hearing and damaged the sponsor's credibility.

Clients have particular concerns when they contract with an office or corporation that has a stellar cast of individuals who can direct an evaluation. The concern is the subsequent discovery that someone else has been assigned to the client's project who "smiles broadly and announces, 'Six months ago, I couldn't even spell *evaluator*' . . . and you know the rest" (Gunn, 1987, p. 11).

Therefore, naming the individuals who will conduct the evaluation and briefly describing their level of expertise is important for the client in negotiating the contract. The client may want the contractor to use experienced evaluation specialists, experts on testing and measurement, psychologists, sociologists, political scientists, statisticians, survey specialists, or program content specialists (Gunn, 1987, p. 14).

In evaluation contracts with federal or state agencies, the vitae of the evaluation team typically are a component of the technical specifications section of the contract. In any case, their specific duties for the evaluation should be stated in the Statement of Work section. The contract also should specify that any changes in key personnel are to be approved in advance by the client. This provision prevents the "'bait-and-switch' tactics of some profit-oriented contractors (known affectionately in Washington, D. C. client circles as 'beltway bandits' or 'Potomac River robber barons')" (Gunn, 1987, p. 15).

Identification of the Object to be Evaluated

The directive "evaluate this program" is often a vague charge because (1) program boundaries are not clear and (2) the rationale for conducting the evaluation has not been clearly established. Thus, the first step is to define the program, project, instructional materials, organizational pattern, or policy that is the focus of the evaluation (Guba & Lincoln, 1981). A curriculum, for example, may be a lesson, a program of a comprehensive high school, or the educational program of a nation (Stake, 1967, p. 4). Further, a curriculum may be specified in terms of the topics, issues, and activities that the student will be exposed to and/or in terms of what the teacher will do (p. 4). If, for example, a computer software program in middle school science is the object of an evaluation, teacher attitudes toward technology and implementation efforts are also important. Thus, the program to be evaluated consists of the software + technology attitudes modeled by the teacher + teacher implementation activities. Also important during the negotiations is to discuss the goals of the intervention. The purpose of this information is to identify potential questions that the evaluation should address.

The contract should specify the program documents and related information that the client will make available to the evaluator. Related information consists of the conceptual framework for the policy or program, the extent of teacher training required, teacher skills required to implement the intervention, and the essential support resources (see Chapter 12). The client should be informed that this information is essential in order to determine the extent to which the implemented program is consistent with the intended program. Also, the client should be informed if the evaluator intends to obtain descriptions from the various stakeholders (Guba & Lincoln, p. 271).

Identification of the Evaluation Purpose

Misunderstandings about purpose are the most likely single reason for evaluations to misfire or to result in findings that are of no use (Guba & Lincoln, 1981, p. 273). For example, if the evaluator conducts a formative evaluation when the client requires a summative or impact evaluation, the information obtained will not address the client's concerns.

Sometimes the client has a specific purpose for the evaluation. In the Boulder Valley retention study, the purpose was (1) to examine the process whereby children are retained in kindergarten and (2) to determine the effects of 2-year kindergarten programs (Shepard & Smith, 1985). At the time the study was conducted, a district policy on retention was not in place. Each school developed its own policy; thus some schools were high retaining, and others were low retaining. Therefore, determining the process whereby children were retained was of major importance.

Often, the stated purpose is not clear-cut or seems inappropriate to the evaluator. That is, the client typically expresses one of three directives for the evaluation that require further negotiation. One type of directive is that the client may insist on a particular set of questions slanted to elicit positive responses from a constituency. In such a situation, the evaluator has reason to suspect a public relations study (see Chapter 17). If more substantive questions cannot be agreed upon for the evaluation, the evaluator should decline the contract.

A second possible directive is that the client may suggest information that is superficial and lacks depth. The client may request some low-level management or monitoring information when, instead, the same evaluation effort can generate important information about implementation. A third possible directive is that the initial charge may be vague and general in scope.

In all these situations, the key to redefining the purpose is negotiation (Guba & Lincoln, 1981). The evaluator and the client discuss possible alternatives in the process of clearly defining the purpose and the information needs of the various audiences. It is important in this discussion for both the evaluator and the client to clarify the conceptual framework for the program (if this information is available), the extent of role change required of the teachers, and the essential resources for the intervention. This information can indicate important questions to ask in the evaluation, such as questions about the adequacy of teacher training and teacher difficulties in implementing the intervention.

This information also is important to avoid evaluating a "no-treatment" project. For example, the new curriculum may require teachers to be facilitators of small group problem-solving inquiries into open-ended problems. If the teachers are accustomed to a direct teaching model in which they teach procedures to the entire class, they will experience difficulty in implementing the new curriculum. Thus, one purpose of an evaluation of the new curriculum is the extent to which teachers are able to adapt to very different roles.

The nature of teacher training also becomes an issue when an intervention requires role change by the teachers or other deliverers of the intervention. For example, a federal agency recently issued a contract for the development of problem-solving lessons in mathematics to be delivered electronically to classrooms. The teacher training component specified in the development involves teleconferencing with feedback to and discussions with the teachers by electronic mail. For teachers who may be apprehensive about using technology and/or have no experience with technology, this training and support mechanism may introduce problems that the evaluation should identify.

Summary

The evaluation contract is important because it establishes the obligations and responsibilities of both parties, and it is the key to avoiding ethical dilemmas. Prior to negotiating the contract, the evaluator should determine the feasibility of the evaluation by developing some information about the intervention and analyzing the budget and time frame for the study.

The contract for an evaluation may vary from a simple letter of agreement to a lengthy detailed document. Regardless of format, the contract consists of the context of the evaluation, the conduct of the evaluation, and the technical specifications.

Establishing the context for the evaluation consists of identifying the client, the contractor, the object of the evaluation, and the purpose. Both the client and his or her authority to initiate and contract for an evaluation should be clearly established. The identification of the evaluator also is important and should specify the expertise of the individual or individuals within the agency assigned to the study. Vitae of the evaluators typically are provided in the technical specifications of the contract. Also, the contract should state that changes in key personnel are to be approved by the client.

Defining the program, policy, or other intervention that is the focus of the evaluation is particularly important. A curriculum, for example, may range in scope from a lesson to the educational program of a nation. Understanding the nature of the program also provides information for developing the evaluation questions. The contract also should indicate the program documents that the client will make available to the evaluator.

Misunderstandings about the purpose of the evaluation are the primary cause of misdirected evaluations. When the stated purpose is not clear or seems inappropriate to the evaluator, negotiation is the key to focusing the study. The three types of directives that require further negotiation are (1) a request for low-level management information, (2) insistence on a particular set of questions slanted to elicit positive responses, and (3) a vague directive to evaluate the intervention.

CONDUCT OF THE EVALUATION

The contract may specify an evaluation of a program or policy already implemented or only one phase of a multiyear developmental and evaluation effort. For example, the contractor may be evaluating phase one of a program such as the development and formative testing of new curriculum materials in mathematics. At the end of phase one, the evaluator submits a detailed plan for conducting the next phase, and a new contract is negotiated. Or, a multiphase contract may be agreed on initially by the sponsor and the contractor, with the contingency that the contractor's plan of work for the next phase is to be approved by the client prior to execution. Regardless of the extent of the evaluation, topics related to the conduct of the evaluation that are specified in the contract are the methods of inquiry, evaluator responsibilities and authority, protection of subjects, access to records, and reporting (Guba & Lincoln, 1981).

Methods of Inquiry

The methods of inquiry stated in the contract should identify the general types of data to be collected and the rationale. However, the contract should allow some flexibility for the evaluator to make decisions as the study progresses.

Some federally funded evaluations are an exception to this general policy, however. In these evaluations, the RFP (which is prepared by the agency commissioning the evaluation) may specify the methodology to be used in the study, as well as the design, the sample size, and the statistical analysis (Cronbach & associates, 1980). An example is the evaluation of an alternative program for high school dropouts (CIP) in which the RFP specified the details of the control group design, which included 4 hours of pretesting (Fetterman, 1983).

The evaluator can submit ideas during the negotiation process; thus, the RFP is not the final word (Cronbach & associates, 1980). The sponsoring agency, although it may accept the suggestions of the evaluation contractor, typically strives for concreteness to the extent of rigidifying the study. The bureaucracy cannot accept research with unspecified operations; such research is unpredictable and, therefore, risky (Cronbach & associates, 1980, p. 229).

One mechanism for ensuring some flexibility is for the contract to specify data collection in successive waves, beginning on different dates in different sites. In this way, unexpected results or problems observed at one site can become a focus of inquiry in a second wave (p. 229).

Even if staggered data collection cannot be specified in the contract, some flexibility can be assured. The evaluator can study process variables that emerge as important and can add outcome measures when new variables emerge. An example is the evaluation of a U.S. AID program in infant nutrition in Guatemala (Cronbach & associates, 1980, p. 230). The original hypothesis for the study was that adding protein to the diet would critically influence both physical and intellectual growth. Expectant mothers in two villages received as much of a protein-rich supplement (atole) as they wished. Mothers and children in the two control villages received a protein-free sweet drink (fresco) that provided calories. Preliminary data indicated that growth was associated with the number of calories of the supplement (regardless of type), and review of the normal village diet indicated no protein deficiencies. Because supplement intake had been recorded at each site, the study was redirected to the effects of extra calories on growth.

Evaluations that are sponsored by clients other than bureaucratic agencies typically are more flexible. For example, the client in the Boulder Valley retention study specified the purpose of the evaluation. The evaluators developed the questions and the methods based on a literature review of the practice of retention and other information.

Of major importance in the consideration of methods of inquiry is that the breadth and depth of the methods to be implemented must be within the scope of the budget. Personnel consumes the largest portion of the budget, and extensive on-site observations are personnel intensive. For example, an ethnographic perspective to understanding program implementation may be possible only if (1) the budget has been planned to include extensive on-site visits by ethnographers, or (2) doctoral students in training conduct many of the visits under the direct supervision of an ethnographer.

Protection of Subjects and Record Access

The contract should state that the confidentiality and anonymity of the individuals who are sources of information will be protected (see Chapter 17 for details). Although the evaluator routinely implements such procedures, a contract statement also holds the client to this principle.

The contract also should stipulate which records under the control of the sponsor or the program staff are to be made accessible and the processes to be followed in gaining access to them (Guba & Lincoln, 1981, p. 276). In the event that personnel may make this task difficult, the contract also should provide for direct appeal to sponsors or administrators for this contingency (p. 276).

Evaluators should be aware that a promise of confidentiality to the study participants does not protect information from disclosure in a legal proceeding (see Chapter 17). Thus, the evaluator should code and aggregate data so that individuals cannot be identified. Also, in the event of a challenge to the data in the final report, the evaluator could be required by a court to open his or her files (Guba & Lincoln, 1981, p. 277). Unless the final report clearly illustrates coding systems and other analyses, the evaluator conducting a qualitative study should maintain records illustrating the methodology for connecting field notes to the analyses and conclusions in the report (p. 277).

Evaluator Responsibilities and Authority

The evaluation contract is a formal statement that describes the basic conditions, requirements, and approach to be taken in the study (Guba & Lincoln, 1981). The evaluator is responsible for executing the basic plans described in the contract, for example, test administration, interviews, records analysis, observations, data compilation, data analyses, and interpretations. The evaluator also is responsible for obtaining informed consent of evaluation participants and for clearing with appropriate administrators any visits to schools and other settings.

The contract, however, does not address all contingencies. Situations can arise in which professional decisions are required of the evaluator. Therefore, Guba and Lincoln (1981, p. 279) suggest that a statement be included in the contract that specifies the autonomy of the evaluator to make a professional decision in these situations. An example of this need occurred in the Guatemala study in which new information indicated that protein supplements were not the key to growth for young children.

In some situations, an advisory panel is selected to provide suggestions during the progress of the evaluation. One advantage of an advisory panel is that the members are exposed to all the issues, potential solutions, likely consequences, and limitations of the study. Further, if they make relevant suggestions that are utilized in the study, they are likely to develop a sense of ownership of the evaluation.

If an advisory panel is to be used, the contract should describe the size of the panel, audiences to be represented, and their function. Specification of the panel's advisory functions is particularly important to the client (Gunn, 1987). With this provision, the panel cannot take it upon itself to change the objectives of the study and decide to do something different from the original focus (Gunn, 1987, p. 12). The contract also may stipulate that members of the advisory panel should be approved by both the evaluator and the client.

Reporting

Reporting may be either formal or informal and may involve several audiences (Cronbach & associates, 1980; Guba & Lincoln, 1981). If draft reports are to be disseminated to representative members of target audiences for their review and comments, the responsibility for this dissemination should be indicated in the contract.

The evaluator also should have the option of reporting to various audiences identified during the evaluation (Guba & Lincoln, 1981). In addition to the sponsor, who receives the formal reports, these audiences may consist of local program staff, project site personnel, parents, and others.

Difficulties are most likely to develop with the final evaluation report. The two most likely problem areas are the content of the report and the authority to release the report. In general, the evaluator must insist that he/she has sole responsibility for content (Guba & Lincoln, 1981, p. 279). The sponsor or audience members are entitled to raise questions about factual accuracy, but judgments and interpretations are the responsibility of the evaluator.

Potential problems in this area can be resolved in one of two ways. The right to edit the report may be accorded to another party with the provision that the evaluator can reserve the right to change any editing if, in his or her judgment, essential meanings are altered (Guba & Lincoln, 1981, p. 279).

The other alternative is to provide for full scrutiny of the report by a panel of qualified reviewers who are not aligned with the sponsoring agency (Cronbach &

associates, 1980, p. 211). Gunn (1987) suggests that the final report receive a wide circulation for review and comments by members of the intended target audience, evaluation experts, and program officials, prior to delivery to the client. Such a review makes it difficult for a bureaucrat in the agency to develop a vague yet scathing review after report delivery and thereby block dissemination (p. 17).

Reports can be disseminated through various channels, such as formal presentations at board meetings, mail distribution, newspaper or television news releases, and so on. The contract should specify the distribution process or the negotiation process by which these decisions will be made (Guba & Lincoln, 1981, p. 280).

Summary

Conduct of the evaluation consists of methods of inquiry, provisions for the protection of subjects, access to records, evaluator responsibilities and authority, and reporting. Although federally sponsored evaluations may specify methodology, design, sample sizes, and statistical analyses, the evaluator can submit ideas during the negotiation process. Of importance in negotiating this portion of the contract is that the structure should be sufficient to provide direction and flexible enough to address new developments as the evaluation progresses.

The evaluator is responsible for protecting the confidentiality and anonymity of individuals who provide information in the study. The contract should hold the client to this principle and also stipulate the records to which the evaluator has access.

The evaluator is responsible for executing the basic plans in the contract, but he or she should have the autonomy to make professional decisions in the course of the study. The functions of an advisory panel (if included), the nature and timing of reporting, and editorial privilege and dissemination of the reports also are specified in the contract. Clients may be accorded the right to edit a final report if the evaluator reserves the right to refuse edits that change meaning. An alternative is to submit draft reports to an advisory committee or a panel of evaluation experts who are not associated with the commissioning agency.

TECHNICAL SPECIFICATIONS

The technical specifications section of the contract consists of the qualifications of the individuals conducting the evaluation, the schedule of major activities in the evaluation, the budget, the products to be delivered to the client, and the conditions for payment.

Evaluator Qualifications and Schedule of Activities

The qualifications of the individuals conducting the evaluation may be in the form of "boiler plate" paragraphs that describe the individuals' capabilities, or they may be in the form of curriculum vitae. The funding agency usually determines the format. A client who is dealing with a large agency may also require that individuals' names be attached to major activities listed in the Statement of Work. When this provision is made, changes in personnel must first be approved by the client.

Of importance in developing the schedule of activities is that it should not be so detailed as to inhibit flexibility. A general sequence of major activities, such as "evaluation of draft materials" and "on-site interviews" with associated completion dates, should comprise the schedule. Also stated are the delivery dates of interim and final reports. The evaluator will, of course, maintain a schedule of specific activities within these major categories, and a copy may be provided to the client as a separate document if the client is concerned about the completion of specific activities within the allotted time frame. (See Chapter 13 for a discussion of issues related to time lines.) However, to incorporate a detailed schedule into the contract does not serve a useful purpose in the evaluation and may also restrain flexibility.

A typical problem with evaluation contracts made with federal agencies is that they are rarely executed on time. The contract may not be final until 2 to 5 months into the proposed work schedule. Fetterman (1983) notes that the RFP for the program for disadvantaged teenage dropouts (CIP) was delayed approximately 4 months, but the time lines for program start-up and operation and delivery dates for interim evaluation reports were not changed. As a result, the first draft report was based on observations of the only site in full operation (although observations of all sites were required) and led to programmatic difficulties for the other three sites because of a report reference to their not being in full operation (p. 70). Thus, whenever possible, the evaluator should negotiate a provision for contract modification in the event of a late start.

Budget

A major component of the technical specifications is the budget, which consists of both direct and indirect costs. Direct costs are expenditures such as fees to consultants, telephone and postage, duplication costs, supplies, travel, and project salaries.

The largest single expenditure in the budget is personnel, and the amount may range from 60% to 80%. An evaluation project with an ethnographic component is particularly labor intensive. The budget determines the size of the team for the evaluation because it sets the ceiling on expenditures (Guba & Lincoln, 1981, p. 287).

The ceiling on the number of team members for a particular budget may be estimated by determining the number of full-time equivalent personnel that the budget will buy and dividing that number by .20. The .20 represents 1 day per week or 20% of the individual's effort (Guba & Lincoln, 1981, p. 287). A budget that will support four full-time equivalents will theoretically support 20 individuals who are working 1 day per week. However, a more realistic number is 15, both from a managerial and a logistical perspective. Projections of the number of personnel that can be used will also vary if an institute within a university setting is the contractor. Advanced doctoral students often are hired on assistantships by institutes of research and evaluation, and they work under the supervision of full-time faculty in a particular area of expertise. The students gain hands-on experience, and the expenditure for personnel is reduced. All or part of the student's assistantship is charged to the project for which the work is being done.

The budget that is a part of the proposal lists expenditures in various categories. Salaries for personnel and their association with the evaluation for a 1-year project may be listed as follows:

Evaluation Staff

Marjorie Smith, Project Director (full-time)	$ 60,000
James Roberts, Qualitative Evaluator (1⁄2 time)	25,400
Janice Smith, Statistician (1⁄2 time)	18,500
Marianne Davis, Joe Evans, David Mathews & Mark Johnson (advanced doctoral students, 1⁄2 time, 1 year @ $9,000 each)	36,000
Judy Anderson, Secretary (1⁄4 time)	7,000

These assignments and expenditures are based on an analysis by the evaluation contractor of the types of expertise that will be required to evaluate the program and the tasks that will be conducted during the evaluation. For example, the contractor will determine specific activities that are to be undertaken (such as literature review, development of the program definition, on-site observations and interviews, and data analysis) and approximate time frames for each activity (see Chapter 13 for a description). The contractor will then "cost out" these activities and determine the total amount of individuals' time that will be required. For example, the secretary's time will be heavily required during certain phases of the project, such as when interim and final reports are to be prepared. At other times, the workload will be light, but it is estimated to average out at about one fourth of the secretary's time. Because she is already on staff with the agency or evaluation institute, one fourth of her time overall is assigned to this project. (The remainder of her time is assigned and charged to other projects or operating expenses of the agency or institute.) Some agencies may require personnel expenditures to be reported in terms of the number of days allocated to the project for different individuals. In these cases, the evaluator estimates the number of days the individual will work on the project and multiplies by the daily salary or fee.

Table 11.1 illustrates direct costs (other than staff salaries) that are a part of the budget. Consultant fees and travel and per diem for staff and consultants are based on the number of days for specific tasks, such as on-site observations and interviews. Similarly, if telephone interviews or conference calls with an advisory committee are a part of the evaluation, estimates for these costs must be made. Equipment purchases for the agency or institution typically are not allowed. However, equipment rental, such as for tape recorders, may be required and is permitted.

Table 11.1
Estimation of direct evaluation costs exclusive of project salaries

Expenditure	Calculation
Consultants	Multiply consultant's daily rate by number of days allocated to the project. (Fringe benefits are not paid to consultants.)
Printing and duplication	Estimate printing of documents and reports and xeroxing.
Consumable supplies	Estimate the costs of paper, pencils, typing supplies, and audio– and video-tapes.
Travel and per diem	Estimate mileage and multiply by the institutional or agency rate. For air travel, estimate ticket cost, ground transportation, and parking. Estimate per diem costs for lodging and meals for the number of days each staff member and consultant will be in the field. (Per diem estimates vary widely for different parts of the country.)
Telephone and postage	Estimate daily service costs for telephone plus long-distance calls; include regular postage, express air service, and packages in postage estimates.
Data processing and library searches	Estimate the time required for mainframe computer use and multiply by the rate charged by the data processing center. If advanced doctoral students are not available to code and enter data, estimate the hourly costs of data processors. Estimates should allow for data reanalysis and additional analyses that may be needed. Estimate fees for library searches.

Indirect costs consist of the percentage of the total budget charged to overhead by the institution (for use of its building facilities and offices). Universities and consulting agencies usually employ personnel who provide assistance in computing indirect costs when contracts are negotiated with state and federal agencies, as the percentages of the total budget allowable for this category sometimes change.

Products and Method of Payment

The products to be developed in the evaluation also are identified in the technical specifications. Products are the interim reports that are completed at certain stages of the work and a final report. These reports often are referred to as "the deliverables," and payment to the contractor is based on submission of these reports. A certain percentage of the total funding may be paid upon the receipt of each interim report with a final portion paid on the delivery of the final report. The conditions of payment and associated amounts also are described in the contract.

Summary

Items delineated in the technical specifications are the qualifications of the individuals conducting the evaluation, the schedule of major activities, the budget, products to be delivered, and provisions for payment. Typically, the schedule describes major activities, such as "completion of on-site interviews" (with associated dates), rather than day-by-day activities. Too detailed a schedule inhibits the flexibility of the evaluation. Important in the assignment of completion dates is a provision for late start-up of the evaluation.

Unlike the schedule of activities, the evaluation budget is highly detailed, with expenditures allocated to specific categories in direct and indirect costs. Also described are the products to be developed in the evaluation, typically, interim and final reports and the delivery dates. Method of payment also is specified, and payment typically is associated with the delivery of the required reports.

GUIDELINES FOR CONTRACT NEGOTIATIONS

Step 1. Determine the feasibility of the contract.
     1.1   Develop a preliminary knowledge base for the intervention.
     1.2   Analyze the adequacy of the budget and the time frame.

Step 2. Confirm the negotiating authority of the client and the evaluation expertise required for the study.
     2.1   Check the lines of command in the agency, district, or institution.
     2.2   Draft a brief description of the required areas of evaluation expertise and affirm the availability of selected individuals.

Step 3. Clarify the focus of the evaluation with the client.
     3.1   Define the nature of the program or policy and the needed resources.
     3.2   Determine the purpose of the evaluation.
     3.3   Negotiate refinement or redirection of the evaluation, if necessary.

Step 4. Establish the evaluation framework.
     4.1   Develop general evaluation questions and methods of inquiry.
     4.2   Negotiate the methodological approach with the client, if necessary.
     4.3   Provide for the confidentiality and anonymity of evaluation participants.
     4.4   Negotiate evaluator autonomy in professional decisions.
     4.5   Negotiate the types of reports and submission dates.

Step 5. Develop the technical specifications.
     5.1   Document evaluator qualifications.
     5.2   Develop a general schedule of work.
     5.3   Develop the budget.
          5.3.1   Calculate personnel costs.
          5.3.2   Estimate office and travel expenses.
          5.3.3   Calculate indirect expenses.

CHAPTER QUESTIONS

1. What is the purpose of an evaluation contract?

2. What is the rationale for specifying the members of the evaluation team in the contract?

3. What are the three types of directives the evaluator is often likely to receive from the client?

4. What are the evaluator's alternatives when the RFP specifies the details of the sample, the design, and the methods?

5. What are the types of expenditures in an evaluation budget?

REFERENCES

Cooley, W., & Bickel, W. (1986). *Decision-oriented educational research*. Boston: Kluwer-Nijhoff.

Cronbach, L. J., Ambron, S., Dornbusch, S., Hess, R., Hornik, R., Phillips, D., Walker, D., & Weiner, S. (1980). *Toward reform of program evaluation*. San Francisco: Jossey-Bass.

Fetterman, D. (1983). Guilty knowledge, dirty hands, and other ethical dilemmas: The hazards of contract research. *Human Organization, 42*(3), 214–224.

Fetterman, D. (1986). Conceptual crossroads: Methods and ethics in ethnographic evaluation. In D. Williams (Ed.), *Naturalistic evaluation. New Directions for Program Evaluation, 30*, 23–26.

Guba, E., & Lincoln, Y. (1981). *Effective evaluation*. San Francisco: Jossey-Bass.

Gunn, W. (1987). Client concerns and strategies. In J. Nowakowski (Ed.), *The client perspective on evaluation. New Directions for Program Evaluation, 36*, 9–18.

Shepard, L., & Smith, M. (1985). *Boulder Valley kindergarten study: Retention practices and retention effects*. Boulder, CO: Boulder Valley Public Schools.

Sieber, J. (1980). Being ethical: Professional and personal decisions in program evaluation. In R. Perloff & E. Perloff (Eds.), *Values, ethics, and standards in evaluation. New Directions for Program Evaluation, 7*, 51–61.

Stake, R. E. (1967). Toward a technology for the evaluation of educational programs. In R. Tyler, R. Gagné, & M. Scriven (Eds.), *Perspectives of curriculum evaluation* (pp. 1–12). Chicago: Rand McNally.

CHAPTER 12

Development of a Program Definition

One of the problems of the early evaluations was that they were unable to address the causes of program success or failure. However, explanations of how and why a program works is essential if the program is to be transferred elsewhere (Cook & Shadish, 1986; Cronbach, 1982). Subsequently, two of the utilitarian perspectives on evaluation addressed the issue of developing detailed information about the program. Two important stages in the Provus (1969, 1971) approach address the operational elements of a program. They are program definition and program installation. In the evaluation of the program definition (Stage I), the evaluator first addresses the adequacy of information about the program. That is, Does the definition describe the purposes of the program; required conditions and events; required student entry behaviors; staff qualifications and training; and essential media, facilities, and administrative conditions? Next, the evaluator analyzes the program definition for clarity, internal consistency, and comprehensiveness (Provus, 1969). Guidelines for this analysis were not provided, however.

The purpose of the analysis of the program definition was twofold. First, a program should be terminated if resources do not meet minimal levels for program operation, if program components are inconsistent with each other, or if the program cannot be comprehensively defined (Provus, 1969). In the event the program definition is comprehensive and consistent, it becomes the blueprint against which to judge the installation of the program (the second purpose of the definition).

The countenance perspective developed by Robert Stake (1967), described the task of program definition somewhat differently. The countenance model provided for descriptive data in three major categories: antecedents, transactions, and outcomes. For each of these three categories, the evaluator documented "intents" and "observations." Next, the evaluator determined the logical contingencies between intended antecedents, intended transactions, and intended outcomes. Then, the evaluator documented the observed antecedents, transactions, and outcomes, as well as the empirical contingencies among them. In addition, observations were to be compared with intents in order to determine the congruency. However, this approach did not provide explicit guidelines for developing the needed information.

As indicated in Chapter 11, some basic information about the program is important at the time of contract negotiations so that important issues may be addressed in the evaluation. The evaluator should develop as much information as possible about the four components of a program definition prior to the start of the evaluation and complete the task as soon as the evaluation is underway. The four components are:

1. The conceptual framework for the program with notations about gaps and contradictions
2. Essential program elements
3. Support resources required to implement the program
4. The causal links between program events and anticipated outcomes

The conceptual framework consists of the basic beliefs, assumptions, and theories that are the basis for the intervention. Current literature and research on the intervention or similar developments also are a part of the conceptual framework. Essential program elements are the activities, learning experiences, and types of evaluation that are the heart of the innovation. Support resources are the materials, equipment, and teacher training required to implement and maintain the program. Finally, the causal links are the immediate and intermediate events that bridge the gap between implementation and outcomes. For example, a key causal link in a distance education program that is broadcast by television is, Was the program received at the distant site by the students?

The purpose of this chapter is twofold. First, the important functions of a program definition are discussed. Second, the specific steps in constructing a program definition are described.

THE FUNCTIONS OF A PROGRAM DEFINITION

One of the beliefs associated with the early evaluations was that any generalist could adequately evaluate any program by applying the appropriate methodology. Reactions to those early evaluations indicated that knowledge of the particular program was essential in order to conduct a fair evaluation. In addition, a well-constructed program definition fulfills four general functions in an evaluation:

1. The program definition can "red flag" a policy or program that has little or no potential for success.
2. In the early stages of development and formative testing, a program definition provides important information for design.

3. The information contributes to the development of the evaluation plan by indicating some specific actions to be taken in conducting the evaluation.

4. When the evaluation is completed, the program definition is a key component in explaining program effects and can contribute to the larger body of knowledge about program dynamics.

Identification of a Policy or Program With Minimal Potential for Success

A major function of a program definition is to "red flag" a policy or program that has little chance of success. Leonard Ruttman (1980) goes so far as to say that if the assumptions are not credible and the planned change does not make sense conceptually, then evaluation resources should not be wasted on the program. An example is a program to use prison guards as counselors. The assumption that prison guards can learn counselor attitudes, beliefs, and skills is highly suspect.

An example in the educational setting of a faulty conceptual framework is the performance contracting study. The policy specified that school systems would contract with private firms that hired teachers and provided instructional materials for disadvantaged students. The firms were to be paid only on the basis of achievement results. The belief was that firms that were successful at teaching underprivileged children would thrive, and school boards would have choices of educational materials based on outputs (Gramlich & Koshel, 1976, p. 152).

In reality, the firms found it difficult both to hire local teachers and to obtain the support of local teachers and school officials. In addition, school officials resented the extra paperwork—preparing lists of potential student participants, arranging for classrooms, and addressing teacher morale. The technology available in the project classes, the scheduling disruptions resulting from the experimental classes, and the higher salaries earned by the experimental teachers were all sources of hostility. "Even such seemingly reconcilable matters as the fact that experimental teachers often did not have cafeteria duty often snowballed into great problems" (Gramlich & Koshel, 1976, p. 162). In other words, the belief in institutional change from an external agency with the power to implement technology, "reward" students for doing their homework, and hire teachers with perceived special privileges was naive at best.

Assistance in Program Design

Programs or curricula in early stages of development often undergo formative testing with classroom teachers to identify problems with the materials. Program definition at this stage of development is an invaluable tool. First, it identifies the conceptual framework on which the program is based, and these assumptions may be tested in preliminary pilot tests of the intervention. Second, it identifies specific immediate consequences from implementing particular activities (e.g., students are more attentive) and intermediate outcomes. The information generated in the program definition may be tested in the early stages of program development to determine breakdowns in cause-effect relationships before the materials and activities are set in concrete. An evaluation that checks out the causal links in a program early allows the program to be revised before outcome data is collected (Cronbach & associates, 1980, p. 258).

Contributions to the Evaluation Plan

Perhaps the most important function of a program definition from the evaluator's perspective is the information provided for planning the evaluation. First, the documentation of essential components and supporting resources serves as a blueprint for determining the extent of implementation of the program. In this way strong representations of the program may be separated from weak implementations.

Second, the gaps and contradictions identified in the conceptual framework and the causal links identified for the program indicate important evaluation questions to ask in the study. On occasion, a program with a strong philosophy but poorly defined activities has been put in place, and the school district or other agency has requested an evaluation. A summative evaluation at this stage of the program is risky at best. The evaluation is likely to be disappointing, and more importantly, it may well doom a promising innovation before it legitimately has a chance to make a difference.

Third, gaps in the conceptual framework and between the causal links and stated aims can indicate unrealistic expectations for the intervention. These expectations should be reconceptualized into achievable goals. Fourth, a careful review of the program definition can reveal potential side effects that the evaluation plan should incorporate as possible outcomes. Fifth, a well-constructed program definition may reveal complexities in the decision making or other essential processes in the intervention that are potential trouble spots in the implementation. The evaluation plan must be sensitive to assessing the nature of these events.

Table 12.1 illustrates the specific types of information indicated by the program definition and the associated courses of action in the evaluation. As illustrated in the table, a program definition provides valuable input to the task of planning the evaluation.

Identification of Essential Program Elements.   A typical practice in the large-scale evaluations of the 1970s was to combine program sites with the same label and calculate "average effect." One problem with this practice is that strong and weak representations of the program are combined and the "average effect" is misleading. Therefore, the description of essential program activities and support resources can serve as a blueprint to determine the extent of implementation at a program site. In this way, different levels of implementation may be identified. For example, Tyler (1991) used a list of 51 characteristics of activity schools to group sites into strong, moderate, and weak examples of the curriculum.

Identification of Potential Evaluation Questions.   Each of the causal links documented for the intervention becomes a potential question for the evaluation to

Table 12.1
Specific informational functions of a program definition

1. Identifies essential elements in program implementation	1. Use as a program blueprint to identify strong and weak implementations
2. Identifies gaps and contradictions in the conceptual framework and causal links	2. Develop evaluation questions to address these issues
3. Identifies unrealistic expectations for the intervention	3. Reconceptualize program aims into attainable outcomes
4. May reveal potential side effects	4. Implement procedures to document unplanned effects
5. May reveal ambiguities or complexities in decision making	5. Implement observational or policy-capturing methods to identify variations in program decision making

address (Cronbach & associates, 1980). Casual reports or observations in passing are sufficient to confirm some causal links, such as the availability of software on classroom microcomputers. Others, however, require specific procedures. An example is the USAID project in Nicaragua that broadcast radio messages about the treatment for a common infant illness. An important causal link in the success of the broadcasts is the adequacy of the mother's knowledge base to understand the information. Therefore, a key evaluation focus is the knowledge base of the audiences who receive the messages.

As already stated, in the absence of a program definition, the evaluation may focus on ultimate impact. However, the program definition indicates intermediate outcomes that are essential if ultimate impact is to be realized. In the USAID example, critical evaluation questions are, Which mothers received the messages? Did the mothers who received the messages understand them? and Were the ingredients available to the mothers to implement the treatment?

Indication of Unrealistic Expectations.   Detailing the specific activities intended to lead to the attainment of program goals may indicate gaps between project events and stated aims. In such situations, the aims should be reviewed and more realistic outcomes identified. The Head Start goal of fostering the social development of the child is an example. This goal may translate into "learning to respect the property and rights of others." Specific program links may be learning to take turns and learning to ask permission to borrow another child's supplies.

Identification of Possible Side Effects.   Unplanned side effects of an intervention may be either negative or positive. A policy or program that is an outgrowth of untested maxims or of an incomplete theory that has not been tested in empirical research may harbor unexpected side effects. For example, one accepted belief of pupil retention prior to first grade is that the children are better off and do not suffer emotionally from being retained at an early age. When this belief was tested in an evaluation of the policy, negative emotional effects were found both for the retained children and their parents. Semi-structured interviews conducted with 30 parents of retained children indicated difficult adjustment to perceived failure, problems with discrepancies between age and grade, interfamily conflict, and conflict with the school (Shepard & Smith, 1985, p. 122).

In contrast, a program may have developed activities that are likely to generate unplanned positive effects. For example, children in a reading program in Appalachia were encouraged to take the booklets and other materials home to share with their families. An increased interest in reading and improved achievement of the children's siblings are potential unplanned positive effects of this activity.

Discovery of the Complexity of Policies and Decisions.   Often, policies or program decisions that appear to be fairly simple are instead subject to ambiguities and various styles or mechanisms of implementation. These problems may be revealed in a review of the literature on the intervention or a review of program documents.

An example is the practice of retention prior to entry into first grade. Children that are identified as "at risk" for succeeding in first grade are often retained in kindergarten or placed in a transition room or pre-first grade. However, in a search of the literature, Shepard and Smith (1985) found that a variety of pupil characteristics, weighted in different combinations, were used by different schools and school districts as a basis for retention. Among the characteristics that were combined in various ways to make retention decisions were perceived social maturity, gender, academic performance, and date of birth.

Awareness of the complexity of retention decisions led to the examination of school records to determine the type of student that is retained and the "policy capturing" study with the kindergarten teachers in the high-retaining schools (described in Chapter 9). The results indicated that the teachers in the high-retaining schools emphasized academic skills and social maturity more than the other characteristics. However, the teachers varied considerably on the other factors to the extent that no consistent combination of characteristics was used.

Assistance in Explaining Program Effects

An important requirement of evaluations is to develop inferences from the data and to make recommendations for subsequent action about the program or innovation. Other important requirements according to Cronbach and associates (1980) are (1) to add to the knowledge base about the innovation and (2) to inform educators, researchers, and evaluators in the broader community beyond the context of the particular evaluation.

In order to fulfill these requirements, evaluation reports must provide more information than simply a description of the findings. Reports should provide explanations of the effects and should relate the explanations to the characteristics of the context in which the program was implemented. If the program is unsuccessful in achieving one or more objectives, the evaluation should identify the reasons. Likely reasons for lack of success are (1) that the underlying basis for the program is defective, (2) that the program elements do not match the underlying theory, and (3) that one or more elements of the program were not implemented as planned. The program definition is a key component in the identification of reasons for lack of success. The program definition describes the elements in the program rationale and theory, notes contradictions and gaps, documents the essential activities and resources, and identifies the causal links between activities and anticipated effects. Documentation of actual program events and outcomes is then compared with the program definition to develop the explanation.

The same process is implemented for programs that are successful. That is, the evaluator should have sufficient information either (1) to support the conceptual basis and implementation of prescribed program events or (2) to identify the particular situational factors responsible for success. Change, for example, may result from the actions of an enthusiastic, dedicated project director who improvises to bridge the gap between a weak conceptual framework and the observed outcomes. The basis for developing an adequate explanation of positive effects in the program definition is then confirmed or disconfirmed by on-site observations.

Summary

Both the Provus Model and the Stake's countenance approach addressed the need to develop information about the conceptual framework and essential elements of programs to serve as part of the framework for evaluation. The functions of such information in an evaluation are several. First, in the early stages of program development, this information provides the basis for testing the conceptual framework of the intervention, weaknesses in the support framework for implementation, and breakdowns in cause-effect relationships. Second, in an impact evaluation, the program definition is a major source of information for the questions that the evaluation is to address. The program definition serves as a blueprint to identify strong and weak implementations, identifies unrealistic aims, and may reveal potential side effects or ambiguities in the decisions made in the program. Third, when the evaluation is completed, the definition can provide an explanation for program effects.

COMPONENTS OF A PROGRAM DEFINITION

A program definition consists of four types of information. As stated earlier in the chapter, they are:

1. The conceptual framework for the program with notations about gaps and contradictions

2. Essential program elements

3. Support resources required to implement the program

4. The causal links between program events and anticipated outcomes

A program definition is similar to a program theory of action as identified by Weiss (1972) and supported by Cronbach and associates (1980). In their view, a theory of action consists of supporting beliefs, program elements, and the causal links between program elements and intermediate outcomes. A program definition, however, addresses two additional types of information (see Figure 12.1). One is information external to the program that may support or raise questions about the soundness of the program rationale. Examples are the history of similar programs and published or unpublished research on the variables the program is expected to influence. Second, a program definition also indicates the resources essential for program operation. Both are important for identifying potential problems in the implementation.

An appropriate mechanism for recording the development of a program definition is a summary document with columns for the types of information. This format allows one to compare entries across columns and note gaps, contradictions, or other problems.

Figure 12.1

Components of a program definition

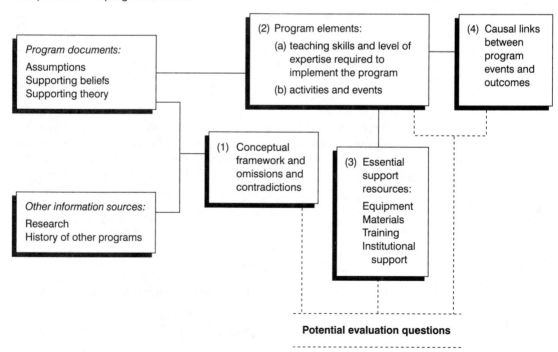

The Conceptual Framework and Analysis

The conceptual framework of a program consists of the assumptions, beliefs, and/or supporting theory on which the program is based. If the assumptions or theory are in error, the success of the intervention is in jeopardy.

An example of a set of assumptions is the beliefs that undergirded the 1960s chemistry curriculum CHEM. The beliefs are (1) that laboratory experimentation is essential for students to deduce the operating principles of chemistry, (2) that deducing the principles of chemistry is a key component in critical thinking in science, and (3) that critical thinking enhances intellectual development and, consequently, achievement.

These beliefs, however, were untested. Thus, they indicate three critical questions that the evaluation should have addressed: (1) Does deducing the principles of chemistry facilitate critical thinking in science? (2) Does critical thinking enhance intellectual development? and (3) In what ways is intellectual development related to school achievement? (Also, definitions were needed for the terms *critical thinking* and *intellectual development*.)

Documents that can provide information about the conceptual framework include proposals submitted to funding agencies, program rationales and descriptions developed to communicate to administrators and teachers, letters to parents, brochures, and teacher training materials. Also, an agency's archives may contain prior evaluation reports or data from past years that may be helpful (Cronbach & associates, 1980).

Sometimes a program is directly derived from an explicit theory. An example is the High/Scope Cognitive Development Curriculum, which is based on Jean Piaget's cognitive development theory. A central principle of the theory is that children's cognitive development is enhanced by their self-directed exploration of the environment and construction of knowledge. The program, therefore, focuses on providing for children's self-directed experimentation on the environment.

As indicated in Chapter 2, the more typical situation is that programs are derived from general beliefs about the potential of a particular intervention to address a problem or unmet need. (The CHEM curriculum is an example.) Further, these beliefs may be implicit rather than explicit. Examination of the program rationale followed by discussions with program developers as to the reasons for implementing certain types of activities may be required to identify the supporting beliefs.

Documenting the social theory and/or research that support a program is one part of the evaluator's homework. Planners, however, are unlikely to have paid attention to voices that challenge their views. The evaluator, therefore, should also search out these critics (Cronbach & associates, 1980, p. 253). Sources of information are the history of similar programs, research on variables addressed by the program under study, and other theoretical positions.

An example of an evaluation that was sensitive to the discrepancy between a policy rationale and other theory and research is the kindergarten retention study for a Colorado school district conducted by Shepard and Smith (1985). The policy of kindergarten retention is supported by the writings of one psychologist who believed in maturational unfolding; that is, children will "grow into" readiness for school. A search of the literature, however, revealed (1) that the maturational belief is countered by several opposing theories; (2) that empirical research does not support the proposed benefits of kindergarten retention; and (3) that the practice of retention is increasingly popular in schools. In other words, despite theoretical and empirical evidence to the contrary, the practice of school retention was flourishing. This information alerted the evaluators to two major directions to pursue in the study. One was to document the effects of kindergarten retention, and the other was to determine the beliefs and retention criteria operating in the high-retaining schools in the district.

Using a ledger-sheet format, the conceptual framework and analysis may be recorded in three columns headed Program Rationale (assumptions, beliefs, and/or supporting theory); Other Relevant Theory and/or Data; and Questions about Gaps and Contradictions. Table 12.2 illustrates this mechanism. As illustrated in the table, column three indicates potential questions to be pursued in the evaluation.

Essential Program Elements

Program elements refer to (1) the activities and essential day-to-day events required in the course of the program and (2) the teaching skills and level of expertise required to implement the program. Examples of educational activities are one-on-one tutoring, small group inquiry, self-directed laboratory experiments, and so on. A

Table 12.2
Examples of conceptual analysis

Program Rationale (Assumptions, beliefs, and/or supporting theory)	Other Relevant Theory and/or Data	Questions About Gaps and Contradictions
1. Laboratory experimentation is essential for students to deduce the operating principles of chemistry.	David Ausubel's subsumption theory, which supports meaningful direct instruction.	1. Is hands-on experimentation a necessary requirement for the process of deduction?
2. Deducing the principles of chemistry is a key component in critical thinking in science.	[No information available in the 60's.]	2. Does deducing the principles of chemistry facilitate critical thinking in science?
3. Critical thinking enhances intellectual development and, consequently, achievement.		3. In what ways is intellectual development related to school achievement?
		4. How does the project define "critical thinking" and "intellectual development"?

separate column on the program summary headed Essential Expertise and Program Activities may be used to record this information.

Documenting the level of expertise required to implement the program is important for two reasons. First, it provides a standard with which to compare the effectiveness of the teacher training. Second, it is an indicator of the degree of role change required to implement the innovation. The greater the required role change, the more flexibility is required of the institution or system, as well as a greater investment of resources (McLaughlin, 1976; Tyler, 1991).

In addition, the possibility of partial or incomplete implementation increases with the degree of required role change. An example is the adoption of a program to help students become self-directed problem solvers in a school that previously emphasized acquisition of facts and information. The new program requires both teachers and students to develop new conceptions of learning. Teachers must focus on giving students the responsibility for their own learning. Therefore, the teacher must develop new skills for stimulating, guiding, and rewarding learning, as well as new ways of evaluating and recording student progress (Tyler, 1991, p. 7).

The restructuring of the mathematics curriculum in California initiated in the mid-1980s is another example. Instead of emphasizing the memorization of rules and procedures and right answers, the new curriculum goals emphasize learning to reason mathematically. Based on the view that learners construct knowledge for themselves, the new curriculum requires teachers to be facilitators who help students learn to reason with and communicate mathematics. In small group and class sessions, the teacher encourages students to offer alternative solutions to problems and to collaborate in figuring out the logical approaches. This perspective, however, differs from most teachers' views of mathematics as a set of truths or rules to be learned. It also establishes a role different from that of the direct instruction model in which the teacher presents rules and procedures and provides student practice with the content.

In such situations, the implementation of a new program is far more difficult and demands more time if it requires different teaching skills or different kinds of teacher-student interactions than the old program. Thus, this information is important in determining the degree of implementation of the innovation (see Chapter 14).

Support Resources Essential for Implementation

Two types of support are important in the installation of a new program. One, which may be referred to as indirect support, consists of the attitudes of administrators, the endorsement of directions and goals for staff members, and the activities undertaken to elicit enthusiasm and support for the innovation in the school and community. The extent of indirect support may be determined when the evaluator meets with administrative personnel and visits project sites.

Direct support, in contrast, refers to the institutional arrangements essential for the program. These arrangements are the structural context described by Charters and Jones (1973) and are an important phase in program implementation. This support includes employing individuals (such as teacher aides), changing job titles, forming and appointing committees, assigning responsibilities, purchasing materials and equipment, and scheduling classes (p. 6). Class schedules, for example, may be rearranged so that members of a teacher team may have a common planning period. Sources of information on these resources are curriculum frameworks, program descriptions, and teacher training materials. An individualized language arts program, for example, may require an aide in the classroom. A computer-based program, however, depends on the availability of appropriate software in addition to microcomputers. A separate column on the program summary document headed Essential Support Resources may be used to record this information.

Rarely, a program description will specify essential resources in detail along with specific roles and responsibilities. An example is Reading Recovery, an intensive one-on-one intervention program for the poorest readers (lowest 20%) in first grade. The Teacher Leader, experienced both in teaching young children and in directing teacher in-service training, is first trained in a year-long clinical course at Ohio State University. The following year, the Teacher Leader trains and works with 10 to 12 teachers. In addition to a summer workshop, the participating teachers participate in a year-long course, in addition to working with four children (for a period of up to 16 weeks). The weekly sessions of the course involve observing and discussing two live demonstration lessons in which the teachers share their insights about the demonstration lessons. In subsequent years, the teachers meet at least four times a year, preferably in half-day sessions. These continued sessions are important in preventing "teacher drift" from the diagnostic model (Pinnell, DeFord, & Lyons, 1988).

Causal Links

Specific activities are planned and resources are marshalled in order to effect some intermediate and long-term change. Documenting the causal links of a program or policy is the process of recording the hypothesized sequence from events and activities to immediate and intermediate effects (Cronbach & associates, 1980; Weiss, 1972). Among them are the activities involved in installing the program, the day-to-day operations of program delivery, early changes in program recipients, and intermediate outcomes. In other words, the causal links are the demonstration of the developer's beliefs or theory as to the ways the program produces its effects (Cronbach & associates, 1980, p. 254).

An example of a social program in which the causal links were identified is a USAID program in Nicaragua (mentioned earlier in this chapter) that broadcast information on a remedy for infant diarrhea. The project was part of a larger program that broadcast essential health messages to the populations of various Third World countries. The announcements in Nicaragua were broadcast repeatedly up to 10 times a day for over 12 months. Figure 12.2 indicates the key events and their relationships required for the broadcasts to be effective.

The causal links for the program are important because they indicate potential breakdowns during the implementation. They are the intermediate or process

Figure 12.2
Causal links in USAID radio programs to Nicaragua

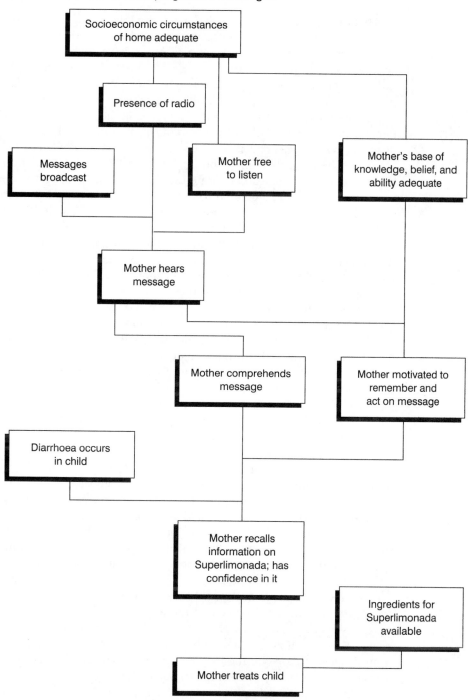

From *Toward Reform of Program Evaluation* (p. 257) by L. J. Cronbach and associates, 1980, San Francisco: Jossey-Bass. Reprinted by permission.

effects of program activities that influence the longer-range effects of the intervention. For example, a science program may emphasize student-directed experiments as a means of developing students' problem-solving skills. Important links in this endeavor are the results of teacher training for the program. Examples are teacher skills in implementing the materials and teacher acceptance of the classroom uncertainties associated with student-directed activities. In other words, the causal sequence should indicate the changes expected in the teachers after training, the different actions they should undertake in the classroom, and the hypothesized immediate and intermediate effects of program activities on the students.

The schematic diagram is one mechanism for illustrating the relationships between essential events and intermediate and final outcomes. A less complex mechanism is simply to add a column to the project summary headed Intermediate Variables. The first step in completing this column is to review the Essential Activities and Level of Expertise and Essential Support Resources columns to determine the immediate effects. Then, in discussions with the program developers or project staff, the evaluator adds other variables that may have been missed. The evaluator then mentally takes note of the arrows that link a process or a procedure to a subsequent process (Cronbach & associates, 1980, p. 255).

Documenting the causal linkages also provides information for selecting questions to be answered in the evaluation. For example, in the absence of a causal analysis, the major evaluation question for the USAID radio broadcast program might have been, Did the radio announcements change adult behavior? However, Figure 12.2 reveals that important questions for the evaluation are, Which mothers received the messages? Did the mothers have a sufficient knowledge base to act on the message? Did the mothers who received the message understand it? and Were the ingredients available to implement the message? If these events do not occur, then there is no hope of ultimate impact. All of these linkages are also important for implementations of similar broadcasts.

Documenting the expected causal links often reveals gaps between program activities and stated aims or goals. Social programs, in particular, are characterized by broad goals "that are so grandiose or so distant in time as to go beyond the grasp of the evaluation. Thus, the goals should be subjected to critical analysis" (Cronbach & associates, 1980, p. 169). For example, one of the Head Start goals was to foster the social development of the child. Essential program activities should have been reviewed to determine the specific aspects of social development the projects could influence and then reconceptualize the broad aim into attainable outcomes.

The USAID example in Figure 12.2 is a situation in which many of the essential events are not under the control of the implementers of the program. Educational programs operate in a narrower setting (the classroom) than that of most social programs. They are, however, also subject to factors that are beyond the developer's control. These factors are the extent of institutional support, the motivation of the teachers, the availability of essential resources, and the types of students in the classroom. An important task in the evaluation is to obtain information on these factors as well as information on program implementation and effects.

ROLE OF THE EVALUATOR

The task for the evaluator in the early stages of learning about the intervention is to be "more than a passive notetaker trying to locate variables to study" (Cronbach & associates, 1980, p. 170). Instead, the evaluator takes an active role in developing information about the program.

The evaluator begins by reviewing funding proposals, project descriptions, teacher training materials, brochures (if available), or other information provided to administrators, parents, teachers, and others. The evaluator also conducts a review of the literature for research on similar programs and any published histories of similar programs. From these documents, the evaluator abstracts information for the project definition summary, making notes about gaps in the information and unanswered questions. Discussion with project developers and the agency or institutional personnel who commissioned the evaluation follow. These discussions are to clarify missing information or to identify the specific focus of the evaluation.

Evaluations often must be conducted within tight time lines, and the evaluators may initially conclude that time does not permit the development of a program definition. However, developing the information should not be an extended task. Moreover, time spent on developing a program definition is important in several ways:

1. Unwelcome surprises are avoided.
2. Evaluation questions can be focused relatively quickly and adequately defended.
3. Potential problems in the evaluation are identified.
4. The evaluator has a framework for defending the findings of the evaluation, should such a situation arise.

Depending on the nature of the evaluation and the issues identified in the program definition, the evaluator completes any of several other tasks. They are:

1. Developing evaluation questions to address essential linkages
2. Developing guidelines to determine the extent of implementation of the program
3. Renegotiating the nature of the evaluation
4. Working with staff to fill in conceptual gaps and restructure ultimate outcomes

Independent Decisions

In some situations, a client, such as a school district or other educational office, contracts with the evaluator to determine the impact of a program that has been in place for some time in the schools. The clearly specified purpose of the evaluation is that the district or other agency plans to use the information to make a decision about continuing or discontinuing the program.

In such a situation, the evaluator collects data on the variables the program or policy is intended to impact. The evaluator also documents program definition and implementation. However, the program definition is developed from sources other than the project sites. Program documents, program developers, and published articles on pilot projects or similar or related programs are sources of information. The reason for excluding project sites as information sources about the conceptual basis for the program is that an evaluation to determine program impact should be as unobtrusive as possible. Discussions with program implementers is typically accompanied by increased attention to the evaluation, and inquiries about specific program elements may precipitate some changes in program operation.

An example of the use of external sources to establish a program definition is an evaluation of the outcomes of the New York City experiment with activity schools (Tyler, 1991). As to the nature of the activity program, school personnel responded that it was the program recommended by faculty at Teachers College, Columbia. After some discussion with the university faculty, a list of 51 characteristics was developed, such as (1) students and teachers work together in planning the activities and (2) students apply their learning to their own out-of-school activities (Tyler, 1991, p. 4). This information was used by the evaluators to determine the level of implementation of the activity curriculum in the experimental schools.

Similarly, the school board of a Colorado district contracted with two university faculty to evaluate the impact of kindergarten retention on children (Shepard & Smith, 1985). At that time, schools within the district developed their own policies on retention, and existing practices had been in place several years. Some of the schools were high retaining (16% to 25% of the kindergarten children) and others were low retaining (0% to 4%).

A search of the literature revealed that the conceptual framework for retention was in question. That is, the policy was not supported either by the weight of psychological theory or by existing research. Research indicated achievement differences to be small between older and younger first-grade children and no emotional benefits for retention. This information indicated that, in addition to assessing impact, identifying and describing teacher belief systems was important in the evaluation. Therefore, one question asked in the evaluation was, To the extent that teachers differ in their philosophy about retention, how might these differences be typified?

Cooperative Decisions

In some situations, a program director or an agency has commissioned an evaluation to determine the effects of a program, but possible termination of the program is not an issue. In such situations, the evaluator works with the intended information users to identify important questions about linkages (Patton, 1986) and, if necessary, to scale down unrealistic outcomes. (This process is referred to by Patton [1986] as "filling in the conceptual gaps".) Cooperation is important because it ensures maximum utilization of evaluation results (Patton, 1986).

Ideal candidates for such an evaluation, in terms of the stage of conceptual development, were the early curricula constructed to foster critical thinking. As already indicated, the conceptual links in the CHEM curriculum between laboratory experimentation, deducing the operating principles of chemistry, and critical thinking had not been tested. These relationships should have been substantiated before assessing the impact of the curriculum on school achievement.

SUMMARY

Educational and social programs are complex multidimensional entities that require the concerted efforts of different individuals in order to succeed. Rarely derived from explicit theory about the learning process, programs often are supported by untested beliefs and accepted practice. Therefore, an important task for the evaluator is to develop a knowledge base about the program or policy prior to conducting the evaluation. This information, referred to as a program definition, fulfills several general functions. They are:

1. To identify a program or policy that has little chance of success
2. To provide information about program design (for programs in early stages of development)
3. To contribute to the development of an evaluation plan
4. To provide an explanation of program effects

The specific contributions of the program definition to the evaluation plan are:

1. To serve as a blueprint for determining the extent of program implementation
2. To identify gaps and contradictions in the conceptual framework and causal links
3. To identify unrealistic expectations for the intervention
4. To reveal possible side effects of the intervention

The program definition consists of four major components. They are:

1. The conceptual framework (with notes about gaps and contradictions)
2. Essential program components
3. Essential support resources
4. Causal links between program events and anticipated outcomes

Included in the conceptual framework are the assumptions, beliefs, and supporting theory on which the program is based, and any contradictions to these assumptions found in the history of similar programs, published research, or other theories. This information may be recorded in a project summary with the following columnar headings: Program Rationale, Other Theory or Data, and Questions (about gaps and contradictions).

Essential program elements are (1) the activities and events required in the program and (2) the level of expertise essential for program implementation. Examples include small group inquiry and student-directed exploration. The former depends on teachers with expertise in planning small group activities; the latter depends on the creative assembly of materials with opportunities for exploration and skills in asking probing questions.

Support resources refer to indirect institutional support (endorsement of the policy or program) and direct support (classroom personnel, materials, and equipment). On the project summary, program elements may be listed in a column headed Essential Activities and Level of Expertise, and support resources may be listed in a separate column.

Finally, the causal links in the program are the expected immediate and intermediate effects of implementing the essential activities and associated support. They are important because they indicate potential breakdowns during implementation of the program; they also indicate potential questions for the evaluation. For example, causal links include the expected effects of teacher training, the expected immediate and intermediate effects of small group cooperative learning, and so on. Documentation of intermediate effects also may indicate gaps between project activities and stated project aims. Reconceptualization of program goals into more achievable expected outcomes may be required. Information on the causal links, obtained from other columns in the project summary and, possibly, from discussions with program developers, may be entered in a column headed Intermediate Variables.

Constructing a program definition begins with a review of available program documents and related literature and continues, if necessary, with discussions with programs developers and project staff. Depending on the nature of the evaluation and the issues identified in the program definition, the evaluator then develops priority evaluation questions, renegotiates the evaluation, and works with staff to restructure program outcomes or resolve conceptual issues.

GUIDELINES FOR THE DEVELOPMENT OF A PROGRAM DEFINITION

Step 1.   Document the conceptual basis for the program or policy and identify gaps and contradiction.

    1.1   Consult program documents, brochures, teacher training materials, funding proposals (if available), and instructional materials.

    1.2   Summarize basic assumptions, supporting beliefs, and supporting theory.

    1.3   If the belief systems are implicit rather than explicit, consult with program developers or other experts to clarify the conceptual framework.

    1.4   Review related literature, both theoretical and empirical.

    1.5   Document any contradictions between the program framework and other materials.

Step 2.   Identify key program elements (events and activities).

    2.1   Identify the essential types of teacher-student interactions.

    2.2   Document teaching skills and/or level of expertise required to implement the program.

      2.3   Document the degree of role change required to implement the innovation.

Step 3. Document the essential support resource required for implementation.
      3.1   Describe the essential institutional arrangements.
      3.2   Document the type, delivery mechanism, and duration of teacher and administrator training.
      3.3   Describe ongoing institutional support required for implementation (e.g., a program coordinator).
      3.4   Identify essential equipment and materials.

Step 4. Identify the causal links between program activities and expected outcomes.
      4.1   Identify expected effects of staff or teacher training.
      4.2   Identify hypothesized immediate effects of implementing program activities.
      4.3   Identify intermediate effects that bridge the gap between activities, immediate effects, and expected outcomes.
      4.4   With project staff, reconceptualize project aims, if necessary.

CHAPTER QUESTIONS

1. How can a program definition assist in the evaluation of an intervention that is in the early stages of development?

2. In what ways does the program definition contribute to the evaluation plan?

3. What is the role of the conceptual framework of a program in planning the evaluation?

4. What is the relationship of the program's causal links to the expected outcomes?

5. In what situations does the evaluator develop a program definition without consulting project staff?

6. Read the description of the proposed Promoting Learning and Understanding (PLUS) curriculum in the appendix. List the major supporting points in the conceptual framework. What gaps or omission do you detect?

REFERENCES

Charters, W., & Jones, J. (1973). On the risk of appraising non-events in program evaluation. *Educational Researcher, 2*(11), 5–7.

Cook, T. D., & Shadish, W. R. (1986). Program evaluation: The worldly science. In M. R. Rosenzweig & L. W. Porter (Eds.), *Annual review of psychology* (Vol. 36, pp. 193–232). Palo Alto, CA: Annual Reviews, Inc.

Cronbach, L. J. (1982). *Designing evaluations of educational and social programs*. San Francisco: Jossey-Bass.

Cronbach, L. J., Ambron, S., Dornbusch, S., Hess, R., Hornik, R., Phillips, D., Walker, D., & Weiner, S. (1980). *Toward reform of program evaluation*. San Francisco: Jossey-Bass.

Gramlich, E., & Koshel, P. (1976). The case of educational performance contracting. In W. Williams & R. F. Elmore (Eds.), *Social program implementation* (pp. 149–166). NY: Academic Press.

McLaughlin, M. (1976). Implementation as mutual adaptation: Change in classroom organization. In W. Williams & R. F. Elmore (Eds.), *Social program implementation* (pp. 167–182). New York: Academic Press.

Patton, M. Q. (1986). *Utilization-focused evaluation*. Beverly Hills, CA: Sage.

Pinnell, G., DeFord, D., & Lyons, C. (1988). *Reading recovery: Early intervention for at-risk first graders*. Arlington, VA: Educational Research Service.

Provus, M. (1969). Evaluating ongoing programs in the public school system. In *NSSE 68th Yearbook, Part II* (pp. 242–283). Chicago: University of Chicago Press.

Provus, M. (1971). *Discrepancy evaluation*. Berkeley, CA: McCutchan.

Ruttman, L. (1980). *Planning useful evaluations: Evaluability assessment*. Beverly Hills, CA: Sage.

Shepard, L., & Smith, M. L. (1985). *Boulder Valley kindergarten study: Retention practices and retention effects*. Boulder, CO: Boulder Valley Public Schools.

Stake, R. W. (1967). The countenance of educational evaluation. *Teachers College Record, 68*, 523–540.

Tyler, R. W. (1991). General statement on program evaluation. In M. W. McLaughlin & D. C. Phillips (Eds.), *Evaluation and education: At quarter century. 90th Yearbook of the National Society for the Study of Education, Part II* (pp. 3–17). Chicago: University of Chicago Press.

Weiss, C. (1972). *Evaluation research*. Englewood Cliffs, NJ: Prentice Hall.

CHAPTER 13

Development of an Evaluation Framework

The evaluation framework consists of the evaluation questions and the associated methods of inquiry, the design for the evaluation, and the management plan. Two important points to remember in developing a framework are (1) that the task involves innumerable choices and (2) that the choice of questions and the selection of investigative methods are inseparable (Cronbach & associates, 1980, p. 214). That is, issues of design do not begin after the questions are selected (Cook & Campbell, 1979; Cronbach & associates, 1980). Equally important, given the diversity of programs, settings, and possible investigations, is that "firm directives to guide evaluation practice are not to be hoped for" (Cronbach & associates, 1980, p. 214). Chief considerations in developing an evaluation framework are (1) that the selected questions are those that will have the greatest leverage with the policy-making community and (2) that the design and sampling strategies will yield the most definitive information within the resource limitations of the study (Cronbach & associates, 1980).

DEVELOPMENT OF THE EVALUATION QUESTIONS

Clarification of the purpose of the evaluation and development of the program definition generate a set of possible questions for the study. Two other sources of questions are (1) the nature of the evaluation, formative or summative, and (2) the needs of stakeholders. After these issues are addressed, the final selection is based on potential benefits of the questions and cost.

Formative and Summative Evaluation

The model developed by Ralph Tyler (1950) used information about student performance on course objectives to modify and revise curriculum. In contrast, the large-scale curriculum projects of the 1960s sought to identify programs that produced the highest achievement. The terms later coined by Scriven (1967) for these two different roles for evaluation are *formative* and *summative*. Specifically, formative evaluation is conducted for the purpose of improving the intervention, whereas summative evaluation involves evaluating the final, refined product of the development process (p. 41).

Formative Evaluation.   After more than 20 years of use, a number of misconceptions about formative evaluation have emerged (Scriven, 1992, p. 19). Among these misconceptions are:

1. It is a very different process from summative evaluation.
2. It is an informal and in-house process.
3. It primarily indicates areas or directions for needed improvement.
4. The real test of a formative evaluation is the extent of improvement that follows it.

These views of formative evaluation, however, are in error, according to Scriven (1992). First, formative and summative evaluations can make use of the same methods. For example, interviews may be used during formative evaluation to identify student problems and during summative evaluation to determine teacher attitudes. Second, exclusive reliance on an in-house evaluation tends to produce a favorable report, rather than to identify problems. Examples are computer software products that are seriously flawed in ways that could have been identified by even slight efforts at formative evaluation (Scriven, 1992; Vargas, 1986). Third, formative evaluation must address any underlying weaknesses in the intervention, such as a faulty conceptual framework. Finally, a formative evaluation can only be judged on the merit of its findings, and not whether or not they were implemented. Adoption of the findings depends on willingness and the ability to implement change (Scriven, 1992).

In the early stages of program development (referred to as the "breadboard" stage by Cronbach & associates, 1980), nothing is fixed, and the role of evaluation is to shape and reshape the proposed intervention (p. 237). Subsequent phases in formative evaluation address other questions, such as, What are the immediate effects of implementing program activities? What problems do students experience with the materials or activities? What installation and implementation problems are identified by teachers? and so on.

An example of the role of formative evaluation in course design is the first aid course developed for the Bell systems of AT&T by American Institutes of Research (Markle, 1967). The objective of the development contract was to produce a course (1) that would require only 7½ hours (1 work day) instead of the 10-hour standard first aid course and (2) that would yield at least the same level of employee performance. Three tryouts of the materials followed by revisions after each implementation with a different sample of employees were required to meet project goals. Among the changes were (1) the addition of instructor guides for the practice sessions of first aid procedures, (2) editing of the student workbooks, and (3) the addition of six brief emergency job-related situations to introduce different course segments. Administration time for the materials decreased from 12 hours (version 1) to 10 hours (version 2) to 7½ hours (version 3). In a comparison with the regular first aid course, posttest performance of employees on the new materials was substantially higher (Markle, 1967).

Summative Evaluation.   The term *summative* originally referred to the evaluation of the product of the final refined development process. The term soon was applied to any evaluation in which outcomes were measured and some determination of the worth or value of the intervention was made. Often, however, interventions have not undergone a prior formative evaluation process to identify and remedy flaws and weaknesses. When a client requests an impact study of such an intervention, the evaluator should negotiate to redirect the study. If the study cannot be redirected to provide information for program improvement, the evaluator's task becomes that of documenting the workings of the innovation in addition to measuring outcomes. In other words, "the formal study of outcomes is almost never sufficient in itself" (Cronbach & associates, 1980, p. 61).

In an impact study, the evaluator should be wary of two potential questions that are simplistic and have little or no potential to generate useful information. One question is, How close did the service and results come to the stated goals? This question connotes a readiness to find fault (Cronbach & associates, 1980). The implication is that, unless the intervention comes very close to meeting its goals, it is a failure. However, if the program has unrealistic goals, unqualified success is impossible.

The second question is, Has the underlying problem been relieved, and if so, by how much? (Cronbach & associates, 1980, p. 148). The problem may be deeply ingrained and not entirely under the control of project staff. A negative response may only demoralize the program staff when failure to alleviate the problem may be the result of circumstances beyond their control.

Instead, the questions selected for the evaluation should reduce uncertainty about the intervention and provide useful comprehensive information for making decisions about the program. Among the legitimate questions that may be asked are, How much service was rendered? Is the program reaching a significant group of those in need? and Is the program overstaffed, given the extent of service that was rendered? (Cronbach & associates, 1980, p. 148). Guidelines for selecting questions and additional examples are discussed in the section entitled Evaluation of Potential Questions.

The Role of Stakeholder Needs

The stakeholder concept emerged in response to criticisms of the early evaluations as tools of bureaucratic sponsors that ignored the interests of less powerful groups

(House, 1980). Initiated by the National Institute of Education (NIE), the stakeholder concept refers to those who have a share in the success and failure of the program or policy (Stake, 1983, p. 18). The intent was to involve diverse groups, each with a stake in the program or policy and with different interests, in the design and conduct of evaluations. This involvement was expected to increase both the relevance of information and to build support for the evaluation findings (Weiss, 1986).

Efforts to involve stakeholders in two large-scale federal projects led to several unforeseen problems. Among them were (1) that it required a role change for evaluators (for which they were ill prepared), (1) that it preserved existing tasks while adding others, and (3) that it seemed to exacerbate differences among the interested parties (Cohen, 1983). Specifically, the evaluators were required to become political managers and negotiators in the orchestration of the involvement of diverse groups (Weiss, 1986). Also, evaluators found that problems arise when groups are asked to articulate their concerns and information needs, but a particular group's concerns are given little weight in the final mix. Thus, stakeholder evaluation can elicit a variety of views, but it cannot contain them (Weiss, 1983, p. 92).

Although less than successful in two evaluations, the stakeholder concept contributed to changes in evaluation practice. Primarily, it took evaluation "down from the pedestal and put it in the middle of the fray" (Weiss, 1986, p. 183). It contributed to the emerging concept of evaluation as a conveyor of information, not a deliverer of truth (p. 154). It placed evaluation at the service of diverse groups and legitimized their interests.

Involving different groups in every phase of an evaluation is a time-consuming and risky task that is no guarantee of improving the quality of the study. However, this approach is useful when (1) the intervention or policy to be evaluated is controversial and (2) data or published literature are ambivalent or nonexistent. In such situations, an advisory panel composed of representatives from different constituencies can provide useful input (see Chapter 17).

In other studies, stakeholder concerns and needs can be identified by asking the questions, Who or what will be hurt if the program or policy is discontinued? and Who or what would be hurt if it is continued? For example, a legitimate concern for the Communities-in-Schools (CIS) project involved the question, Are CIS loyalties being formed at the expense of family and neighborhood ties? (Stake, 1983, p. 27).

Two ways of identifying legitimate concerns are (1) to conduct a review of the literature and (2) to interview selected representatives (key informants) of different groups. Of importance in this process is that the evaluator be sensitive to possible program effects on the poor and the powerless. The reason is that the economically and politically disadvantaged do not have a seat at the negotiation table when evaluations are initiated (House, 1990; 1991). (See Chapter 17 for a description of the social justice concept in evaluation.)

Evaluation of Potential Questions

One of the problems faced by evaluators is that the list of potential questions is almost endless, but the resources for studying the questions are quite limited (Cronbach & associates, 1980, p. 224). Answers typically are sought in a short time, and financial resources are limited. Therefore, the evaluator, often in consultation with the client during contract negotiations, must reduce the list to a manageable set.

Four considerations are important in the selection of evaluation questions (Cronbach & associates, 1980). They are prior uncertainty, leverage, cost, and information yield (p. 227). These four considerations are applied jointly in reviewing the proposed list of questions.

Prior Uncertainty and Leverage.   These two criteria are referred to as "external" considerations because they relate to the broader community to whom the evaluation is addressed. Prior uncertainty refers to differences in the policy-making community in beliefs about the intervention. Specifically, the important issue is to know whether there are divided beliefs or some questions about the process of implementation, the kinds of outcomes, or other characteristics of the intervention. If the policy-making community differs in basic beliefs, then questions that address the divisions are of major importance in the evaluation.

Leverage, in contrast, refers to the type of new information that would influence subsequent discussion and action. It refers to "the probability that the information— if believed—will change the course of events" (Cronbach & associates, 1980, p. 265). Facts that participants in the political process indicate are useful to them can be expected to have leverage.

Questions that rate high on both uncertainty and leverage are top candidates for thorough study. An example is the Boulder Valley retention study. Schools in the district were divided in their beliefs about the value of retention as a policy. Therefore, a key question for the evaluation was, What are the cognitive and emotional benefits of retention?

The issue of leverage is reflected in the two subquestions about cognitive achievement listed in Table 13.1. Each meets the criteria for leverage with different groups. Standardized test results often are key information for administrators and some parents. However, the literature indicates that others, particularly teachers, believe that standardized test results provide only partial information and that teacher ratings of pupils can reveal dimensions of student performance important for academic success.

Questions 2 and 3 address the stated evaluation purpose of determining the ways that retention decisions are made. Thus they meet the criterion of prior uncertainty and the requirement to document implementation of a program or policy. Chronological age is cited in the conceptual framework of the maturational theory of development as the basis for retaining children. However, some studies indicate that children are retained for other reasons. (See Gredler, 1992, for a review.) Therefore, the specific questions about the relationship of age to retention decisions and school success were important.

Applying the considerations of prior uncertainty and leverage can prevent the arbitrary elimination of questions related to stakeholder needs. Often a stakeholder concern is one that questions the conventional wisdom, and data have not been previously obtained to test those beliefs.

Table 13.1
Summary of questions in the Boulder Valley retention study and supporting rationales

Evaluation Questions[1]	Evaluation Purpose	Prior Uncertainty	Leverage	Low Cost/High Info.	Stakeholder Need	Implementation
			Rationale			
1) What are the cognitive and emotional benefits of kindergarten retention?	X	X			X	
1a) What is the cognitive achievement of retained and nonretained children in first grade as measured by standardized tests?	X		X			
1b) How do first-grade teachers rate the academic performance of their pupils?	X	X	X		X	
2) What are the characteristics of children that lead to retention?	X	X			X	X
To the extent that teachers differ in their philosophy about retention, how are these differences typified?	X	X	X		X	X
3) Is age related to retention decisions and subsequent academic performance?	X	X			X	X
Would a change in entrance age lead to fewer retentions or more success in school?	X	X			X	X
4) What is the predictive validity of the Gesell readiness test and other readiness instruments?	X	X		X	X	X

[1]Summarized from Shepard and Smith, 1985.

Cost and Information Yield.   The considerations of cost and information yield are "internal" considerations (Cronbach & associates, 1980, p. 227). A given investment can only accomplish so much in reducing uncertainty. Questions of equal importance may differ in the investment required to obtain reasonably dependable information. Thus, cost is a concern when a decision must be made between questions of equal importance or when a minor question may possibly be added to the evaluation. For example, a minor question asked in the retention study was, What is the predictive validity of the Gesell test and other selected readiness measures? These tests are popular, but the validity of the Gesell in particular has been questioned. This issue was addressed with a review of published studies on the instrument. Addressing this question cost little in the evaluation.

Cost is not a factor in removing a question of primary importance. For example, observers and interviewers may be required to address the extent of implementation of an innovation, and extensive observations and interviews are costly in both time and personnel. However, the cost is justified when the alternative is the risk of evaluating a "no-treatment" project.

Summary

Sources of information for evaluation questions are the purpose of the study, the program definition, the nature of the evaluation (formative or summative), and identified stakeholder needs. Final selection of questions is based on potential benefits of the questions and cost.

Formative evaluation is conducted to improve the intervention, whereas summative evaluation involves evaluating the final, refined product of the development process. Characteristics of formative evaluation are that it can use the same methods as summative evaluation, it should not be an in-house process, it must address fundamental flaws, and it should be judged on the merit of the findings.

The term *summative evaluation* has been applied to studies in which an innovation has not undergone formative evaluation. In the event that the evaluator cannot negotiate a redirection of the study, he or she should document the conceptual framework and workings of the intervention. Questions that are simplistic and connote a readiness to find fault in the evaluation should be avoided. Instead, potential questions should be those that reduce uncertainty about the intervention.

Information about possible stakeholder needs may be obtained from literature reviews and interviews of key informants. Stakeholders can be involved in all phases of an evaluation when the intervention is controversial and the published literature is ambivalent or nonexistent. Also important in addressing stakeholder needs is the evaluator's sensitivity to possible program effects on the poor and the powerless.

Four considerations important in the selection of evaluation questions are prior uncertainty, leverage, cost, and information yield. Prior uncertainty refers to differences in the policy-making community in beliefs about the intervention. Leverage refers to the information that would influence subsequent discussion and action. Questions that rate high on both considerations are top candidates for thorough study. Cost is a consideration when a decision must be made between questions of equal importance or when a minor question may possibly be added to the evaluation.

SELECTION OF THE DESIGN AND METHODS

The units to be studied, the issues in choosing designs, the types of designs, and the choices among methods are issues in developing the framework of the evaluation.

Units To Be Studied

The purpose of an evaluation typically is to obtain an understanding of the workings and ramifications of some policy, program, curriculum, or other service implemented to address a need or problem. An intervention influences the recipients (e.g., students or school dropouts) and others (e.g., teachers and parents). The Boulder Valley retention study, for example, studied the decision-making behavior of kindergarten teachers, in addition to obtaining achievement data on retained and nonretained children.

The units studied in an evaluation also may be communities, schools, or clinics (Cronbach & associates, 1980, p. 232). If the unit is a classroom or site, then the sites that are studied are the sample. Evaluations that address implementation of an innovation may study both sites and individuals. In an impact study, process data may be classroom specific or school specific, but outcome data may involve either classrooms or individuals.

Further, an evaluation with a substantive ethnographic component will focus on the values, communication patterns, and rituals of the particular culture that influence the intervention. In the evaluation of the Career Intern Program (CIP), for example, the ethnographic component studied communities (school sites + neighborhoods), students, school staff, and federal agencies.

Once the units to be studied are identified, the evaluator must determine the ways that those units will be sampled. When an innovation is adopted in several classrooms in a district or a state, at least three factors should enter into site selection. The first consideration is the stage of implementation of the policy, curriculum, or program. When classrooms or schools are at different stages of implementation, each stage should be represented in the evaluation. The second consideration is the stage of implementation of the program or policy. Given different stages of implementation, the client may prefer that schools from the different stages be sampled or that only those at routine use or above be evaluated.

The third consideration is the types of school populations that receive the intervention. A program that gets good results with one ethnic minority may fail with another, and a program that succeeds in schools with above-average students may not be effective in other schools (Cronbach & associates, 1980, p. 279). In such situations, separate substudies with different subpopulations may be needed.

Particularly for programs or policies that are controversial, the evaluator should take care so that the basis for the study findings cannot be strongly contested. In such situations, sampling and design can be critical issues. The Boulder Valley retention study is an example, because some individuals supported retention and others did not. To determine the effects of retention, the evaluators compared retained children with a matched sample of nonretained children from similar schools. A two-stage sampling procedure was used. First, the high-retaining schools were matched with similar low-retaining schools. Then for each first-grade child who had been retained in kindergarten, the evaluators identified a control from a similar low-retaining school. The children were matched on gender, socioeconomic status, second language, school entry ability (as determined by a readiness test), and birth month. The birth months were lagged by a year so that the retained and nonretained children were the same age when they entered kindergarten. This attention to sample selection was important, given the importance of the outcomes to the school district.

Design Issues

As already indicated, evaluations typically address the effects of an intervention (1) on the primary recipients of the intervention and (2) on program implementers and secondary groups influenced by the intervention. A major task in planning the evaluation is designing the portion of the study that will address program effects on the recipients.

Issues in developing evaluation designs are:

1. The type of evaluation, formative or summative
2. Prior knowledge about the intervention
3. The need to rule out rival hypotheses
4. Information leverage

Formative evaluation may be viewed as a series of reviews and pilot tryouts of an emerging course or program. Typically, summative evaluations address interventions that have been installed in an institution or a system for a particular purpose.

The role of prior knowledge in design is to assist in determining the need for a control group in the evaluation (Cronbach & associates, 1980, p. 279). A control group is not likely to produce new information if (1) the program addresses a problem that is not addressed by current policies or practices and (2) the problem will not improve spontaneously. An example is the Superlimonada study in which radio messages were to broadcast a new treatment for infant illness to mothers (Cronbach & associates, 1980). If the treatment is new to the culture, pre-post figures on the illness can establish treatment effectiveness. "Only heroic imagination could construct a scenario that attributes appreciable frequency of medication use to anything but the broadcast" (p. 289).

The third consideration in planning the evaluation design is the possible need to rule out rival hypotheses. That is, events other than the intervention may account for positive outcomes. Possible rival hypotheses are the effects of concurrent events and maturation or growth. For example, proponents of kindergarten retention maintain that the additional year is essential in order for the children to perform adequately when they reach first grade. A study of retention, therefore, should address the alternative hypothesis that candidates for retention, who do not receive the extra year, can perform adequately in first grade.

The fourth consideration is information leverage. Sometimes the client who commissions the evaluation has the impression that only a control group design can yield definitive information. The situation may not warrant a control group; however, the client views credible information as synonymous with comparative data. In such a situation, one alternative is to implement a cohort design. As indicated in a subsequent section of this chapter, a cohort design provides an estimate of growth. It also provides comparative data without the expense and time investment of a control group study.

Among the designs that may be considered for assessing the effects of an intervention are the cyclic design, the control group design, the cohort design, the comparison of program variations, and pre-post designs.

The Cyclic Design

Formative evaluations typically use a cyclic design that consists of a recurring sequence of tryout, data selection, and feedback to developers. Scriven (1992) describes four phases in the process. They are:

1. Critique by in-house colleagues or external experts
2. Field trials with hand-holding involving typical consumers
3. Hands-off field trials at remote sites with typical users
4. Full-scale commissioned evaluations (the "review preview" phase) (p. 21)

Sometimes phases 2 and 3 are run together, and phase 4 often is omitted. The focus of the initial critique (phase 1) is to determine if beliefs and principles can be translated into practice. When the difficulties identified in the early tryouts are corrected, the materials, course, or program is ready for field trial. The focus of the field test is the appraisal of outcomes and the factors that contribute to success or nonsuccess (Cronbach & associates, 1980, p. 238). The development and evaluation of the first aid course for AT&T is an example.

The Control Group Design

Issues in considering a control group design are the potential problems and the prerequisite conditions for its use.

Potential Problems.   Three potential problems are associated with the use of a control group in evaluation. One is the possibility of equivocal findings. One of the causes of such an outcome is a lack of clear differences between the innovation and the experiences of the control group. In a study of Individually Guided Education

(IGE), Hall and Loucks (1977) found that 63% of the non-IGE schools were implementing key features of Individually Guided Education. Thus, no significant differences were found between IGE and non-IGE schools on reading and mathematics achievement. A second cause can be reactions of control group participants that invalidate the findings, such as the John Henry effect and resentful demoralization. A third cause can be the loss of subjects from the study that alters the composition of one or both of the groups.

A second problem associated with some control group studies is the ethical issue of denying important services to a needy or disadvantaged group. Special needs students or dropouts attracted to an innovation that provides reentry into the system should not be denied the opportunity to participate because they were arbitrarily assigned to a "no-treatment" control.

A third potential problem is the division of resources that the design requires (Cronbach & associates, 1980). Expenses required for a comparison may cut spending on the treatment group by as much as half (p. 281). Moreover, cost is not restricted merely to expenditures of funds. The evaluator's time and energy also are expended in maintaining contact with control group members and keeping a watchful eye on their behavior.

Prerequisite Conditions.   Cronbach and associates (1980) identify two situations in which a control group is appropriate in evaluation. One situation is to answer comparative summative questions about a defined pair of treatments. An example is comparing science "wet labs" with computer/videodisc "dry labs."

The other situation is one in which an effect could be persuasively explained away in the absence of a control group (p. 291). An example of a study in which a control group was essential is the Boulder Valley retention study. The literature on retention indicates that kindergarten retention does not provide cognitive benefits to the retained children that are different from those of nonretained children (see Gredler, 1992, for a review). However, different schools in the district implemented different retention policies. Therefore, in order for the study to be credible for the clients, a comparison of retained children and nonretained children who were eligible for retention was important.

The Cohort Design

In the educational setting, a plausible alternative explanation for program effects in some situations is that of growth or maturation. In the absence of the intervention, the possibility exists that the children may have achieved the same outcomes. Another plausible explanation for program effects is that the intervention differs little in key characteristics from existing programs. Thus, a benchmark is needed that is an indicator of performance on important outcomes if the intervention were not implemented.

The cohort design makes use of the fact that individuals in schools and businesses pass through education and training in groups on a regular basis, specifically, "institutional cycles" (Cook & Campbell, 1979). Cohorts are "groups of respondents who follow each other through formal institutions or informal institutions like the family" (p. 127). Thus, an earlier group or cohort that received extant services may be compared to a current cohort that receives the innovation.

Figure 13.1 illustrates an expanded variation of the cohort design. In this hypothetical example, a curriculum to enhance problem-solving skills is implemented with tenth-grade students in the 1995-96 school year. Problem solving and achievement measures are obtained on the 1994-95 tenth-grade cohort in June 1995. These measures (O_1, O_2, and O_3) obtained for high, average, and low achievers serve as a benchmark for the assessment of program effects on the 1995-96 cohort that receives the new program. Measures of problem solving and achievement obtained in June 1996 on program recipients can be compared with their pretest scores and the post-year scores of the nontreatment cohort.

Figure 13.1
Expanded variation of the basic cohort design

	September			June	
					Post-course Measures
			High		O_1 O_2 O_3
1994–95 [prior cohort of 10th graders]		*Prior Achievement*	*Average*		O_1 O_2 O_3
			Low		O_1 O_2 O_3
		Pretest Measures	*Intervention*		*Posttest Measures*
	High	O_4 O_5 O_6	Program to enhance problem-solving skills	*High*	O_7 O_8 O_9
1995–96 *Prior Achievement*	*Average*	O_4 O_5 O_6		*Average*	O_7 O_8 O_9
	Low	O_4 O_5 O_6		*Low*	O_7 O_8 O_9

Comparison of Program Variations

Comparing program variations may occur in one of two ways. First, in formative evaluation, program components may be varied by design in order to determine the effects of different configurations. Second, information from different implementation sites is likely to identify different levels of installation of the intervention. Data from weak implementations can be analyzed separately or the study can compare high, adequate, and weak implementations to determine both problems and effects.

Pre-Post Designs

The "hands-off" field trials of a program or set of materials that are undergoing formative evaluation are usually pre-post designs. A sample of representative students is pretested; they complete the program and are posttested.

A pre-post design also is appropriate when an intervention is developed to address a need or problem that is not likely to improve spontaneously (or through maturation) and no other policies or practices address the problem or related issues. An example is the Superlimonada study in which the treatment was new to the culture.

Considerations in Selection of Methods

A variety of methods may be used in formative evaluation to determine which components of an intervention are working and the nature of the problems. For example, in early stages of development, when a small group of three to five is working through computer-based materials, videotapes supplemented by interviews can identify major problems. Recordings of "talk-aloud" protocols also are useful. In later stages of program tryout, on-site observations of an intervention using rating scales or checklists can document program events. Interviews with teachers and others can identify implementation problems. In later field trials of a program, student interviews can document students' perceptions of classroom priorities. Davinroy, Bliem, and Mayfield (1994), for example, found that the emphasis in reading had shifted little from reading for accuracy after 1 year of efforts to implement performance assessment in the classroom.

In an impact study, the three considerations in the selection of data collection methods are prior uncertainty, leverage, and cost. Prior uncertainty refers to the available information or lack of it about an intervention. If the components of a program are well defined, then an observation checklist may be sufficient to determine the extent of implementation. If not, on-site observers may be required to develop field notes and/or answer analytic questions about the implementation based on 1-week visits to each site.

In addition to prior uncertainty, leverage is an important consideration for choosing the types of data to be obtained. Leverage refers to the credibility of the data for the audiences of an evaluation. As indicated earlier, administrators and parents often are interested in standardized test results, but teacher ratings may have more credibility with other audiences for the evaluation findings.

Cost is a consideration when two methods may provide comparable information but one is more costly than the other. Cost refers to both the financial investment and the time investment required to implement a particular data collection approach. For example, one choice may be between developing observer rating scales to document implementation or conducting on-site semi-structured observations followed by the observers completing an analytic questionnaire. Both the development of observer rating scales and the analysis of data from unstructured observations are time consuming. If the program is a multisite project, the development of rating scales that are transportable to several sites is warranted.

Cost also is a factor if an ethnographic approach to program implementation is being considered. An ethnographic approach is labor intensive and requires extensive on-site time. A separate team is required, and ideally, the project should be a multiyear effort to permit sufficient time for tentative data analysis and subsequent visits.

The evaluation questions and the methods selected to answer them should combine to provide a complete picture of the intervention. Table 13.2 from the Boulder Valley retention study is an example. The evaluation (1) addressed the impact of retention on children both cognitively and emotionally, (2) compared the cognitive achievement and adjustment of retained children with nonretained children who met the criteria for retention, and (3) provided in-depth information about the processes involved in retention decisions.

The methods selected for the study met the criteria of prior uncertainty and leverage. The literature indicated a lack of unanimity in retention decisions, but little was known about the foundations of such decisions. Thus, in-depth interviews of the kindergarten teachers were needed. A checklist or questionnaire asking teachers how they make decisions would not have revealed the depth of teacher beliefs. These beliefs, in other words, were tacit unarticulated knowledge. Second, information from the interviews were credible data and they explained, in large measure, the different retention rates in different schools.

Of particular importance is that the methods can contribute to answers to more than one evaluation question. As indicated in Table 13.2, the methods implemented to answer questions 1 and 2 also address question 3. Similarly, the methods used to determine the extent of implementation of a program or policy can also determine if the intermediate effects (causal links) are occurring. Observations and student interviews can determine the extent to which essential resources are in the classroom, the types of activities implemented, and some of the immediate effects. For example, in evaluating the CHEM curriculum, the difference between CHEM experiments and those in other chemistry courses, the extent of open-ended inquiry in the classroom, and the availability of media and materials can be determined through observations. Student reactions to the activities and their descriptions of classroom priorities can be identified through interviews of students at different achievement levels.

Methods selected to measure outcomes depend, in part, on the purpose of the program. The CHEM curriculum, for example, was to enhance critical thinking in science. First, an operational definition of "critical thinking in science" is needed. Then, depending on the specifics of the definition, situations similar to the examples devel-

Table 13.2
Summary of questions and methods implemented in the Boulder Valley retention study

(1) What are the cognitive and emotional benefits of kindergarten retention?	(a) CTBS scores of matched pairs of retained and nonretained children. (b) First grade teacher evaluations of their pupils. (c) Parent interviews.
(2) What are the characteristics of children that lead to retention? To the extent that teachers differ in their philosophy about retention, how are these differences typified?	(d) Pupil profile analysis and decision making by kindergarten teachers. (e) Semi-structured interviews with kindergarten teachers.
(3) Is age related to retention decisions and subsequent academic performance? Would a change in entrance age lead to to fewer retentions or more success in school?	(f) Nature of the sampling. (g) Also, (a), (b), (d), and (e).
(4) What is the predictive validity of the Gesell readiness test and other selected readiness instruments?	(h) Review of the literature.

Summarized from Shepard and Smith, 1985.

oped by Tyler (Smith & Tyler, 1942) and Scriven (1994) may be designed to supplement other indices of achievement. Such situations also can address the conceptual framework questions about the program.

Summary

Selection of units to be studied, selection of the design for assessing effects on program recipients, and choices among methods are issues in developing the evaluation framework. The units to be studied may be individuals, communities, schools, or clinics. Also an evaluation may study several units, such as communities, students, and project staff.

When the units are identified, the evaluator must determine the ways they will be sampled. Two factors that enter into site selection are the stage of implementation of the policy or program and the types of populations that receive the intervention. When the program or policy is likely to yield controversial findings, sampling and design are critical issues. The sample in a comparison study, for example, must be carefully selected so that the findings cannot be set aside by policy detractors.

The four major considerations in selecting the design are the nature of the evaluation, prior knowledge about the intervention, the need to rule out rival hypotheses, and information leverage. Prior knowledge and the possibility of rival hypotheses assist in determining the need for a control group.

Formative evaluations typically use a cyclic design that consists of a recurring sequence of tryout, data collection, and feedback to developers. In later stages, the field trials often are pre-post designs.

Potential problems in a control group design concern the possibility of equivocal findings, reactions of participants, and the ethical issue of not denying important services to needy groups. Another issue is the division of resources required by the design. Two appropriate uses for a control group are (1) to compare a defined pair of treatments and (2) to address rival hypotheses that may be persuasive explanations of program effects.

The cohort design is a plausible alternative to the control group design when growth or maturation may be cited as a cause of observed improvement. A cohort is a group of respondents who progress through a formal institution in the same way as program recipients. Thus, an earlier cohort that received extant services may be compared to a current cohort that receives the intervention.

Other designs include the comparison of program variations and pre-post designs. Program components may be varied by design in a formative evaluation to determine the effects. Also, high, adequate, and weak implementations of a program may be compared with each other.

Three considerations in the selection of data collection methods are prior uncertainty, leverage, and cost. If the program components are well defined, for example, an observation checklist may be sufficient to determine the extent of implementation. If not, on-site observations may be required. Leverage refers to the types of data that are credible for different types of audiences. Finally, cost is a consideration when two methods may provide comparable information, but one is more costly than the other. Cost also is a factor if an ethnographic component is part of the study.

The evaluation questions and the selected methods should combine to provide a complete picture of the intervention. Also, methods can contribute to answers to more than one evaluation question. Methods selected to measure outcomes depend, in part, on the purpose of the program. A program to facilitate critical thinking, for example, should make use of test situations that assess students' abilities to address complex situations in a systematic way.

DEVELOPMENT OF A MANAGEMENT PLAN

The typical characteristics of evaluations include a limited time frame and adequate, but not abundant, resources. An evaluation typically undergoes a start-up phase, a data collection phase, and an analysis and communication phase. Events in each of these phases must be managed carefully in order to complete the evaluation.

An important management task for the evaluator is to plan the execution of specific tasks in the evaluation so that resources are available when needed and contract deadlines are met while allowing for minor unforeseen events. A management plan should consist of two components. One is a worksheet of essential tasks and personnel. The other is a mechanism that illustrates both the time frames for the evaluation tasks and their interdependence.

Project Worksheet

The rough information for the project worksheet is prepared at the time the budget is developed for the evaluation contract. The details of the worksheet are then fleshed out as an initial task in the evaluation. The project worksheet consists of three types of information. They are the tasks to be completed, the estimated time frame for each task, and the personnel to be assigned to that task.

Table 13.3 lists a sample of project tasks and associated time frames for each. If the contract is with personnel who are working part time on the evaluation, dollar amounts should be attached to each task. In this way, the total days that the evaluator is to work on the project can be apportioned adequately across all the tasks.

Time Management Guidelines

Although the worksheet records general time frames for particular tasks, it does not indicate potential conflicts in time schedules or potential logjams. Two mechanisms for managing the available time are PERT charts and Gantt charts.

PERT Charts.   The acronym *PERT* stands for Program Evaluation and Review Technique. The method was developed by the U.S. Department of Defense as a management mechanism for large projects. Later adapted for use in evaluation, PERT charts are blueprints of the interrelated activities in a project and the paths among them.

Table 13.3
Sample of project worksheet entries

Task	Personnel and Estimated Time Frame
Conduct literature review	Evaluator and graduate assistant (10 days each) (First month)
Select sites and arrange visits	Evaluator (7 days) (First month)
Review program documents, conduct informal interviews, and develop observational methods	Two evaluators (30 days [6 weeks]) (First and second month)
Train classroom observers	Evaluator and three graduate assistants (9 days each) (Third month)

Figure 13.2 illustrates the construction of a partial PERT chart. As indicated, the chart indicates (1) the activities that must be completed prior to the initiation of other activities and (2) the activities that can be conducted simultaneously. If a PERT chart is used, the evaluator should develop realistic time estimates for each of the solid lines.

PERT charts are difficult to construct and are only useful if they reflect all the essential activities, regardless of their mundane nature. PERT charts are most useful in large, complex projects in which several activities must proceed simultaneously in order to achieve a particular goal.

Gantt Charts.   In contrast to PERT charts, a Gantt chart is easy to construct. It is a time-oriented graph that displays a line with a beginning and ending point for each activity. The horizontal axis is the time frame for the evaluation, which may be partitioned by weeks or by months. The vertical axis lists project tasks, and the graph illustrates the projected time frame for each. Figure 13.3 is an example.

As indicated in Figure 13.3, the overlapping lines indicate potential problems in scheduling personnel. Of importance in scheduling interdependent activities, such as on-site observations and data analysis, is to allow some unallocated time between them, even if it is only a week. This time lag allows for some recovery from unanticipated delays in completing the observations.

Figure 13.2
Example of a PERT network

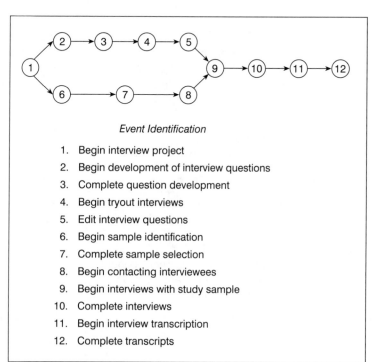

Event Identification

1. Begin interview project
2. Begin development of interview questions
3. Complete question development
4. Begin tryout interviews
5. Edit interview questions
6. Begin sample identification
7. Complete sample selection
8. Begin contacting interviewees
9. Begin interviews with study sample
10. Complete interviews
11. Begin interview transcription
12. Complete transcripts

Figure 13.3
Example of a partial Gantt chart

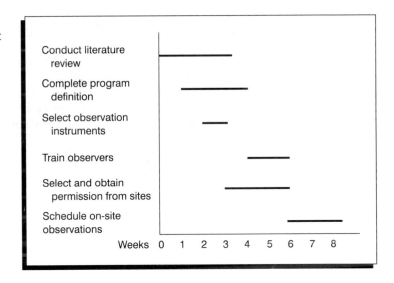

If the evaluation is addressing a policy or program that is already in place, some minor problems can be anticipated with the time schedule. For example, individuals may not be available for interviews in the weeks identified, and interviewers may be required to return later to a particular site. These problems can be accommodated in the Gantt chart by not scheduling events into restrictive time frames; that is, some slippage is allowed for each event. Also, a useful rule of thumb is to allow 3 to 4 weeks at the end of the project in which to prepare the final report and to communicate with various audiences. Much of that time is likely not to be there when the project is underway, as a result of other activities requiring more time than was estimated. However, this allocation provides a cushion for completing other required evaluation activities.

In a developmental project, in which the evaluators are dependent on others for product design and delivery, the time schedule can be altered as a result of factors that are not under the evaluator's control. In such situations, a wise course of action is to plan as realistically as possible and also to be prepared for worst-case scenarios. For example, the evaluator may be responsible for obtaining expert reviews of draft scripts of television lessons prior to production. The evaluator should have a contingency plan for obtaining fast turnaround time on the reviews in the event the drafts are received late.

In developing a Gantt chart of evaluation activities, a good rule of thumb is to asterisk any activity on the chart that is dependent on the delivery of products or the completion of activities by others and to develop a contingency plan for delays.

In summary, the evaluator should maintain a worksheet of essential tasks and personnel and a mechanism that illustrates the time frames for evaluation tasks and their interdependence. Although PERT charts are useful in large, complex projects, a Gantt chart can indicate ongoing tasks and their overlap.

GUIDELINES FOR THE DEVELOPMENT OF AN EVALUATION FRAMEWORK

Step 1.   Review the potential sources of evaluation questions.
1.1   Review the purpose of the evaluation.
1.2   Develop questions from the program definition, and negotiate the nature of the evaluation (formative, summative, or impact).
1.3   Determine the information needs of stakeholders.

Step 2.   Evaluate potential questions.
2.1   Select questions that meet the criteria of prior uncertainty and leverage.
2.2   Apply the criteria of cost and information yield to identify other questions.

Step 3.   Identify the units to be studied.
3.1   Identify sites and the groups of individuals to be studied.
3.2   Select sites, based on stage of implementation and populations served.
3.3   Select and implement a sampling strategy.

Step 4.   Develop a design and select data collection methods.
4.1   If a formative evaluation, plan the tryout and revision cycles.
4.2   If an impact study, review the need for a control group.
4.3   Select a design appropriate for the questions and type of study.
4.4   Select inquiry methods appropriate for the questions that meet the criteria of prior uncertainty, leverage, and cost.
4.5   Review the design and methods for consistency and completeness.

Step 5.   Develop a management plan.
5.1   Complete a project worksheet.
5.2   Develop a Gantt chart.

CHAPTER QUESTIONS

1. What are the current misconceptions about formative evaluation?
2. What are some ways to identify stakeholder priorities in an evaluation?
3. Name the four considerations important in the selection of evaluation questions.
4. Discuss the issues important in considering the use of a control group design.
5. Describe the advantages of the cohort design.
6. What are the advantages of a Gantt chart as compared to a PERT chart?

REFERENCES

Cohen, D. (1983). Evaluation and reform. In A. Bryk (Ed.), *Stakeholder-based evaluation. New Directions for Program Evaluation, 17,* 73–81.

Cook, T. D., & Campbell, D. T. (1972). *Quasi-experimentation: Design and analysis issues for field settings.* Chicago: Rand McNally.

Cronbach, L. J., Ambron, S., Dornbusch, S., Hess, R., Hornik, R., Phillips, D., Walker, D., & Weiner, S. (1980). *Toward reform of program evaluation.* San Francisco: Jossey-Bass.

Davinroy, K., Bliem, G., & Mayfield, V. (1994, April). *"How does my teacher know that I know." Third graders' perceptions of math, reading, and assessment.* Paper presented at the annual meeting of the American Educational Research Association, New Orleans.

Gredler, G. R. (1992). *School readiness: Assessment and educational issues.* Brandon, VT: Clinical Psychology Publishing Company.

Hall, G., & Loucks, S. (1977). A developmental model for determining whether the treatment is actually implemented. *American Educational Research Journal, 14*(31), 263–276.

House, E. (1980). *Evaluating with validity.* Beverly Hills: Ca: Sage.

House, E. (1990). Methodology and justice. In K. Sirotnik (Ed.), *Evaluation and justice: Issues in public education. New Directions for Program Evaluation, 45,* 23–26.

House, E. (1991). Evaluation and social justice: Where are we? In M. McLaughlin & D. C. Phillips (Eds.), *Evaluation and education: At quarter century. Ninetieth yearbook of the National Society for the Study of Education, Part II* (pp. 233–247). Chicago: University of Chicago Press.

Markle, D. (1967). The development of the Bell system first aid and personal safety course. Palo Alto: American Institutes for Research (AIR-E814/67-FR).

Scriven, M. (1967). The methodology of evaluation. In R. Tyler, R. Gagne, & M. Scriven (Eds.), *Perspectives of curriculum evaluation. AERA monograph series on curriculum evaluation.* Chicago: Rand McNally.

Scriven, M. (1992). Beyond formative and summative evaluation. In M. McLaughlin & D. Phillips (Eds.), *Evaluation and education at quarter century. Ninetieth yearbook of the National Society for the Study of Education* (pp. 19–64). Chicago: University of Chicago Press.

Scriven, M. (1994, April). *Death of a paradigm: Replacing multiple choice with multiple ratings.* Invited address presented at the meeting of the American Educational Research Association, New Orleans.

Shepard, L. & Smith, M. L. (1985). *Boulder Valley kindergarten study: Retention practices and retention efforts.* Boulder, CO: Boulder Valley Public Schools.

Smith, E. R., & Tyler, R. W. (1942). *Appraising and recording student progress.* New York: Harper Brothers.

Stake, R. (1983). Stakeholder influence in the evaluation of Cities-in-Schools. In A. Bryk (Ed.), *Stakeholder-based evaluation. New Directions for Program Evaluation, 17,* 15–30.

Tyler, R. (1950). *Principles of curriculum construction.* Chicago: University of Chicago Press.

Vargas, J. (1986). Instructional design flaws in computer-assisted instruction. *Phi Delta Kappan, 67*(10), 738–744.

Weiss, C. (1983). Toward the future of stakeholder approaches in evaluation. In A. Bryk (Ed.), *Stakeholder-based evaluation. New Directions for Program Evaluation, 17,* 83–96.

Weiss, C. (1986). The stakeholder approach to evaluation: Origins and promise. In E. House (Ed.), *New Directions in Program Evaluation* (pp. 145–157). London: Falmer Press.

CHAPTER 14

Documentation of Program Implementation

A major shortcoming of the evaluations of the 1960s and 1970s was their inability to identify the causes of program success or failure. Compiling a program definition is one step toward developing the information that can explain program effects. The second step is documenting the nature and extent of the implementation.

FACTORS THAT INFLUENCE IMPLEMENTATION

As indicated in Chapter 2, implementation can take any of several different forms. These forms include implementation as planned, mutual adaptation, co-optation, and non-implementation (also referred to as the no-treatment project). The key influences on implementation are the specific local conditions that interact with the innovation (Fullan, 1982; Hall, 1992; McLaughlin, 1976; McLaughlin, 1990). These factors are:

1. The relationship of the innovation to the system
2. The extent of institutional support
3. The influence of local beliefs and practices
4. Teacher belief systems
5. Degree of required role change
6. Experience with the innovation

Relationship of the Innovation to the System

Two general characteristics of programs or policies are related to the potential for problems during implementation. The first characteristic is the extent to which the innovation seeks to change the system. That is, Is the innovation intended to change the practices of teachers or others within the system, or will project personnel be responsible for the intervention? The second characteristic is the extent to which the program is well defined. The less explicit the intervention, the greater the likelihood it will be implemented in different ways.

Figure 14.1 illustrates the interaction of these two characteristics. The extent to which the program seeks to impact the system (vertical axis) and the degree of program specificity (horizontal axis) interact to produce four types of programs. They are indicated by sectors I, II, III, and IV.

Figure 14.1
Relationship of degree of program definition to intended systemic change

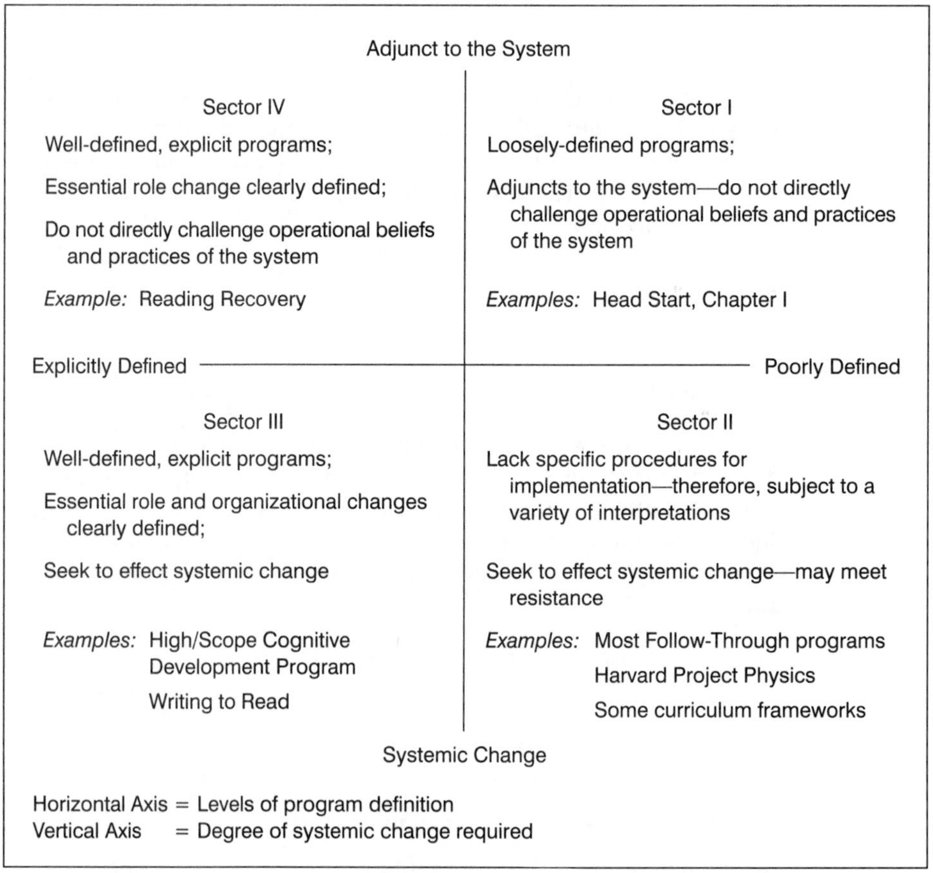

Adjunct to the System	
Sector IV	Sector I
Well-defined, explicit programs;	Loosely-defined programs;
Essential role change clearly defined;	Adjuncts to the system—do not directly challenge operational beliefs and practices of the system
Do not directly challenge operational beliefs and practices of the system	
Example: Reading Recovery	*Examples:* Head Start, Chapter I
Explicitly Defined ———————————— Poorly Defined	
Sector III	Sector II
Well-defined, explicit programs;	Lack specific procedures for implementation—therefore, subject to a variety of interpretations
Essential role and organizational changes clearly defined;	
Seek to effect systemic change	Seek to effect systemic change—may meet resistance
Examples: High/Scope Cognitive Development Program Writing to Read	*Examples:* Most Follow-Through programs Harvard Project Physics Some curriculum frameworks
Systemic Change	

Horizontal Axis = Levels of program definition
Vertical Axis   = Degree of systemic change required

Each of the four types of programs presents different considerations in documenting implementation. Sector I programs do not seek to bring about systemic change; they are adjuncts to the institution. However, the programs also are loosely defined. Both the populations of students served and the program elements will vary from school to school.

Programs in sectors II and III seek change within the system. New approaches and methods are developed for groups such as elementary mathematics teachers, first-grade reading teachers, or physics teachers. However, the innovations may evoke unexpected reactions from those outside the program. Tyler (1991, p. 9) noted that, in many situations, teachers, parents, and students who are not in the innovation "heap criticism, sarcasm, and jest on teachers learning new things." Also, David Weikart, the developer of a Piagetian cognitive-development curriculum for preschool children and the early grades, recalls that teachers often faced critical opposition from people outside the model. He notes that a principal told one teacher to "do things the way those Ypsilanti people want them done" only when the High/Scope consultants were in the schools. Also, a non-project teacher complained that Follow Through had not taught the children self-discipline. However, his definition of self-discipline was that children would do exactly as they were told (D. Weikart, personal communication, 1995). These and similar reactions add to the implementation problems and also contribute to changes in the innovation.

The primary difference between sector II and III programs is the explicitness of materials, procedures, and activities. Sector II programs, as a result, are likely to be implemented in different ways at different sites. Harvard Project Physics, for example, consisted of a variety of materials and media. However, teachers had considerable latitude in the choice of units and materials. Thus, implementation differed in different classrooms. Sector III programs, in contrast, are fully developed programs with well-defined activities, procedures, and role descriptions. They are more likely to be implemented in a fairly consistent manner, given sufficient institutional support and experience with the innovation. An example is Writing to Read, a program to teach reading in first grade.

In terms of relative ease of implementation, Sector IV programs are an evaluator's dream. The projects are well defined and explicit, and they do not seek to change the priorities or beliefs of the ongoing system. Like sector I programs, personnel roles are defined in terms of the innovation. Thus, other things being equal, sector IV programs have the most potential for successful implementation. An example is Reading Recovery, the program for the most disadvantaged first-grade readers described in Chapter 12.

Institutional Support

Although money is essential in initiating a project, resources alone are insufficient for project acceptance or implementation (McLaughlin, 1990). Instead, the active commitment of district leadership is essential for success. As indicated in Chapter 12, both indirect and direct support are essential for successful implementation. Particularly important to teachers in the program are the attitudes and active endorsement of the program by administrators and district staff (McLaughlin, 1990). Teachers may be willing or eager to undertake a new direction; however, they may not participate or do so only on a pro forma basis because the institutional setting is not supportive (p. 15).

Direct support activities, however, vary in their likely impact on staff behavior. For example, school faculty may pay little attention to changes in job descriptions or titles, but the daily presence of a paraprofessional in the classroom brings inescapable consequences for the teachers (Charters & Jones, 1973, p. 6).

Equally important is that the institutional support cannot be limited to a few changes established at the initiation of a new program or policy. Instead, the support must be ongoing. The Rand study found that, in addition to building broad-based commitment to a new project, effective implementation strategies included extended teacher training, classroom assistance from project staff, regular project meetings that focused on practical issues, and principals' participation in training (McLaughlin, 1990). All of these strategies are expressions of institutional commitment to the success of the innovation.

Influence of Local Problems and Practices

Early analysis of implementation factors indicated that different local problems and characteristics lead to different responses to new policies and programs (McLaughlin, 1987, p. 172). For example, parent involvement in urban districts presents different problems and issues than parent participation in rural settings. Similarly, bilingual education issues in Puerto Rican New York City neighborhoods differ from those of a Massachusetts community with large numbers of Vietnamese and Thai children.

On occasion, a new program or curriculum initiative may be at cross purposes with existing programs. The mathematics curriculum framework introduced in California in 1985, for example, is incompatible with a district Achievement of Basic Skills (ABS) program for low socioeconomic schools. They differ in philosophy, goals, and delivery of instruction (Peterson, 1990). The curriculum framework, based on the concept that individuals construct knowledge from experience, is a group-based experiential perspective. ABS, in contrast, is a direct-instruction skills-based program.

The effects of local differences in interpretation of policy concepts also precipitates different local responses. Western Australia funded six high schools in the district to implement curriculum innovations associated with technology education (Rennie & Treagust, 1993). Each of the six schools developed a different approach. Their plans varied in (1) the choice of a whole school or a particular subject-related focus, (2) percentage of resources allocated to personnel and technology, and (3) methods of teacher involvement (Rennie & Treagust, 1993).

Degree of Role Change

Implementation of a new policy, program, curriculum, or set of instructional materials ultimately depends upon the individual responsible for delivering the service.

Thus, "change ultimately is a problem of the smallest unit. What actually is delivered or provided under the aegis of a policy depends finally on the individual at the end of the line" (p. 174). In most educational programs, the classroom teacher is the direct agent of change. A policy or program is not implemented until the teachers change, and that goal is achieved on an individual basis (Hall, 1992).

The extent to which the teacher can successfully implement the innovation is the result of several factors. One is the extent of the role change required of the teacher. Tyler (1991) noted that implementation would be a fairly straightforward task if the new program did not introduce a new conception of education, did not attempt to alter familiar teacher-student interactions, did not address different objectives, and did not require new skills of the teachers (p. 6). In other words, the only change that does not require extensive accommodation by the teacher is the adoption of a new textbook in a curriculum in which the content is not altered (Tyler, 1991).

The more extensive the role change required of the teacher, the more resources and time will be required. Weikart (personal communication, 1995) admits that, like other project directors, he initially assumed that verbal description of a model with charts and diagrams in a 5-day workshop would lead to radical modification of teaching behavior the following year. Instead, consultants, classroom aides, and periodic discussions and workshops were required.

The importance of staff training and support is indicated in the technology initiative in Western Australia. Of six high schools funded to integrate technology into the curriculum, only two were successful. Although the two schools differed in both philosophy and approach, they shared one important characteristic. Both schools allocated 90% of their funding to faculty released time so that the teachers could develop both new ways of thinking and new ways of teaching (Rennie & Treagust, 1991).

Teacher Belief Systems

In the absence of resources targeted to assist teachers to construct alternative conceptions of teaching, new practices are likely to be adapted to fit teacher belief systems. For example, one project to assist teachers to develop performance-based assessments found that teachers whose beliefs about mathematics teaching emphasized computation and memorization adapted the new practices to fit their existing beliefs. That is, "a teacher who believed children learn by being told would show children how to use base ten blocks in a directive manner" (Flexer, Cambo, Borko, Mayfield, & Scott, 1994, p. 26).

In a different project, teachers at high levels of implementation of portfolio assessment reported that the philosophy of alternative assessment fit their own beliefs (Lamme & Hysmith, 1991, p. 638). Teachers at low levels of implementation viewed portfolio assessment as an "add-on" to their duties and had difficulty in understanding why they should use this type of assessment (p. 638).

A newly discovered problem associated with role change is that teachers may not perceive major differences between their usual practices and the innovation. The

California Study of Elementary Mathematics found this situation in a study of the 1985 mathematics curriculum framework. Some teachers saw no contradiction between teaching the memorization of facts and procedures and the framework that emphasizes learner construction of knowledge and mathematics as a form of inquiry. One teacher, for example, viewed the framework intent of "teaching for understanding" as understanding the applications of mathematical procedures and "insight" as being able to do mathematics work quickly and correctly (Weimer, 1990). Another viewed "understanding" as following directions (Wilson, 1990). A third teacher believed that the framework validated her practice of teaching facts, rules, and procedures "with understanding" (Ball, 1990, p. 254). This teacher found the manipulatives and concrete activities provided with the new textbook to be very useful in helping children "understand" the procedures.

These classrooms illustrate a lesson from detailed studies of the implementation process (McLaughlin, 1987). The lesson is that teacher failure to implement innovations fully and accurately is not the result of laziness or resistance to change. Instead, teacher responses to innovations may represent their best efforts to do their job in a complex fluid setting. In other words, as teachers and students attempt to progress from familiar practices to new ones, they often "cobble new ideas onto familiar practices" (Cohen, 1990, p. 312), and the result may be a no-treatment project.

Experience With the Innovation

Another factor in implementation is that the extent and accuracy with which a new policy, curriculum, or program is translated into practice varies with the teacher's experience in using the innovation. Implementation is not an all-or-nothing activity. For the classroom teacher, implementation and use of an innovation is a developmental phenomenon during which teacher concerns and practices evolve and change (Hall, 1992). In other words, "teachers construct meaning of the innovation and interpret the innovation differently at different times in the change process" (p. 892).

Early studies of the clinical experiences and case notes of change agents indicated eight levels in the nonuse/use continuum (Hall, Loucks, Rutherford, & Newlove, 1975; Hall, Wallace, & Dossett, 1973). These levels primarily reflect teacher experience with the innovation and are illustrated in Table 14.1. (These levels are refinements of the "role performance" stage of a school program in the Charters and Jones [1973] analysis discussed in Chapter 2.)

This analysis was applied to classrooms that were implementing Individually Guided Education in reading and mathematics (Hall & Loucks, 1977). Table 14.1 illustrates the percentages of teachers at each level for reading. As indicated, 20% of the IGE classrooms are non-users, and 16% are only mechanical users. Therefore, only 64% of the classrooms were implementing IGE at routine (adequate) use or above. Hall (1992, p. 894) notes that summative evaluation should not be undertaken with users who are only at Level III (Mechanical Use). When use is disjointed, the teacher's focus is near-time and inefficient.

Table 14.1
Analysis of individualized reading in IGE schools according to levels of use and nonuse

Level of Use	Behavioral Indices of Level	Percentage of Classrooms N=68
VI Renewal	The user is seeking more effective alternatives to the established use of the innovation.	0
V Integration	The user is making deliberate efforts to coordinate with others in using the innovation.	12%
IVB Refinement	The user is making changes to increase outcomes.	15%
IVA Routine	The user is making few or no changes and has an established pattern of use.	37%
III Mechanical	The user is using the innovation in a poorly coordinated manner and is making user-oriented changes.	16%
II Preparation	The person is preparing to use the innovation.	4%
I Orientation	The person is seeking out information about the innovation.	13%
0 Nonuse	No action is being taken with respect to the innovation.	3%

Summarized from Hall, 1992; Hall and Loucks, 1977.

Different levels of implementation also were documented in the first year of a school-based project in portfolio assessment. The pre-kindergarten to grade 2 teachers in the school completed questionnaires about (1) the aspects of portfolio assessment that were easy or difficult and (2) their concerns that might be addressed in future in-service workshops. Each teacher was then interviewed about the strategies and portfolios in her classroom, and classrooms were observed (Lamme & Hysmith, 1991).

Table 14.2 illustrates the different levels of use of portfolio assessment and the associated attitudes at the end of the first year. Like the Hall and Loucks' (1977) scale, this listing illustrates various degrees of implementation from superficial to fully integrated. It also illustrates the relationship of teacher belief systems to practice.

Summary

Implementation of an intervention can occur in at least three unplanned ways. They are mutual adaptation, co-optation, and non-implementation. The factors that influence implementation primarily involve (1) the extent of systemic and individual change the innovation requires and (2) the beliefs and experiences of the implementers.

The extent to which the programs seek to effect systemic change and the degree of program specificity interact to produce four types of programs. They differ in the problems they present for implementation. Loosely defined programs that are adjuncts to the system will be implemented in a variety of ways across sites. Loosely defined programs that are intended to change teacher practice are likely to be distorted in both implementation and their aims. In contrast, well-

Table 14.2
Stages of implementation of portfolio assessment in one elementary school

First Stage (Non-use)
No systematic collection of anecdotal records or samples of student writing in portfolio format.

Second Stage[1]
Purposes:
    To indicate a child's level of progress.
    To show if a child is accumulating the necessary prerequisite knowledge and skills.
    To tell us what a child doesn't know.
    To see what skills I need to reteach.
Content:
    A collection of the child's tests and writings on assigned topics.
    The county's exit skills checklist.
Process:
    Teacher collects with no child input.
Attitudes:
    Teacher says he/she likes more structured assessment.
    Teacher wants to be told what must be included.
    Teacher feels need for documentation of county exit skills checklists.

Third Stage[1]
Purposes:
    To collect and keep more in-depth records of what child is doing.
    To tell me what skills to teach.
    To make decisions about promotion and retention.
Content:
    Collections of children's work.
    County exit skills check lists.
    School-issued forms used with no alterations or personal innovations.
    Observations of total group responses to various aspects of the curriculum such as SSR.
Process:
    Teacher keeps anecdotal records in his or her head.
    Teacher selects what goes into portfolios.
    Teacher integrates county exit skills with curriculum.
Attitudes:
    Teacher claims that there isn't time for county-mandated forms and portfolio assessment.
    Teacher tries various ways to record information.
    Teacher states that we need consistency and uniformity by grade level.
    Teacher feels the need for more experience to determine the purpose of anecdotal records.

defined programs that seek systemic change are more likely to be successful if given the essential support for implementation. Finally, well-defined programs that are adjuncts to the system are most likely to be implemented according to the project plan.

The types of both direct and indirect support for an intervention as well as local problems and practices also influence implementation. Ongoing support and the

---

Fourth Stage[1]

Purposes:

Teacher understands reasons for portfolios: the importance of determining how children actually use skills rather than just whether they know them or not.

Teacher uses information to inform teaching.

There are authentic reasons for the showcase portfolio—teacher provides an audience with whom children can share their best work.

Content:

Teacher uses a variety of strategies for collecting data: observations, checklists, scales, anecdotes, and artifacts.

Teacher keeps a log or record of what has been taught.

Process:

Children select work for their showcase portfolios.

Teacher observes systematically (i.e., 5 children a day, each curricular area, etc.)

Attitudes:

Teacher is concerned about time and the management system.

Teacher says, "I can now see the progress of each child more clearly."

Fifth Stage[1]

Purposes:

To inform instruction.

To display and celebrate good work.

For students to assess their growth.

Content:

Teacher analyzes artifacts that are kept and student logs, reading journals, etc., so that the portfolio is not merely a collection of things, but contains interpretive data as well.

Teacher utilizes records to reflect on instruction.

Process:

Children reflect on why they put work in portfolios and can explain why the work is good.

Teacher keeps a log on what has been taught to each child.

Teacher moves away from systematic observation to recording information as it occurs.

Students keeps logs on what they are learning.

Innovations occur on assessment systems.

Attitudes:

Enthusiastic sampling of new ideas.

[1]The correspondence with the stages in the Hall and Loucks' (1977) model are generally as follows: Second Stage (teacher is taking initial steps) Level II; Third Stage, Level III; Fourth Stage, Level IVA; Fifth Stage, Level IVB.

---

lack of conflict between the new program and existing programs are important for successful implementation.

Three teacher characteristics that interact with implementation are the degree of expected role change for the teacher, the teacher's belief system, and his or her experience with the innovation. The greater the expected role change, the more difficult the implementation. Similarly, the more divergent the innovation is from the teacher's belief system, the more it is likely to be perceived as an "add-on" to existing responsibilities. Finally, implementation is not an all-or-nothing event. Instead, it is a developmental process for the teacher that consists of several stages. Implementation may range from non-use through haphazard use to mechanical use and then be integrated into classroom practice. Summative evaluations should not be conducted on new classroom practices that are implemented at less than mechanical use.

SELECTION OF AN EVALUATION PERSPECTIVE

Assessing the implementation of a new curriculum, program, or policy should provide information about the operations of the program in the local setting. Either an issues-oriented or an ethnographic perspective may be used to document implementation.

Major Considerations

Four major considerations guide the planning of documentation activities. One consideration is that plans should be sensitive to the influential local factors already described. The second consideration involves the absolutely essential observation of the intervention at the individual level. Testimonials about use from principals, district staff members, or others is not reliable (Hall, 1992, p. 894). Also, as indicated in the case studies of five California mathematics teachers, teacher self-report is not a reliable indicator of the nature of the innovation in a particular classroom. Thus, a major task in the evaluation is planning the type and extent of classroom observations.

The third consideration that influences the organization of evaluator time and the types of activities selected to address implementation is the stage of development of the program. For a program in the early stages of design and development, the evaluator may be participating in pilot tryouts of the innovation. The primary purpose of developing information is for program improvement. The evaluator also may be assisting in program development and refinement. Feedback to program staff may be informal for the most part, supported by data organized into an interim written report.

In contrast, a funding agency, school district, or other institution typically seeks information about the effectiveness of a particular program. Data about implementation are important in order to determine whether modification of the program is an option and to develop more effective implementation strategies.

Regardless of the developmental stage of the program, the evaluation team should not alter the classroom configuration in order to assess implementation. In the early field tests of the Sesame Street television program in Mexico (Plaza Sesamo), six experimental children were selected randomly every day and were separated from the other children in the experimental group. The six children were placed in a special room with their own television set. Two assistants sat at either side of the group and recorded their attention for every program segment. The results of the study indicated that the field test yielded positive effects for Plaza Sesamo, but the final tryout indicated no differences between the two groups. The monitoring of the experimental children in the field test may have conveyed the impression that this program was important and thus increased the children's attention to the program when they returned to the regular room. In other words, an artifact of the field trial may have contributed to the positive effects in that tryout (Diaz-Guerrero, Reyes-Lagunes, Witzke, & Holtzman, 1976).

The fourth consideration is that the evaluation team may choose either an issue-oriented or an ethnographic perspective to document implementation. Issue-oriented approaches, using the program definition as a basis for developing specific questions, focus on extent of use, intermediate effects (if any), and any implementation problems. An ethnographic approach, in contrast, seeks to understand the nature of the program culture and the school environment as the participants experience it.

An Issue-Oriented Approach

The issue-oriented approach takes the program definition and develops specific questions to be answered about the intervention. These questions take into account the factors discussed in the prior section of this chapter.

Table 14.3 illustrates an overview for documenting implementation of Project CHEM, an innovative chemistry curriculum of the 1960s. CHEM was a curriculum project with sets of activities and materials that did not adequately address the task of implementation. Thus, it was a sector II program, indicating that extensive site variation was likely. On the overview, "institutional climate" identifies specific local conditions that influence implementation. "Support for teacher role change" targets the specific activities (ongoing training, consultant and/or aide assistance, teacher meetings to work out problems, and so on) used to move implementation of the innovation from a pro forma effort to a vital program. Such activities are particularly important for sector II programs, both to survive and to influence the nature of teaching and learning. Finally, "conceptual framework questions" and "documentation focus" are derived directly from the program definition. Together, the categories in the overview orient the evaluation team to the essential information about implementation.

The overview identifies program type and the specific focus to be addressed for an identified program. This information is important in answering three key questions about the curriculum or program. These questions are, What target population is the intervention serving? To what extent are essential program elements being

Table 14.3
Overview of assessment plan for the implementation of Project CHEM

Type of program: Sector II

Extent of role change:

Philosophy of learning and teaching (major redirection)
Methods (major redirection)

Institutional climate:

Administrative support
Related programs, policies, & practices
Nature of support for teacher role change. Are classroom aides, consultants, or other
  support available to the teacher? Is periodic training and review available?
Direct program support. Are lab materials, student manuals and workbooks, and
  media available and in use?

Conceptual framework questions (from program definition):

1. Is hands-on experimentation a necessary requirement for the process of deduction?
2. Does deducing the principles of chemistry facilitate critical thinking in science?

Specific documentation focus:

(a) Types of students in the program.
(b) Nature of "hands' on" experimentation and frequency.
(c) Teacher beliefs about the role of experimentation in chemistry.
(d) Student reactions to the activities.
(e) Classroom activities that flow from experimentation (e.g., is there open-ended inquiry in the
  classroom?).
(f) How is CHEM experimentation different from experiments in other chemistry courses?

implemented? and What are the intermediate effects on students, teachers, and others? For each of these three key questions, the evaluation should determine the factors that contribute to the observed events.

The two major categories of data essential in answering these three questions are intents and observations. (These categories are the two major types of data in Stake's countenance model, discussed in Chapter 3.) The data categories, the key implementation questions, and the associated information sources are illustrated in Table 14.4.

Identification of the Target Population.   Determining the population actually served by the intervention is extremely important because the group described in the program definition may not be receiving the services. Recall the bilingual instruction program intended for children of Hispanic origin with a limited command of English, which was discussed in Chapter 2. The evaluators found that the program was not implemented with that group.

Table 14.4
Key implementation questions and information sources

	Questions	Overview Item	Intents	Information Source — Observations
1.	(a) Is the innovation reaching the designated target population?	(a)	Program definition	Project records; school assignment and enrollment data; school attendance records; classroom observations
	(b) Why or why not?			Informal interviews with administrators, teachers, program staff, and others; project records
2.	(a) Are the critical elements of the innovation in place?	(b,c,f)	Program definition	Classroom observations
	(b) If not, why not?			Program records; classroom observations; informal interviews of stakeholders
3.	(a) Are the hypothesized intermediate effects occurring?	(d,e)	Program definition Program staff	Classroom observations; student products (e.g., lab work workbooks, portfolios, and/or test scores) student interviews
	(b) If not, why not?			Classroom observations; semi-structured interviews of administrators, teachers, and students
	(c) What other intermediate effects are occurring?	(1,2)	Analysis of weaknesses in program definition	Classroom observations; student products; student interviews

283

Sometimes high absentee rates or dropout rates occur, and they may negate the presumed existence of a program. Cooley and Bickel (1986) found this problem in an urban school district that had expanded Title I services in remedial reading into ten high schools. Dropout rates ranged from 9% to 44% of the total program enrollment in each school. Also, depending on the within-school structure, maximum possible attendance varied from 1 to 4 days per week. Thus, the maximum possible attendance in a semester ranged from 12 to 165 class periods. Absentee rates also varied; in four schools the daily absentee rate was 20% or higher. In other words, some of the schools were examples of the no-treatment project problem discussed in Chapter 2.

The project evaluation found that the school district lacked an adequate system for recording and monitoring student enrollment in programs. A major recommendation of the evaluation was the development of a computer system to track enrollment and attendance by program and school.

Documentation of Actual Program Activities.   The essential program elements are (1) the activities and prescribed day-to-day events that impact students or program recipients and (2) the teaching skills and level of expertise required to implement the program. As already indicated, adequate evidence of curriculum, program, or policy implementation requires observation of the individual units where implementation is to take place. This task varies somewhat, given the relationship of the program to the institution or system. An essential task for sector I and II programs is to determine the various program interpretations that are in place. For these programs, the equipment and various activities implemented in different sites are determined and compared for consistency with the basic program philosophy.

Sector III and IV programs, unlike the others, are constructed from conceptual frameworks that have been translated into specific classroom methods, activities, and procedures. Therefore, observation guidelines or checklists derived from descriptions of essential program elements may serve as the basis for classroom observations. Hypothesized intermediate effects, such as increased student confidence in conducting independent inquiry, also should be included so that they may be assessed during later observations of the program. The observation guidelines also should differentiate between mechanical, routine, and refinement levels of implementation. That is, a superficial or "go through the motions" effort should be differentiated from an integrated use of activities and materials. Classroom observations may then be used to identify strong, adequate, weak, and no-treatment implementations.

Of major importance is that the evaluation should not rely on self-report questionnaires or teacher interviews to determine the nature and extent of implementation. First, it is almost impossible to design questionnaire items on implementation without cueing respondents as to the desired answers. For example, a self-report questionnaire on a new tutoring program that asks about the frequency and duration of tutoring sessions is likely to yield inflated responses.

Moreover, the respondents may unknowingly be inaccurate reporters of critical program events in their classrooms. The case studies in the California Mathematics

Study revealed teacher misconceptions about the new curriculum leading to their beliefs that they were implementing the new policy in their classes.

Informal and semi-structured interviews (as described in Chapter 9) are useful for developing information about the contextual and attitudinal factors that are influencing classroom practice. In this way, institutional commitment, teacher philosophies about learning, the extent of teacher training and subsequent support, and school and district priorities may be identified. Program documents, such as teacher training materials and equipment checkout records, also should be reviewed for information about the teachers' level of expertise.

Documentation Example.   One documentation example is the California Study of Elementary Mathematics. The curriculum framework in elementary mathematics is a sector II program in that it seeks to effect changes in mathematics teaching in elementary classrooms across the state. Data were collected in three school districts at four levels: state, school district, school, and classroom. State-level informants, school district administrators, and school principals were interviewed about state-level and school district policies, procedures, and practices (Peterson, 1990). The purpose was to develop an understanding of the policy context in which the teachers were functioning (p. 243).

Twenty-three second- and fifth-grade teachers participated in the study. Site visits of 2 weeks in December 1988 and 2 weeks in March 1989 consisted of (1) a 2-hour interview with each teacher and (2) a 2-day observation of the teachers' mathematics instruction, accompanied by pre- and post-observation interviews about the particular lessons. The focus of the 2-hour interview was teacher knowledge of the curriculum policy; the meaning of teaching for understanding; assessment, teaching, and learning in mathematics; resources needed to implement the policy; and the demands of the policy on practice from the perspective of the teacher. Teachers also responded to questions on specific mathematics topics (such as subtraction with regrouping), in terms of their classroom approach. They were asked about the children's difficulties in learning the topic, their approach to teaching the topic, and how material in the textbook is used (Peterson, 1990, p. 244). The conversations in the post-observation interviews addressed what the teachers were trying to teach, why they were teaching it, how they were trying to teach the material, and their views of what the students got out of the lesson (Peterson, 1990, p. 244).

Each classroom was audiotaped (each teacher wore a wireless microphone), and observers took field notes. They also wrote narrative summaries the same day. In addition, the observer wrote responses to a set of analytic questions on an analytic guide. The questions addressed mathematical content being taught, apparent goals, representations and mathematical tools used by the teachers and students, extent of opportunities to "unpack" ideas or use mathematics tools, and the nature of teacher and student discourse. The researchers developed case studies of each teacher constructed from the interview transcripts, field notes, summaries, and audiotapes.

Determination of the Intermediate Effects.   A new curriculum, policy, or program is developed to address some unmet need or unsolved problem. Implementing the new perspective should begin to change actions and perceptions in the classroom, referred to as intermediate effects. For example, teachers in one project who began using performance-based assessments and similar instructional activities reported that their students were enjoying mathematics more (Flexer et al., 1994).

The identification of expected intermediate effects is a component of the program definition. As indicated in Chapter 12, program documents may not be specific about transitional classroom changes. In such a situation, program staff may be asked what they expect to occur in the classroom when the program is implemented. Sources of information for intermediate effects are classroom observations, interviews of students, and student work, such as lab workbooks, portfolios, teacher observation checklists (e.g., observation records of oral reading), and classroom test scores.

Three caveats are of primary importance in efforts to document intermediate effects of an innovation. First, only innovations implemented at level IVA-Routine or above can be expected to lead to observable, relatively stable changes in the classroom. Lower levels of implementation are superficial and haphazard and may not be consistent with the program philosophy and intent. In one study, an 11-member team worked with 14 elementary school classroom teachers to develop performance assessments for their classes. Twenty-six children were interviewed three times during the school year on their perceptions of assessment and instruction. In the spring interviews, the children seemed to recognize and appreciate that reading involves meaning making (a goal of the new curriculum focus). However, they viewed meaning as word identification. They perceived reading aloud as the primary way the teacher knows they can read, and they reported, " . . . she puts checks down for how we read and the words we have trouble with" (Davinroy, Bliem, & Mayfield, 1994, p. 14). Thus, their basic concepts about reading had changed little during the year. Similarly, children perceived the focus in mathematics as computation with emphasis on "right answers, wrong answers, that's about it" (Davinroy et al., 1994, p. 15).

Second, as Charters and Jones (1973) indicated, changes in students are the last change to occur when a new curriculum, program, or policy is installed. Therefore, intermediate effects in terms of student change should not be assessed until the students have had adequate exposure to the innovation and experience with different activities and ways of thinking.

Third, in the early stages of implementation, confusion and lack of clear direction are likely intermediate classroom effects. Further, these effects are more likely for sector I and II programs that are not explicitly defined and that provide minimal teacher training and support. Therefore, assessment of intermediate effects should be planned in light of the factors described in the introduction section of this chapter.

An Ethnographic Perspective

An issue-oriented approach to documenting program implementation uses program intents, the nature of the program, and local climate and characteristics as a framework for answering key questions about the intervention. In contrast, an ethnographic approach seeks to provide in-depth understanding of a program culture from the perspective of the insiders. This perspective is referred to as contextual because it can provide a wealth of information about the context in which the program is attempting to function, the actual activities of the program, perceptions of participants, and the factors influencing the direction of the innovation (Britain, 1978).

The frame of reference for an ethnographic study of program implementation is the ways that participants construct the program and its effects in terms of their social realities and meaning systems (Dorr-Breme, 1985, p. 67). A primary data collection mechanism in ethnography is participant observation. The purpose is to understand the cultural setting as the participants do by engaging in their day-to-day activities. The evaluator first becomes familiar with the operational structure, language, and functioning in that setting. In a school setting, one typically begins with a tour of the physical facility conducted by an administrator or designated staff member. The evaluator then spends time in the teacher's lounge, on the playground (elementary school), in the cafeteria, in faculty and staff meetings, joining the teachers during bus duty, attending PTA meetings and school assemblies, and so on. Important aspects of this period are respectful listening, interest in the school and the particular program under study, and a nonjudgmental perspective. These characteristics are the building blocks of developing mutual respect and trust between the evaluators and the participants, which is essential to the study.

During these activities, the ethnographer begins to develop information about rituals (including informal authority structures and subgroups), rites of passage (if appropriate to the setting), and other data that indicate the ways that the school functions and the belief systems of the participants.

Participant observation is also supplemented by information from other sources. They are project documents, curriculum materials, prior faculty meeting minutes (if appropriate), and key informant interviews. Gaps in knowledge and other issues typically are addressed through interviews of knowledgeable and perceptive participants, referred to as key informants.

Of importance is that site visits should be of sufficient length to permit the evaluator to develop in-depth information about the program and the participants' perspectives. Some time also should be scheduled between site visits for reflection, developing questions, and later, data analysis.

An ethnographic study of program implementation can yield rich and detailed information about the program and its operation. The ethnographic component of the CIP intern study yielded 32 adaptive and 37 maladaptive relationships at the classroom, project management, and federal agency oversight levels that influenced program operation. Specific recommendations in the study were based on these discoveries. Among the adaptive relationships discovered were that "the 'firm but caring' attitude of instructors toward the interns is a primary motivating factor that promotes their continued participation in the programs," that "staff criticism of inappropriate intern behavior (in informal and formal settings) is interpreted positively by interns as a form of caring" and that "the accelerated nature of the program motivates interns to 'get down to it'" (Fetterman, 1988a, p. 268). Among the maladaptive relationships discovered were that inadequate administrative support "bottlenecked" necessary requests (for materials, for example) and frustrated the staff and that hiring policies ignored philosophical and attitudinal qualifications (p. 268).

A disadvantage of the ethnographic approach to understanding program implementation is the time requirement. However, this approach is particularly important in settings where there is little information and for innovations that attempt to address long-standing problems in a different way.

ALLOCATION OF RESOURCES

Four issues are important in the scheduling of time and resources to assess implementation. The first issue concerns the implementation or intermediate records of learning that were built into the project. Such records are more likely to be found in sector III and IV programs. These records should be identified and incorporated into the evaluation plan.

The second issue concerns the stage of development of the project and the requirements of the evaluation contract. If the innovation is in the early stages of development, the contract may call for an evaluator on site during all field trials to provide feedback to the development team. Otherwise, the contract, if negotiated in view of the critical role of implementation by the evaluators, should require identification of adequate and less than adequate project or school examples, and recommendations for future implementations.

The third issue pertains to the length of the evaluation. If, for example, a 1-year contract is in effect and the innovation, according to policymakers, has been in place 1 year or more, the evaluation can conduct a two-stage assessment of implementation. The first stage is preliminary, and the purpose is to identify the extent of implementation at different sites (i.e., no evidence of implementation or evidence of implementation that is weak [mechanical use], adequate [routine use], and strong [refinement level and above]). The second stage of the evaluation, depending on the purpose of the evaluation, may examine in depth the sites identified at the routine or higher levels. Factors hindering implementation at lower levels also may be identified if resources and time are available. A multi-year evaluation, in contrast, may document changes in implementation and effects over time.

The fourth issue in the scheduling of time and resources to assess implementation involves the scope of the implementation. If the initiative is state sponsored, for example, but implemented in volunteer schools only, all sites should be evaluated, if resources permit. If the initiative is a directive that is intended to be implemented statewide, then some selection of schools is required. A logical choice is schools in two or more districts that differ in size and socioeconomic level that are perceived by state and district personnel to be implementing the new directive.

As indicated in Chapter 13, the number of sites selected, the length of each site visit, and the number of visits depend, in large measure, on the budget and personnel available for the task. To adequately assess the level of implementation at any one site visit, two evaluators would be required and approximately 1 week should be scheduled (issue-oriented approach). This time frame allows for school schedule changes and other unanticipated events, as well as time for interviews of personnel at different levels within the school. If ten schools are to be visited during a 1-month period, for example, six observer/interviewers are needed.

Level of expertise of the observer/interviewers is a critical element in assessing implementation. Ideally, an evaluation team, such as the team that assisted the teachers in implementing performance assessments (Davinroy et al., 1994; Flexer et al., 1994), should consist of individuals with different types of expertise. A subject-matter expert, a researcher knowledgeable in school change, an ethnographer, and a measurement expert would be ideal, for example. Team members can then be responsible for training others for conducting observations and interviews. Such training also requires volunteer classes so that the trainees may practice and refine their skills prior to participating in the evaluation study. If the expertise for training is not available on the evaluation team, this service must be contracted out, at a further expense to the evaluation budget.

SUMMARY

Four major considerations should guide the planning of documentation activities:

1. Sensitivity to local factors
2. A reliance on observation
3. The stage of development of the innovation
4. The conceptual approach taken by the evaluation team

An issue-oriented approach develops specific program-related questions from the program definition and addresses three key issues about the implementation. These issues concern the target population, the occurrence of critical elements of the program, and intermediate effects. The evaluation also provides information about likely causes of implementation problems and omissions.

An ethnographic perspective, in contrast, uses fieldwork to develop a holistic picture of the program from the perspective of the insiders. The evaluator participates in the daily activities of the program and the setting to develop an understanding of the latent agendas and processes that influence program operation. The information obtained from this involvement is also checked against the information provided in key informant interviews and document analysis.

Among the considerations in scheduling evaluation activities for assessing implementation are the stage of development of the project or innovation, the scope of the implementation (a few schools or a large number of schools), the length of the evaluation contract, and the expertise of the evaluation team. Also important is the training of observer/interviewers, which must include practice with feedback in classrooms and with teachers that volunteer for this effort. Training must be completed prior to assessment of the implementation of the program or policy.

GUIDELINES FOR THE DOCUMENTATION OF PROGRAM IMPLEMENTATION

Issue-oriented approach:

Step 1. Determine the relationship of the innovation to the system.

    1.1   Review program documents to identify purpose, target population, and implementers (e.g., project personnel or regular classroom teachers).

    1.2   Classify the innovation as a Sector I, II, III, or IV intervention and note potential implementation problems.

    1.3   Gauge the extent of active support provided by administrators (and district staff, if appropriate).

    1.4   Identify any competing programs or priorities to the innovation (e.g., a skills-based program versus problem-solving curriculum frameworks).

    1.5   Identify direct support provided and degree of role change required.

Step 2. Identify the specific documentation focus.

    1.1   Address the conceptual framework questions identified in the program definition.

    1.2   Identify specific factors related to the intervention to target in observations and interviews.

    1.3   Select methods to document the population reached by the intervention, the presence of critical elements (level of implementation), and the intermediate effects.

Ethnographic approach:

Step 1. Gain entry into the field.

    1.1   Obtain the permission of administrators.

    1.2   Develop a social map and a temporal map of the setting through an informal tour.

    1.3   Begin to sort and categorize individuals who can serve as information sources.

    1.4   Begin to collect anecdotes, stories, and myths.

Step 2. Develop a data record.

    2.1   Record events and interactions in field jottings and convert to field notes with contextual information added.

2.2	Collect information about rituals, myths, and other data that indicate belief systems of participants.
2.3	Check perceptions and gaps in knowledge through unstructured or semi-structured interviews.
2.4	Review curriculum materials, teacher handouts, and other materials.
2.5	Corroborate information with other information sources.

Step 3. Develop a report of the implementation.
3.1   Construct a case study of each site.
3.2   After analyzing the data (see Chapter 15), describe functional and maladaptive linkages and relationships in the program.

CHAPTER QUESTIONS

1. What are two specific recommendations that should be made to the school districts implementing the 1985 mathematics curriculum framework described in the curriculum study project?

2. What are the implications of extensive role change for implementation?

3. The issue-oriented approaches and the ethnographic approach to the analysis of implementation rely on many of the same methods. What are the key differences?

4. Review the program definition you developed for the Promote Learning and Understanding (PLUS) curriculum (in the appendix) when you read Chapter 12. What are some of the likely implementation problems for this program?

5. Using an issue-oriented approach to assessing implementation, what are some of the events and effects you would look for?

REFERENCES

Ball, D. (1990). Reflections and deflections of policy: The case of Carol Turner. *Educational Evaluation and Policy Analysis, 12*(3), 247–259.

Britain, G. (1978). The place of anthropology in program evaluation. *Anthropology and Education Quarterly, 6*(4), 28–34.

Charters, W., & Jones, J. (1973). On the risk of appraising non-events in program evaluation. *Educational Researcher, 2*(11), 5–7.

Cohen, D. (1990). A revolution in one classroom: The case of Mrs. Oublier. *Educational Evaluation and Policy Analysis, 12*(3), 311–329.

Cooley, W., & Bickel, W. (1986). *Decision-oriented educational research.* Boston: Kluwer-Nijhoff.

Davinroy, K., Bliem, G., & Mayfield, V. (1994, April). *"How does my teacher know that I know." Third graders' perceptions of math, reading, and assessment.* Paper presented at the annual meeting of the American Educational Research Association, New Orleans.

Diaz-Guerrero, R., Reyes-Lagunes, I., Witzke, D., & Holtzman, W. (1976, Spring). Plaza Sesamo in Mexico: An evaluation. *Journal of Communication,* 145–154.

Dorr-Breme, D. (1985). Ethnographic evaluation: A theory and method. *Educational Evaluation and Policy Analysis, 7* (l), 65–83.

Fetterman, D. (1988a). A national ethnographic evaluation: An executive summary of the ethnographic component of the career intern program. In D. Fetterman (Ed.), *Qualitative approaches to evaluation in education* (pp. 262–273). New York: Praeger.

Flexer, R., Cambo, K., Borko, H., Mayfield, V., & Scott, M. (1994, April). *How "messing about" with performance assessment in mathematics affects what happens in classrooms.* Paper presented at the annual meeting of the American Educational Research Association, New Orleans, LA.

Fullan, M. (1982). *The meaning of educational change.* New York: Teachers College Press, Columbia.

Hall, G. (1992). The local educational change process and policy implementation. *Journal of Research in Science Teaching, 29*(8), 877–904.

Hall, G., & Loucks, S. (1977). A developmental model for determining whether the treatment is actually implemented. *American Educational Research Journal, 14*(3), 263–276.

Hall, G., Loucks, S., Rutherford, W., & Newlove, B. (1975). Levels of use of the innovation: A framework for analyzing innovation adoption. *The Journal of Teacher Education, 26*(1), 52–56.

Hall, G., Wallace, R., & Dossett, W. (1973). *A developmental conceptualization of the adoption process within educational institutions.* Austin: Research and Development Center for Teacher Education, The University of Texas.

Lamme, L., & Hysmith, C. (1991). One school's adventure into portfolio assessment. *Language Arts, 68,* 629–640.

McLaughlin, M. (1976). Implementation as mutual adaptation: Change in classroom organization. In W. Williams & R. F. Elmore (Eds.), *Social program implementation* (pp. 167–182). New York: Academic Press.

McLaughlin, M. (1987). Learning from experience: Lessons from policy implementation. *Educational Evaluation and Policy Analysis, 9*(2), 171–178.

McLaughlin, M. (1990). The Rand change agent study revisited: Macro perspectives and micro realities. *Educational Researcher, 19*(9), 11–16.

Peterson, P. (1990). Doing more in the same amount of time: Cathy Swift. *Educational Evaluation and Policy Analysis, 12*(3), 261–280.

Rennie, L., & Treagust, D. (1993). *Factors affecting the successful implementation of whole-school curriculum improvement.* Paper presented at the annual meeting of the American Educational Research Association, Atlanta, GA.

Tyler, R. (1991). General statement on program evaluation. In M. McLaughlin & D. C. Phillips (Eds.), *Evaluation and education at quarter century* (pp. 3–17). Ninetieth Yearbook of the NSSE. Chicago, IL: University of Chicago Press.

Weimer, N. (1990). Transformation and accommodation: A case study of Joe Scott. *Educational Evaluation and Policy Analysis, 12*(3), 281–292.

Wilson, S. (1990). A conflict of interests: The case of Mark Black. *Educational Evaluation and Policy Analysis, 12*(3), 293–310.

CHAPTER 15

Data Analysis and Interpretation

An important stage in program evaluation is the analysis and summarization of the data obtained in the study. Also, if hypotheses were tested on samples in the study, inferential statistics are calculated to determine the significance of the relationships or the differences in the population from which the sample was drawn. The two broad types of data obtained in evaluations are qualitative and quantitative.

QUALITATIVE DATA ANALYSIS

A range and variety of research traditions in sociology, psychology, and education yield qualitative or nonnumerical data. Some of these perspectives focus on social structures, whereas others focus on meanings. Also, some are holistic, whereas others study "micro" events or processes. As a result, there is no single method of analyzing qualitative data. However, discussions of analysis techniques often present idiosyncratic approaches as though they were "the" method. Thus, the field now has a series of manuals for "particular makes of vehicle (often asserting they are the only cars on the road), with little general literature on automotive engineering" (Richards & Richards, 1992, p. 42). Nevertheless, several characteristics of qualitative data analysis are shared by the various methods, and they are discussed in this section.

Overview

Four characteristics are common to the various methods of qualitative data analysis. They are:

1. Data are divided into relevant and meaningful units for analysis while maintaining a connection to the whole.
2. The data units or segments are categorized according to an organizing system that is predominantly derived from the data.
3. The analysis process is systematic and comprehensive but not rigid.
4. Analysis is often concurrent with data collection or cyclic (Tesch, 1990, p. 954).

The essence of the data analysis process is the division of a whole phenomenon into its components and then the reassembly of the phenomenon under various new rubrics (Goetz & LeCompte, 1984, p. 192). This process also is referred to as decontextualizing and recontextualizing the data (Tesch, 1990).

An example of an inductive qualitative analysis is the study of teacher values conducted by LeCompte (1978). The data consisted of teacher verbalizations recorded during classroom observations. The data first were subdivided into relevant segments of the class period, such as "getting settled," "homework review," and so on. The unit of analysis for the study was the verbal episode, and the recorded data were read and reread to identify the regularities and patterns in teacher statements. Among the values that emerged from the data that became categories for the verbal episodes were emphases on work, rule setting, and time schedules.

In addition to the inductive nature of the analysis, the relationship between data collection and analysis in ethnographic studies is recursive. The tentative data categories developed from the preliminary analyses are tested and revised through further data collection and analysis (Goetz & LeCompte, 1984, p. 165).

Other perspectives, however, are quasi-inductive. For example, when observations or interviews are conducted for a particular purpose in evaluation, some of the data categories are developed from other sources. Examples are theory, existing literature, research questions, or a combination of these sources. However, whether the approach to developing data categories is inductive or only partially inductive, the analysis consists of three major steps. They are (1) segmenting the data record, (2) deriving a categorization system and applying it to the data, and (3) interpreting the recontextualized data.

Segmentation of the Data Record

Segmentation of the data record involves two important tasks. One is that of dividing the data into manageable portions for analysis. This task is part of the process referred to by Goetz and LeCompte (1984) as mundane data coding. The other task is that of identifying units of analysis for the data (perceptual divisions of the data that are to be analyzed and interpreted in detail).

Mundane Data Coding.   The process of mundane data coding involves first the identification of the context of the data collection, that is, location, time, participants, and type of activity. This information is recorded at the time the data are collected. The second phase is that of subdividing the data record into manageable portions. This step is necessary because participant and nonparticipant observations, as well as documents and interviews, yield a voluminous data record. The researcher, therefore, identifies descriptive categories that represent logical subdivisions of the data. For example, classroom observations may be subdivided into events such as getting settled, reviewing homework, introducing a new lesson, and so on. Observations taken at several times of day in different school settings may be segmented into designations such as homeroom, lunch, recess, faculty meeting, math class (transition), math class (new lesson), and so on. For data that are responses in semi-structured or structured interviews, answers to the questions form natural segments of the data.

Selection of Units of Analysis.   In an interpretative study, analysis units are the perceptual divisions of the data that are the focus of further data analysis. The unit of analysis for a particular study may be, for example, verbal episodes, thought units, settings, social interactions, or some other unit meaningful for the particular study.

The basis for formulating units of analysis depends on the purpose of the research, the researcher's theoretical perspective, and the data that are gathered. One anthropological perspective, for example, focuses on "bounded phenomena" or social units of behavior, referred to as "strips" (Agar, 1986). The data analysis focuses on identifying the regularities and patterns found in various social interactions among members of a culture. Other perspectives suggest other units. In ethnographies of communication, language units, such as words, patterns, utterances, or speaking turns, are important (Tesch, 1990). This perspective focuses on the micro processes of social interaction (Jacob, 1987). Ecological psychology, another micro approach, focuses on specific behaviors and behavioral episodes.

Another approach to selecting the unit of analysis is to draw on a set of classifications developed from another source. Lofland (1971), for example, developed a set of categories based on structural-functionalist social theory (Goetz & LeCompte, 1984, p. 184). According to Lofland, social phenomena are assumed to be divisible into any of six categories. These categories are acts, activities, meanings, participation, relationships, and settings. Observations initially are sorted into one of the six basic groups, and a classification scheme within the category is developed from the data. The disadvantage of such a classification scheme, however, is that it mandates those units of analysis that are intrinsic to its construction.

Development of a Categorization System

Two general perspectives for developing categories for the data are the ethnographic approach and a quasi-inductive approach. They differ to the extent that a classification system is developed from the data record itself.

The Ethnographic Perspective.   For the analysis unit selected for the study, the researcher begins by searching the data for regularities and patterns. The general questions asked are, Which things are occurring on a regular basis? and Which things are like each other? (p. 171). The search involves going through the data record, reading and rereading it, and jotting down notes and observations (Goetz &

LeCompte, 1984). This process of scanning the data for regularities, developing tentative hypotheses about the provisional descriptions of emerging categories, and testing the categories is referred to as analytic induction (Glaser, 1965; Goetz & LeCompte, 1984).

The tentative categories are tested and revised in several ways. Among them are the testing of rival hypotheses, searching for negative cases, and the process referred to as constant comparison. In this process, each new data item is compared with prior items as it is coded into a category. Categories also are compared during analysis (Glaser, 1965; Goetz & LeCompte, 1984). These comparisons lead to revised categories, new categories, and the discovery of relationships across categories.

Another useful process for evaluating tentative categories is enumeration. The relative number of data instances in each classification can indicate categories that perhaps should be subdivided. In the study of teacher behavior conducted by LeCompte (1975), one large group of teacher verbalizations was labeled "taking responsibility" (Goetz & LeCompte, 1984, p. 194). Examination of this large cate-

Table 15.1
Coding categories for teacher interview analysis

PRE-KINDERGARTEN	FIRST GRADE	FIRST
PRESCHOOL - Mention of, beliefs about	Beliefs about first grade	FIRSTVIEW
SENDHOME - Mention of keeping 5 year olds out	Contact with first grade teachers (or lack of) including Backward Transitions, influence by 1st	FIRSTCONT
% QUAL-K - % of 5 year olds qualified for kindergarten	*BELIEFS ABOUT DEVELOPMENT*	BEL-DEL
PreK-QUAL - Qualifications for entry into kindergarten	Origin of beliefs in experience, research or theory	BEL-ORG
PRECAUSE - Causes of differences in qualification	smooth curves, fixed stages, blooming	
KINDERGARTEN	rate of development belief discrepancies from "norm"	BEL-RATE
K-PURPOSE - Beliefs about the purpose of kindergarten	comparative judgments regarding development	DEL-COMP
K-DESC - Description of kindergarten practices	tractability of development attention span theory	DEL-TRACT ATTENSPAN
K-GROUP - Dealing with heterogeneity in grouping		
K-EXPECT - Expectations for kindergartners		
PRODUCT - Indications of a "process/product orientation"		
K-QUAL - Endpoints of kindergarten; what are the qualifications for successful exit?	*CONTEXT*	
	School characteristics & influence	
K-QUAL-CHAR - Characteristics of the unqualified	Parent characteristics & influence Teacher characteristics (spread of effect)	C-SCHOOL C-PARENT C-TEACH

gory revealed two related but diverse subsets that were renamed as separate categories. These subsets were "following teacher's orders" and "student self-direction and initiative."

The Quasi-Inductive Approach.   In evaluation, qualitative data often are collected for specific purposes. In such situations, tentative categories may be developed from the research questions and other sources in addition to the data. An example is the Boulder Valley study of kindergarten retention that included semi-structured clinical interviews. The purpose of the interviews was to determine the teachers' tacit belief systems about child development, school readiness, and the relationship of schooling to development. The categories for the data were developed from (1) the evaluation questions, (2) the parent interviews, and (3) the coding of one third of the data.

Table 15.1 lists the categories that were applied to teacher statements in the interviews. These categories reflect the specific views expressed by individuals and those found in published anecdotal reports.

K-QUAL-EVID - Evidence of unqualification	Principal characteristics	C-PRINC
K-QUAL-TIME - How soon is unqualification evident?	"Downward Pressure" (the curricular press of content into lower grades)	DOWN
K-QUAL-SEVER - How bad does it have to be? (tolerance differences)	Contact with other K teachers, (spread of theory)	CONTACT
K-QUAL-TRACT - Can unqualification be remedied?	NORMATIVE IMPRESSIONS (other children influence judgment of the development of 1)	C-NORM
K-QUAL-FIX - What to do with the unqualified?		
K-QUAL-CATCH - Is it possible to catch up?	*GESELL*	
K-QUAL-CAUSE - Causes of unqualification (PH = physiological, H - heredity, T = teacher, P = parents, PR = program, EX = exposure to stimulation)	Use of, belief in Gesell Test	GESTEST
	Mention of Gesell Philosophy	GESTPHIL
K-EXTRA - Extra help provided to the unqualified and view of	*MISCELLANEOUS*	
RETENTION	"Parent Blame"	PAR-BLM
R-DEC - Description of decision to retain	"Consequences of Pushing"	PUSH
R-CRIT - Criteria for retention	"Struggle"	STRUGGLE
BENE/RISK - View of risks of not retaining; predictions/benefits of retention	Staffing	STAFF
	COMPETE	
ALT-RET - Alternatives to retention		
R-REACT - Child/parent reactions to retention		
%-RET - Percent retained; explanations		

From *Boulder Valley Kindergarten Study: Retention Practices and Retention Effects* (Appendix C) by L. Shepard and M. Smith, 1985, Boulder, CO: Boulder Valley Public Schools. Reprinted by permission.

Categorizing Data Coding and Regrouping

After the categories are developed, tested, and revised, the category names are attached to the basic units of field research data (Glaser, 1965). This process is referred to as coding. Table 15.2 illustrates the coding of an excerpt from an interview in the retention study. The example is the response to the question about the point in the school year that the teacher can determine the child's readiness for first grade.

After the data are coded, the data record is separated into segments according to the categories and regrouped under the category names. Three approaches to regrouping the coded data segments physically are (1) the cut-up/file folder approach (Bogdan & Biklen, 1982), (2) the file card system (Bogdan & Biklen, 1982), and (3) electronic data handling. Both the file folder and file card methods are manual procedures for coding and regrouping the data.

The Cut-Up/File Folder Approach.   Important preliminary steps are numbering all the pages sequentially, making several photocopies, and filing one copy as an intact chronological record of the data (Bogdan & Biklen, 1982; Lofland & Lofland, 1984).

Table 15.2
Example of coding from the Boulder Valley retention study

Paragraph Excerpt	Code
(At what point during the year can you make a judgment about whether a child is going to be ready for first grade?) Sometimes you can get the feeling at the	K-QUAL-TIME
beginning of the year, but not always. I don't like to make judgments like that, because as I told you, children can change so quickly.	DEL-RATE
So I would say by March the pattern is there. If they are still having difficulty understanding and doing the things that the majority of the other children find easy to do, I begin to question the parents on whether they would be willing to let their children stay another year in kindergarten. Teachers disagree with this, even the first grade teachers here. I contend	K-QUAL-CHAR C-NORM DEL-COMP R-DEC
that a child gains more repeating first grade. But I'm not sure that these first grade teachers	ALT-RET
agree with me. I think that they think if a child is going to come into first grade, it is going to be a year of struggle and maybe a loss of self-image.	BENE-RISK FIRST-CONT STRUGGLE

From *Boulder Valley Kindergarten Study: Retention Practices and Retention Effects* (p. 127–128) by L. Shepard and M. Smith, 1985, Boulder, CO: Boulder Valley Public Schools. Reprinted by permission.

The next task is to add appropriate "source information," because the origin of a particular segment cannot be identified after it is cut apart and placed in a file folder. One mechanism is to write an interview number or other identification next to each segment to be coded (Bogdan, 1982, p. 166). Another mechanism is to use colored markers that represent physical settings, teachers observed, and/or interviewees. The appropriate colors may be run down the center of each page from top to bottom because they do not obliterate the words (Tesch, 1990, p. 128).

After the segments are identified, one photocopy is coded according to the mundane categories selected for the data, such as "recess," "homeroom," and so on. The coded copy is then cut apart and each labeled segment is placed in a file folder with the same label. Then another copy is coded in the margins according to the analytic categories, cut apart, and placed in the appropriate folder for each category.

When the inductive approach to developing categories is implemented, the researcher may cut apart one copy of the data according to the segments to be analyzed (analysis units) and sort and re-sort the segments into tentative groups (Tesch, 1990, p. 129). The segments are then coded with an alphabetical, numerical, or alphanumerical code and placed in the appropriate folder.

The File Card System.   Unlike the file folder approach, the file card system creates a secondary set of data that leaves the original data record intact (Tesch, 1990, p. 129). However, the method is not conducive to developing a set of categories from the data. Instead, the assumption is that categories already exist. The process involves (1) numbering each page and line of data, (2) preparing a set of note cards for the data categories, and (3) recording on each category the page and line numbers of data segments that are in that category. Brief notes about the nature of the entry, such as "observer's comment," may also be made next to a card entry (Bogdan & Biklen, 1982, p. 169).

The outcome of this process is a set of cards that indicates the location of material relevant for each category, but the material itself is elsewhere (Tesch, 1990). (For this reason, this process is sometimes referred to as data indexing rather than data coding.)

Electronic Data Handling.   In recent years, computer software programs have been developed specifically to address the decontextualization and recontextualization requirements of inductive data analysis (Tesch, 1990, 1992). Such programs are referred to as "chunking and coding" programs (Lee & Fielding, 1992, p. 5). The two basic functions conducted by the programs are (1) the mechanical task of attaching codes to the text as the evaluator goes through the material and (2) searching for text segments according to codes and assembling them (Tesch, 1990, p. 150). The programs can display the codes or combinations of codes together with the associated text (Lee & Fielding, 1992, p. 5). Among the auxiliary functions of different programs are selecting segments that satisfy a particular condition (such as the transcriptions from female interviewees) and counting the number of times a given code has been used (Tesch, 1990).

The advantages of these programs are that they save time, they are accurate, and they have the potential for greater thoroughness (Tesch, 1990, p. 25). However, John Seidel (1992), the creator of the computer program ETHNOGRAPH, notes a potential problem with electronic data analysis. In his view, the capability of handling large volumes of data may lead to trading depth for breadth of analysis in efforts to collect ever larger volumes of data simply because the technology is available.

Interpretation of the Data

The two tasks associated with interpreting the data are (1) to review the recontextualized data as it appears under the classification categories and (2) to relate the findings to an empirical or theoretical framework.

Review of the Recontextualized Data.   After the data are recontextualized in categories, the evaluator reviews the categories for completeness. The set of categories should be a typology of the data; that is, they should fully represent the phenomenon. An example is the typology of student behaviors developed in a study of a rural third-grade classroom (Goetz, 1976). The focus of the study was to discover the mechanisms of behavior and belief that maintained the sociocultural environment of the classroom and the teacher's and pupils' perceptions and interpretations of the social reality of the classroom. The principal methods of data collection were participant observation and intensive interviews of the teacher and pupils over one semester.

Table 15.3 illustrates the typology of categories that were discovered in the study. As indicated, patterns of student behavior divided into two major classifications dependent on context orientation: situational behaviors and pervasive behaviors. The two subcategories of situational behaviors were initiating acts (behavioral patterns originated by the children independent of communication or conscious cues from the teacher) and emerging acts (behaviors responsive to some specific teacher action). The subcategories of emergent actions differentiated the behavioral patterns largely controlled by the teacher (dictated behaviors) and those actions in which students possessed a range of options (respondent behaviors).

Identification of Linkages to an Empirical or Theoretical Framework.   After the coding categories are reviewed for completeness, relationships across the categories are developed, and the findings are interpreted. In the study of teacher norms, for example, Goetz (1976) found that, despite differences in teacher values, a common core of categories existed that involved classroom management. This group of behaviors, which were labeled "the management core," was differentiated from other teacher behaviors, which were labeled "discretionary behaviors" (Goetz & LeCompte, 1984).

In evaluation, the broader issues or framework may be identified in advance of the data collection. An example is the Boulder Valley retention study. The teacher statements (coded according to the 48 categories illustrated in Table 15.1) were orga-

Table 15.3
Typology of student behaviors in a rural third-grade classroom

I.   *Situational behaviors* = contingent upon the nature of ongoing events
  A. *Emergent actions* = responsive to some specific action of the teacher
    1. *Dictated behaviors* = explicitly directed by the teacher
      a. *Academic performance*
        (1) Writing
        (2) Copying (handwriting)
        (3) Letter writing
        (4) Proof reading
        (5) Correcting assignments (own and others)
        (6) Test taking
        (7) Story making and telling/creative writing
        (8) Tape recording
        (9) Responding/answering (oral)
        (10) Responding/answering (written)
        (11) Constructing
        (12) Reading
        (13) Measuring
        (14) Mapping
        (15) Listening/attending
        (16) Drawing
        (17) Checking references
        (18) Working problems
        (19) Simulation gaming
        (20) Reporting
      b. *Nonacademic performance*
        (1) "Sharing"
        (2) Dancing/exercising
        (3) Lining up
        (4) Hand raising
        (5) "Leading" (i.e., introductory exercises)
        (6) Administrating
        (7) Housekeeping
        (8) Recess games (limbo, etc.)
    2. *Respondent behaviors* = implicitly directed by the teacher
      a. *Academic supportive*
        (1) Choosing (activities and time sequence)
        (2) Work pairing
        (3) Assistance seeking (from teacher or other)
          (a) Repetition requesting (from teacher)
          (b) Word requesting ("How do you do this?")
          (c) Procedure requesting ("How do you do this?")
          (d) Clarification requesting
          (e) Meaning requesting ("What does this mean?")
          (f) Spelling requesting
        (4) Sharing materials
        (5) Browsing (among books, learning games)
        (6) Challenge requesting ("Make it real," etc.)
        (7) Assisting other students
        (8) Settling in (getting ready to work)
          (a) Sharpening pencils
          (b) Solitary seeking (for private place to work)
          (c) Obtaining materials
          (d) Arranging materials for work
      b. *Nonacademic supportive*
        (1) Permission requesting (to go to office, etc.)
        (2) Requesting teacher to intercede with another student
        (3) Policing (supervising other students' behavior)
        (4) Succorance seeking ("I'm sick.")
        (5) Self-maintenance
          (a) Washing hands
          (b) Grooming

continued

Table 15.3, *continued*

    (c) Using bathroom
    (d) Getting drinks
    (e) Eating
    (f) Self-nursing

B. *Initiating actions* = behaviors largely unsolicited by the teacher in authority role

  1. *Social reciprocating*
    a. Conversing
      (1) Normally
      (2) Whispering
      (3) Exchanging notes
      (4) Exchanging gestures
    b. Partner seeking
    c. Gaming
    d. Joking/teasing/tall-tale telling
    e. Hugging/arm linking
    f. Playing
    g. Kibbutzing

  2. *Conflict generalization/resolution*
    a. Tattling
    b. Feuding
    c. Disagreeing
    d. Physical fighting (recess)
    e. Mediation appealing (to teacher/other adult)
    f. Self-managing
      (1) Reconciliating
      (2) Consensus reaching

  3. *Reactive behaviors* (stalling, off-task, defending, distracting, adaptive, attention-avoiding)
    a. Crying
    b. Fiddling/squirming
    c. Watching other children
    d. Fixed staring
    e. Yawning
    f. Fumbling in desk
    g. Leg swinging/foot propping/rocking
    h. Misplacing things

      i. Wandering
      j. Rationalizing
  4. *Activity generation*
    a. Suggesting academic topics and procedures
    b. Suggesting organized reaction activities (basketball, etc.)

II. *Pervasive behaviors* = exhibited across the range of event settings

A. *Rewarding/accepting*
  1. Praising (verbal and nonverbal)
  2. Touching
  3. Clapping
  4. Giving Presents

B. *Punishing/rejecting*
  1. Complaining
  2. Excluding (another student)
  3. Reprimanding
  4. Booing

C. *Attention-seeking*
  1. Displaying
  2. Boasting
  3. "Calling out"/interrupting

D. *Personal integrating* (behaviors engaged in by a student are usually spontaneous, in which s/he relates in some manner to an environmental stimulus)
  1. Modeling
  2. Demonstrating (a process, movement, etc.)
  3. Anecdoting
    a. Own experiences
    b. Experiences of someone in primary group
    c. Vicarious experience
  4. Commenting
    a. Labeling
    b. Translating
    c. Summarizing
    d. Observing/evaluating
    e. Comparing/contrasting
  5. Solitary verbalizing/self-reciting/Eurekaing

From "Behavioral Configuration in the Classroom: A Case Study" by J. Goetz, 1976, *Journal of Research and Development in Education, 9*(4), pp. 40–41. Copyright 1976 by *Journal of Research and Development in Education.* Reprinted by permission.

nized according to the eight major issues that differentiate teacher perceptions about development and early learning described in the literature on school retention. These issues are development, rate of development, evidence of child's lack of preparation, possibility of catching up, possibility of influencing a child's preparation for school, the causes of lack of preparation, what the teacher can do, the endpoints of kindergarten, and how to deal with heterogeneity (Shepard & Smith, 1985).

Analysis of the coded teacher comments categorized according to these issues revealed that teacher beliefs varied on two major dimensions. These dimensions were (1) perceptions about the fundamental processes of child development and (2) whether teachers can alter the level of preparation of individual children and the nature of an effective intervention (Shepard & Smith, 1985, p. 129). The analysis also yielded four distinct belief systems that vary on these two dimensions. The four belief systems and their characteristics are summarized in Table 15.4.

These findings are important because they reveal a greater range of teacher belief systems than would be predicted from either prior research or the literature on retention. Also, the analysis indicates the relationships between variations in teacher practice and beliefs.

On occasion, metaphors can be useful for interpreting findings and relating them to a larger context. Metaphors are tools for revealing the special properties of an object or event. An example is the metaphors used to describe the types of visitors to the National Museum of Natural History. Three of the types were the commuter, the nomad, and the cafeteria type (Wolf & Tymitz, 1978). Metaphors must be used carefully, however, so that they serve as a means of illumination (Denzin, 1978). Also, metaphors convey connotations, so they should be checked to determine the exact messages they communicate (Patton, 1990).

Summary

The essence of qualitative data analysis is the division of the data into relevant and meaningful units of analysis and the development of a categorization system from the data. The first step is to segment the data into manageable portions for analysis and to select the unit of analysis for the particular study. The initial segmentation, referred to as mundane data coding, consists of location, time, participants, and descriptive categories for the data. Examples of descriptive categories are "homeroom" and "recess." Analysis units, in contrast, are perceptual divisions of the data that are to be analyzed in detail. Examples are language units, behavior episodes, and social interactions. Sources for selecting units of analysis are theory, prior research, or classifications derived in a similar setting.

The process of developing a categorization system may be either inductive or quasi-inductive. In the inductive approach, tentative categories are developed through analysis of the data. The tentative categories are then tested and revised through the testing of rival hypotheses, constant comparison, and enumeration. In the quasi-inductive approach, tentative categories are developed (1) from sources such as the research questions, prior research, and/or preliminary interviews and (2) by coding a portion of the data.

Table 15.4
Four teacher beliefs about development and schooling

Nativists	Diagnostic/Prescriptive	Interactionists	Remediationists
Development is a physiological evolutionary unfolding of abilities that is smooth and continuous (a child who is behind in September will be behind in May).	Specific abilities either develop normally or dysfunctions can develop. Rates of development are uneven and unpredictable.	Children go through natural stages, but parents and teachers influence the progression. Within broad limits, rate of development is not predictable.	Within a broad range of pupil abilities, learning is largely a function of experience, the learning program, and the environment.
Initial screening provides supporting evidence for teacher observation that the child is not developmentally prepared for school.	Multifactor diagnosis of specific traits and abilities by clinical specialists can identify any dysfunction.	Assessment of readiness is context-dependent; readiness tests are only partial indicators.	Teacher observation throughout the year to reveal lack of academic preparation and social immaturity.
Intervention is largely futile and extra help or remediation causes pressure and frustration.	Deficits can be remedied by intervention designed for the dysfunction.	The teacher can influence psychomotor development, attention, and emotional maturity.	The teacher, parents, and other aspects of the environment can make a difference.
Teacher can provide children with more time to mature through retention, transition rooms, or lowered expectations.	Teacher can identify problem area, build up or work around problem area, adapt instruction, and provide assistance to correct disordered ability.	Teacher can arrange the environment so every child can be successful, set up cooperative peer teaching, and individualize instruction.	Teacher can provide additional academic help, accommodate achievement differences, hold high expectations, and reinforce and train.

Summarized from Shepard and Smith, 1985; Smith and Shepard, 1988.

After the categories are developed, tested, and revised, the data segments are coded with the category names. Then the coded text is separated according to the categories and regrouped under the category names. Two methods for physically regrouping the data in an inductive or quasi-inductive study are the cut-up/file folder approach and electronic data analysis. The former results in several folders that each contain similarly coded portions of the data. In electronic data analysis, a computer software program is used to assign codes to the text. The program can then display and print out the category names (or combinations of names) and the associated text, as well as perform one or more auxiliary functions. A third method of regrouping the data, the file card system, creates a secondary data set on note cards. However, this method is not conducive to developing categories from the data.

After the data are recontextualized in categories, the evaluator reviews the categories for completeness. Then relationships among the categories are developed, and the findings are interpreted. In the Boulder Valley retention study, for example, the data were regrouped into the eight major issues concerning development, readiness, and school retention. Analyses of these categories and the associated text revealed four different teacher belief systems that varied both in basic assumptions and preferred teacher practice.

QUANTITATIVE DATA ANALYSIS

Qualitative data consist of words, objects, and pictures that are analyzed using words. Evaluators also collect numerical data in various forms, such as frequencies, ratings, rankings, and test scores. These data are summarized in indices referred to as descriptive statistics. In addition, inferences about the magnitude of the differences between groups and the relationships among variables are facilitated through the use of statistical methods. Important concepts in the use of quantitative data are:

1. Levels of measurement
2. Methods of summarizing quantitative data
3. Methods assessing associations among variables
4. Methods for interpreting group differences
5. Methods for generalizing sample results to populations

Levels of Measurement

The three levels or scales for measuring quantitative variables are nominal, ordinal, and interval. Nominal measurement consists of counting the individuals, objects, or events in a particular classification. An example is counting the individuals in different groups, such as parents, teachers, and principals, who respond to a district survey on school issues. Another example is counting the students in "mastery" and "nonmastery" categories on key course objectives.

Some variables, in contrast, may be measured on scales that indicate "more" or "less" of the particular trait. When individuals, objects, or events are rank ordered on a particular trait, the measurement is referred to as ordinal. For example, a social studies teacher may rank his or her students on achievement from highest to lowest. A ranking indicates relative standing; however, the ranks do not represent equal distances. The difference between the rankings of one and two, for example, is not necessarily the same as the difference between the rankings of six and seven.

A well-known example of ordinal measurement is percentile scores. A student who scores in the 80th percentile, for example, has scored higher than 80% of the norming group for the test. However, there is not a one-to-one correspondence between students' raw scores on a test and their percentile scores; percentile scores indicate relative standing only. (As discussed in Chapter 6, on norm-referenced tests, the percentile scores from 40 to 50 and 50 to 60 are closer together than the percentile scores from 0 to 10 and 80 to 90 because there are more students at the center of the score distribution.) Course grades are another example of ordinal measurement. They indicate relative standing in a course. An *A*, for example, is not equivalent to an *F* in terms of the range of performance that the grade represents.

Unlike ordinal measurement, interval measurement indicates precise differences among individuals or objects because the differences between the points on the scale are equal. That is, an interval scale is based upon predetermined equal intervals. For example, the difference in height between 5 feet 4 inches and 5 feet 3 inches is the same as the difference between 4 feet 4 inches and 4 feet 3 inches.

On classroom achievement tests, for example, the distance between the scores of 30 and 40 is the same as the distance between 80 and 90. Similarly, the raw scores earned on norm-referenced achievement and intelligence tests also are interval scores.

Summarization of Quantitative Data

The data collected in an evaluation must be summarized in some way in order to be interpretable. Types of summary or descriptive methods that are typically used are (1) percentages and crossbreak tables, (2) the median and the mean, and (3) the standard deviation.

Percentages and Crossbreak Tables.   Percentages and crossbreak tables are appropriate for summarizing nominal data. For example, the numbers of students who have mastered key course objectives can be converted to percentages of the total class. Similarly, reports of questionnaire results often indicate the percentages of respondents in different categories, for example, teachers, principals, and parents. (In addition, the percentages of respondents and nonrespondents may be reported.)

Respondents to workshop or course satisfaction instruments are often asked to indicate the methods or activities that were most beneficial in their learning. The percentages of individuals who selected the different activities, such as small-group discussions, films, and hands-on exercises, may be reported.

Percentages are useful when one characteristic or trait is involved, such as gender or respondent group. When data are to be reported in two categories, the data are often displayed in crossbreak tables. An example is reporting the numbers of individuals responding to a questionnaire according to group membership and gender (see Table 15.5).

The Median and the Mean.   When a group of individuals is measured on some continuous variable, such as achievement, the result is a distribution of scores or other data that range from higher to lower values. Important information in summarizing the distribution is the typical or average score in the set of data. Such indices are referred to as measures of central tendency.

For ordinal data, the appropriate index of central tendency is the median, or the midpoint of the set of data. The median is the score or other data point that separates the distribution into two equal parts, with 50% of the scores above and 50% of the scores below the median. Depending on the nature of the distribution, the median may or may not be an earned score. For a data set with an even number of scores or data points, for example, the median is the average of the two middle scores.

The median is appropriate for both ordinal and interval data. However, the most used index of central tendency for interval data is the mean. It is simply the arithmetic average of all the data points. The mean is calculated by summing all the numerical values in the data set and dividing by the number of cases. For example, for the set of scores 25, 26, 26, 29, 30, and 35, the mean is 28.5.

The mean is not an appropriate measure of central tendency for ordinal data. The mean is based on a sum; a sum that does not reflect equal intervals, that is, ordinal data, is not meaningful.

The Standard Deviation.   Information about the spread of test scores or other interval data is also important. Two groups may have approximately the same mean, but the scores of one group may be more diverse than those of the other group. Thus, an index that provides information about the variability or spread of test scores is also important in comparing the two groups. The index that is used with interval data is the standard deviation. Briefly, the standard deviation represents an average deviation of data points from the mean of the distribution. (It is computed

Table 15.5
Summary of questionnaire respondents

	Administrators	Teachers	Counselors	Total
Males	21	71	18	110
Females	9	108	24	141
Total	30	179	42	251

by first subtracting each score from the mean. Then, these differences, referred to as deviation scores, are individually squared, and the squares are summed. This sum is referred to as the variance of the set of data. The square root of the variance is the standard deviation.)

The importance of the standard deviation is that the greater the spread of the data in the distribution, the larger the standard deviation will be. The smaller the spread of test scores, the smaller the standard deviation. Suppose the standard deviation of one group of test scores is 2.3, and the standard deviation of another group of scores is 6.7. The second group, on the variable being measured, is more heterogenous than the first group.

When interval data are obtained on the participants in a new program or intervention, the researcher or evaluator is obligated to report the means and standard deviations for the relevant groups. These indices can provide important information about the effects of new curricula, technology, counseling methods, or other innovations that may be implemented in an educational setting. For example, suppose the mean of a group is higher with a particular method, but the standard deviation is large as compared to a control group. The new method is raising the scores of some of the students, but the large standard deviation indicates that the scores are more diverse for some reason. An examination of student characteristics and implementation of the method is warranted in order to provide an explanation.

Methods of Assessing Relationships Among Variables

In addition to descriptive statistics on key variables, evaluators may be interested in the relationships among variables for an identified group. For example, an evaluation issue may be the relationship between student perceptions of school climate and dropout rate for the students enrolled in a particular innovation.

Relationships between two (or more) variables that are each measured on a continuum are identified by calculating correlation coefficients. Although there are several different correlation coefficients, two well-known methods are the Spearman-rho and Pearson product-moment correlations. The Spearman-rho is appropriate for ordinal data, and the Pearson product-moment correlation applies to interval data. These correlations, however, are restricted to two-variable situations.

A positive relationship is indicated when subjects with high ratings or scores on one variable also have high ratings or scores on the second variable, and low-scoring individuals on the first variable similarly score low on the second. The relationship between achievement motivation and standardized achievement test scores is an example.

A negative relationship is an inverse relationship. That is, low scores on one variable are associated with high scores on the second and vice versa. The relationship between test anxiety and performance is an example. High test anxiety is associated with low test scores, and low anxiety is associated with higher performance. Correlation coefficients may vary from +1.00 (a perfect positive relationship) to

-1.00 (a perfect negative relationship). These perfect relationships are rarely found, however.

Coefficients between .40 and .60 indicate a moderate relationship between the variables. However, a correlation of at least .60 must be obtained for even a crude prediction of performance on one variable from performance on the other.

Although correlations between two variables can be useful, many social situations are far more complex. That is, a combination of variables may be related to some identified outcome variable. For example, the Boulder Valley retention study found that gender, age, size, academic skills, and social maturity were all characteristics involved in teachers' decisions about end-of-year placement for children. The method that indicates the relationship between combinations of variables to an outcome variable is referred to as multiple regression. The statistic calculated in the analyses is a coefficient of multiple correlation, which is symbolized by R.

Methods for Interpreting Group Differences

Evaluations may compare the students in an innovation to a prior cohort or a concurrent comparison group, or the study may compare strong, adequate, and weak implementations of the new program. The evaluator's task is to determine how large a difference between the groups must be in order to be important. Two approaches to evaluating the magnitude of the differences among groups are (1) using information about known groups and (2) calculating effect size.

Information About Known Groups.   The use of a prior cohort in an institutional setting as well as other classes that receive different programs can provide a frame of reference for evaluating the performance of students in the innovation. In a study of critical thinking, for example, the end-of-year group mean for eleventh graders in the special curriculum was higher than the typical mean scores of eleventh graders. Moreover, the scores were close to the mean of a group of college students and far ahead of the scores of a comparison group (Fraenkel & Wallen, 1990, p. 210). This information from other groups indicated the importance of the gains of the special-curriculum group.

Effect Size.   The term *effect size* refers to a group of statistical indices, each of which is a method for clarifying the magnitude of the difference between two group means. A commonly-used index, referred to as delta (Δ), is calculated by first subtracting the comparison group mean from the mean of the students in the innovation. That number is then divided by the standard deviation of the comparison group. Most researchers consider that an effect size of .50 or larger is an important outcome (Fraenkel & Wallen, 1990). An effect size of .50 indicates that the average performance of the students in the innovation exceeded the average performance of the comparison group by one half of the standard deviation of the comparison group's scores.

Methods for Generalizing Sample Results to Populations

An evaluation or a component of an evaluation may involve random samples taken from some identified larger group. The larger group, referred to as a population, may be all middle school students in district X, elementary guidance counselors in suburban schools in district Y, first-year rehabilitation counselors in state agencies, and so on. The purpose of using a sample of the population may be to test variations of an innovation on a subgroup, for example. In such situations, the evaluator wishes to make generalizations about the larger group based on the findings from the sample.

The methodology appropriate for this purpose is referred to as inferential statistics. Their function is to test hypotheses about relationships in a defined population based on findings from a sample. Of major importance is that inferential statistics are not designed to evaluate the magnitude of the sample results. Instead, their function is to assist in making inferences about the larger group from which the sample was drawn.

Important topics in inferential statistics are (1) the logic of hypothesis testing, (2) methods for determining the covariation of variables in a population, and (3) methods for determining differences between or among populations on one or more variables.

The Logic of Hypothesis Testing.   The purpose of hypothesis testing in quantitative research is to test relationships between or among variables in defined populations. The hypothesis (or hypotheses) to be tested is stated, a sample is drawn from the population, and data are collected on the sample. The inferential statistic appropriate for the type of hypothesis and nature of the variables is calculated, and a decision to reject or not reject the proposed hypothesis is made.

The three types of hypothesis-testing studies are relational, experimental, and post hoc (also referred to as causal-comparative). Relational hypotheses address the covariation of two (or more) variables in a population. Experimental and post hoc studies investigate differences in groups that result from (1) a preexisting condition (post hoc study) or (2) the manipulation of an intervention (experimental study). For example, an experimental study may compare the effectiveness of program A and program B on the group means on achievement. In contrast, a post hoc study may compare the consequences of gender on the verbal fluency of ten-year-old children.

Two types of hypotheses are used in inferential quantitative studies. One is the null hypothesis, which is the hypothesis that is tested by the inferential statistic. Specifically, the null hypothesis states that (1) there is no significant relationship between the variables in a population; or (2) for an experimental or post hoc study, there is no difference between populations on the variable of interest. That is, the null hypothesis states that (1) the relationship between the variables in the population is zero, or (2) the difference between two population means (interval data) or ranked scores (ordinal data) on the variable of interest is zero.

The second hypothesis is the research hypothesis that states the expected relationship if the null hypothesis is rejected. For example, the research hypothesis may state that the mean of 10-year-old girls will be significantly higher on linguistic ability than the mean of 10-year-old boys. At the conclusion of the study, if the null hypothesis is rejected, the research or alternative hypothesis is accepted. If the null hypothesis is not rejected, no other inferences about hypotheses can be made.

Although a random sample is the best guarantee of obtaining a sample that represents the population, no sample is a perfect replica of the population. Therefore, as a result of sampling error, the statistics calculated on a sample will not be exactly the same as the population value. Suppose that the null hypothesis states that there is no significant difference in the mean of students in the population taught by method A and that of students in the population taught by method B. Even if the hypothesis is true, the difference between the two sample means will not be exactly zero. Theoretically, one could draw sample after sample of the same size from the two populations, calculate the observed differences between the two sample means, and construct a frequency distribution of all the obtained differences (a sampling distribution). Thus, one could determine the differences in sample means that occur more or less frequently when, in fact, the difference in the population means is zero.

Instead of implementing such a procedure, statistics that provide estimations of such values are used. For example, in comparing the effects of methods A and B on group means on achievement, the researcher calculates a t-statistic. Then the researcher compares the value of the statistic obtained in the study with the sampling distribution of the statistic. This comparison informs the researcher of the likelihood of obtaining the value observed in the study when the null hypothesis is true. For example, what is the likelihood of a 5-point difference between the two group means for a sample size of 40 when there is no difference in the population means?

The question arises, of course, as to the point at which an observed difference between two sample means is too great to be considered as simply the result of sampling error and, instead, as indicative of a real difference between the population means. In other words, what is the cut-off point at which one rejects the null hypothesis?

The decision as to the *value* to be used to reject the null hypothesis is not made on the basis of the data collected in the study. Instead, a point is selected on the sampling distribution of the statistic that represents an unlikely outcome if the null hypothesis is true. This point on the sampling distribution is the decision point for rejecting the null hypothesis. Typically, in education studies, the rejection point is the value of the statistic that can occur 5% of the time or less when the null hypothesis is true. The decision point is referred to as .05 probability level or .05 level of significance. If the obtained value of the statistic in the study is one in which the likelihood of obtaining that value (when the null hypothesis is true) is only 5 times (or less) in 100, the null hypothesis is rejected. The logic of this decision is that obtaining such results in the sample is an unlikely outcome if there is no relationship among the variables in the population(s). Therefore, the researcher rejects the null hypothesis, which states, for the methods study, that there is no difference in population means. (Sometimes the 1% or .01 level is used in hypothesis testing.)

Although the statistics that are used in different studies vary according to the nature of the hypotheses being tested and the nature of the data (nominal, ordinal, or interval), the hypothesis-testing process is the same. That is, one or more null hypotheses about the population(s) are stated, a probability or significance level for testing the hypothesis is stated, data are collected on a sample of the population, an inferential statistic is calculated, and a decision is made about the null hypothesis(es).

Statistics for Testing Relationships.   Three well-known statistics for testing hypotheses about relationships between variables are Chi square (x^2), the Spearman-rho correlation coefficient, and the Pearson product-moment correlation coefficient.

Chi square is appropriate for testing hypotheses about relationships among categorical variables. For example, the null hypothesis may state that there is no significant relationship between gender and type of school (urban or suburban) for elementary school counselors in the state. The data are collected on a random sample of 100 counselors. If there is no relationship, then the number in each cell of the 2 × 2 table should be the same, or 25. The formula for the statistic compares the actual numbers in each cell (observed frequencies) with the expected frequencies in each cell, in this case, 25. The resulting Chi square statistic is compared with the sampling distribution for the statistic. The null hypothesis is rejected if the obtained value is one that would occur 5 times or less in 100 if the frequencies in the cells were independent of each other (the categories are not related).

As already indicated, the Spearman-rho correlation is appropriate for ordinal data and the Pearson product-moment correlation is calculated for interval data. The paired observations for each individual are listed, and the formula for the appropriate statistic is applied to the data.

Methods for Testing Differences.   Experimental and post hoc studies posit changes in one or more dependent variables resulting from either different interventions or differences in existing characteristics or prior experiences. Parametric statistics, one group of methodological techniques, require interval data and a distribution of the variable of interest that approximates a normal distribution. The two major inferential techniques are (1) the t-statistic for group means when only two groups are involved in the study and (2) analysis of variance when the study involves two or more groups and/or more than one independent or dependent variable. Analysis of variance (ANOVA) yields a ratio, referred to as the F-ratio, which compares the variation across groups with an estimate of random variation or error.

Parametric statistical methods are appropriate when the dependent variable(s) is/are interval data and the distribution of the dependent variable approximates a normal distribution. When these requirements cannot be met, nonparametric methods are appropriate. Specifically, nonparametric statistics should be used when the dependent variable is ordinal, when the data represent an ordinal scale, when the nature of the distribution of the variable is not known, or when one or more of the assumptions essential for parametric tests has been greatly violated (Freed, Ryan, & Hess, 1991).

Table 15.6 summarizes frequently used parametric and nonparametric inferential statistics. (See Freed et al., 1991, for a complete listing.) Among the applications are designs referred to as factorial designs. Advantages of factorial designs (two-way between subjects ANOVA) are (1) that the effects of more than one variable can be determined and (2) that the effect of the interactions among independent variables can be determined. For example, if the independent variables are methods of instruction and prior achievement, the effects of the intervention for high, average, and low achievers can be determined.

Table 15.6 also lists analysis of covariance (ANCOVA) as a mechanism for removing variables that are systematically related to the dependent variable from the calculation of the effects of the dependent variable. Of primary importance, however, is that ANCOVA should not be implemented as an effort to equate nonequivalent groups. The problem is that nonequivalent groups differ in a variety of characteristics, such as learning-related skills. Statistical methods cannot compensate for group differences in the ways that they approach and manage their learning.

Summary

Unlike qualitative data, quantitative data consist of numbers and are summarized and interpreted using numerical methods. The three methods of measuring quantitative variables are nominal, ordinal, and interval. Nominal measurement consists of counting the objects or individuals that are in particular categories. When individuals are ranked on the amount of a particular trait they possess, the measurement is ordinal.

Table 15.6
Summary of frequently used parametric and nonparametric statistics for testing group differences

| Situation | Inferential Statistics | |
	Parametric	Nonparametric
Two independent groups	t-test for independent means	Mann-Whitney U test
Dependent measures (pre- and posttest on the same group)	t-test for correlated means	The sign test
Two or more independent groups	One-way ANOVA	Kruskal-Wallis ranks test for K-independent samples
One group is measured on two or more occasions	One-way repeated measures on ANOVA	Friedman two-way ANOVA by ranks
Two or more independent groups and more than one independent variable (referred to as a factorial design)	Two-way between-subjects ANOVA	
Use of a continuous independent variable to reduce the estimate of error in the dependent variable	Analysis of covariance (ANCOVA)	

Interval measurement consists of frequencies or scores that are equidistant from each other.

Methods for summarizing data are percentages and crossbreak tables (nominal data), the median (ordinal data), and the mean (interval data). The median and the mean are referred to as measures of central tendency. Also, for interval data, the standard deviation is used to indicate the variability of a distribution. Both the mean and standard deviation should be reported for interval data.

Describing the relationships between characteristics of individuals or events may also be a focus of a study. When the variables are categories of individuals, crossbreak tables are used to illustrate the relationship.

Relationships between two variables that are each measured on a continuum are identified by calculating correlation coefficients. A positive relationship is indicated by a high-high, low-low correspondence of scores or ratings on the two variables. In contrast, a negative relationship is a high-low, low-high correspondence. When the data are ordinal, a Spearman-rho correlation is calculated. A Pearson product-moment correlation is computed for interval data.

Evaluators may compare the students in an innovation to other classes or groups. Two methods for evaluating the magnitude of observed group differences are using information about known groups and calculating effect size on the difference between two group means. A general rule is that an effect size of .50 indicates an important difference.

When random samples are selected from a population for the purposes of identifying relationships or testing different program components, for example, inferential statistics are needed. The purpose of inferential statistics is to test relational, experimental, or post hoc hypotheses about populations. Data are collected on a sample from the population, and the appropriate inferential statistic is used to reject or fail to reject the null hypothesis. The basis for this decision is the sampling distribution of the statistic. If the value of the statistic obtained in the study is an unlikely event when the null hypothesis is true, then the null hypothesis is rejected. Different statistical methods are appropriate for different situations, depending on the nature of the hypothesis, the type of variable, and specific features of the situation, such as the number of groups in an experimental study.

GUIDELINES FOR CONDUCTING DATA ANALYSIS

Qualitative data:

Step 1.   Prepare the data for inductive analysis.
   1.1   Divide the data into manageable portions for analysis (mundane data coding).
   1.2   Select the unit of analysis (verbal episodes, thought units, settings, etc.).

Step 2.   Develop a categorization system for the data.

Inductive:

2.1   Use analytic induction to develop tentative categories from the data.

Quasi-inductive:

2.1   Develop categories from the evaluation questions, information related to the innovation, and coding a portion of the data.

Step 3.   Analyze and interpret the data.

3.1   Attach the category names to the basic units of data.
3.2   Separate the data record into segments, and regroup the data under the category names.
3.3   Review the recontextualized data for completeness.
3.4   Develop relationships across the categories, and interpret the relationships.

Quantitative data:

Step 1.   Summarize the data.

1.1   Calculate the mean and standard deviation for interval data and the median for ordinal data.
1.2   Organize nominal data into tables.

Step 2.   If relationships between variables in the sample are of interest, develop the appropriate information.

2.1   Present nominal data in crossbreak tables.
2.2   Calculate the appropriate correlational coefficient for the type of data (ordinal or interval).

Step 3.   If differences between groups are of interest, evaluate the magnitude of the differences.

3.1   Compare mean performance of students in the innovation to the mean performance of known groups.
3.2   Calculate effect size on the difference between the mean of the innovation and a comparison group.

Step 4.   If hypotheses about a population are to be tested, implement the appropriate procedures.

4.1   Set a probability level for testing the null hypothesis.
4.2   If the hypothesis is correlational, calculate the appropriate coefficient of correlation.
4.3   If the hypothesis addresses differences between or among groups, calculate the appropriate inferential statistic.
4.4   Reject or fail to reject the null hypothesis.

CHAPTER QUESTIONS

1. What are the common characteristics of the various qualitative data analysis methods?
2. What is the task referred to as mundane data coding?
3. What are the two approaches to developing a categorization system?
4. What are the two major tasks in interpreting the recontextualized qualitative data?
5. What is the key difference between ordinal and interval data?
6. What is the role of inferential statistics in data analysis?

REFERENCES

Agar. M. (1986). *Speaking of ethnography.* Beverly Hills, CA: Sage.

Bogdan, R. (1982). *Qualitative research for education: An introduction to theory and methods.* Allyn & Bacon.

Bogdan, R., & Biklen, S. (1982). *Qualitative research for education.* Boston: Allyn & Bacon.

Denzin, N. (1978). *Sociological methods.* New York: McGraw Hill.

Fraenkel, J. R., & Wallen, N. E. (1990). *How to design and evaluate research in education* (2nd ed.). New York: McGraw-Hill.

Freed, M., Ryan, J., & Hess, R. (1991). *Handbook of statistical procedures and their computer applications for education and the behavioral sciences.* New York: American Council on Education and Macmillan.

Glaser, B. (1965). The constant comparative method of qualitative analysis. *Social Problems, 12,* 436–445.

Goetz, J. (1976). Behavioral configurations in the classroom: A case study. *Journal of Research and Development in Education, 9*(4), 36–49.

Goetz, J., & LeCompte, M. (1984). *Ethnography and qualitative design in educational research.* New York: Academic Press.

Jacob, E. (1987). Qualitative research traditions: A review. *Review of Educational Research, 57*(7), 1–50.

LeCompte, M. (1978). Learning to work: The hidden curriculum of the classroom. *Anthropology and Education Quarterly, 9,* 22–37.

Lee, R., & Fielding, N. (1992). Computing for qualitative research: Options, problems and potential. In N. Fielding & R. Lee (Eds.), *Using computers in qualitative research* (pp. 1–13). Newbury Park: Sage.

Lofland, J. (1971). *Analyzing social settings: A guide to qualitative observation and analysis.* Belmont, CA: Wadsworth Publishing Company.

Lofland, J., & Lofland, L. (1984). *Analyzing social settings.* Belmont, CA: Wadsworth.

Patton, M. (1990). *Qualitative evaluation and research methods.* Newbury Park, CA: Sage.

Richards, L., & Richards, T. (1992). The transformation of qualitative method: Computational paradigms and research processes. In N. Fielding & R. Lee (Eds.), *Using computers in qualitative research* (pp. 38–53). Newbury Park: Sage.

Shepard, L., & Smith, M. (1985). *Boulder Valley kindergarten study: Retention practices and retention effects.* Boulder, CO: Boulder Valley Public Schools.

Seidel, J. (1992). Method and madness in the application of computer technology to qualitative data analysis. In N. Fielding & R. Lee (Eds.), *Using computers in qualitative research* (pp. 107–116). Newbury Park: Sage.

Smith, M. L., & Shepard, L. (1988). Kindergarten readiness and retention: A qualitative study of teachers' beliefs and practices. *American Educational Research, 25*(3), 307–333.

Tesch, R. (1990). *Qualitative research.* London: Falmer Press.

Tesch, R. (1992). Software for qualitative researchers: Analysis needs and program capabilities. In N. Fielding & R. Lee (Eds.), *Using computers in qualitative research* (pp. 38–53). Newbury Park: Sage.

Wolf, R. L., & Tymitz, B. (1978). *Whatever happened to the giant wombat: An investigation of the impact of the ice age mammals and emergence of man exhibit.* Washington, DC: Smithsonian Institutes, National Museum of Natural History.

CHAPTER 16

Communication of Evaluation Events

The early conception of evaluation was that of the stand-alone study. The program is established; the evaluator sets up the investigation and then waits for the program to do its work. At the designated time, the evaluator returns, measures the effects, and submits a final report to a decision maker who makes a "go-no-go" decision (Cronbach & associates, 1980, p. 57).

The expectation was that policymakers and program managers would willingly adopt and disseminate programs identified as successes and terminate or radically alter ineffective programs (Cook & Shadish, 1986; Suchman, 1967). This view of decision making is a formal, linear decision model. A study is released, recommendations are made based on the findings, and a decision that reflects the findings is made (Weiss, 1981). In this hypothetical sequence, utilization of evaluation findings was automatic. Therefore, the preparation of a final report that summarized the evaluation and described the findings was sufficient to influence decision making. However, as indicated in Chapter 2, this view of decision making was in error. First, the evaluator is not remote from the program, waiting for it to wind down. Instead, he or she is negotiating the evaluation with the sponsors, observing program events to determine the nature of implementation and the influence of the context, and perhaps interviewing program participants.

Second, evaluation results become part of a larger context in which many priorities are operating. As a result, decision and policy development processes are often diffuse, and "decisions" may percolate up or down an organizational structure (Cooley & Bickel, 1986; Weiss, 1980). Policymakers also are influenced by various constituencies, from teachers and principals to parents and taxpayers. Given this broad context, clear communication to diverse audiences about the workings of a program and the effects is essential. Cronbach and associates (1980) note that "communication counts as much toward the contribution of an evaluation as the adequacy of an evaluation itself" (p. 186).

Studies of the utilization of evaluations have identified two major types of use. They are instrumental and conceptual (Leviton & Hughes, 1981; Rich, 1981; Weiss, 1981). Instrumental use refers to documented situations in which information is explicitly applied to make a decision or solve a problem. In contrast, conceptual use refers to the influence on people's perceptions and their thinking about an issue or a problem. Conceptual use, in other words, changes the landscape in which the issue or problem is considered. According to Cronbach and associates (1980), a well-designed evaluation influences conceptual use. Success in this role depends on effective communication to a variety of audiences. Factors essential to communicating with evaluation audiences are understanding the nature of the dissemination process in evaluation and understanding the issues in developing effective communication.

DISSEMINATION IN EVALUATION

Two major components in the dissemination process in evaluation are the differences between research and evaluation and the dimensions of the communication process.

Characteristics

Communicating evaluation information differs in several ways from the dissemination of research results. First, research and evaluation are addressed to different audiences. Published research is addressed primarily to one's colleagues in a particular discipline. The research is reviewed and analyzed by others in the field whose major concerns are both the concepts and hypotheses that are tested and the methodology of the study. In contrast, evaluations are addressed to a policy-making community that consists of agency officials, sponsors, recipients of the program or curriculum, and others. Their interests typically are action oriented, and a major obligation of the evaluator is to get the story out to those who have the greatest power to act on it (Cronbach & associates, 1980, p. 174).

Second, research conclusions are typically reported in terms of some type of significant finding. In empirical studies, the focus is often that of statistical significance. In contrast, evaluations are decision oriented. They should provide recommendations for action to be taken about the program, curriculum, or policy.

Third, research findings are disseminated at professional meetings and in published reports in professional journals. However, published reports of evaluations are not sufficient to influence decision making in the policy-making community. Verbal communication is at least as important as the written word (Cooley & Bickel, 1986, p. 131). A legislator cannot take time to wade through lengthy reports, but he or she can listen to a visitor who provides a succinct overview and then responds to specific questions (Cronbach & associates, 1980, p. 185).

Fourth, the timing of dissemination differs for research and evaluation. Research is typically reported after the study is concluded and the data analysis is completed.

In contrast, in many evaluations, various phases of the study may be communicated to sponsors or stakeholders as they occur. Evaluators conducting the study of Alaskan village high schools, for example, contacted identified stakeholders, informed them of the general purpose of the study, and asked them about specific questions to be answered and any pitfalls they saw for the study. The purpose was not to shape the study to partisan interests but to obtain an expanded view of the phenomenon to be studied (Kleinfeld & McDiarmid, 1986). In formative situations, the evaluator may serve as a member of the development team. The feedback to the developer may be fairly continuous, or it may be in stages following each of a series of pilot tests or materials revisions.

Communications for summative evaluations or other information-gathering efforts also are usually spaced in time (Cronbach & associates, 1980, p. 174). That is, the findings may be reported in sequence to different audiences. An example is the reporting of the results of the 1980 needs assessment for the Pittsburgh public schools described by Cooley and Bickel (1986). As illustrated in Table 16.1, the presentations were organized in stages, with the initial presentations to the major decision makers—the superintendent and the board of education. The next series of presentations were to district administrators and supervisors who would be responsible for implementing policies related to the priority areas. Then closed-circuit television meetings were held with each school faculty to discuss the needs assessment

Table 16.1
Stages of presentation of needs assessment results

Format	Audience
Preliminary presentation of results to test clarity of concepts and smoothness of slide presentation	Superintendent, president of the board, and a key central administration official
All-day Saturday session at a nearby, secluded college campus (January)	Nine-member board of education, superintendent, and one board staff member
A.M. Issue-oriented slide presentation with emphasis on open discussion of results	
P.M. Board deliberated without evaluator and voted on priorities	
Press release from superintendent's office the following Monday on general priorities approved by the Board	General public
Series of meetings with different components of district staff (February–March)	District administrators and supervisors; subject area consultants
Closed-circuit television discussion of results by superintendent and two senior researchers (February–March)	Each school faculty
Press conference-presentation of detailed findings	General public

Summarized from Cooley and Bickel, 1986.

findings and to answer the teachers' questions about the implications for their schools.

These examples illustrate that, for evaluation, dissemination is not a specific event. Instead, it is often integrally related to all phases of the evaluation—from design to data analysis. In other words, dissemination should be thought of as part of a continuum (Cooley & Bickel, 1986, p. 128).

Dimensions of the Communication Process

Communication may be analyzed in a variety of ways. Three important dimensions for evaluation, however, are the degree of formality, the form of the communication, and the breadth of communication.

The Degree of Formality.   Communications about an evaluation may vary on a continuum from informal to formal. The variation is related, in part, to the type of evaluation. In formative evaluations, when the evaluator is a member of the development team, communications often are highly informal. They may consist of conversations and discussions with developers, memos, and brief written summaries of observations. The sole audience for these communications often is the development team.

Evaluations that make use of advisory or steering committees also make extensive use of informal communications throughout the study. Examples are informal memos, discussions, and brief summaries that are issued periodically. However, some of the communication should be interactive. In the study of Alaskan village high schools, the evaluators maintained telephone contact with identified stakeholders, in addition to periodic meetings.

Many summative or impact evaluations tend to rely on formal written communication as their only product. However, the capability of such reports for influencing use is, at best, minimal. Instead, informal and usually oral statements are likely to be far more influential (Cronbach & associates, 1980, p. 185). One strategy consistent with this view is an oral presentation to policymakers and other major stakeholders prior to submission of the final report. Such a presentation incorporates questions and challenges from the interested groups. This strategy can assist evaluators in relating the findings to the frame of reference of the particular audience.

Meetings that combine presentation of information with discussion are working meetings that are more structured than conversations and telephone calls. However, they also emphasize interaction among the participants. An example is the presentation and discussion of needs assessment findings to the school board described by Cooley and Bickel (1986).

Although informal communication often is important, formal communications do play a role in evaluation. First, they serve to disseminate the evaluation to a wide audience. Presentations at professional associations and other groups are examples, as are summaries in organization newsletters, articles in professional journals, and final reports. Second, written reports and other documents are important for the institutional memory of events (Cooley & Bickel, 1986). Agencies and institutions address a variety of priorities that do not remain static. A record of program events and findings is important for future staff personnel and others. However, the final formal report is basically an archival document; it is not a live communication (Cronbach & associates, 1986, p. 185).

Forms of Communication.   The form of communication may involve combinations of any of several visual, print, and verbal formats. Media formats range from illustrative charts, diagrams, and slides to audio- and videotapes. Further, an often untapped resource for communication is other individuals and organizations. In the study of Alaskan village high schools, for example, advisory committee members communicated evaluation findings to others by word of mouth. Also, the Alaska Association of School Boards was asked to disseminate the findings to the members using materials developed by the evaluators (Kleinfeld & McDiarmid, 1986). Other organizations, such as the PTA, teacher organizations, and curriculum groups, publish newsletters; and they often look for copy (p. 399).

When possible, the results of an evaluation should be communicated through many media and at several levels of detail and precision (Cronbach & associates, 1980, p. 186). These considerations are important because much information is lost to the policy shaping community as a result of inappropriate packaging (p. 186). For example, the presentation of needs assessment results to the school board discussed in the prior section used slides organized around major priorities identified by the different constituencies who responded to the surveys. Each section of the presentation began with a clear statement of the policy implications indicated by the data with an emphasis on broad, thematic statements (Cooley & Bickel, 1986, p. 128). Data also were presented in the form of visuals—charts, diagrams, and slides. Each section of the presentation also was accompanied by an executive summary that was distributed to the board members as that section was introduced. Particularly important is that the presentation was an open discussion of the findings on each priority as it was presented. Thus, the board members had ample opportunity to question and challenge the findings prior to voting on the priorities.

A slide presentation plus discussion is appropriate when face-to-face meetings can be easily organized. Types of media opportunities for dialogue employed when individuals cannot meet together are interactive teleconferences and electronic networks.

The advantage of using individuals, conferences, and electronic networks for the dissemination of events is the opportunity for interaction among evaluators and interested stakeholders. Cooley and Bickel (1986) observe that, whether written or verbal, the opportunity for exchanging ideas and for dialogue between the evaluators and the potential users can strengthen the dissemination process and enhance the quality of the findings that are shared (p. 132). The perspectives of different stakeholders can alert the evaluators to difficulties, constraints, and problems that later may be raised to question the evaluation findings. If reports are cast in concrete without the evaluators' knowledge of these potential problems, doubts will be cast on the evaluation itself. Addressing these concerns in communications about the evaluation enhance its credibility.

Breadth of Communication.   Conducting an evaluation is not a leisurely activity. An evaluation is a time-bound enterprise. In addition, the schedule of activities is usually quite compressed, and unexpected events that can disrupt the schedule are the rule rather than the exception. Thus, when the evaluation is about to wind down, communicating evaluation findings to a variety of audiences is often not a priority. However, Cronbach and associates (1980, p. 189) suggest that the evaluator should be as active in communication as the contract permits, so that good use will be made of the work. Fulfilling this goal, however, suggests that planning communications should be a part of the contract negotiations and should be built into the evaluation schedule of events.

Evaluations that can inform a broad community of educators, other practitioners, and other interested parties should be disseminated to a wide audience. However, initial communications should be to the sponsors or those identified in the contract, such as an advisory committee, steering committee, or an expert panel. Then, after these obligations are met, the evaluation may be disseminated to a broader audience, if the contract permits. For example, during the study of Alaskan village high schools, researchers aired a series of radio broadcasts about the schools and the evaluation directed to Eskimo and Indian village parents, who were unlikely to read an evaluation report (Kleinfeld & McDiarmid, 1986, p. 399).

Summary

Dissemination in evaluation differs in several ways from the dissemination of research findings. Evaluation reports are addressed to a policy-making community rather than professional colleagues, and the information is related to decisions rather than the testing of constructs. Further, evaluations provide recommendations for actions to be taken. The focus is not that of the significance of a construct or principle in the development of theory. Finally, information about an evaluation may be effectively communicated in both verbal and written forms and may also be disseminated throughout the evaluation rather than only at the conclusion of the study. When findings are reported, they often are communicated to several audiences at different points in time.

The three important dimensions of communication in evaluation are the degree of formality, the various media forms, and the breadth of the communication. Evaluations with advisory or steering committees and formative evaluations routinely use informal communications throughout the study. Although many summative or impact evaluations tend to rely on formal written communications as their only product, formal reports alone are insufficient for influencing use in a major way. Other strategies are (1) to obtain feedback from major stakeholders prior to submission of the final report and (2) to present the major findings in a series of meetings with various audiences. Written reports are important, however, for institutional memory.

The form of the communication may involve any of several visual, verbal, or print formats. Media formats range from illustrative charts, diagrams, and slides to audio- and videotapes. Another important resource is other individuals, teleconferences, and electronic networks. Forms of communication that provide the opportunity for exchanging ideas or dialogue between evaluators and potential users can strengthen the dissemination process and enhance the quality of the findings.

Some evaluations (e.g., formative evaluations) are communicated only to a small group. However, evaluations that can inform a broad policy shaping community should be communicated to a wide audience. Initial communications should be directed to the sponsors and others identified in the contract, such as an advisory committee or an expert panel. Then the evaluation should be disseminated to parents, teachers, other agencies, the professional community, and others.

DEVELOPMENT OF EFFECTIVE COMMUNICATIONS

Several studies have investigated the characteristics of evaluations that contribute to their later use. A review of 65 studies of evaluation utilization found that relevance and communication quality were identified as influential in a majority of cases (Cousins & Leithwood, 1986). Factors that contribute to relevance and quality are language, content and organization, the use of visual displays, the use of a variety of written communications, and the demonstration of insight.

Language

An important characteristic of written communications about an evaluation is readability (Cousins & Leithwood, 1986). The compressed academic style found in published research articles is not appropriate for evaluation reports. Sentences should use action words and be free of deadwood, and paragraphs should be short and to the point.

Avoiding jargon is also of primary importance. Jargon is a shorthand language used by specialists in a certain discipline. However, it does not communicate to outsiders, and it can elicit negative reactions to the evaluation. For example, a consultant working with a large hospital indicated that the words *independent variable* and *dependent variable* must not be used. These terms did not communicate to clients and also gave the impression of a lack of relationship between the evaluation and the real world (Braskamp, Brandenburg, & Ory, 1987). In other words, an excess of jargon can obscure the most salient findings (Fetterman, 1988).

Further, the language should be as straightforward and clear as possible. Therefore, words such as *parameters* and *school practitioners* should be replaced by words such as *limits* and *teachers,* respectively, and terms such as *finalize* and *viability* should be avoided (Murray, 1982, p. 766).

Content and Organization

A common error in evaluation reports is communication overload. Many evaluations are reported with "self-defeating thoroughness" (Cronbach & associates, 1980, p.

184). The problem is that the reader can assimilate only so many numbers and words and "when an avalanche of words and tables descends, everyone in its path dodges" (p. 186). In contrast, the needs assessment summaries of the methodology and results prepared by Cooley and Bickel (1986) was 16 pages in length.

An evaluation summary also may be visually organized. An example is the chart essay (Haensly, Lupkowski, & McNamara, 1987). A chart essay is a restructured form of a report in which the problem statement, methods, results, and implications are arranged into a series of charts. The set of charts represents a sequential unfolding of the study from the problem to results and implications. Each chart essay summarizes a portion of the report, such as the purpose and evaluation questions or the design of the inquiry (Haensly et al., 1987, p. 67).

Organization is also important for written reports. The report should begin with an executive summary that serves as an advance organizer. The summary is then followed by a chapter on each section that the summary addressed. It is also important to summarize the major points for each section at the beginning of that section. Smith and Robbins (1984) also suggest capturing the meaning of the subsequent information in a meaningful heading for a report section instead of a heading that functions only as a label. For example, instead of "Parent Attendance Patterns," use "Few Parents Attended PAC Meetings" (p. 130).

The report also should present findings that are of interest to different audiences. Smith and Robbins (1984) identified three different audiences for their multisite study of parent involvement. The audiences were congressional representatives, program office staff, and the local project audience. First, to accommodate the different information needs of these audiences, the text focused on major and secondary findings only. Second, illustrative vignettes, which were mini-case studies, appeared in the form of figures. Third, each section contained tables that summarized the data from each site (p. 130).

Visual Displays of Information

Audiences for evaluation reports have different information needs. Researchers and evaluators, for example, tend to look for tables that present means and standard deviations, percentages of students in certain categories, tables of beta weights for regression analyses, and so on. Others, however, are more comfortable with some visual display of the data. In oral presentations, the data displays should be selected to fit the information needs of the particular group. In written reports, both visual and tabular formats should be used whenever possible. Pie charts, bar graphs, and line graphs are effective visual devices.

Visual displays can be particularly effective in illustrating growth or change. An example is the portrayal of outcomes of the implementation of Reading Recovery (a program for the poorest first-grade readers) in New Hampshire. The charts illustrate the progress of "discontinued" children (those who have completed the program), the progress of children remaining in the program, and the range of scores of 52 randomly selected first graders. Figure 16.1 illustrates writing vocabulary, and Figure 16.2 illustrates text reading level. These charts illustrate the improvement from September to June of the children in the program.

An example of different data presentations for different audiences is the reporting of findings for the policy analysis component of the Shepard and Smith (1985) retention study. (Chapter 9 describes the pupil profiles and the two decisions that were made about each profile by the first-grade teachers.) Each teacher's judgment data were analyzed using multiple regression. The evaluators reported the policy

Figure 16.1
Progress of children who completed Reading Recovery Program on writing vocabulary

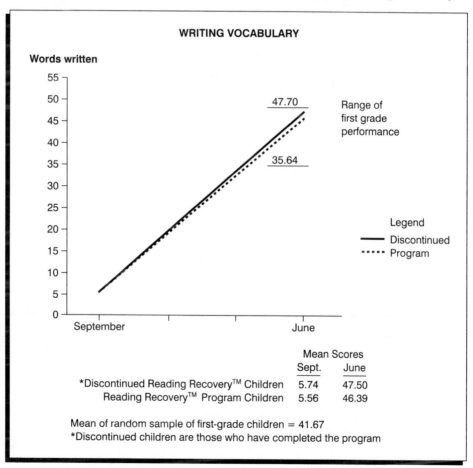

From *Report of Results and Effectiveness: Reading Recovery Pilot Project* (p. 21) by H. Schotanus, C. Chase, and A. Fontaine, August 1991, Concord, NH: New Hampshire Department of Education. Reprinted by permission.

Figure 16.2
Progress of children who completed Reading Recovery Program on text reading level

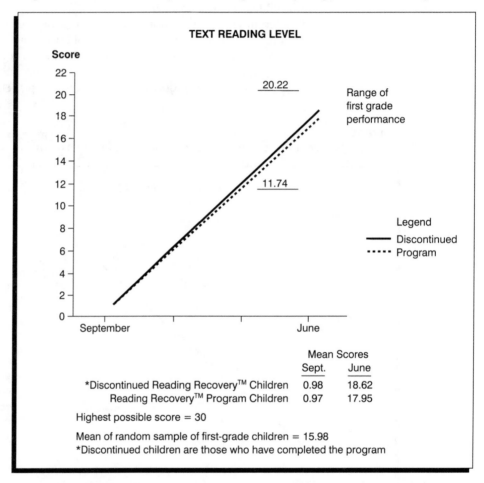

From *Report of Results and Effectiveness: Reading Recovery Pilot Project* (p. 23) by H. Schotanus, C. Chase, and A. Fontaine, August, 1991, Concord, NH: New Hampshire Department of Education. Reprinted by permission.

weights (standardized beta weights) for each cue (gender, age, size, academic skills, and social maturity) and the multiple correlation coefficients for each decision for each teacher in a table. (With only three exceptions, the multiple correlations were 84 or higher.) In addition, the report presented the results in a visual diagram (see Figure 16.3). The position of each circle in Figure 16.3 indicates the relative weight given to academic skills and social skills, whereas the shading indicates the role of age, gender, and/or size in the teacher's decisions. The diagram illustrates the variability in the decision making process.

Figure 16.3
Representation of major factors considered by teachers in their judgments about children's chance for success in first grade

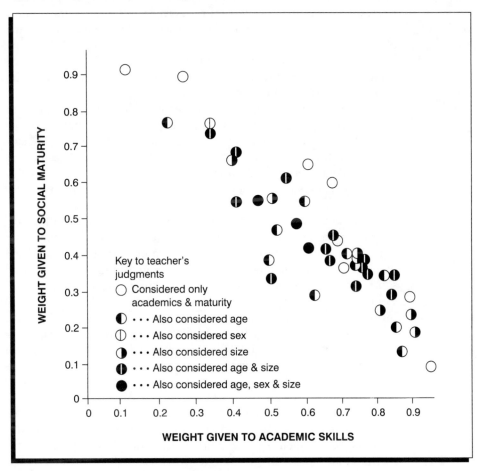

From *Boulder Valley Kindergarten Study* (p. 187) by L. Shepard and M. Smith, 1985, Boulder, CO: Boulder Valley Public Schools. Reprinted by permission.

Types of Written Communication

The evaluation contract typically requires the submission of interim and final reports to the client or funding agency. These products serve as evidence that the work specified in the contract has been conducted, and payment typically is contingent on their completion. Although the final report describes the findings and conclusions of the study, the format is not effective for communicating to a wide audience.

Other written forms of communication, referred to as research briefs by Macy (1982), can effectively communicate to different audiences. A research brief is a written and condensed statement that provides information about the evaluation (p. 180). The content and style may vary according to the intended audience. Five types of research briefs are the report summary, the executive summary, memos, the news item, and the abstract. The report summary often appears at the end of a final research report. Its strength is that it provides comprehensive information about an evaluation in a small amount of text (Macy, 1982, p. 181). The report summary can serve as a stand-alone document, however. Recall that Cooley and Bickel (1986) presented a 16-page report summary on the needs assessment to the board of education at the initial presentation of findings.

The executive summary is a shorter version of the report summary. It is typically placed at the beginning of a final research report, but it can be effective as a stand-alone document. One executive summary condensed a 52-page report into 2 pages that described project objectives, evaluation design, results, and recommendations (Macy, 1982, p. 182). A frequent use of executive summaries is in large public school districts in which evaluations findings are reported periodically to boards of education.

Memos are particularly useful in reporting interim findings or in reporting progress in the evaluation. A memo written early in a project may describe the selection of schools, participants, and plans for interviewing, for example. One advantage of the memo is mobility, because it can circulate without being attached to a cumbersome report. It also provides the evaluator an opportunity to personalize communication. A memo may be sent to Dr. Jones, for example, with copies to Smith and Brown (Macy, 1982, p. 184).

News items are similar to the report summary, but they are more flexible in content and emphasis (Macy, 1982). They may appear in newspapers, newsletters, and in news columns or departments in serial publications. Several professional journals and newspapers have a "research notes" or a "research in progress" column where these items may appear.

The oldest research brief is the abstract. Abstracts are found in journals and data base collections of research and evaluation. Although concise and informative, they serve only the audience of the journal or the data base reproduction service (Macy, 1982).

Research briefs can extend the network to whom the evaluator can communicate. One disadvantage of research briefs, however, is their brevity. Bias in selecting the content can mislead the audience through incomplete information. Therefore, the evaluator should be sensitive to the priorities of the target audience (Macy, 1982, p. 188).

Demonstration of Insight

An important aspect of the evaluation is to develop inferences from the evaluation data and to make recommendations for subsequent action about the program or intervention. Perhaps the single most important characteristic that contributes to instrumental and conceptual use of evaluation findings is the demonstration of insight into the evaluation context. The evaluator should remember that the intervention is only one element in a complex network of relationships, goals, priorities, interests, and problems. The demonstration of insight into this network begins with the questions the evaluation is to address. Equally important, however is the presentation of the conclusions and recommendations.

The conclusions should relate the data to the practical concerns of the clients, and they should be stated in concrete terms. A purely descriptive study is not useful to policymakers. Furthermore, to describe findings in terms of unfamiliar categories and concepts reduces the credibility of the evaluation to the client.

An example of context-relevant conclusions is the Shepard and Smith (1985) evaluation of kindergarten retention. The study compared first-grade children in high-retaining schools with matched controls from low-retaining schools. The study compared the performance of both groups on the district-administered Comprehensive Tests of Basic Skills (CTBS) in reading and mathematics. First-grade teachers also rated the children on learner self-concept, social maturity, and attention level. The only difference between the two groups was a 1-month gain in reading achievement for the retained children. The report concluded that providing 2 years of schooling prior to first grade is "an extremely costly but minimally effective solution to a short-term problem" (Shepard & Smith, 1985, p. 10). The report then stated the dollar cost of retention, which was $3,130 per child, and described the minimal gains.

Recommendations for further action should take into consideration the context in which the intervention is operating. If the recommendations do not address these daily realities, they will not be credible. Instead, the client's working knowledge of the context will compete with the evaluation findings (Kennedy, 1983). In such a situation, the client's working knowledge is likely to function as "conventional wisdom" to discount the findings.

The recommendations of the Shepard and Smith (1985) study reflect an understanding of the policy context of retention. Prior to the study, each school developed its own policy on retention. Thus, the district consisted of some high-retaining and some low-retaining schools. In the high-retaining schools, from 16% to 25% of the children were not promoted into first grade; and in the low-retaining schools, from 0% to 4% of the children were not promoted into first grade. Given this disparity, any recommendations for a single district policy would be upsetting, as well as divisive, to some of the school personnel. Therefore, the evaluators developed a "Statement of Policy Implications" (Shepard & Smith, 1985, pp. 10–11). First, they indicated that the absence of a district policy resulted in the creation of 22 minipolicies. The report also recognized that individuals within the district have "strong intellectual commitments and interests that are supported or attacked by the results of the study" (p. 11). The report than suggested two possible avenues. One avenue was that of discussion and education in which several questions should be pursued. Among these questions were:

1. What is the function of 2-year programs if so few positive effects are demonstrated?

2. Must the level of classroom instruction be set for the needs of older and more prepared children and segregate the others?

3. Are there alternative ways to address individual differences?

The report also noted that many teachers in low-retaining schools implemented variable standards and shared with the first-grade teachers a willingness to work with individual differences (Shepard & Smith, 1985, p. 11).

The report acknowledged, however, that discussion and dialogue might not be possible. Therefore, a second course of action was suggested. Among the recommended steps were:

1. The issuance of disclaimers to parents that 2-year programs have not produced average benefits in measured achievement or affective areas

2. The promotion of workshops that enhance teacher skills in working with diverse children in the classroom

3. The expansion of academic assistance programs

4. Revision of the kindergarten curriculum to emphasize learning to learn and socialization rather than counting to a certain number and a certain level of reading readiness

5. Revision of the first-grade curriculum so that a certain level of reading readiness is not a required prerequisite for entry into first grade (Shepard & Smith, 1985, p. 12)

Note that the report did not recommend that the district issue a policy eliminating kindergarten retention. Although such a recommendation is a logical extension of the report findings, the polarization and other negative reactions would exact too high a price. Instead, the report suggests practical and defensible courses of action.

Summary

Factors that contribute to the communicability of evaluation reports are language, content and organization, the use of visual displays, the use of a variety of written communications, and the demonstration of insight in the reporting. Written communications should be easy to read, avoid jargon, and use language that is straightforward and to the point. Communications should be organized so that they are free of deadwood and present a logical sequence of information. A report should begin, for example, with an executive summary followed by a chapter on each major topic in the summary.

Data that are reported should be designed for the particular audience. Some individuals prefer data tables, and others prefer visual displays. Examples include pie charts, bar graphs, line graphs, and other two-dimensional displays.

Among the types of written communication that are useful in evaluation are reports, report summaries, executive summaries, memos, news items, and abstracts. A report summary is a condensed version of the report, and an executive summary is a shorter version (two to five pages) of the report summary. Memos are useful in expanding the distribution of findings; and they also can report interim events effectively. News items are brief accounts that may appear in newspapers, newsletters, and the news columns of professional journals. Of these types, the abstract communicates to the smallest audience, that is, journal readers and those who use various document reproduction services.

Perhaps the single most important characteristic that contributes to both instrumental and conceptual use of evaluation findings is the demonstration of insight into the context of the evaluation. The data must relate to the practical concerns of the clients and provide concrete recommendations. Recommendations also should be sensitive to the local situation. They should address the findings of the report in a way that allows the client to make use of the information.

CHAPTER QUESTIONS

1. What are some differences between the dissemination of evaluation findings and research findings?

2. How does the reporting of formative evaluation findings differ from that of summative evaluations?

3. What are the two most important requirements for communicability in an evaluation report?

4. What are the differences between executive summaries and memos?

5. What should an evaluator do to demonstrate insight in a final report?

REFERENCES

Braskamp, L., Brandenburg, D., & Ory, C. (1987). Lessons about client expectations. In J. Nowalski (Ed.), *The client perspective on evaluation. New Directions for Program Evaluation, 36*, 63–74.

Cook, T. D., & Shadish, W. R. (1986). Program evaluation: The worldly science. *Annual Review of Psychology, 37*, 193–232.

Cooley, W., & Bickel, W. (1986). *Decision-oriented educational research.* Boston: Kluwer-Nijhoff.

Cousins, J., & Leithwood, K. (1986). Current empirical research on evaluation utilization. *Review of Educational Research, 56*(3), 331–364.

Cronbach, L. J., Ambron, S., Dornbusch, S., Hess, R., Hornik, R., Phillips, D., Walker, D., & Weiner, S. (1980). *Toward reform of program evaluation.* San Francisco: Jossey-Bass.

Fetterman, D. (1988). A national ethnographic evaluation: An executive summary of the ethnographic component of the Career Intern Program study. In D. Fetterman (Ed.), *Qualitative approaches to evaluation in education* (pp. 262–276). New York: Praeger.

Haensly, P., Lupkowski, A., & McNamara, J. (1987). The chart essay: A strategy for communicating findings to policymakers and practitioners. *Educational Evaluation and Policy Analysis, 9*(1), 63–76.

Kennedy, M. (1983). Working knowledge. *Knowledge, Creation, Diffusion, Utilization, 5*(2), 193–211.

Kleinfeld, J., & McDiarmid, G. (1986). Living to tell the tale: Researching politically controversial topics and communicating the findings. *Educational Evaluation and Policy Analysis, 8*(4), 393–401.

Leviton, L. C., & Hughes, E. (1981). Research on the utilization of evaluations: A review and synthesis. *Evaluation Review, 5,* 525–548.

Macy, D. J. (1982). Research briefs. In N. Smith (Ed.), *Communication strategies in evaluation* (pp. 179–190). Beverly Hills, CA: Sage.

Murray, D. (1982). Write research to be read. *Language Arts, 59*(7), 760–768.

Rich, R. (1981). *Social science information and public policy.* San Francisco: Jossey-Bass.

Schotanus, H., Chase, C. & Fontaine, A. (1991). *Report of results and effectiveness: Reading Recovery pilot project.* Concord, NH: New Hampshire State Department of Education.

Shepard, L., & Smith, M. (1985). *Boulder Valley kindergarten study: Retention practices and retention effects.* Boulder, CO: Boulder Valley Public Schools.

Smith, A. G., & Robbins, A. E. (1984). Multimethod policy research: A case study of structure and flexibility. In D. Fetterman (Ed.), *Ethnography in educational evaluation* (pp. 115–132). Beverly Hills, CA: Sage.

Suchman, E. A. (1967). *Evaluative research: Principles and practice in public service and social action programs.* New York: Russell Sage Foundation.

Weiss, C. H. (1980). Knowledge creep and decision accretion. *Knowledge: Creation, Diffusion, Utilization, 1,* 381–404.

Weiss, C. H. (1981). Measuring the use of evaluation. In J. Ciarlo (Ed.), *Utilizing evaluation: Concepts and measuring techniques* (pp. 17–33). Beverly Hills, CA: Sage.

CHAPTER 17

Ethical Issues in Evaluation

E ducational and social programs and policies are not developed and implemented in a vacuum. Instead, they are, in part, the "creatures of political decisions" (Guba & Lincoln, 1981, p. 298). Attached to them are the expectations
of sponsors, perhaps the careers of administrators and the jobs of the staff, and the
hopes of the developers. Against this tapestry, the evaluation (whether formative or
summative) is expected to make definitive statements and recommendations about
the program or policy. Further, the evaluation itself takes place within the operating
context of the program, and the evaluator has a responsibility to those associated
with the intervention who are sources of information or data. Given these parameters, conducting an evaluation can give rise to any of several ethical issues. Discussed
in this chapter are the evaluator's obligations to individuals affected by an intervention and potential conflicts of obligation and interest.

OBLIGATIONS TO PARTICIPANTS IN SOCIAL SCIENCE RESEARCH

Both social research and evaluation address the effects of contexts, interventions,
programs, or services on human beings. Thus, researchers and evaluators interact
with recipients of social and educational services in various ways. Of major importance in these interactions is that the individuals providing information are treated
ethically and fairly. Concern for the ethical treatment of participants in biomedical
and behavioral research was enacted into law by Congress in 1974. The legislation,
referred to as the National Research Act (PL 9348), also is applied to social science
research. The Act established institutional review boards for research in institutions

that receive federal funds for research. However, because many data collection activities in the social sciences pose little or no risk to research subjects, many projects were exempted from the review process in 1981. Among them are (1) research in school settings, such as research on the effectiveness of curricula or methods, (2) research using educational tests when the subjects remain anonymous, and (3) the collection or study of documents if the sources are available to the public or if the obtained information remains anonymous.

Another provision of the Act established the National Commission for the Protection of Human Subjects of Biomedical and Behavioral Research. The commission identified three basic principles of human interaction that are the foundation for ethical conduct in human research. These principles are beneficence, respect, and justice.

Beneficence

The principle of beneficence refers to two responsibilities. They are to maximize good outcomes and to avoid harm (Sieber, 1980). The three components in avoiding harm are (1) avoiding the use of harmful procedures, (2) ensuring participant anonymity, and (3) protecting the confidentiality of data records.

Maximization of Good Outcomes.   One aspect of the standard is the issue of social value. The research should contribute to knowledge related to improving the human condition. Much of the research and evaluation in the educational setting is conducted with the explicit intent of improving the welfare and/or educational experiences of students. The purpose often is to identify the various principles, practices, and conditions that enhance learning.

The question of social value is also one that evaluators should address, according to Cronbach and associates (1980). An evaluation should produce social benefits by contributing to a broader base of knowledge about a particular policy, program, curriculum, or set of materials or procedures. Consistent with this view, an evaluator should decline a contract that qualifies as busywork or is noninformative (p. 199).

The maximization of good outcomes also implies that members of an eligible population should not be denied remedial services simply for the purposes of research and evaluation. This requirement raises an ethical issue in the use of control groups in implementing and evaluating programs (House, 1990a). An example is the design prescribed by the sponsoring agency for the evaluation of the Career Intern Program (CIP). Disadvantaged urban dropouts who expressed an interest in the program had to be assigned to either the program or a no-treatment control through a lottery (Fetterman, 1983). Thus, some of the teenagers who were disenchanted with "the system" and decided to return to the school setting were denied a second chance by virtue of the experimental/control group requirement. Fetterman (1982, p. 263) reports the sense of dejection and parental concerns about the rejected teenagers' behavior—falling back into bad habits and hanging around with hoodlums. According to Fetterman (1982), the denial of an innovative curriculum to a middle- or upper middle-class student is not the same situation as that of denying a lower income dropout a second chance to enter the mainstream. Further, the social costs of denying treatment to an individual with few alternatives to enter the legitimate social system far outweigh any benefits derived from a no-treatment control (p. 264).

Avoidance of Harmful Procedures.   A few extreme examples of research in which deception led to subsequent pain and trauma for the participants are believed to be the basis for the current ethical guidelines. One of these studies was the Milgram (1974) obedience study. Subjects were ordered to deliver increasingly severe shocks to another subject who was hidden from view. No shocks were actually administered; however, the study generated widespread controversy.

The current ethical standards specify the avoidance of procedures that can generate negative physical or psychological effects. An example would be a social program that introduces a housing allowance for the purpose of determining the effects (Cronbach & associates, 1980). Families who accept the allowance may move out of rent controlled quarters. However, if the program is short lived, the families are worse off because the rent controlled housing no longer is available to them (p. 200). In such a study, the evaluator takes on a professional obligation to individual participants; and if necessary safeguards for participant welfare are lacking, he or she should decline the contract.

The code of ethics subscribed to by ethnographers goes beyond the avoidance of harm to participants. The code specifies that the researcher does no harm to either the people or the community under study (Fetterman, 1989, p. 120). Thus, the ethnographer exercises care so as to not trample the feelings of natives and to not desecrate events, objects, rituals, and traditions that the culture identifies as sacred (p. 120). This respect for the social environment ensures both the rights of the people and the integrity of the data developed about the community.

Assurance of Participant Anonymity.   A major component of the 1974 Privacy Act is that identifiable information about individuals may not be disclosed outside the agency that collected the information without the prior consent of the individuals concerned (Feinberg, Martin, & Straf, 1985, p. 20). The law applies directly to researchers and evaluators who contract with a federal agency. Evaluations of federal programs are examples.

The data become anonymous when the identifiers are removed *and* "the individual is included in a group sufficiently large for the data subject to get lost in the crowd" (Bing, 1986, p. 86). This requirement typically is not a problem in the quantitative measurement of outcomes. Code numbers are assigned to individual scores, and data typically are reported in the form of frequency distributions, means, and standard deviations.

Protecting the anonymity of individuals can be a problem in a qualitative study where losing the individual in the small "qualitative crowd" is more difficult (Akeroyd, 1991, p. 98). One of the suggested mechanisms for preserving subject anonymity is to use pseudonyms in any references to individual participants. However, pseudonyms may not be sufficient to protect the identity of individuals when only one or two persons, such as a school principal and/or a guidance counselor, are in a position to make particular observations (Guba & Lincoln, 1981, p. 278). In such situations, the evaluator should seek to present the information in another way or to use other sources (Fetterman, 1989, p. 134).

A practice that should not be used to protect subject anonymity is that of combining elements from several real cases into a more "typical" picture (Guba & Lincoln, 1981). Discussing teacher performance in implementing a particular curriculum innovation by presenting a composite rather than a discussion of actual cases with their idiosyncratic deviations is an example. This practice results in misleading information unless the reader knows that the situations or persons are not real and are only representational artifacts (p. 379).

Case studies, anecdotal reports, and ethnographic evaluations also use pseudonyms to disguise the identity of locales such as project sites, schools, and districts. A practice that is not recommended is that of disguising the location and other identifying features with misleading descriptors. This practice both distorts the data and introduces the risk that the disguise may mistakenly suggest another locale or community and raise questions about that group. For example, Appell (1978) disguised case materials for a course in terms of ethnic group, geographic location, and actors. On one occasion, he was approached by an anthropologist who demanded to know how Appell had secured his case. In disguising the case, Appell had placed the events in the hemisphere in which the anthropologist had worked, and the sequence of events was similar to his own fieldwork (Appell, 1978, p. 10).

Protection of Confidentiality.   Public awareness of issues of privacy and confidentiality has increased over the past several years (Feinberg et al., 1985). In part related to the escalating use of computers in business and government, respondents express concern over invasion of privacy; and public discussion has sensitized investigators to this issue (p. 21).

The term *confidentiality* refers to an explicit promise or contract to reveal no personal information provided by or about an individual except under conditions agreed to by the subject. The rationale for confidentiality in an evaluation is that informants may be penalized when an evaluator's report exposes individuals to censure or sanction (Cronbach & associates, 1980, p. 200).

Maintaining the anonymity of participants in evaluation reports is one aspect of confidentiality. The evaluator also faces two other key responsibilities with regard to confidentiality. One is the safeguarding of personal and confidential information from unauthorized access and disclosure (Akeroyd, 1991). This responsibility is of particular concern when computers are used to analyze qualitative data. The evaluator's records, particularly those derived from key informants, often contain personal information that neither has been obtained from nor confirmed by the referent (p. 91). The data record may contain a great deal of information that is open and generally known, some that is confidential and restricted, and some that is known but not stated openly or acknowledged (p. 91).

Evaluators should be aware that the use of a password to protect one's files on the mainframe against unauthorized access can be ineffective if the password is not "robust." The user should, for example, avoid easily guessed passwords, such as first names, surnames, street names, names of famous characters, acronyms common to computer professionals, and common dictionary words (Highland, 1990, p. 286). Also, the safeguards in mainframe networks and workstations often vary considerably. Restricting access and the right to view files to defined categories of users does not secure the files against intrusion if unauthorized use of override controls is easy to obtain. Users typically have greater immediate control over microcomputers. The exception is networking, which presents security problems (Akeroyd, 1991). Commercial companies currently are developing software that can assist in guarding access for the user.

The Concept of Privileged Communication.   The second responsibility regarding confidentiality is that of encoding or aggregating information in the evaluator's files, so that it cannot be traced to particular informants (Cronbach & associates, 1980, p. 201). For qualitative data that may contain sensitive information, the evaluator may use codes in field notes for individuals and settings and/or remove some data to the personal diary as field notes are reviewed (Brajuha & Hallowell, 1986). This caution is related to the fact that evaluators can be compelled to disclose their data records in a legal proceeding.

The evaluator and the participants in a study regard confidentiality as a contract to protect personal and private information. However, the accepted legal expression for confidentiality is "privileged communication." The privilege refers to a person's rights in a special relationship to prevent the disclosure in a legal proceeding of information provided in confidence in that relationship (Fischer & Sorenson, 1991). At present, legal statutes identify communications between physicians and patients, clergy and penitents, husbands and wives, and attorneys and clients as privileged. Some states also have enacted statutes that protect the communications between reporters and informants.

Privileged communication, however, does not extend to researchers and evaluators. Thus, a promise of confidentiality to participants in a study is not sufficient to protect the information from disclosure in a court of law. At Stanford, for example, law enforcement officials claimed access to the data from a questionnaire on drug use administered to high school students as a baseline for evaluating an intervention (Cronbach & associates, 1980).

Another situation involved a protracted legal battle over the release of confidential data records. The data files of a doctoral student in sociology, who was researching the restaurant business, were subpoenaed in New York City. The restaurant in which he was working burned down, and the detectives suspected arson. Because the researcher had promised confidentiality to participants, he refused to submit his records to the court. His attorney filed a motion to quash the subpoena based on constitutional First Amendment rights and the New York State shield law, which protects privileged communications by those engaged in disseminating knowledge to the public (Brajuha & Hallowell, 1986, p. 458). A complicated 26-month legal battle followed in which the case was heard finally by the U.S. Court of Appeals, Second Circuit. The court eventually ruled that the researcher could declare as protected those parts of the field notes that involved confidentiality or privacy claims. The federal district attorney's office eventually agreed to accept the notes without claimed confidential material as fulfilling the subpoena (p. 462).

Respect

The principle of respect refers to the protection of the autonomy or freedom of persons and the well-being of nonautonomous persons (e.g., children and prisoners) (Sieber, 1980, p. 54). The key to this protection of individuals is the process referred to as informed consent. The individual is informed about the nature of the study and freely consents in writing to be a participant. Assurances of confidentiality also are a part of the consent form. In a large corporation or agency, initial written permission from the institution should be followed by verbal consent from each individual in discussing a particular topic (Fetterman, 1989).

Informed consent is not necessary when test data that are a part of institutional records are used for an evaluation and scores cannot be traced to individuals. Informed consent is needed, however, when individuals are to be assigned to different programs or there is some other manipulation in the educational setting that requires their participation.

Informed consent involves three important characteristics. The first characteristic is that the consent must be based on knowledge. Individuals should be informed of the general purpose of the study and any risks associated with their participation. For example, families participating in a housing allowance study should be informed of the risk to their future lives on leaving rent controlled housing (Cronbach & associates, 1980). The researcher or evaluator must disclose enough information, so that the individuals can make an informed choice (Jacob & Hartshorne, 1991).

The second characteristic is that the individual must be competent to make legally binding decisions. Unless specific circumstances have been identified, adults who are 18 years old or older are considered to be legally competent. When children are to be involved in a study, informed consent is sought from their parents.

The third characteristic is that the consent must be voluntary. It must be obtained without coercion, misrepresentation, or undue inducement. For example, an evaluator should not tell teachers that information he/she is collecting is to meet a district requirement, if this is not the case. Further, the individual must be free to discontinue participation at any time during the study. In other words, individuals should have a real choice about participation.

Justice

The term *justice,* when applied to classical research studies, refers to the "equitable treatment and equitable representation of subgroups within society" (Sieber, 1980, p. 54). In most human research, the justice standard is operationally defined as equitable subject selection (p. 54). The individuals who are studied should be those who will benefit from the research; and the participants in a research project should not be overstudied (Sieber, 1980, p. 54).

Social Equity.   In program evaluation, justice also refers to social equity, which is interpreted both as equitable assignment to treatments and equitable design and measurement. First, in any comparison study, relevant subgroups should be represented in each version of programs, methods, or curriculum.

In addition, the evaluation design and the selected measurements should not penalize the particular population that is under study. For example, one of the instruments used to measure outcomes in the Follow Through evaluation was the reasoning test, Raven's Progressive Matrices. The rationale for using the test was that it was nonverbal; however, the abstract nature of the items penalized disadvantaged children.

Also, recall the ex post facto design used in the Westinghouse-Ohio State evaluation of Head Start discussed in Chapter 2. The comparison group, although from similar socioeconomic situations, differed in other important ways from the disadvantaged Head Start children. Thus, the design was not equitable.

A subsequent design suggestion to use children on the waiting lists for Head Start as a comparison group also is faulty because the most severely disadvantaged were typically admitted into the program. Thus, these groups were not equivalent in their ability to learn.

Social Justice.   The second interpretation of social equity is that of social justice (House, 1980, 1990b, 1991). A key responsibility of the evaluator in the social justice view is to serve the interests of the larger society and its various groups, as well as those of the sponsor (House, 1990b, p. 24). Thus, evaluation, as a social practice, involves the ethic of public responsibility. Further, social justice means that the evaluation must be sensitive to program effects on the poor and the powerless. For example, a nursing home may be adequately meeting the physical needs of the residents. However, it may be at the expense of their freedom of movement, their freedom of individual expression, and their right to privacy (Smith, 1983). The evaluator who is sensitive to the residents' needs will document and report these effects.

An example of an unjust evaluation, according to the concept of social justice, is the evaluation of the Follow Through programs (House, 1990b). The same achievement tests were administered to all the programs, and the programs were ranked based on the test results. As indicated in Chapter 2, the variation within programs was greater than the variation between programs. Although researchers stated that the programs could not be compared, the Office of Education supported ranking them (House, 1990b). The injustice in the evaluation is that the interests of large numbers of disadvantaged children were not adequately served in the evaluation (p. 26). That is, the findings of the study would mislead a poor district that wanted to adopt the best Follow Through program.

House (1991) notes that the stakeholder concept, which consists of the values of different individuals in the negotiation process, is inadequate for ensuring social justice. Typically, the stakeholder values reflected in negotiation are those of sponsors, managers, and participants. Criteria for the evaluation are then developed from these values (p. 244). Because the economically and politically disadvantaged do not have a seat at the negotiation table, evaluators must be sensitive to the extent to which the program meets their needs (House, 1980).

Summary

A major obligation in the evaluation of programs, policies, curricula, and materials is the just, respectful, and fair treatment of subjects who are recipients of the program or who are providing information about the program or policy. First, the evaluation design should not exclude members of the needy population for whom there is no alternative. Second, the procedures used in the evaluation should not inflict physical or psychological harm to individuals or communities. The right to privacy, confidentiality, and anonymity of individuals must be protected; individuals must have free choice about participation or nonparticipation; and deceptive methods should not be used to obtain information.

Third, both the design and measurements used in the evaluation should ensure social equity. The individuals who are studied should be those who will benefit from the evaluation. Also, relevant subgroups, such as disadvantaged children, should be represented in each of the different program versions. In addition, if comparison groups are used in the evaluation, disadvantaged children should not be compared to children with more adequate learning skills and greater opportunities to learn.

Some evaluators also advocate a responsibility to represent the needs of the economically and politically disadvantaged. These groups often are not represented in the planning of the evaluation. Therefore, the evaluator should document and report the extent to which the program meets the needs of these groups.

POTENTIAL CONFLICTS OF OBLIGATION AND INTEREST

The evaluator accepts considerable responsibility in attempting to influence actions that affect the public and the political system (Cronbach & associates, 1980, p. 197). In addition to the protection of the rights of individuals in the program, the evaluator has other ethical responsibilities. Among them are to fulfill the contract terms, acquaint the sponsor with unsound program practices, develop a balanced report, and make the results available to audiences with legitimate rights to the findings (Anderson & Ball, 1978; House 1990a).

Evaluators may face potential conflicts of obligation and interest in their efforts to benefit the larger system with commitments to the clients, informants, program participants, and their professional reputations. Three general types of conflicts are discussed in this section. They are sponsor originated conflicts, evaluator related conflicts, and conflicts arising from the controversial nature of a program or policy.

Sponsor Originated Conflicts

The sponsor or client who has commissioned an evaluation may initiate the study for self-serving purposes. Such studies are described by Stufflebeam (1980) as pseudo evaluations. Such studies are a service to private interests, but they are not legitimate evaluation (House, 1980). Stufflebeam (1980) identifies two types of pseudo evaluations. They are the politically controlled study and the public relations inspired study.

Politically Controlled Studies.   The client's purpose in the politically controlled study is to secure assistance in acquiring, maintaining, or increasing his/her sphere of influence, power, or money. Generally, the client wants the obtained information to be as technically accurate as possible. However, the client also wants to guarantee that he/she can control the dissemination of the information (Stufflebeam, 1980, p. 25). For example, an official in an upper echelon commissions an evaluation and specifies that reports are made only to him or her (Cronbach & associates, 1980). The sponsor is therefore free to ignore the findings, suppress them, or edit and transmit them selectively (p. 205). The evaluator's role in such a situation is that of confidential consultant, similar to that of the company lawyer or the chief financial officer (p. 205).

Politically controlled evaluations also can occur in small decentralized studies in which the evaluator allies himself or herself with the staff or community to be observed. The evaluator is expected to make all reports to and through the staff and is not authorized to release information to a higher authority or the public. The evaluator, in such a situation, signs away his/her rights in that the commissioners of the evaluation decide the data to be released and the data to be suppressed (Cronbach & associates, 1980, p. 204).

An example is the evaluation of an alternative program for disadvantaged dropouts (CIP) (Fetterman, 1989). The contract specified that draft reports were to be delivered to the sponsor and the agency disseminating the programs. The evaluator anticipated that the disseminating agency would share the information with the project sites for comments. However, the agency informed the evaluator that two of the sites would not receive the reports (one was a new program and the other was vying with the agency for control) (Fetterman, 1983).

The research corporation responsible for the ethnographic evaluation solved the problem without violating its contractual responsibilities. Reports were delivered to the sponsor and the disseminating agency, accompanied by a letter stating that the evaluator would request comments from each program by the end of the month. Further, the letter indicated that if a response was not received, the evaluator would assume that report had been "lost in the mail," and he would contact the program directly (Fetterman, 1989, p. 124). In this way, the ethnographer fulfilled his ethical responsibility to share the findings with the participants without violating the reporting requirements of the contract.

A key issue with client managed situations is that they lack an essential characteristic of social inquiry. In legitimate social inquiry, data and interpretations are made available, so that peers can question assumptions, offer alternative interpretations, and cross-check the conclusions (Cronbach & associates, 1980, p. 206). When free exchange is not possible, these corrective processes cannot operate. The crucial issue in such a situation is the evaluator's freedom to communicate during and after a study, subject to legitimate concerns for privacy, national security, and governance of the institution or agency (Cronbach & associates, 1980, p. 209).

Public Relations Inspired Studies.   The purpose of this type of pseudo evaluation is to create a positive public image for a school district, program, or process (Stufflebeam, 1980, p. 26). The questions that guide the study are derived from the client's conceptions of the questions that would be most popular with school, district, or program constituents (p. 26). In other words, the agenda is to obtain information that will contribute to public support for the program or policy. An example is the superintendent who requested a community survey of his district that would yield a positive report on the performance of the district (Stufflebeam, 1980, p. 26).

On occasion, a client who has been instrumental in developing a program also commissions the evaluation (Sieber, 1980). In such a situation, the client is likely to hold strong opinions about the types of data to be collected. If the evaluation is formative, this situation does not present a major problem. However, if the evaluation is summative, conducting an unbiased study is next to impossible. Cooley and Bickel (1986, p. 36) suggest that an evaluator should not conduct a summative evaluation when the program developer or implementer is the sole client.

The issue in the public relations inspired evaluation is that the focus is a particular partisan intent, and not the public interest. The evaluator functions only as a hired gatherer of data (Sieber, 1980, p. 57).

Evaluator Related Conflicts

Undertaking the evaluation of an educational or social program can subject the evaluator to conflicts during the conduct of the study. These conflicts are related to the evaluator's value system and the role(s) to which he or she is obligated.

Evaluator Values.   At the time an evaluator accepts a commission, his or her values are an important consideration (Cronbach & associates, 1980). First, an evaluator should not attempt to evaluate a program with aims that are counter to his or her basic value system. For example, a pacifist who agrees to conduct a neutral evaluation of an ROTC program will be torn by conflict (p. 209).

Moreover, an evaluator should avoid conducting a summative evaluation of a program or policy for which he or she is a passionate advocate. The evaluator will experience conflict in attempting to detect imperfections or problems and in viewing the program through the eyes of others. The posing of the questions may—myopically or intentionally—favor the interests of the developer or the sponsor (Cronbach & associates, 1980, p. 208). Further, the evaluator may be tempted to adopt the statistical technique that makes a treatment effect appear to be statistically significant even though a more appropriate technique leads to a weaker conclusion (Cronbach & associates, 1980, p. 201).

Role Maintenance Conflicts.   The problem of role maintenance is one faced by the ethnographer who is participating in a contract evaluation for a sponsor or client. Role maintenance involves two issues. The first issue is that of balancing conflicting roles and interests encountered in the field as the ethnographer attempts to determine how the system works from an insider's perspective (Fetterman, 1983, p. 215).

An ethnographic evaluation of an alternative program for disadvantaged urban dropouts (CIP), for example, involved collecting information in the street, the classrooms, the individuals' homes, the local and national disseminating organizations for the program, the city governments, and the two federal agencies that were involved. Further, each of these levels consisted of conflicting groups. Thus, maintaining rapport with rival groups required that the ethnographer establish himself or herself as an independent entity sensitive to each set of concerns and interested in information from all perspectives (p. 216).

The second issue in the ethnographer's role in evaluation is that he or she has a contractual obligation to the sponsor. In conventional ethnography, informant information may alert the ethnographer to a more pressing research concern, and the line of inquiry may be redirected. However, in a contract evaluation, field information is rarely considered sufficient to drop the topic of investigation (Fetterman, 1983, p. 216). This priority of investigation can lead to conflict for the ethnographer.

The "Guilty Knowledge" Issue.   A problem likely to be encountered by ethnographers in particular during an evaluation is the "guilty knowledge" issue. The ethnographer's primary task is to understand and describe a social and cultural context from the insider's perspective (Fetterman, 1989, p. 12). This task requires extended stays in a community, spending time with people, and participating in the daily activities of people.

For example, evaluating a program for urban dropouts requires an intimate knowledge of dropouts and their activities, which can involve extralegal and, on occasion, illegal activities (Fetterman, 1983, p. 216). One student, who befriended the evaluator, showed him around the neighborhood. After introducing him to some of the leaders who ran the street, the student took the evaluator to a neighborhood health food bar for a cold drink and a snack (Fetterman, 1986). The student winked at the proprietor and told him to give his friend a granola bar. The granola bar was accompanied by a tiny bag of marijuana. Not wanting to pass judgment, the evaluator accepted it. Two policemen who were walking by and observed the transaction smiled and walked on (Fetterman, 1983, 1986).

The ethical dilemmas in this situation concerned incriminating information (guilty knowledge) and "dirty hands" (a situation in which the field worker cannot emerge as innocent) (Fetterman, 1983, p. 217). The ethnographer's response was (1) to record the event in detail to provide context information on the pressures on the students and (2) to not take an active role, which would be a breach of confidence regarding the student. However, the ethnographer did discuss the issue of police corruption with city officials on his own time and provided a description of the corruption in the evaluation report (p. 217). These decisions were based on timing (the study had just begun), trust, a professional responsibility to respect environmental norms or rules, and a responsibility to complete the evaluation (p. 217).

Controversial Programs or Policies

A program or a policy may be considered controversial for any of several reasons and may pose ethical dilemmas for the evaluator. One dilemma is that of choosing an appropriate course of action in the absence of prior information about a program or published reports in the literature. This situation typically involves a relatively expensive program that attracted little prior attention until tight budget times. Such programs have both advocates and detractors, and there may be little or no information available on the effects of the program. Further, the program or practice may be one that was developed to address a local problem, and no research data or theoretical bases can be found that address these issues. Thus, a clear course of action is not indicated from the research literature.

An example is the village high schools in Alaska. At the time of the evaluation, the state was undergoing a period of severe revenue decline and was seeking ways to contain school expenditures. Other concerns were those of school personnel, who feared that the small high schools would be blamed for the complex social and educational problems of the often disorganized native communities (Kleinfeld & McDiarmid, 1986). Further, some of the native village parents supported the village high school, and others preferred the boarding schools; and some state agency staff believed some schools should be closed and the students transported elsewhere.

The evaluators developed a three-step strategy to enhance both the quality of the evaluation and the later acceptability of the findings. First, they compiled a list of the various gatekeepers, stakeholder groups, and individuals and their worries, fears, and interests. Such an exercise provides a broad view of the situation and a map that indicates the land mines (Kleinfeld & McDiarmid, 1986, p. 395).

The second step, prior to selecting the evaluation questions, was to telephone each of the major stakeholders for their suggestions. The evaluation was described in general terms, and the stakeholders were asked questions such as, What questions do you think should be addressed? What pitfalls do you see for research in this area? What is your organization doing successfully that might be valuable for others? and Whom do you suggest should serve on a steering committee to direct the evaluation? (Kleinfeld & McDiarmid, 1986, p. 396).

In the third step, the evaluators established a steering committee that represented the major stakeholders and the range of political opinion on the issue. Particularly important in such a strategy is that the committee members must be those who hold the respect and confidence of the stakeholding groups. The downside of relying on a steering committee is the costs and risks that are involved. The personal communications and arranging of meetings are highly time consuming, and the committee also absorbs funds that might be allocated elsewhere (Kleinfeld & McDiarmid, 1986). Further, the possibility exists that the steering committee will "run away with the research," using their authority to direct the study away from the difficult issues (p. 396).

However, careful selection of committee members reduces the possibility of the risk factor. Moreover, the positive advantages are that the steering committee (1) identifies issues that can be addressed prior to completion of the evaluation and (2) plays a key role in legitimizing the findings and transforming them into politically appropriate policy recommendations.

Another type of politically controversial intervention is one in which the research data do not support the intervention, but the practice continues in some communities. Key questions for the evaluation are, Why does the practice persist? and What local factors sustain the practice?

An example is the practice of kindergarten retention. Evaluating the practice in a district in which each school developed their own policy required an evaluation strategy sensitive to the potential controversy over the findings. The evaluators (1) identified and documented the context differences between high- and low-retaining schools and (2) addressed the conventional wisdom cited to support kindergarten retention (e.g., that the children are happier with less stress and that retention does not hurt them). The evaluation found several context features that supported reten- tion (e.g., pressures from teachers in higher grades to ensure the learning of certain skills) as well as flaws in the conventional wisdom about the lack of negative effects of retention on the children (Shepard & Smith, 1985).

Summary

Evaluations of educational and social programs take place in a context dominated by various layers and types of human interactions in relation to diverse goals, interests, and agendas. This context can lead to conflicts of obligation and interest. Evaluation sponsors or clients may commission a study for a particular agenda other than that of serving as a comprehensive information source about the program. These pseudo evaluations may be politically controlled studies in which the client wants a high degree of technical accuracy but selects and controls the information to be dissemi- nated. Other pseudo evaluations are for the purpose of public relations only. That is, only questions designed to elicit positive answers are asked. Both types of pseudo evaluations are not legitimate social inquiry and should be avoided.

The evaluator also may contribute to conflicts of obligation and interest. First, the evaluator should not attempt to evaluate a program with aims that are counter to his or her basic value system. Further, the evaluator should not conduct a summative evaluation of a program or policy for which he or she is a passionate advocate.

Particular problems faced by ethnographers conducting program evaluations are role maintenance conflicts and the guilty knowledge issue. Role maintenance involves (1) balancing conflicting roles and interests encountered in the field and (2) continuing in the contractual investigation when a more pressing line of inquiry emerges from early fieldwork in the setting. The guilty knowledge issue involves incriminating knowledge and unknowing participation in a situation from which the evaluator cannot emerge as innocent. Two of the considerations in decisions about possible actions are the bond of trust and confidence with the informant and profes- sional responsibility to complete the research.

Another set of conflicts can emerge from the nature of the program or policy itself. A program that is controversial has both advocates and detractors, and such a situation can pose ethical dilemmas for the evaluator. One type of controversial intervention is that of a relatively expensive program that falls under scrutiny in tight budget times. A proposed strategy is (1) to compile a list of gatekeepers and stake- holders and their concerns and interests, (2) to consult stakeholders for their sug- gestions, and (3) to establish a steering committee that represents the major stakeholders. Careful selection of committee members can reduce the risk of a committee that redirects the evaluation to nonproductive ends.

A second type of controversial intervention is one in which research data do not support the intervention, but the practice continues in some communities. An example is the practice of kindergarten retention. Important in an evaluation of such a practice is to document the context differences between sites with and without the practice and to collect data on conventional wisdom that supports the practice.

CHAPTER QUESTIONS

1. What is the problem with assigning students to a control group for programs that address special needs?
2. What particular problems face ethnographic evaluators with regard to ethics?
3. What are the three requirements for an informed consent?
4. What is the evaluator's responsibility according to the social justice concept?
5. What are some evaluator strategies for addressing controversial programs?

REFERENCES

Akeroyd, A. (1991). Personal information and qualitative research data: Some practical and ethical problems arising from data processing legislation. In R. Lee & N. Fielding (Eds.), *Using computers in qualitative research.* Newbury Park: Sage.

Anderson, S., & Ball, S. (1978). *The profession and practice of program evaluation.* San Francisco: Jossey-Bass.

Appell, G. N. (1978). *Ethical dilemmas in anthropological research: A case book.* Los Angeles, CA: Crossroads Press.

Bing, J. (1986). Beyond 1984: The law and information technology in tomorrow's society. Data protection and social policy. *Information Age, 8*(2), 85–94.

Brajuha, M., & Hallowell, L. (1986). Legal intrusion and the politics of fieldwork. *Urban Life, 14*(4), 454–478.

Cooley, W., & Bickel, W. (1986). *Decision-oriented educational research.* Boston: Kluwer-Nijhoff.

Cronbach, L. J., Ambron, S., Dornbusch, S., Hess, R., Hornik, R., Phillips, D., Walker, D., & Weiner, S. (1980). *Toward reform of program evaluation.* San Francisco: Jossey-Bass.

Feinberg, S., Martin, M., & Straf, M. (1985). *Sharing research data.* Washington, DC: National Academy Press.

Fetterman, D. (1982). Ibsen's baths: Reactivity and insensitivity. A misapplication of the treatment-control design in a national evaluation. *Educational Evaluation and Policy Analysis, 4*(3), 261–279.

Fetterman, D. (1983). Guilty knowledge, dirty hands, and other ethical dilemmas: The hazards of contract research. *Human Organization*, *42*(3), 214–224.

Fetterman, D. (1986). Conceptual crossroads: Methods and ethics in ethnographic evaluation. In D. Williams (Ed.), *Naturalistic evaluation. New Directions for Program Evaluation*, *30*, 23–26.

Fetterman, D. (1989). *Ethnography step by step.* Newbury Park, CA: Sage.

Fischer, L., & Sorenson, G. P. (1991). *School law for counselors, psychologists, and social workers.* New York: Longman.

Guba, E., & Lincoln, Y. (1981). *Effective evaluation.* San Francisco: Jossey-Bass.

Highland, H. J. (1990). Demise of passwords, part III. *Computers and Security*, *9*(4), 286–290.

House, E. R. (1980). *Evaluating with validity.* Beverly Hills, CA: Sage.

House, E. R. (1990a). Ethics of evaluation studies. In H. J. Walberg & G. D. Haertel (Eds.), *The international encyclopedia of educational evaluation* (pp. 91–94). Oxford: Pergamon Press.

House, E. R. (1990b). Methodology and justice. In. K. Sirotnik (Ed.), *Evaluation and justice: Issues in public education. New Directions for Program Evaluation*, *45*, 23–26.

House, E. R. (1991). Evaluation and social justice: Where are we? In M. McLaughlin & D. C. Phillips (Eds.), *Evaluation and education: At quarter century. Ninetieth yearbook of the National Society for the Study of Education, Part II* (pp. 233–247). Chicago: University of Chicago Press.

Jacob, S., & Hartshorne, T. (1991). *Ethics and law for school psychologists.* Brandon, VT: Clinical Psychology Publishing Company.

Kleinfeld, J., & McDiarmid, G. (1986) Living to tell the tale: Researching politically controversial topics and communicating the findings. *Educational Evaluation and Policy Analysis*, *8*(4), 393–401.

Milgram, S. (1967). Behavioral study of obedience. *Journal of Abnormal and Social Psychology*, *67*, 371–378.

Shepard, L., & Smith, M. (1985). *The Boulder Valley kindergarten study: Retention practices and retention effects.* Boulder, CO: Boulder Valley Public Schools.

Sieber, J. (1980). Being ethical: Professional and personal decisions in program evaluation. In R. Perloff & E. Perloff (Eds.), *Values, ethics, and standards in evaluation. New Directions for Program Evaluation*, *7*, 51–61.

Smith, N. (1983). *Dimensions of moral and ethical problems in evaluation* (Paper and Report Series, No. 42). Portland, OR: Northwest Regional Educational Laboratory, Research on Evaluation Programs.

Stufflebeam, D. (1980). Alternative approaches to evaluation. In G. Madaus, D. Stufflebeam, & M. Scriven (Eds.), *Evaluation Models.* Boston: Kluwer-Nijhoff.

Description of Program PLUS

Program PLUS (Promote Learning, Understanding, and Self-fulfillment), based on research on perceived classroom goal structures, is designed for middle school social studies. The purpose of the program is to develop positive beliefs about school and self through group exploratory learning and, as a result, to improve students' approaches and strategies to school tasks and student mastery of important objectives in the curriculum.

Your state has been selected for a summative trial of the program. Formative evaluation conducted by the developers indicated that some teachers experienced difficulty in removing the emphasis on grades and comparative achievement information. Administrators expressed concern that not every teacher would be suited to the nondirective nature of the curriculum. Also, participating schools initially may be penalized on district and statewide assessment measures. Therefore, middle school students in participating schools will be exempted from such assessments for 2 years.

BACKGROUND

Research (Ames & Archer, 1988; Dweck, 1989; Elliott & Dweck, 1988; Stipek & Daniels, 1988) indicates that the perceived goal structure in a classroom influences students in (1) their beliefs about themselves, (2) task-related effort, and (3) achievement. Specifically, classrooms may be described as either "performance oriented" or "learning oriented." The focus in the performance-oriented classroom is to perform well in competitive situations. Students seek judgments of high ability through high normative performance or the appearance of success with little effort. In performance-oriented classrooms, Stipek and Daniels (1988) found that children were divided into stable learning groups for at least one subject area. Written assignments were graded, and only the grade of A or "mostly correct" papers were displayed on bulletin boards. Students took tests and received positive and negative feedback, sometimes in a public context. Also, letter grades were assigned and appeared on report cards sent to the parents.

In contrast, the emphasis in the learning- or mastery-oriented classroom is on learning new skills and improvement and progress in learning. An emphasis on learning places the classroom focus on student effort and strategies that will facilitate learning. Characteristics of learning-oriented classrooms (Stipek & Daniels, 1988) include flexible instructional groups, variations in assignments according to the students' skill levels, discouragement of normative comparison, frequent group projects, encouragement of peer assistance, and substantive comments rather than grades on report cards.

Students in performance-oriented classrooms tend to give up easily on difficult tasks and to exhibit anxiety when they make errors. When given a choice of tasks, they avoid challenging tasks and choose ones that have the potential for them to display competence or to avoid displaying incompetence. However, students in learning-oriented classrooms view errors as part of learning; tend to persist at difficult tasks; and, given a choice, select challenging tasks.

PROGRAM PLUS

Program PLUS has been developed in part from the research on classroom goal structures. Activities in the program are designed to establish learning-oriented (instead of performance-oriented) classrooms. In Program

PLUS, the social studies curriculum for grades 6 and 7 is organized around understanding various cultures in the world. It is based on the view that the world is one community, and survival of that community begins with understanding.

The program includes curriculum guides, activities, and resource materials. Units in the course are based on themes, such as food gathering, family roles, child raising, cultural rituals, and others. The purpose of the curriculum is for the students, in small groups, in pairs, and in total class activities, to develop a shared knowledge about different cultures related to the course themes.

The curriculum guide recommends that the class work in small groups to study different cultures, spending 2 to 3 weeks in exploring and studying each culture. Pictures, artifacts, and other materials are suggested as useful stimuli for discussion. After the groups complete their study of one culture, they present their findings to the class, followed by question-and-answer sessions. Then the class is regrouped in small groups to study another type of culture. At the conclusion of the second 2- to 3-week period, the class spends a few days in drawing comparisons and contrasts across the cultures presented to date.

Mastery tests on specific concepts related to the ways that different cultures solve their problems are included in the curriculum, and the students also keep journals about their thoughts and observations.

Student grades in the course are based on (1) mastery of the course objectives, that is, the ways that different cultures relate to the major theme; and (2) the student's contributions to group research projects.

A major expectation of the developers is that students participating in the program will become more interested in learning and become self-directed learners through their responsibilities in the group. Another expectation is that students will develop skills in researching and organizing information about particular topics, in addition to learning about different cultures. A third expectation is that students will develop more positive attitudes toward social studies, school, and self.

TEACHER TRAINING

A 4-day workshop explains the principles of learning-oriented classrooms. Guidelines accompanied by videotapes of teachers implementing the curriculum and discussions of ways to address problems comprise the majority of the training.

IMPLEMENTATION

Program PLUS was implemented in six middle schools in your state selected from school districts and schools that volunteered. Teachers who implemented the program in the 1994–95 school year attended a 2-week workshop prior to the beginning of the school year. A program coordinator visited each school every 2 weeks to meet with the teacher and to provide support, assistance, and feedback. Teachers who participated in the program were given an additional planning period because of the time required to complete responsibilities such as reviewing student journals and identifying materials.

REFERENCES

Ames, C., & Archer, J. (1988). Achievement goals in the classroom: Students' learning strategies and motivational processes. *Journal of Experimental Psychology, 80*(3), 260–267.

Dweck, C. S. (1989). Motivation. In R. Glaser & A. Lesgold (Eds.), *The handbook of psychology and education*, (Vol. 1, pp. 187–239). Hillsdale, NJ: Erlbaum.

Elliott, E. E., & Dweck, C. S. (1988). Goals: An approach to motivation and achievement. *Journal of Personality and Social Psychology*, 54(1), 5–12.

Stipek, D. J., & Daniels, D. H. (1988). Declining perceptions of competence: A consequence of changes in the child or in the educational environment? *Journal of Educational Psychology*, 80(3), 352–356.

APPENDIX B

The Program Evaluation Standards

Summarized from the Joint Committee on Standards for Educational Evaluation, 1994. *The Program Evaluation Standards* (2nd ed.). Thousand Oaks, CA: Sage.

The 1994 *Program Evaluation Standards* are a revision of an earlier set of evaluation standards for educational programs, projects, and materials completed in 1981. Like the earlier standards, the current revision was undertaken by a Joint Committee on Standards for Educational Evaluation. The original committee was composed of individuals appointed by the 12 sponsoring organizations. The present Standards are sponsored by 15 professional organizations in the United States and Canada.

The term *evaluation standard* is defined by the committee as "a principle mutually agreed to by people engaged in the professional practice of evaluation, that, if met, will enhance the quality and fairness of the evaluation" (The Joint Committee on Standards for Educational Evaluation, 1994, p. 2).

The 30 standards are grouped into four broad categories that represent the characteristics of a sound and fair evaluation. The categories are utility, feasibility, propriety, and accuracy. The standards in these categories are intended to serve as guidelines for the design, use, and critique of evaluations of programs, projects, and materials (p. 4). That is, they form "a working philosophy for evaluation" (p. xviii). In addition to people and organizations that conduct evaluations, intended audiences for the standards are those who commission evaluations and those who use evaluation findings.

The standards are summarized in the following pages, and each is accompanied by a rationale reflected by the discussion of the standard in the 1994 revision.

UTILITY STANDARDS

The focus of the seven utility standards is the factors important in developing evaluations that are informative, timely, and influential (The Joint Committee on Evaluation Standards, p. 5).

U1. *Stakeholder identification.* The evaluator should identify the individuals who are involved in or affected by the evaluation in order to meet their information needs (p. 23).

Rationale: Projects and programs almost always involve "multiple and diverse stakeholders" (p. 25). An evaluation that does not address information needs may result in a misguided study that is ignored or criticized because it lacks relevance. The standards note, however, that stakeholders include clients and other decision makers, administrators, legislators, project and instructional staffs, individuals who will be affected by the findings, community organizations, and the general public (p. 25).

U2. *Evaluator credibility.* The individuals who conduct an evaluation should be both trustworthy and competent to design and implement the evaluation. These qualifications are essential for maximum credibility and acceptance of the completed evaluation (p. 23).

Rationale: Evaluation credibility depends on the training, knowledge, competence, experience, integrity, and public relations skills of the evaluation team (p. 31). In addition to integrity, trustworthiness depends on "consistent, open and continuing communication and approachability with clients and other stakeholders while offering expertise and maintaining impartiality" (p. 31).

U3. *Scope and selection of information.* The evaluator should broadly select the information so as (1) to address relevant questions about the program and (2) to respond to the needs and interests of clients and other identified stakeholders (p. 23).

Rationale: Appropriate scope of information depends on (1) relevance to decision makers' objectives and important stakeholders concerns and (2) attention to all important variables, such as the assumptions and values underlying the program, harmful side effects, costs, responses to learner needs, and feasibility (p. 37). The Standards note that all information is not of equal importance and that the evaluator should use reports of previous evaluations, other theoretical and research literature, and discussions with stakeholders to first cull unimportant classes of information and then specific items of information (p. 32). The Standards caution that required evaluation procedures, such as standardized tests, should not drive practice because such a requirement reduces the focus of the study almost exclusively to test results (p. 38).

U4. *Values identification.* The viewpoints, methods, and rationale used to interpret the evaluation findings should be carefully described (p. 24).

Rationale: The information generated in an evaluation will be of little use unless it is interpreted in terms of pertinent and defensible concepts of what constitutes merit (p. 43).

U5. *Report clarity.* The evaluation report (whether oral or written) should clearly describe (1) the program or project and its contexts and purposes and (2) the purposes, procedures, and findings of the evaluation (p. 49). The Standards define *clarity* as "explicit and unencumbered narrative, illustrations and descriptions" (p. 24).

Rationale: Credibility of the report, as well as audience understanding and application, depend, in large measure, on the clarify of the report(s).

U6. *Report timeliness and dissemination.* The evaluator should disseminate significant interim findings and report to users (p. 24).

Rationale: Information should be provided to intended users when it can best be used. The Standards define intended users as those individuals who legitimately should be informed of evaluation findings. Five such groups are (1) clients who commissioned the evaluation;

(2) persons who are legally responsible for the program; (3) persons who funded the program or project through taxes, monetary gifts, or contributions of time and effort; (4) persons who provided substantial amounts of information for the evaluation; and (5) other stakeholders, such as program developers, persons whose careers or professional status will be affected by the evaluation or who are cited in the report, and parents, students, or representatives of the mass media (p. 53).

The Standards note that evaluations and clients share responsibility for dissemination. However, the evaluator is responsible to both the client and intended users. The Standards suggest that the authority to meet this responsibility should be stated clearly in the formal agreement for the evaluation. Thus, in the event the client violates the agreement by distorting or withholding evaluation findings, the evaluator must inform the client and then take steps to inform other intended users (p. 54).

U7. *Evaluation impact.* The planning, conduct, and reporting of evaluations should be executed "in ways that encourage follow-through by stakeholders" (p. 24).

Rationale: Planning and conducting evaluation activities with utilization of the evaluation as a goal enhances the likelihood that the information will be used (p. 59).

FEASIBILITY STANDARDS

The focus of the feasibility standards is the factors that are important in insuring the realism, prudence, diplomacy, and frugality of the evaluation (p. 63).

F1. *Practical procedures.* In order to minimize disruption, the procedures used in the evaluation to obtain information should be practical (p. 63).

Rationale: Procedures that are theoretically sound, but unworkable, "consume resources without yielding valuable and/or usable results" (p. 65).

F2. *Political viability.* Planning and conducting evaluations should be undertaken with anticipation of the different perspectives of various interest groups. The purpose is to obtain their cooperation and thus avert or counteract possible efforts to curtail evaluation activities or to bias or misapply the findings (p. 63).

Rationale: Evaluations have political implications in that they can lead to decisions that reallocate resources and influence (p. 71). Evaluators who are sensitive to political pressures can avoid or reduce efforts to manipulate their work. The Standards define an interest group as any group that seeks "to influence policy in favor of some shared goal or concern" (p. 71).

F3. *Cost effectiveness.* The evaluation should produce information of sufficient value in an efficient manner so that the expenditure of resources can be justified (p. 63).

The standards note that "an evaluation is cost effective if its benefits equal or exceed its costs" (p. 77). In addition to financial expenditures, costs also include the human and physical resources used in the evaluation. Benefits refer to the value of all the evaluation findings, including ways to reduce program costs without reducing services and facilitating understanding of program components from different perspectives (p. 77).

Rationale: The selection of designs and methods from among the many alternatives should be made in order to provide the most useful information for an efficient expenditure of resources, whenever possible (p. 77).

PROPRIETARY STANDARDS

The focus of the proprietary standards is the factors involved in ensuring a legal and ethical evaluation that is sensitive to the welfare of individuals involved in the evaluation and those who are affected by the findings (p. 81).

P1. *Service orientation.* Evaluations should be designed to assist organizations in their broad purpose of addressing and effectively serving the needs of the various targeted participants (p. 81).

Rationale: One purpose of the evaluation is to serve the community and society in addition to program participants. Standard P1 addresses this purpose.

P2. *Formal agreements.* Written agreements of the obligations of the formal parties to an evaluation should be executed (p. 81).

Rationale: The process of preparing a formal written agreement provides both the client and evaluator an opportunity to clarify their respective expectations, rights, and responsibilities and prevent potential misunderstandings (p. 87).

P3. *Rights of human subjects.* Each evaluation should be designed and executed "to respect and protect the rights and welfare of human subjects" (p. 81).

Rationale: Evaluators should be knowledgeable about and implement both legal and ethical human rights requirements (p. 93).

P4. *Human interactions.* Evaluators should interact with persons associated with an evaluation in ways that respect human dignity and worth. The purpose is to avoid threat or harm to evaluation participants (p. 81).

Rationale: Evaluators who do not understand or respect the feelings of evaluation participants may offend them or generate hostility toward the evaluation (p. 99).

P5. *Complete and fair assessment.* The evaluation should be both thorough and fair in assessing and reporting strengths and weaknesses of the program (p. 82).

Rationale: An evaluation should address both positive and negative aspects of a program in order to provide the kinds of information that are useful to intended users (p. 105).

P6. *Disclosure of findings.* The formal parties to an evaluation should ensure that the complete set of evaluation findings including pertinent limitations are made accessible to (1) persons affected by the study and (2) persons with a legal right entitling them to the findings (p. 82). Exceptions to this standard are (1) the endangerment to public safety or (2) the abridgement of individual freedoms that disclosure of the findings would precipitate (p. 109).

Rationale: Without the full set of findings, persons or groups affected by an evaluation cannot (1) make use of the findings or (2) identify flaws in either the procedures or the data (p. 109).

P7. *Conflict of interest.* Conflict of interest should be addressed with openness and honesty in order to prevent the compromising of evaluation processes and findings (p. 82). The Standards note that conflict of interest may occur when (1) the evaluator's financial or personal interests may affect or be influenced by the evaluation or (2) the client or a stakeholder "has an inappropriate personal or financial interest in an evaluation or a program being evaluated" (p. 115).

Rationale: Conflicts of interest can bias an evaluation by distorting or corrupting the investigation or its findings.

P8. *Fiscal responsibility.* The assignment and expenditure of resources should (1) reflect sound fiscal accountability procedures and (2) be both prudent and ethically responsible (p. 82).

Rationale: Alleged misuse of funds can be used as a means to discredit an evaluation. Thus, evaluators must use extreme care in both their allocation of funds and their methods of documenting expenditures (p. 121).

ACCURACY STANDARDS

The focus of the accuracy standards is the broad requirements for developing and conveying information that is technically adequate about the (program) features that determine the merit of the program (p. 125).

A1. *Program documentation.* The program should be described and documented with both clarity and accuracy (p. 125).

Rationale: A comprehensive understanding is essential in order to develop an evaluation that is of maximum use.

A2. *Context analysis.* The context surrounding a program should be studied in sufficient detail to identify likely influences on the program (p. 125).

Rationale: Understanding the context of a program is essential to develop an evaluation that is realistic. In addition, explication of contextual components can assist individuals in judging the similarity of the program setting to other settings in which the evaluation findings may be applicable (p. 133).

A3. *Described purposes and procedures.* The evaluation objectives, intended use of results, and methods of an evaluation should be monitored and documented in sufficient detail to permit both identification and assessment (p. 125).

Rationale: These descriptions are essential for evaluations of the evaluation and to inform the conduct of similar evaluations in other locales (p. 138).

A4. *Defensible information sources.* The various sources of information tapped in a program evaluation should be described in sufficient detail to assess the adequacy of the information that was obtained (p. 125).

Rationale: Evaluators usually are unable to obtain all the information that potentially is available. Therefore, information sources, methods of selection, and methods of obtaining information should be documented to allow others to assess the adequacy of the information for the evaluation questions (p. 142).

A5. *Valid information.* The procedures and methods for obtaining information should be selected (or developed) and implemented to assure valid interpretation for the intended use (p. 126). The Standards define validity as the soundness or trustworthiness of inferences made from the evaluation findings (p. 126). The Standards also state that evaluators should collect evidence to support the interpretations and uses of the data collected in the evaluation. Further, the evaluator should measure multiple outcomes and implement multiple methods for obtaining information. The purpose of the recommendation is twofold: (1) to assess all important variables and (2) to compensate for the fallibility inherent in every single data source (p. 146).

Rationale: An evaluation that is not sound misleads clients and other stakeholders.

A6. *Reliable information.* The methods and procedures for obtaining information should be selected (or developed) and implemented to assume sufficiently reliable information for the intended use (p. 126).

The Standards define reliability as the degree of consistency of the information obtained by the evaluation methods and procedures (p. 153). The Standards also state that effort should be directed toward "reducing and/or describing the amount and impact of unwanted sources of variability upon the evaluation results and findings" (p. 153).

Rationale: Lack of dependable information calls into question the evaluation findings.

A7. *Systematic information.* The information that is developed and reported in an evaluation should be reviewed systematically and identified errors should be corrected (p. 126).

Rationale: Numerous possibilities for error exist in collecting, scoring, coding, finding, analyzing, and reporting information. Therefore, care should be taken to check accuracy at every stage and to keep the data secure.

A8. *Analysis of quantitative information.* Quantitative information should be analyzed appropriately and systematically. The purpose is to effectively answer the evaluation questions (p. 126).

Rationale: A variety of methods for analyzing quantitative data exist, but each is based on a number of assumptions. Therefore, it is important that appropriate methods are selected for the particular evaluation.

A9. *Analysis of qualitative information.* Qualitative information should be analyzed appropriately and systematically. The purpose is to effectively answer the evaluation questions (p. 126).

Rationale: Qualitative analysis often involves an inductive and interactive process. Therefore, the evaluator must seek confirmatory evidence from more than one source and seek independent verification of inferences (p. 172).

A10. *Justified conclusions.* Evaluation conclusions should be justified explicitly so that they may be assessed by the stakeholders (p. 126).

Rationale: Alternative explanations may seem plausible initially to individuals who were not involved in the evaluation. Therefore, evaluators provide explanations that rule out alternative explanations and provide supporting information for the conclusions.

A11. *Impartial reporting.* Reports should fairly reflect the evaluation findings, and reporting procedures should guard against distortion resulting from the personal feelings and bias of individuals or groups associated with the evaluation (p. 126).

Rationale: Evaluations are conducted in contexts in which different individuals and interest groups hold different perspectives, and the evaluation has the potential to reallocate resources and roles. These factors can exert pressure on the evaluation.

A12. *Metaevaluation*. The evaluation itself should be evaluated against pertinent standards, both formatively and summatively. The purpose is (1) to guide the conduct of the evaluation and (2) to permit stakeholders to closely examine its strengths and weaknesses on completion of the evaluation (p. 126).

Rationale: Metaevaluation is an evaluation of an evaluation and should be conducted (1) to enhance the credibility of particular program evaluations, (2) to support the fair treatment of competent evaluators when users seek to discredit unfavorable results, and (3) to support advances in evaluation practice (p. 186).

Subject Index

Name Index

Agar, M., 297
Ajzen, I., 169
Akeroyd, A., 339, 340, 341
Ames, C., 14, 354
Anderson, L. W., 172, 173, 174
Anderson, N., 190
Anderson, S., 344
Angelo, N., 150
Appell, G. N., 340
Archbald, D., 132, 133, 149
Archer, J., 14, 354
Arnstein, G., 66

Baker, E., 13, 107, 115, 127, 128, 129, 130, 131, 136, 137, 139, 140, 141, 147, 148, 149
Ball, A., 160, 161
Ball, D., 276
Ball, S., 344
Bandura, A., 167, 168
Banet, B., 26
Barker, R. G., 192, 198
Barone, T. E., 68
Baxter, G., 139
Beck, J., 156
Bell, R., 159
Berk, R. A., 116, 117, 129
Berlak, H., 12

Berman, P., 25
Bernard, H. R., 180, 195, 199
Bickel, W., 16, 45, 97, 98, 99, 100, 120, 181, 215, 284, 321, 322, 323, 325, 328, 332, 346
Bing, J., 339
Bixby, J., 147
Bliem, G., 261, 286
Block, M., 160
Bloom, B., 106, 112, 113, 115
Boas, F., 190
Bogdan, R., 300, 301
Borick, D., 11
Borko, H., 140, 185
Boruch, R. F., 33
Brajuha, M., 341
Brandenburg, D., 327
Braskamp, L., 70
Breland, H., 136
Britain, G., 204
Brophy, J., 33
Brooks-Gunn, J., 33
Bulmer, M., 190
Burstein, L, 184

Cadwell, J., 185
Calfee, R., 147, 151, 152
Cambo, C., 140, 275

Camp, R., 136
Campbell, D. T., 28, 29, 33, 34, 180, 249, 250, 259
Carlson, D., 67, 68
Cavanaugh, S., 115
Chambers, P., 139
Champagne, A., 130, 133
Chapman, C., 132
Charters, W. W., 25, 27, 239, 274, 276, 286
Chase, C., 329, 330
Chesterfield, R., 197, 205
Chi, M., 112, 136
Choppin, B. H., 107
Clarke-Stewart, K., 31
Clayton, S., 127, 147
Clyne, S., 64, 67, 68
Cohen, D., 10, 23, 27, 28, 30, 31, 252, 276
Conlan, G., 139
Cook, T. D., 7, 21, 22, 23, 28, 29, 34, 36, 229, 321
Cooley, W., 16, 45, 97, 98, 99, 100, 120, 181, 215, 284, 321, 322, 323, 324, 325, 328, 332, 346
Cosaro, W., 193
Cousins, J., 327

371